THE PURSUIT
OF JUSTICE

THE PURSUIT OF JUSTICE

LORD WOOLF

Edited by Christopher Campbell-Holt

OXFORD
UNIVERSITY PRESS

OXFORD
UNIVERSITY PRESS

Great Clarendon Street, Oxford OX2 6DP

Oxford University Press is a department of the University of Oxford.
It furthers the University's objective of excellence in research, scholarship,
and education by publishing worldwide in

Oxford New York

Auckland Cape Town Dar es Salaam Hong Kong Karachi
Kuala Lumpur Madrid Melbourne Mexico City Nairobi
New Delhi Shanghai Taipei Toronto

With offices in

Argentina Austria Brazil Chile Czech Republic France Greece
Guatemala Hungary Italy Japan Poland Portugal Singapore
South Korea Switzerland Thailand Turkey Ukraine Vietnam

Oxford is a registered trade mark of Oxford University Press
in the UK and in certain other countries

Published in the United States
by Oxford University Press Inc., New York

© Lord Woolf 2008

The moral rights of the author have been asserted
Database right Oxford University Press (maker)

Crown copyright material is reproduced under Class Licence
Number C01P0000148 with the permission of OPSI
and the Queen's Printer for Scotland

First published 2008

British Library Cataloguing in Publication Data

Data available

Library of Congress Cataloging-in-Publication Data

Woolf, Harry, Sir, 1933–
The pursuit of justice / by Lord Woolf; edited by Christopher Campbell-Holt.
p. cm.
Includes bibliographical references and index.
ISBN 978-0-19-921709-0 (hardback : alk. paper) 1. Rule of law—Great Britain.
2. Justice, Administration of—Great Britain. 3. Constitutional law—Great Britain.
4. Judicial power—Great Britain. 5. Judicial review—Great Britain.
I. Campbell-Holt, Christopher. II. Title.
KD3995.W66 2008
347.42—dc22

2008004178

Typeset by Cepha Imaging Private Ltd., Bangalore, India
Printed in Great Britain
on acid-free paper by
Antony Rowe, Chippenham, Wiltshire

ISBN 978–0–19–921709–0

1 3 5 7 9 10 8 6 4 2

PREFACE

A common misunderstanding is that English law is certain. The reality is that the law is often uncertain. Judges have become increasingly willing to adopt a more purposive approach to the interpretation of statutes to ensure that justice is done when the legal rule or principle to be applied to the facts of a case is unclear or has become outdated. This is in contrast to a more traditional approach where judges have assumed a narrow application of the law would lead to justice or have considered it was not their place to interfere. If justice is to be done in the English courts, then the common law must not become stagnant or archaic while society moves forward. It must be accessible, intelligible, and change with the times, responding to the realities of modern life. In recent times, no judge has tried more than Lord Woolf to show how this is being done.

This book publishes for the first time a collection of lectures and papers written and delivered by Lord Woolf between 1990 and his retirement in 2005 from the office of Lord Chief Justice. The title, *The Pursuit of Justice*, reflects Lord Woolf's determination to see that justice is done in the courts. A key theme in the papers is that to do justice according to law the judiciary must deliver pragmatic decisions on the facts of each case and the applicable law.

The papers cover developments to which Lord Woolf has personally contributed in a variety of legal areas that continue to be relevant in contemporary society, including the rule of law and the constitution, the role of judges, human rights, access to justice and civil justice, asylum, terrorism, crime, sentencing and prisons. Each paper discusses the way the challenges in English common law have been solved or attempted to be solved to ensure that justice is done: so there are fair hearings, accessible lawful remedies and the elimination of unnecessary costs and delays.

The Introduction provides fresh first-hand insight into Lord Woolf's career in the law, from his early days as a law student, to time practicing as a barrister, and later as the most senior judge in England and Wales. It also provides an overall assessment of some of the most recent changes to the English legal system in the areas referred to in the papers.

A conscious effort has been made to make this book as accessible as possible to lawyers and anyone concerned with the reform of the law. It will be of interest to legal specialists and the general public.

The papers have been updated and the law is as stated on 30 November 2007.

Chris Campbell-Holt

ACKNOWLEDGEMENTS

We are very grateful to everyone involved with the publication of this book. In particular, we would like to thank Jane Kavanagh, Annabel Moss, Marjorie Francois, Faye Judges and the publishing team at Oxford University Press for their assistance and patience throughout this project. Peter Lu, a law student at University College London, assisted with some reference confirmation during the final stages of publication. Fiona Evans, Head of Know-how at the law firm Norton Rose LLP, provided an account of the current vocational training arrangements at the leading English law schools. Pam Ellis, a secretary at Norton Rose LLP, assisted in her free time with the initial typing of the first two chapters. Erica Peters, a content editor, assisted with transferring a list of amendments to the provisional manuscript. Sylvia Lough and Maggie Stevenson, Lord Woolf's secretaries, are also thanked here for their support and encouragement.

CONTENTS

Chronology   xi

Introduction   1

I. The English Legal System

1. A Question of Balance   19
2. Remedies   45
3. Droit Public—English Style   69
4. The Education the Justice System Requires Today   89

II. The Constitution and the Judiciary

5. Magna Carta: A Precedent for Recent Constitutional Change   101
6. The Rule of Law and a Change in the Constitution   117
7. Judicial Review—The Tensions Between the Executive and
   the Judiciary   131
8. Should the Media and the Judiciary be on Speaking Terms?   149
9. Judicial Independence Not Judicial Isolation   161
10. The Needs of a 21st Century Judge   175
11. Current Challenges in Judging   193
12. The Impact of Human Rights   209
13. Human Rights and Minorities   223

III. Crime and Penal Reform

14. The Strangeways Prison Report: Overview   239
15. Strangeways: A Decade of Change?   259
16. A Justice System the Community Owns   277

17. Do We Need a New Approach to Penal Policy?   281

18. Making Sense of Sentencing   293

IV. Civil Justice

19. Access to Justice Final Report: Overview   311

20. Medics, Lawyers and the Courts—A Defence of the Access to Justice Recommendations   323

21. Are the Courts Excessively Deferential to the Medical Profession?   343

22. Are the Judiciary Environmentally Myopic?   361

23. Environmental Law and Sustainable Development   381

V. International Legal Systems

24. The International Role of the Judiciary   395

25. The Rule of Law and the Development of a Modern Economy in China   405

26. The Rule of Law and Harmony in China   417

Index   427

CHRONOLOGY

1933	Born, Newcastle-upon-Tyne, son of late Alexander Woolf and Leah Woolf (née Cussins)
1946–1951	Fettes College, Edinburgh
1951–1954	University College London, Laws
1954	Called to the Bar of England and Wales, Inner Temple; Commission (National Service), 15/19th Royal Hussars
1955	Secondment to Army Legal Services, Army Captain
1956–1979	Barrister, 1 Crown Office Row Chambers
1961	Married Marguerite Sassoon; three sons, Jeremy, Andrew, Elliot
1972–1979	Recorder, Crown Court
1973–1974	Junior Counsel, Inland Revenue
1974–1979	First Treasury Junior Counsel
1976	Bencher, Inner Temple
1979–1986	Judge, High Court of Justice, Queens Bench Division
1981–	Fellow of University College London
1981–1984	Presiding Judge, South East Circuit
1981–1985	Member of Senate, Inns of Court and Bar
1985–1989	President, Association of Law Teachers
1985–1994	Board of Management, Institute of Advanced Legal Studies
1986–1994	Chairman, Institute of Advanced Legal Studies
1986–1990	Middlesex Advisory Committee on Justices of the Peace
1986–1991	Chairman, Lord Chancellor's Advisory Committee on Legal Education
1986–1992	Lord Justice of Appeal
1987–1993	South West London Magistrates Association
1987–2000	Central Council of Jewish Social Services
1989–1993	Governor, Oxford Centre for Postgraduate Hebrew Studies
1991	The Strangeways Prison Report
1992	Life Peer
1992–1996	Lord of Appeal in Ordinary
1992–1996	Chairman: Butler Trust (Life President)
1993–1997	Special Trustees, St Mary's Hospital, Paddington, London

1994–1996	Association of Members of the Boards of Visitors
1994–2002	Pro-Chancellor, University of London
1996	Access to Justice Report
1996–2000	Master of the Rolls; Lord Chancellor's Advisory Committee on Public Records; Public Records Society; Magna Carta Trust; Visitor, Nuffield College, University of Oxford and University College London
1998–2000	Council of Civil Justice; Rules Committee
1998–	Patron, Centre for the Study of Jewish-Christian Relations
2000–2005	Lord Chief Justice of England and Wales
2001–2005	World Bank International Advisory Council on Law and Justice; Vice-President, Royal Overseas League
2003–	Non-permanent Judge, Hong Kong Supreme Court
2005–	Chairman, University College London Council and Visiting Professor; Bank of England's Financial Markets Law Committee; Chancellor, Open University of Israel
2006–	President, Qatar Financial Centre Civil and Commercial Court; Chartered Arbitrator/Mediator, Blackstone Chambers
2007–	Chairman, BAE Systems 'Ethics Committee'

Honorary Doctorates

Hon LLD, University of Buckingham (1990), University of Bristol (1992), University of London (1993), Anglia Polytechnic University (1994), Manchester Metropolitan University (1994), University of Hull (2001), University of Richmond (2001), University of Cambridge (2002), University of Birmingham (2002), University of Exeter (2002), University of Wolverhampton (2002); Hon DSc, Cranfield (2002); Hon DLit, University of London (2002), University of Oxford (2004). Hon Fellow of the British Academy, the Academy of Medical Sciences, UCL, and the US College of Trial Lawyers. Hon Member of the American Law Institute.

Publications

Protecting the Public: the New Challenge (Hamlyn Lecture, 1990); *The Strangeways Prison Report* (HMSO, 1991); ed with J Woolf, *Declaratory Judgement* (2nd edn, 1993), (3rd edn, 2002); *Access to Justice Report* (HMSO, 1996); ed jtly, de Smith, *Judicial Review of Administrative Action* (5th edn, 1999), (6th edn, 2007).

INTRODUCTION

This book consists of a series of lectures that I gave during my time as a judge. Its title, *The Pursuit of Justice,* was chosen because I believe judges should strive to achieve justice. They should not be content to be merely neutral arbitrators who, having listened to the arguments of both sides, give reasoned judgments. They should be proactive; even fiercely proactive in the pursuit of justice.

This was not the attitude of judges when I started to practice law, but it had become the pattern by the time I retired on 1 October 2005. I was privileged to be able to assist with bringing the changes about. Some of the lectures in this book help to explain why and how the changes occurred. I followed the traditional route to becoming a High Court judge, beginning my legal career as a barrister. Solicitors can also be appointed directly to the High Court bench, but the number who have followed this route is woefully few.

My practice at the bar was admirable preparation for being a judge. It taught you about the needs of litigants. It meant you had a thorough understanding of how courts work. You were aware of the tricks of the trade. Perhaps most importantly you appeared before a great variety of judges and were in a good position to form your own opinion as to different styles of judging. This is a considerable advantage. Until a new judge becomes an appellate judge he will always sit alone and no one will comment on his personal performance. They were given virtually no guidance or training. So it was painfully easy to develop bad habits which remained uncorrected unless you corrected them yourself. You are more likely to make the correction if you suffered as an advocate from judges with similar bad habits. In particular, witnessing the effects of the disease can provide real protection against contracting 'Judgitis'.

What I did not have was personal experience of politics. By the time I became a judge this was, as I would come to learn, a handicap from which virtually all the judiciary suffered. Unlike the previous position, during my career at the bar, it was difficult if not impossible to combine a successful career as a barrister with that of a Member of Parliament. Particularly if you share my good fortune, and serve in succession in the highest judicial offices, you realise that it can be a considerable advantage to have had first-hand experience of politics. You then have a better understanding of the implication of your decisions on the State's ability to carry out its responsibilities to govern.

My role as a barrister and then as a judge stretched over more than 50 years. If anything can justify this book it is not the length of that period, but the fact I was able to witness the transformation of almost every aspect of the legal scene. The scale and the rapidity of the change were without precedent. A legal system that had evolved over at least 800 years was transformed by being bombarded with change both from within and without. In addition, in the case of a great many of the changes, I was a prominent participant. Many of the lectures included in this book provide a first hand contemporaneous account of different aspects of the process of change.

Early days

Equipping myself for the role I was to play in the law began in 1946 with my being sent to the Scottish public school, Fettes, at the age of 13, and then in 1951 to University College London (UCL), of which I am now proud to be Chairman of the Council and a visiting professor. I enjoyed myself thoroughly at both establishments but did not distinguish myself in my studies at either. However, I learnt to stand on my own two feet at Fettes, notwithstanding a degree of prejudice that was counter balanced by the loyal support of my friends. At UCL, I was taught law extraordinarily well, which was fortunate as I spent far less time on my studies than I should have.

Despite my failings as a student I passed my barrister or 'bar' exams and was called to the bar by the Inner Temple in 1954; the night before I joined the army for my National Service. My experience of practising law began while I was in the army. Having been commissioned, I was seconded from my regiment, the 15th/19th Kings Royal Hussars, to the Army Legal Services. This meant that during the majority of my National Service I was exposed to military law and was able to acquire experience of prosecuting, 'in patrols', at court martials. This stood me in good stead for what was to come, as most of my work at the bar initially involved criminal law. It included visits to Germany to defend soldiers before court martials. Having been a gamekeeper, I became a poacher.

One difference between practice when I became a barrister and practice today is that there used to be much less specialisation. This was especially true for those practising on a circuit. In my case, the circuit was the Oxford Circuit.

If you had a specialisation it was in advocacy and court craft. True circuiteers would not dream of declining a brief because it involved an area of law of which up to then they were ignorant. The change to greater specialisation was probably inevitable but not necessarily for the better. You cannot divide the law into watertight compartments and both as counsel and as a judge you need to be able to take a holistic view.

Both in giving judgments and in giving the many lectures that a contemporary senior judge is required to give, of which only a minority of mine are able to be included in this book, I have found my extremely broad experience to be a considerable advantage.

Unusually for a circuiteer at that time I had experience of tax law. This was entirely due to the Inland Revenue's belief in the merits of retaining generalists to act on their behalf in the courts even in the specialist area of tax. My career at the bar changed when I was appointed standing junior counsel to the Revenue, colloquially known as the 'Revenue Devil'. In the eyes of the Revenue, I had one primary qualification; I had never previously appeared in a Revenue case! The Revenue correctly thought they knew all about tax law. What they wanted was counsel who had a general experience of the way in which courts were likely to react to problems, and who could assist them to avoid acting in a way that was not in accord with the standards the courts would expect of a Government Department.

The wisdom of the Revenue's policy was illustrated by one of the first problems on which they asked me to advise. The very clever and conscientious Revenue lawyers wanted me to advise on when it was acceptable for the Revenue to make an application for summary judgment. This involved swearing in an affidavit that there was no arguable defence. However, what was the position if, although the Revenue believed they were bound to succeed after a trial, with their knowledge of tax law, the Revenue were able to identify an ingenious argument that might create a defence, but which they thought would fail? I understood their concerns, but they were not being realistic and I had no difficulty in advising them that the then Rule 14 of the Supreme Court only prevented the making of an application for summary judgment if there was a real possibility of the defence succeeding at trial.

You did not need to be a tax lawyer to give that advice. I was able to refer to my wholly unrelated experience at Oxford City Quarter Sessions. At that court, if a defendant to a criminal charge pleaded not guilty despite overwhelming evidence pointing to guilt, there was always a prospect of there being at least one scientist being on the jury who, in his wisdom, would never be satisfied about anything beyond reasonable doubt and so could always be relied on to have doubts as to the defendant's guilt. In both situations those responsible for making the decision, whether juror or Revenue expert, had to be encouraged to be guided by common sense if justice was to be done.

My experience of Oxford City Quarter Sessions related to my initial period of practice as a member of the Oxford Circuit. It was on that Circuit I learnt my trade as an advocate. John Alliot,[1] who was the next most junior member of 1 Crown Office Row, the barristers' chambers I joined as a pupil and happily remained until I became a judge, explained the approach you should adopt as a young barrister if a solicitor was considering instructing you in a case involving an area of the law about which you know nothing. His excellent advice was to 'Look the solicitor directly in the eye, confess your ignorance and say: "while I know scarcely anything about the subject now, come tomorrow I will know as much as any expert".' What John called his 'total advocacy' always impressed the solicitor who would be won over by his enthusiasm.

It was while I was learning my trade as a circuiteer that the importance of integrity was drilled into me. This required complete frankness with the bench. It was also paramount to treat your opponents at the bar with courtesy and fairness. These are values the circuit system had preserved for hundreds of years. You would not prosper on the Circuit if you failed to observe them.

It is also through the Oxford Circuit that I learnt valuable lessons as to the dangers that can be involved in seeking to reform our legal system. Dr Beeching (of railways fame) was given the task of creating a new structure for the court system. Changes were undoubtedly needed and the reforms he recommended, which were generally accepted by the government, became law in consequence of the Courts Act 1971. They transformed a system which had been evolving since medieval times. Historic Assizes, Quarter and Borough Sessions which had until then been responsible for dispensing criminal justice, disappeared, to be replaced by the new Crown Courts for the whole of England and Wales. This new structure has stood the test of time and is still largely intact today. The recommendations were a remarkable achievement for which Dr Beeching deserves great credit. Yet, despite this, he made at least two basic mistakes. First, he did not recognise the need for justice to be locally administered. He swept away the local

---

[1] Later Mr Justice Alliot.

administration and in its place introduced a centrally administered court service massively increased in size. Secondly, he removed from the judges the responsibility for overseeing the running of the courts and managing their lists. The judges' responsibility was relegated to doing justice in the individual cases that came before them.

I am almost certainly being unfair, but at the time I thought Dr Beeching never really understood the important part played by the old system in the pursuit of justice. I still find it difficult to understand how he could abolish the Oxford Circuit without justifying what he was doing. It was done as part of a tidying up operation by the simple device of redrawing the boundaries of the other six circuits. The result was that the 800-year-old proud Oxford Circuit ceased to exist.[2] History sometimes repeats itself. Could there be a similar explanation for the manner in which the former Prime Minister, Tony Blair, sought unsuccessfully to abolish the office of Lord Chancellor?

I attempted to address the shortcomings to which I have just referred at various stages of my judicial career. The need for local or community prisons plays an important role in my Prison Report and local justice in which the judiciary are deeply involved are central to my recommendations for access to justice. Both of which are subjects with which the lectures deal. One of the few rays of hope for the criminal judicial scene are community courts such as that which now exists in Liverpool, presided over by a judge committed to the locality.

One significant way in which the deficit created by Dr Beeching was addressed was by the creation and the increasing reliance upon the office of Presiding Judge. For each of the surviving six circuits, there are two Presiding Judges who, 'in partnership' with the Circuit Administrator of the Circuit, are responsible for overseeing the administration of justice on Circuit. When one Presiding Judge is in London, the other is on Circuit. On the Circuit, they are the eyes, ears, and voice of the Chief Justice. They and the Senior Presiding Judge, who coordinates their activities, provide local proactive administration. The importance of their contribution to the system as a whole is not in dispute. They are the means for resolving local concerns and assist in achieving common standards across the system.

---

[2] For a more detailed account of my concerns, see Foreword in G Williams QC, *Death of A Circuit: Being Some Account of The Oxford Circuit and How it was Established* (Wildy, Simmonds and Hill Publishing, 2006).

I use the word 'partnership' to denote a sharing of responsibility. However, in my experience, Circuit Administrators are usually content for the Presiding Judges to take the lead unless it is an issue where the judiciary and Ministers have not been able to agree on common objectives. This concept of 'partnership' has been central to my thinking in relation to the development of an effective justice system. While the administration has day-to-day responsibility for the effective running of the courts, it does so in concert with the judiciary. As civil servants, administrators are now ultimately answerable to the Minister of Justice and Lord Chancellor. But they also have a separate responsibility to support the judiciary and, under the Constitutional Reform Act 2005, the Minister of Justice, as Lord Chancellor has a special duty to uphold the independence of the judiciary. In many of the lectures in this book you will find that I repeatedly come back to this theme of partnership. If the executive wholeheartedly gives effect to the concept of partnership, the relationship between the executive and the judiciary prospers, as do the interests of the public. But when the executive acts independently the relationship falters and administration of justice suffers. A demonstration of this is provided by a paper included in this book, the Essex Lecture, 'Judicial Independence, Not Judicial Isolation'.[3]

Revenue and Treasury Junior

Following my 18 months as Revenue Junior my career at the bar took another change of direction. In 1974 I was appointed the Common Law Treasury Junior or Treasury Devil, the senior post at the junior common law bar. I was then 40 years of age. My appointment carried with it the expectation that I would at the end of my term of office, usually five years, be appointed a High Court judge. This is what happened.

While, as Revenue Junior, I had been responsible for one Government Department, I was now responsible for advising and representing the great majority of Government Departments in relation to common law issues. I was also regularly instructed to appear as the friend of the court or amicus curiae when the court had a particularly difficult question of law or legal policy to decide.

The Treasury Devil was appointed by the Attorney-General and was called the 'Devil' because he used to 'devil' or work on cases on which the

---

[3] See Chapter 9 in this book.

Attorney-General's opinion was required. He would appear alongside the Attorney-General as his junior when the Attorney appeared before the courts.

I was appointed at a time when there was a dramatic increase in litigation involving the Government. There were also considerable developments in the vigour with which the courts scrutinised the legality of activities of the Government and other public bodies. The tools the courts used to do this were still the historic prerogative orders, but the circumstances in which they would be granted rapidly developed.[4]

Judicial Review and Human Rights

Being the Treasury Devil gave me unrivalled experience of Judicial Review. I had a unique insight into its strengths and weaknesses at that time. When I became a judge in 1979, Lord Widgery Chief Justice asked me to assist in drafting the 1980 amendments to the relatively new Order 53 of the Rules of the Supreme Court. The changes in procedure created a new motorway over which litigants challenging actions of the Government travelled in ever increasing numbers. I witnessed the effect the new procedure had in making it easier for members of the public to obtain redress for unlawful actions on the part of the Government. I was to deploy the same lesson more than ten years later when I was asked to make the report which became known as the 'Woolf Report' on the 'Access to Justice Reforms'. I knew just how important a part Civil Procedure can play in determining the quality of civil justice. Judicial Review, after the reforms, ceased being a process in which there were chronic delays and technical hurdles to be surmounted. In addition, the creation of an effective procedure gave judges confidence to develop the substantive law. It was in this period that the judiciary established a system of administrative law which was capable of supervising the great expansion in the powers of public bodies and, particularly, central Government, that has taken place over the preceding 25 years.

Lacking a written constitution and without the European Convention on Human Rights being part of our domestic law until 2000, judicial review expanded its reach to fill what would otherwise have been a gap in the safeguards available to protect the public against unlawful executive action.

---

[4] See 'A Question of Balance' in *The Protection of the Public—A New Challenge* (Stevens & Son, 1989), included as Chapter 1 of this book, which describes the situation at that time. This was the first of my Hamlyn Lectures, given at the Institute of Advanced Legal Studies in London.

There remained, however, a great weakness in our system of administrative law. All too often our citizens would have to appeal to the Court of Human Rights at Strasbourg for remedies they could not obtain from their own English courts. It is greatly to the credit of the present Labour Government that shortly after they came into power in 1997 they introduced the Human Rights Act 1998 which incorporated the European Convention into our domestic law. This has proved to be the catalyst, transforming the availability of protection for breaches of human rights in this jurisdiction. But it is not only our citizens who have benefited. The decisions of our domestic courts have over the last few years been increasingly influential in encouraging developments in the Strasbourg jurisprudence.

Immigration, Asylum and Terrorism

The improvements in the effectiveness of Judicial Review and in the use of human rights jurisprudence, after the ECHR became part of our domestic law, were fortunately well timed. The UK has always been considered to be a bastion of the freedom of the individual and a champion of the rule of law. Magna Carta may have been undervalued by the country but its spirit has never been extinguished. In the three situations to which I will now turn, the courts made clear their determination to ensure justice was done irrespective of the lack of sympathy of the media and a section of the public for those whose rights were in issue.

The three situations all concerned individuals who had at some stage come to the UK from abroad and who were denigrated for that reason. Initially, the issues came before special tribunals rather than the ordinary courts.

For those seeking access to the UK as immigrants or seeking to prevent their removal as illegal immigrants, part of the difficulty was the very large numbers involved. Neither the Home Office nor the tribunals were able to cope with the scale of the immigration. The problems were accentuated by the fact that an initial hearing before a tribunal could be followed by repeated subsequent applications and appeals, and then the whole process would be repeated on applications for judicial review. The chaotic situation that resulted illustrated the importance of a sensible and proportional procedure designed for the resolution of the issues involved in the proceedings.

At numerous stages of my career I spent many hours with officials trying to find an answer but the political tensions and inadequate resources meant the solutions I suggested were never given the time to prove themselves. Instead, the Government would dream up new initiatives designed more for public consumption than to solve the problems.

What did produce an improvement was the injection, with my agreement, of High Court judges into both the first instance and appellate level of the tribunal system. However, this did not satisfy Government, which continued to intervene with further legislation. The result was a promising initiative that was not able to prove its worth. Despite the efforts of those presiding, an efficient, fair, and proportionate tribunal system for handling immigration cases was never achieved.

Nonetheless, the High Court did ensure that in the cases that reached the High Court, justice was provided to immigrants in the same way as it was provided for any other litigants. It was in an immigration case that it was established for the first time that even a Secretary of State can be liable for contempt of court.[5] The courts' success here was evident from the lengths governments were prepared to go to avoid the consequences of the courts decisions. One tactic was to remove the right to all social benefits from applicants and another was to remove directly the right of access to the courts. To dilute the first tactic, the courts limited the circumstances to which it applied. As for the second tactic, I had the satisfaction of knowing that one of the lectures in this volume contributed to the Government's decision to withdraw the unprecedented proposed legislation intended to exclude any application to the courts.[6] The proposed provision shamefully was in direct conflict with the rule of law.

The second situation involved those seeking asylum. The story is very similar to that in the case of immigration. In both, the judiciary demonstrated their determination to ensure that justice was done according to law.

The third situation involved the detention without charge of suspected terrorists. National security considerations were involved. While there was provision for a hearing before a high level tribunal, even with the use of special advocates the detainees had none of the normal rights to be informed of the case against them. Perhaps if the period of detention had been shorter a different view may have been taken, but detention for many months,

---

[5] See *M v Home Office* [1994] 1 AC 377.
[6] See H Woolf, 'The Rule of Law and a Change in the Constitution', Squire Centenary Lecture, University of Cambridge, 3 March 2004, included in this book at Chapter 6.

even indefinitely, meant the process was inadequate and was rightly struck down by the House of Lords.[7]

The Government then resorted to control orders. Here they have also had setbacks as a result of the courts' decisions. The last word on this subject remains to be pronounced by the House of Lords. I hope, if it is adverse to the Government in the course of giving their opinions, the House of Lords will feel able to indicate what courses are open to the Government to protect the public. In accord with the principles of partnership to which I am committed, when many lives could be at stake the courts should in my view be sensitive to the genuine dilemma in which the Government finds itself. Some way has to be found of squaring the circle. The rights of the public and detainees should be protected equally. The courts have demonstrated that terrorist suspects are entitled to the same protection from the courts as any other citizen, but so are citizens entitled to be protected against terrorists. This is how it should be and I believe a better solution could be achieved than exists under the current control order regime.

A former Home Secretary, Charles Clarke, feels strongly that the Law Lords should have responded positively to his request to meet them to discuss the action he should take to square the circle. However, he overlooks the need for the House of Lords to retain not only its independence, but its appearance of independence in a situation where it is likely that the legality of any scheme discussed informally could be tested before the courts up to the House of Lords level.[8] The discussion he wanted was of a different nature from that which I encouraged between myself, as chief executive of the judiciary, and Ministers. My discussions related to matters of administration and management of the courts and the judiciary, and not issues that could come before the courts for decision in litigation.

Now I am retired as Chief Justice and no longer have any intention to sit as a judge in the Appellate Committee of the House of Lords, I am in a position to comment on the dilemma faced by the Government, although my views are no more worthy of consideration than those of anyone else. It is my belief that the initial mistake was asking a tribunal to adjudicate on the issues rather than the ordinary courts. This is despite the fact that the proceedings in the tribunal are presided over by a High Court judge. Secondly, more effort should have been made for evidence to be heard in

---

[7] See *A v Secretary of State for the Home Department* [2004] UKHL 56, [2005] 2 AC 68.
[8] See House of Lords Sixth Report, 'Relations Between the Executive, the Judiciary and Parliament', HL paper 151 (HMSO, 26 July 2007), for a description of the tensions.

public than occurred. Normal procedures should have been used except where an exception in the public interest was essential. Where an exception was shown to be essential the exception should have been no greater than was strictly necessary. Having, while Treasury Junior, dealt with many cases involving the need for secrecy, I am far from convinced that if sufficient flexibility had been deployed it would not have been possible to adopt normal procedures to a greater extent than occurred. Instead, the procedure introduced special courts, proceedings that did not involve any charge, but only suspicion, and detention for unlimited periods. This can involve such a disregard of the ordinary standards of fairness that it is not surprising they were found to be unacceptable.

Criminal Proceedings and Sentencing

When I became Chief Justice, two separate initiatives in the criminal field for which the Government could claim credit raised expectations that this could be an opportunity to make a difference. The initiatives were the establishment of the Criminal Procedure Committee as a counterpart to the Civil Procedure Committee and a Sentencing Guidelines Council to work in conjunction with the Sentencing Advisory Panel. I was by statute and in reality Chairman of both bodies.

The Criminal Justice Act 2003 focussed on creating a panoply of meaningful non-custodial remedies as an alternative to prison. Both David Blunkett, a former Home Secretary, and I, recognised the possibilities this presented of tackling the serious problems of funds being squandered, overcrowded prisons, and the failure to rehabilitate offenders from crime. David Blunkett was the initiator of this meaningful reform.

Criminal law lacked any sensible or comprehensive procedural code and trials were in need of forceful and effective management. The new Committee set about remedying this situation. Following the precedent of what happened in the case of civil justice, the new Procedural Committee commenced by producing overriding objectives that created, for the first time, an obligation on both the prosecution and defence to cooperate in the management of the criminal process. The defence was required to reveal its hand. Ambush defences were to be a thing of the past.

The support of the judiciary, solicitors, and barristers, was essential if real progress was to be made. This was forthcoming from the majority involved and was, by itself, a significant gain. It resulted in a protocol designed to create proportionate conduct of criminal trials. Trials were to finish usually in not more than three months and at most within six months. I did not and do not believe you can expect a jury to be able to try a case if it does not finish within these periods. Even more importantly, case management was to be part of the trial process.

Sadly, the initial progress achieved by the Procedure Committee and the judiciary was undermined by a clash between the criminal bar and the former Lord Chancellor, Lord Falconer, over fees. The merits of the dispute are too complex to discuss here, but at a time when great change could have been achieved consensually, the momentum was brought to a halt by a refusal of Lord Falconer to make the minor concession needed to obtain progress. The judiciary could have pressed on but our judgment was that this would result in the bar, who felt they had been pushed too far, carrying out their threat to strike. Even if this was too pessimistic a view, certainly the necessary spirit of consensus had dissipated. I can only hope that passage of time has restored the cooperation needed between bar and bench.

Lack of resources also undermined the emphasis on non-custodial sentences. Some of the new sentences have never been implemented. Others were implemented, but not meaningfully. The Probation Service did not have the capacity to provide the necessary support. The Sentencing Guidelines Council also ran into trouble. One of my hopes for the Council was that it would bridge what has been described as a geological fault in the criminal justice system. The fault being due to the fact that it is primarily the judges who sentence to imprisonment but it is the Home Office that is responsible for the prisons. The Council was composed of very senior representatives of the majority of agencies involved in sentencing. The Panel was an expert body who provided the detailed advice on which the Council would act. They were independent bodies. It was to be hoped they would take sentencing out of politics.

This hope proved illusory. The Council had been led to believe there was support for their taking action to reduce the excessive use of prisons and some of the early guidelines were intended to contribute to the dampening of inflation in the use of prison sentences. This, however, infuriated the tabloid press with the consequence that Government support evaporated. We returned to legislation that increased the use of imprisonment. The worst example of this was a huge increase in the tariffs for murder, which I am afraid I regarded as a bad tempered response by the former Home Secretary David Blunkett to the removal by the Court at Strasbourg of the Home Secretary's power to decide when those serving a life sentence should be released.

The result was that by the time I left office as Chief Justice my optimism had been dashed. We now have a population of prisoners we can only house in conditions that reduce to a minimum the prospects of turning prisoners away from crime. It also made a mockery of the sentences passed by the courts—if the judges passed the sentences recent legislation required, those sentences would produce a prison population which could only be accommodated if a regime of early release of prisoners was rigorously practiced. Even if the resources existed for the prisons that needed to be built there was no prospect of this happening in the available timescale.

The Prison and Civil Justice Reports

The Human Rights Act 1998 was enacted when I was Master of the Rolls and implemented in 2000, the year I became Lord Chief Justice. However, it was the reforms that implemented my Prison and Civil Justice Reports that had the most direct influence on our justice system.[9] The subject matter of both reports was different, but the way in which I prepared the reports was similar. Both reports were based on extensive consultation. This was central to the recommendations that were made. Each report involved a two-stage process. For example, with the Prison Report, I first identified the role prisons should perform in our society and then recommended the holistic reforms that were required if the prisons were to be in a position to play this role. While both sets of reforms were holistic they built on what had gone before. Both reports were extraordinarily well received. On publication of the Prison Report the then Home Secretary, Kenneth Baker, accepted all the recommendations it contained on behalf of the Government. In the case of Civil Justice, the former Lord Chancellor, Lord MacKay of Clashfern, accepted my report. There was then a change of Government and the next Lord Chancellor, Lord Irvine, also accepted my recommendations, albeit only after Sir Peter Middleton, a former Permanent Secretary, had endorsed them. Initially, there were significant improvements in the operation of prisons and I was optimistic we would have a prison system in which the UK would be proud.

Unfortunately, my optimism proved to be premature. There developed a war between the main political parties as a result of which the criminal justice system in general and prisons in particular have been the ultimate victims.

---

[9] I was assisted by excellent assessors and many others. For the Prisons Report, there were two stages: an initial report and a final report. His Honour Judge Stephen Tumin and I produced the final report together.

One headline-grabbing change after another has followed, regardless of whether the system had sufficient resources to properly implement them. More attention has been paid to being tough on crime than on the causes of crime. Prisons for a number of years have suffered from such severe over-crowding that it has prevented the prison service and the other agencies in the criminal justice service being able to take the action which is known to be necessary if there is to be a reduction in re-offending. However, at least the Prison Service still regards my Report as being a blueprint for reform. Perhaps there is a prospect that one day it will be recognised, as surely it should be, that present policies are the cause of the chaos that now exists within the prison system. The answer is to put in place, albeit belatedly, such of my reforms that still await implementation.

In the case of civil justice the outcome has been happier and there has been the change of culture which I hoped to achieve. The reform is not complete. While my report was being implemented, the Government made savage cuts to legal aid. It then replaced the vacuum this created with conditional fees and insurance, both of which have grossly increased costs, although they did fill the vacuum created by the savaging of legal aid. In addition, despite its impor-tance to the economy, the civil justice system has been starved of resources due to the mistaken belief that civil justice can be financed out of court fees. This belief is wholly in conflict with the policy I was promoting, that litigation should be a last resort and only used if other methods of dispute resolution are or would be ineffective. This was designed to reduce and did reduce litigation which in turn limited the income available from court fees for the reformers.

Reform of the English Unwritten Constitution

While I was invited to play a leading role in the reform of prisons, civil, and later, criminal procedure, there was a fundamentally different approach adopted by the Government to constitutional reform. This was largely initi-ated without warning and consulting the judiciary as to what was about to happen. Both in relation to the abolition of the Office of Lord Chancellor and the creation of a Ministry of Justice (after I had retired in 2005), there was no proper consultation until after the intended changes had been announced. The Squire Centenary Lecture, 'The Rule of Law and a Change in the Constitution', sets out the dismal sequence of events triggered by a press announcement.[10]

---

[10] See n 6 above.

Fortunately, it was apparent, within hours after the announcement of the proposal to abolish the Office of Lord Chancellor, that this was a change for which legislation would be needed. This led to direct negotiations between the new Lord Chancellor and Secretary of State, Lord Falconer, and myself; the outcome of which was the Concordat followed by the Constitutional Reform Act 2005. This gave full effect to the principles of partnership to which I referred earlier. It also resulted in a new process for judicial appointments, disciplining judges, and a Supreme Court. In addition, Government ministers were placed under a new duty to uphold the continued independence of the judiciary and to ensure they have the necessary resources.[11]

Partnership does, however, require cooperation between the partners. Already there have been very worrying tensions between the Government and the judiciary over a number of further constitutional changes involving the unilateral transmogrifying of the Lord Chancellor's second office of Secretary of State for Constitutional Affairs into that of a Minister of Justice who is not a member of the House of Lords but is a member of the Commons.[12]

As for reform of the Office of the Attorney-General, another great historic legal office of state, a consultation paper has been published and I wait to see if there is to be a meaningful consultation. If there is, it will suggest lessons have been learned and that the necessary cooperation between the Government and the judiciary is possible.

Conclusion

I trust this introduction will enable the reader to place the lectures in their context; a context that has involved an extraordinary volume of change to which I have had the privilege of contributing.

A cottage industry has become a massive legal system. But the changes were not brought about because of a master plan designed in the corridors of Whitehall. Much of the change was the result of single initiatives precipitated by circumstances that had not been anticipated by the Government of the day.

---

[11] See Constitutional Reform Act 2005, s 3. This is supported by the oath the Lord Chancellor has to make on taking office. Ibid, s 17.

[12] See n 8 above.

These lectures are an individual's spasmodic comments on change brought about in this way. However, when read with this Introduction they lead me to the following conclusions:

1. Despite the haphazard manner in which the reforms took place, the English unwritten constitution and legal system have proved to be sufficiently robust to absorb the strains imposed upon them.

2. In any justice system the role of procedure is far greater than generally accepted. Procedural improvements can transform the ability of a legal system to achieve efficient and proportionate justice.

3. The changes that have taken place have improved the English legal system. In many cases the improvement is despite, and not because of, the way Government introduced change. Great credit is due to the judiciary and the Court Service for the way in which, as partners, they have accepted change and driven it forward. In the English system, it is usually and perhaps always the case that to achieve lasting improvement the judiciary and the administration have to act in concert.

4. It is extremely disappointing that the Government has undermined the quality of the English legal system by failing to provide the resources it requires. The English legal profession and judges are rightly admired internationally, but, if our legal system had been adequately resourced, so much could have been achieved.

5. Finally, the judiciary have had to take on heavy additional responsibilities both in the UK and abroad. This has certainly added to the burdens of being a judge. No one becomes a judge today for a quiet life. However, the changes in the role have added to the satisfaction to be derived from being a judge. This is notwithstanding the fact that their current role can bring a judge into confrontation with Government, the media, and sections of the population who have little sympathy for human rights. Despite this, the judiciary can still be relied upon to continue the *pursuit of justice*. Long may this remain the situation.

PART I

The English Legal System

1

A Question of Balance

Abstract This paper provides an introduction to the English legal system, explaining that a distinction, albeit blurred, between public and private law is now an essential feature at the heart of the English administrative law system. It gives an historical account of the procedure for judicial review, being primarily concerned with enforcing public duties on behalf of the public as a whole, vindicating the interests of the individual as part of the process of ensuring public bodies do not act unlawfully and do perform their public duties. It discusses the safeguards in judicial review procedure and notes that courts should use their powers to remedy injustice rather than unnecessarily intervening where there is no injustice. This involves a fundamental change from the traditional approach of English law, which in the past used to equate the rights and duties of public bodies with those of private individuals. It is the base upon which future legal developments have occurred.

Introduction

Lord Denning gave the first Hamlin Lectures 57 years ago in 1949. The title was 'Freedom under the Law'. I was not fortunate enough to hear the lectures, but I have read them and they are, as you would expect, splendid. They are a paean of praise of the English legal system. However, they conclude with a warning delivered in Lord Denning's unique style:

> No one can suppose that the executive will never be guilty of the sins that are common to all of us. You may be sure that they will sometimes do things which they ought not to do: and will not do things that they ought to do. But if and when wrongs are thereby suffered by any of us what is the remedy? Our procedure for securing our personal freedom is efficient, our procedure

---

* This paper was originally delivered as the first of four lectures in the forty-first series of the Hamlyn Lectures. See H Woolf, *Protection of the Public—A New Challenge* (Stevens & Sons, 1990), 1–36.

for preventing the abuse of power is not. Just as the pick and shovel is no longer suitable for the winning of coal, so also the procedure of mandamus, certiorari, and actions on the case are not suitable for the winning of freedom in the new age. They must be replaced by new and up to date machinery, by declarations, injunctions and actions for negligence . . . This is not the task of Parliament . . . The courts must do this. Of all the great tasks that lie ahead this is the greatest. Properly exercised the new powers of the executive lead to the welfare state; but abused they lead to a totalitarian state. None such must ever be allowed in this country.[1]

When, 40 years later, I became the surprising if not eccentric choice of the Hamlyn Trustees to give these 1989 lectures I was unable to resist the temptation to look again at what Lord Denning described as the greatest task of the courts in the 'new age'.

The only justification for my presumption in taking on this task, other than that I inherited Lord Denning's second set of Court of Appeal robes, is that due to two strokes of good fortune I have been involved, intimately first as a barrister and then as a judge, in more than my fair share of cases which have contributed to the development of administrative law. I happened to be the common law Treasury Junior or 'Devil' when the new Order 53, which introduced a new procedure for challenging the abuse of power by public bodies, first came into force in 1977.[2] So, up until that time, I had to work with the procedure which Lord Denning accurately prophesised would prove inadequate for the task. I was also one of the four judges who were nominated for the first time to hear administrative law cases under the second stage of the reform introduced in 1980. As both these roles provide the source of my experience, I should say something about them.

The Treasury Junior or 'Devil'

The Treasury Devil is an office the origins of which it is difficult to trace. However, according to an impeccable source, the former Lord Justice Cumming-Bruce, who believes he received the information from an equally impressive source, Lord Justice Winn (both ex Treasury Devils), the first

---

[1] 'Freedom Under the Law' (Hamlyn Lectures, 1949), 126.

[2] See Supreme Court [Senior Courts] Act 1981, s 31 (soon to be renamed the Senior Courts Act 1981: Constitutional Reform Act 2005, s 59 and Sch 11, para 1). It is to be noted that RSC Order 53 was replaced by CPR Part 54 with effect from 2 October 2000. Part 54 introduced a raft of changes. For example, parties were named 'claimant' and 'defendant' instead of 'applicant' and 'respondent'.

Devil was appointed at the time when Pitt the Younger was Prime Minister. He was appointed because the government, dissatisfied with the service they obtained from the law officers of that day, wanted a member of the Bar who would require the law officers to maintain the proper standards and, if they did not do so, to protest by resigning.

For those unfamiliar with our legal system it is worth saying a few words about the Treasury Devil since he is a constitutional oddity who plays a significant role in our administrative law but, as far as I know, has no precise equivalent in other jurisdictions.[3] The Treasury Devil is accepted as head of the junior Bar. His only badge of office is a textbook, *Manning's Exchequer Practice*, the contents of which are of no possible relevance to the office today, but which record the fact that it has been handed down from one Treasury Devil to another for over a hundred years. The first entry records the transfer from AL Smith to WO Dankwerts in February 1885.

Although he remains an ordinary member of his Chambers, for a period of about five years the Treasury Devil has a general retainer in respect of the government's common law work. This gives him an unrivalled opportunity to obtain an insight into government litigation. However, until he is appointed he may have little or no experience of public law. In my case, although for eighteen months I had been the Revenue Junior,[4] my ignorance of public law was demonstrated by the fact that I had to ask my predecessor, Gordon Slynn,[5] which books I should read in order to prepare myself for my new responsibilities. Fortunately, he suggested de Smith, *Judicial Review of Administrative Action*.[6]

While the Treasury Devil is standing counsel, to most government departments his closest links are with the Attorney-General. The Attorney-General has first call on his Devil's services in respect of both his role as legal adviser to the government and his role as the representative of the public interest in the courts. Because of the Attorney-General's latter role, the Devil is also

---

[3] The nearest of which I am aware is the Solicitor-General in Australia.

[4] My qualification to be the Revenue Junior, which involved representing the Crown in tax cases, was that up until the time I was appointed I had never studied tax or appeared in a tax case. The Revenue consider that they know tax law inside out but require guidance as to how their approach to the law would be perceived by a non-specialist court and so a common law junior with a broad experience of the courts and advocacy would be more likely to supplement their in-house expertise. The practice also avoids their counsel being embarrassed by previous involvement in advising taxpayers.

[5] Now, Lord Slynn.

[6] For the latest version, see S A de Smith, A Le Sueur, J L Jowell, H Woolf (Sweet & Maxwell, 2007).

normally the counsel instructed when the court requires an amicus to argue a difficult point of law from an independent standpoint. In the past, he would always appear in court with the Attorney-General; Lord Rawlinson records in his autobiography that he would never go into court without Gordon Slynn.[7] Today, however, the Law Officer's appearances in court are rare, so John Laws, the current Treasury Devil,[8] often attends by himself in cases where even in my day the Attorney-General would have led.[9] The present law officers have appeared in a number of cases (many before the European Commission, the European Court of Human Rights and the European Court of Justice).

A great strength of the system is that the Crown is being represented by an independent member of the Bar who is briefed and paid[10] for each case he does and is able to take an objective view free from departmental pressures. Yet, during his period in office, the department will make available to him information which is not available to any other outside legal adviser and which indeed can relate to the activities of previous administrations, so it is not even available to ministers. His advice is taken at times by the Prime Minister of the day and he can even be invited to attend Cabinet meetings. If he initially lacks experience of the workings of government, this is compensated for by the quality of his solicitors—the Treasury Solicitor and departmental lawyers who conditionally prepare instructions of the highest quality and who have immense expertise, unrivalled elsewhere, in their specialist field. However, it is only when the Devil has been in office for some time that he is properly equipped to perform his role and the longer he is in office the better able he is to do this and the greater the dependence of the department on his advice. The fact that the Treasury Devil is an independent member of the Bar contributes to the trust which exists between the Treasury Devil and the courts and lawyers appearing for litigants involved in legal proceedings against the Crown. It is accepted that he will not knowingly allow the Crown to abuse its position in the courts. If there is information available to the Crown which should be disclosed, it will be, irrespective of any argument, of a technical nature to the contrary. If a department wishes to use its powers oppressively it will be prevented from

---

[7] *A Price Too High* (1989).

[8] Now, Sir John Laws, Lord Justice of Appeal.

[9] This is still true today for the current Treasury Devil, Phillip Sales QC.

[10] Paid, but modestly! I remember Gordon Slynn (now Lord Slynn) leading me and complaining that while he did not mind being paid less than the leader on the other side, he thought less than one-third of the junior on the other side was going too far.

doing so. Although if rights of audience are extended to employed lawyers cause could be made for declaring the Treasury Devil redundant. I believe this would be a great mistake; it could be bad for standards within the government legal service, bad for the courts and bad for the public. It is all too easy to underestimate the advantages of an independent mind in the inner closets of government.

By the time I was appointed in 1974 there had already been a substantial increase in government litigation and the Treasury Devil certainly could no longer do private work. As my unfortunate pupils will testify, being a Treasury Devil involves frantic activity, rushing from court to court and conference to conference. By the time I became a judge in 1979 the volume of litigation had increased to such an extent that, in order to cope on the common law side, we had a small team. Since that time the team has grown and my successors, having been appointed from this team, have already acquired on appointment the experience which I lacked. However, my Chancery counterpart, Mr Justice Peter Gibson,[11] was then still managing with the majority of Chancery work himself, including some tax cases, and even finding time to join with me, alas, only in some of my cases. I say 'alas', because it remains our proud boast that when we were both briefed to appear together from the Crown we never lost a case. I am afraid my record of appearing on my own was not quite so impressive. With singular lack of success, in a period of little over a year, I appeared in cases such as *Tameside*,[12] *Congreve*,[13] *The Crossman Diaries*,[14] and *Laker Airways*,[15] all of which contributed to the development of administrative law. At the same time, the conventional work progressed very much as it had done in my predecessor's time. The Treasury Devil appeared almost daily before the Lord Chief Justice, Lord Widgery, in the Lord Chief Justice's Court, occupying the seat which was traditionally occupied by the Treasury Devil, the first seat on the left of the central gangway. An astonishing number of cases involving the Crown would be disposed of, frequently on some technicality which would never succeed today, such as insufficient standing or interest or the absence of an error on the face of the record.

---

[11] Now Sir Peter Gibson, former Lord Justice of Appeal, retired on 4 April 2005.
[12] *Secretary of State for Education v Tameside MBC* [1977] AC 1014.
[13] *Congreve v Home Office* [1976] QB 629.
[14] *Attorney-General v Jonathan Cape Ltd* [1976] QB 752.
[15] *Laker Airways Ltd v Department of Trade* [1997] QB 643.

A Nominated Judge

I then became a Judge[16] in time to play a part in drafting the amendment to Order 53. This took effect in 1980 and was the second stage of the reform procedure allowing for the dramatic progress in administrative law which has occurred during recent decades. Like the other four judges who were for the first time nominated to hear applications for judicial review, I found myself called upon to decide cases which a few years earlier would have been quite outside the role of the courts. For example, the part which nurses could lawfully be called upon to play in procuring an abortion,[17] the legality of distributing a pamphlet which described methods of efficiently terminating one's own life,[18] and the lawfulness of a department's guidance on the provision of assistance to girls under the age of 16 as to methods of contraception.[19] Developments were taking place so rapidly that those involved, myself included, were swept along without having time to identify the destination for which we should be heading and without appreciating the hazards we were creating for those who would have to follow behind us. Windeyer J, a distinguished Australian jurist, identified our role when, using a different metaphor, he said:

> A judge is a working hand part of the crew of a vessel, the courts, for which each case is a separate voyage. He has not the time to be a cartographer of lands discovered. This is the task which is undertaken by academic writers.[20]

---

[16] The Treasury Devil does not normally become a Queen's Counsel but goes straight to becoming a judge—it is to be noted that the current Treasury Devil, Phillip Sales QC, has recently become a Queen's Counsel. It might be considered that to appoint a Treasury Devil to be a judge is equivalent to appointing a poacher to be a gamekeeper. In practice, I do not believe it works that way (although I would say that) and in support remember a comment, which I believe was half-serious by my successor (now Lord Brown), that as I had been a judge for about a year it was now no longer necessary always to give judgment against the Crown.

[17] *Royal College of Nursing v DHSS* [1981] AC 800; [1981] CLR 169.

[18] *Attorney-General v Able* [1984] QB 795.

[19] *Gillick v West Norfolk and Wisbech Area Health Authority* [1986] AC 112; [1984] QB 581.

[20] They were selected because of administrative law. It was a recognition, for the first time, that, as in the case of the Commercial Court, judicial review required expert judges. It was a typically English compromise between having a separate Administrative Court of the sort that exists on the Continent and maintaining the English tradition that everyone including public bodies should be subject to the ordinary courts of the land.

The Influence of Academics

In administrative law, the influence of academic writers has been immense. Without the contribution of academics such as Professor de Smith[21] and Sir William Wade,[22] the judges could not have made the progress they have. Of course, even with this help judges can lose their way but on the whole the academic writers have been reasonably kind about what has been achieved.

What has been Achieved

Two publications on the development of administrative law have been highly influential. The first publication was that of the Justice All Souls Review of Administrative Law, *Some Necessary Reforms*.[23] This Review provided the long overdue in-depth examination of administrative justice which most administrative lawyers felt should have been undertaken by the Royal Commission, 'that never was'.[24] The other was the publication of the sixth edition of Wade's *Administrative Law*[25] which was undoubtedly destined, like previous editions, to be the haven to which all lawyers, including judges, would resort with gratitude when at sea in uncharted areas of administrative law.

Both works acknowledged what has been achieved by the courts. The Review recognised that the face of administrative law was being transformed and judicial and professional attitudes were changing even during the period when they were conducting their investigation.[26] Sir William Wade acknowledged

---

[21] Author of the first three editions of *Judicial Review of Administrative Action*.

[22] Author, until his death in 2004, of *Administrative Law*, first published in 1961. The latest edition was co-authored with Professor Christopher Forsyth and published as the ninth edition in 2004.

[23] (Oxford: Clarendon Press, 1988).

[24] The membership of the Committee was broadly based, and included practitioners, academics and administrators. It also had an Advisory Panel which included judges from this country and abroad. I was, with Lord Wilberforce (former Lord of Appeal in Ordinary), one of the two English Judges. The views I express at this lecture will be no surprise for the Committee and in particular the very distinguished Chairman of the committee, Sir Patrick Neill (now Lord Neill), who very generously autographed my copy and in doing so thanked me for my 'friendly advice and some even friendlier criticism'!

[25] (OUP, 1988). The same can also be said of the most recent edition, co-authored by H W R Wade and C F Forsyth (OUP, 2004).

[26] The Review took ten years to complete. I suspect because its thoughts were continuously being overtaken by the speed of developments

that judges do not appear to be 'disposed to retreat from the high ground which they had invaded so vigorously in recent years'. He stated that:

> . . . in defiance of theoretical obstacles they have extended their empire by reviewing the exercise of the royal prerogative, the rulings of non-legal bodies such as the Take-Over Panel, decisions which conflict with published policies or undertakings, and discretionary decisions which an earlier generation of lawyers would have considered impregnable.

Sir William added:

> It might have been supposed in the previous editions that the judicial intervention has been carried virtually to the limit, but the courts have continued to spring surprises and they doubtless have plenty more in store . . . At the same time there has appeared in some areas at least a welcome tendency towards the simplification of doctrine and the upholding of wide general principles.[27]

The Programme

As the state of administrative law was so admirably charted by the Review and Sir William Wade and other academic writers, I will not concentrate in these lectures on the principles of administrative law. Instead, I will take advantage of my practical experience to focus on two objectives. The first will be to identify the features of our system which have enabled administrative law to develop so rapidly in this country. The second will be to identify the way in which the same features could be used to achieve the further progress which I believe is needed.

These being my objectives, my programme is as follows: in my next lecture, I will illustrate how the courts have extended the process of judicial review by the use of declaratory remedies, one of the new and up-to-date pieces of machinery to which Lord Denning referred. I will also contrast this situation with what has happened to injunctions and damages, where much less progress has been made. In my third lecture, I will concentrate on the alternatives to judicial review—what I call non-judicial review—which by complimenting the work of the courts have allowed the courts to focus on what they do best. The emphasis will be on the important, if unglamorous, role of tribunals, which numerically determine many more administrative law problems with greater speed and economy than the courts and the Ombudsman,

---

[27] Wade, Preface, *Administrative Law,* n 25 above.

who has been transplanted from more northerly climes with much success. Linked to my examination of non-judicial and judicial review with the requirement to give reasons we would indeed have a system capable of protecting our freedom in the next four decades. Finally, in my last lecture I will try and highlight a menu of the reforms which I believe still need to be made.[28]

However, I want to concentrate on what will at first sight appear, and for my audience I fear may remain, an unexciting subject, that is our present procedure of judicial review.[29] I will stress its characteristics which I believe explain why it has been possible for there to be this striking judge-propelled progress in administrative law, which is not reflected in other parts of our legal system. These characteristics are the 'safeguards' built into the procedure of judicial review: the requirement on an applicant to obtain the leave of the court to make an application for judicial review, the strictly limited time in which to make the application, the absence in the ordinary way of evidence or discovery and the discretionary nature of the remedy which enables the court only to intervene when it is right to do so. I regard these safeguards as being so important, not because they protect public bodies, but because they protect the public and, in addition, have encouraged judges to develop their power to intervene to control abuse of power in a way which they would not have done otherwise.

Public Law and Private Law Proceedings

To understand my approach it is necessary to appreciate that I regard administrative or public law proceedings as serving a different purpose to private law proceedings. In the case of private law proceedings it is the parties alone who are directly concerned with the outcome of the litigation. The public at large are not usually interested in the outcome of private law proceedings. The public as a whole are concerned only that private law proceedings should provide a fair and efficient manner of resolving disputes between individuals and of enforcing the rights of one individual over another. However, public law proceedings much more frequently directly affect many members of the public or even the public at large as well as the parties to the proceedings.

---

[28] The third and fourth lectures are not included in this book. They can be found in H Woolf, *Protection of the Public—A New Challenge* (Stevens & Sons, 1990), 67–126.

[29] This account is included here for its historical value. For a more up-to-date discussion of a system of judicial review, see 'The Tensions Between the Executive and Judiciary', Chapter 7 in this book.

For example, many members of the public are directly affected by a challenge to a scheme for a new motorway. Some members of the public's interest will be direct and obvious, for example, their home will have to be compulsorily purchased if the scheme goes ahead and they will want to know if and when they will be required to move. Other members of the public will be interested to a lesser extent, for example, they may want to use the motorway when and if it is built and until it is built they will have to put up with the inconvenience of using existing overcrowded roads. Other members of the public's interest will be limited to the fiscal consequences which will be involved in financing the new road, the cost of which will be met out of national or local taxes. The public will also be involved because the case may set a standard for administrative decision-making generally; there may be other decisions which will be taken by other departments as a result and those subsequent decisions may affect them. In resolving a dispute of this type between a public body and the individual citizen the court must always have in mind the wider interest of the public. There are also public law cases which may be of little interest to the public at large; for example, the immigrant who is threatened by removal for alleged deception on entry is concerned about the proposed action but the public in general will not be affected. In his case the court will be largely, if not exclusively, concerned with the merits of his application alone. However, both sets of proceedings are treated under our system as public law proceedings because the decision is taken by a public body performing a public duty.

English administrative law procedure is fortunate in having as its primary source the historical prerogative writs. Those writs, which were used to control inferior courts and public bodies,[30] already had the safeguards to avoid abuse to which I have referred, so that when the new remedy of judicial review was created based on the prerogative remedies it was natural it should inherit the same safeguards. These included a two-stage procedure: a requirement to bring proceedings promptly and a broad discretion to refuse relief.

The historical link between judicial review under Order 53 and the prerogative writs is emphasised by section 31 of the Supreme Court Act 1981. Initially, the change in procedure was introduced by the simple process of amending the Rules of the Supreme Court but section 31 gives retrospective statutory recognition to the procedure of judicial review. Section 31 does

---

[30] See S A de Smith, *Judicial Review of Administrative Action* (4th edn, 1980), Appendix 1, 581–584 *et seq*, on the historical origins of the prerogative writs.

not affect the jurisdiction of the court to grant orders of mandamus, prohibition or certiorari[31]—that remains as it was prior to the new procedure. The proceedings are still brought in the name of the Crown and not in the name of the individual applicant and there is a similar two-stage procedure. Declarations and injunctions can now also be brought by the same procedure, but the High Court, in deciding whether to grant a declaration or injunction, is specifically required by section 31(2) to consider:

> (a) the nature of the matters in respect of which relief may be granted by orders of mandamus, prohibition or certiorari and (b) the nature of the persons and bodies against whom relief may be granted by such orders.

So the basis upon which a declaration or injunction can be granted is linked to and controlled by the circumstances which, prior to the procedural changes, the prerogative remedies could be obtained.[32]

The nature of judicial review as a public law remedy also emerges from section 31(6) which expressly empowers the court to refuse relief where there has been undue delay in making an application for judicial review, if the court considers that the granting of relief would be likely to cause substantial hardship to, or substantially prejudice the rights of 'any person', that is not only a party to the proceedings, or would be 'detrimental to good administration'.

The unusual and probably unique requirement in English law to have regard to the interest of good administration underlines the distinct nature of an application for judicial review. The court has to take into account not only the interests of the applicant and the respondent but also the interests of the public as a whole in good administration.

I recognise that it can be argued that this should not be the approach, and that no distinction should be drawn between the rights of the individual in private law proceedings and his rights in public law proceedings. However, if, as I contend, there is a fundamental difference between the primary purpose and effect of public and private law proceedings then it is perfectly

---

[31] Or 'mandatory, prohibiting or quashing orders' as they are now known. See the Civil Procedure (Modification of Supreme Court Act 1981) Order 2004, which amends certain language within the Supreme Court Act 1981, s 31.

[32] This position has to be contrasted with the position with regard to the power of the court to award damages on an application for judicial review. Here, under s 31(4) of the Act, there is the requirement that the court is required to be satisfied that if the claim had been included in an action the applicant would have been awarded damages. In other words damages can only be recovered if damages could have been recovered in a separate private law action.

acceptable that in order to safeguard the interests of the public at large, not administrators, there should be restrictions upon an applicant's right to bring judicial review proceedings which do not exist and would be unacceptable in the case of ordinary civil proceedings. I also believe that individual applicants do in fact benefit as a result of these safeguards, because, as I have indicated, they encourage the courts to intervene in areas where they would not do so but for the safeguards. However, if there are safeguards involving restrictions which apply only to public law proceedings, inevitably it becomes necessary to identify those proceedings and there must also be, if the safeguards are not going to be ineffective, some form of requirement coupled with a sanction to ensure that the safeguards are not bypassed. Herein lies the problem.[33]

The Attitude of Public Bodies

Before commenting further on the problem, there is one further general point which I should make and that is the critical importance of the courts in public law proceedings maintaining *in the interests of the public* a proper balance between the interests of applicants and public bodies against whom applications are made. So far as applicants are concerned, the growth in the number of applications dispels any fear that the courts are being establishment-minded. I have, however, anxiety with regard to respondents to applications and in particular central government's conception of judicial review.

It should be acknowledged that, so far, the cooperation of government departments with the judicial review process has contributed to its success. For example, when there is a challenge to some departmental decisions, it is the practice for the departments to set out frankly in an affidavit the matters which were taken into account in reaching a decision. The decision-making process is fully disclosed. This has the advantage that in the majority of applications for judicial review it has been possible both to dispense with any order for discovery and to dispose of the application on affidavit evidence

---

[33] I apologise for the emphasis which I place upon the distinction between public and private law proceedings which lawyers who have any familiarity with administrative law will regard as trite (I have dealt with this subject before in more detail in 'Public Law—Private Law: Why the Divide?' (1986) PL 220) but I felt it necessary to do so because this explains and goes to the root of my approach to administrative law. It also explains why I reject the criticisms and proposals which the Justice All Souls Review Report made on the safeguards which are built into the present procedure on an application for judicial review and the criticism that the Review and Sir William Wade made of the decision in *O'Reilly v Mackman*.

without cross-examination.[34] This has contributed to a simple, inexpensive and expeditious procedure. Again, government departments, where there is a bona fide application, are mainly content to hold their hand pending the outcome of the application, thus compensating for the inability to obtain an interim injunction against the Crown.[35]

However, as judicial review has become more and more pervasive there has undoubtedly been increasing anxiety at the highest levels of government as to whether judicial review is inhibiting the implementation of governmental decisions and policy to an extent which is becoming intolerable.[36] This has led to steps designed to reduce the vulnerability of government departments to the consequences of supervision by the courts on judicial review being taken. Some of the steps which have been taken by government in this regard are welcome. They have improved the way decisions are reached and they have made some attempt to explain judicial review to administrators who are on the whole sadly lacking in legal training. For example, nothing but good can flow from the distribution by the Treasury Solicitor to government departments of his pamphlet, *The Judge Over Your Shoulder*, which in clear and simple terms describes the judicial review process.[37] There are, however, also less welcome and more questionable procedures which are being adopted with increasing frequency and which appear to be designed to remove particular decisions from the area of judicial review. About these procedures I am less happy.[38] This unhappiness was shared by a government lawyer at a talk he gave to the Administrative Law Bar Association. He said, while presently public administration is honest, there is a risk that, as a result of judicial review, people will go through

---

[34] Both features of the procedure were criticised by the Justice All Souls Review.

[35] *R v Secretary of State for Transport, ex parte Factortame Ltd* [1989] 2 WLR 997. See *R v Secretary of State for the Home Department, ex parte Al Fayed* [1998] 1 WLR 763, which pre-dated the coming into force of the Human Rights Act 1998, but is a good example of the principle that a decision-maker must allow the person who is the subject of a decision to know the case against him. Otherwise, he cannot properly defend himself, and cannot effectively persuade the decision-maker that his information does not justify an adverse decision. In the *Al Fayed* case, the Secretary of State refused to grant Al Fayed a certificate of naturalisation and declined to give him any reason for his decision. In the face of express statutory words in the British Nationality Act 1981, the Court of Appeal decided that fairness obliged the Secretary of State to notify Al Fayed of the matters causing him concern. The principle is now fortified by the Human Rights Act 1998 and the requirements of Art 6 which protect the right to a fair trial. Incidentally, s 44(2) of the British Nationality Act 1981 was repealed in 2002 and the Immigration and Nationality Directorate now usually give reasons for decisions.

[36] It also resulted in correspondence in *The Times* initiated by Sir William Wade suggesting that the courts were going beyond their allotted role.

[37] For the most recent version, see Edition 4 (Treasury Solicitor, January 2006).

[38] See also AW Bradley [1988] PL 2.

a charade: applicants to put themselves in the best possible position and the authority to defend themselves.[39]

Although it is too much to expect a department to welcome the scrutiny of the courts, they should realise that the effect of that scrutiny is to protect the interests of the citizen and at the same time to raise administrative standards. Nonetheless, I do recognise that complaints are raised by government departments that judges are insufficiently aware of the problems with which administrators are faced and that on occasions they are required to adopt unrealistic standards in order to comply with decisions of the court. It is perhaps unnecessary to determine whether these complaints are justified or not; it is sufficient that some civil servants at the highest level consider they are justified. Action should therefore be taken to remedy the situation. In my view, a contributory factor to the problem, in addition to lack of legal training of civil servants, is that there is virtually no interchange between the judiciary and administrators as to the supervisory role performed by the courts in relation to administrative action. I well understand the difficulty in having discussions on the subject. It is no doubt due to a reluctance on both sides to create the impression that judges and administrators are in cahoots. However, I do regard the situation as being unsatisfactory and I later suggest that an improvement would have been made if judges dealing with applications for judicial review had received training as to the problems of administrators.[40]

The danger which could result from the effect of an over-invasive use of judicial review emphasises the importance of the safeguards which are built into judicial review since they enable the courts to strike a balance between the interests of the administrators and the public, which in some proceedings for judicial review could well increase, with the result that judicial review would afford less effective protection of the public. In seeking to draw attention to this possible counter-productive effect of judicial review, I am of course not suggesting the court should ever be inhibited in interfering as forcefully as necessary with a governmental department if justice requires that intervention. All I wish to ensure is that judges appreciate the consequence of their intervention.

---

[39] Michael Warr, 26 October 1987.

[40] I come back to the subject of training and judges in 'The Needs of a 21st Century Judge', Chapter 10 in this book.

The Safeguards

I turn now to the safeguards against its abuse built into judicial review and in particular the requirement for leave or permission to make an application for judicial review. The requirement of leave is a unique feature of our system, although in some Commonwealth countries, such as India and Israel where the old prerogative orders of certiorari, prohibition and mandamus still issue, there is also a similar procedure.

The requirement to obtain the leave of the court to make an application would probably not exist were it not for the fact that for historical reasons there was always in effect a two-stage procedure to obtain the prerogative writs of certiorari, prohibition and mandamus.[41] In the case of the prerogative orders prior to the new Order 53,[42] the application involved an *ex parte* stage followed if necessary by an *inter partes* hearing.[43] It may well be that when the new procedure was introduced it was unwise to describe the first stage of an application for judicial review as an application for leave. It would have been better if, what would in effect have been the same thing, was described as a two-stage hearing, the first being *ex parte* or *nisi* and the second only taking place if there was a case to answer. I say this because the objection to the requirement of leave is often made as a matter of principle. For example, the Justice All Souls Review argued that:

> The citizen does not require leave to sue a further citizen and we do not think they should have to obtain leave in order to proceed against state and administrative bodies . . . What we regard as wrong in the current situation is that one category of litigant, namely those seeking judicial review, should be subjected to an impediment which is not put in the way of litigants generally.[44]

This reasoning has considerable emotive force but its impact would have been reduced if the same practical result had been achieved by adopting the two-stage procedure which still exists on an application for habeas corpus. However, the fact that the initial stage is an application for leave should not

---

[41] I am therefore not surprised that in new systems (including that of Scotland) which do not have this tradition there is no requirement for leave. Nor am I surprised that where a country has abolished the two-stage procedure, it is not prepared to introduce any requirement for leave.

[42] As noted, Order 53 has been replaced with CPR Part 54.

[43] The position is still the same today in the case of an application for habeas corpus which is governed by Order 54 and involves an initial application *ex parte* followed by an adjourned *inter partes* hearing if this is justified.

[44] *Some Necessary Reforms* (Oxford: Clarendon Press, 1988), 153.

be allowed to obscure the advantages of the present procedure. In practice the requirement, far from being an impediment to the individual litigant, can even be to his advantage since it enables a litigant expeditiously and cheaply to obtain the view of a High Court judge on the merits of his application.[45] But even if this were not the case I believe its retention would be justified in the interest of the public at large. From my discussions with colleagues from many European and Commonwealth countries which do not have this requirement I can confidently say that if the requirement were to be politically acceptable, it is one which they would welcome. The explosion in applications for judicial review has not been confined to this country, but is a phenomenon of most developed legal systems. Most legal systems are from time to time troubled by vexatious applications for judicial review. The requirement of leave acts as a useful filter in respect of such applications. Its effectiveness, however, cannot be assessed by counting the number of applications in which leave is refused. The requirement of leave undoubtedly deters many frivolous applications as litigants do not trouble to make an application if they do not consider that they will get leave.[46] The solution chosen by the Justice All Souls Committee for dealing with frivolous applications, namely an application to strike out the proceedings, does not have the same deterrent effect as the requirement of leave. In addition, there is inevitably a period of uncertainty until an application to strike out can be heard during which the public body is involved in the proceedings and the activities of the public body are brought to a halt contrary to the interests of the public.

The Committee suggested that the requirement of leave is discriminatory and the passages I have quoted from the Report expressed this feeling of the citizen being at a disadvantage to public bodies. However, many applications for judicial review are now made by public bodies including central government and a public body which is an applicant is subject to exactly the same requirement to obtain leave as is the ordinary member of the public.

For those who are not already aware of this, I would emphasise that the procedure for obtaining leave is very inexpensive and simple. It is well within the capabilities of the ordinary litigant to make the application in person and normally involves no more than filling in a simple form and swearing an affidavit in support of the application. An application is then considered,

---

[45] The granting of leave will ensure that if he is eligible there should be less difficulty in his obtaining legal aid. There have since been significant cuts to legal aid.

[46] In fact, during 1988, of 1,229 applications for leave, 574, 47%, were refused. In 2005, the number of applications for leave had increased to 5,382, and 2,396, 45%, were refused.

usually in the first instance by a judge on the papers without the litigant having to attend. If he is refused leave he has the right to renew the application in open court and, if again refused leave to renew it, before the Court of Appeal. It is true, as the Committee points out, that if he is refused leave by the Court of Appeal, the applicant has no right to seek leave to appeal to the House of Lords. While I would not object to the House of Lords being the final arbiter as to whether leave should be given, in practice the number of cases in which it would be appropriate for the House of Lords to consider the application for leave would be minute. Moreover, there is already a practical way of dealing with the isolated case where an applicant could succeed before the House of Lords but not before any other court. What happens is that the High Court judge or the Court of Appeal grants leave and then dismisses the application, so as to give the House of Lords jurisdiction to grant leave to appeal if it wishes to do so.

When these considerations are taken into account and the distinction to which I referred earlier between ordinary (that is private law) legal proceedings and proceedings in the public law field is appreciated, the argument based on principle, I believe, loses much of its force. Nor am I impressed by the alternative proposal which is made by the Review Committee that if it is necessary to have a special safeguard, that safeguard should be that which exists in Scotland, namely a preliminary *inter partes* hearing. It would not assist the applicant to have the respondent present at the preliminary hearing. It is already the practice in England, in the exceptional case where it is felt that this would assist, to require the respondent to be given notice of the application for leave so that the respondent has the opportunity to attend. However, in practice, it has been found that the involvement of the respondent at this early stage has been really of limited help except in the cases of the most complicated applications or where the applicant is acting in person and the court needs the assistance of the respondent to ensure that there is not some point which the applicant has been unable to make clear involved in the application.[47]

If the leave stage was abolished it would also deprive the court of the power to exercise its discretion at the outset of the proceedings. The discretion which the Court has at this stage is much more limited than that which exists at a later stage, although it is still very important. The discretion is

---

[47] It is noteworthy that the defendant or any interested party is not required to attend a hearing of an application for leave unless the court directs otherwise. See Practice Direction 54, para 8.5.

only to deal with the obvious case where, whatever the merits, the court should not intervene, as for example, when there is an alternative and better remedy or because there has been excessive delay. I know there have been problems over the time limit laid down by the Act and the Rules of the Supreme Court. The Rules refer to the need to bring proceedings promptly and in any event within three months. However, this time limit can be and usually is extended if there is an explanation for the delay and the delay is fully and properly taken into account in making the ultimate judgement as to whether, as a matter of discretion, it is proper to grant relief if the application is otherwise successful.

However, the requirement of leave made necessary the decision in *O'Reilly v Mackman*[48] with regard to which the Justice All Souls Report[49] and Sir William Wade joined forces. Both were equally hostile to the decision. In the preface to the sixth edition of *Administrative Law* Sir William Wade expressed his hostility with considerable eloquence and I know that he would have forgiven me for quoting the passage. He said:

> No subject calls out more loudly for reform than the unfortunate procedural dichotomy enforced by *O'Reilly v Mackman* criticised alike in the Review and in this volume. Every admirer of the late Lord Diplock will agree that his speech in that case was a brilliant virtuoso performance. But the misfortune resulting from it is that procedural technicality, always the bugbear of this subject, has become more dominant and more troublesome than ever. A solitary judgment on a single case is not an ideal instrument for proclaiming radical and sweeping changes. In his later years Lord Diplock was inclined to yield to the temptation to restate a whole branch of the law in his own terms. His mastery of administrative law and his contributions to it entitle these *ex cathedra* statements to great respect; but it may not I hope be impertinent to point out their drawbacks as a technique either of codification or of law reform. A feat of Lord Diplock's, however, which as a mere academic I can only envy is his ability to put forward a novel theory in a lecture and then to enshrine it canonically in a speech in the House of Lords.[50]

The whole of Sir William's criticism was not confined to the decision of *O'Reilly v Mackman*; he was also concerned about Lord Diplock's views as to the significance of and distinction between errors going to jurisdiction and

---

[48] [1983] 2 AC 237.

[49] Sir Patrick Neill (now Lord Neill), the Chairman of the Review, and I crossed snakes and ladders on this subject prior to the Report. See H Woolf, 'Public Law—Private Law: Why the Divide?' (1986) PL 220.

[50] Wade, Preface, *Administrative Law*, n 25 above, viii.

errors within the jurisdiction. However, it is clear that Sir William regarded the *O'Reilly v Mackman* decision as one of the great problems of administrative law. Earlier in his Preface he said that within a fortnight of the last edition of his book:

> The House of Lords created the most seismic disturbance that the subject had suffered in many years. By declaiming a rigid dichotomy between public and private law, but without explaining how the line was to be drawn the House of Lords created a host of new problems for litigants which have by no means yet been resolved.[51]

Criticism in these strong terms by Sir William, echoing the Report of the Committee, clearly deserves the greatest respect. The decision of *O'Reilly v Mackman* is undoubtedly immensely important. First of all it gives what I regard as needed emphasis to the fact that there now is a real distinction between public and private law. In drawing the distinction the House of Lords was doing no more than recognising that our legal system has a feature derived from the ancient prerogative writs which is common to most if not all other advanced legal systems, though the boundary is drawn differently in virtually every country.[52] I appreciate, as Sir William pointed out, that boundary is blurred. It does not have a Berlin Wall, but this, far from being a defect, could be a strength. In the days of privatisation and the creation of non-statutory regulatory bodies it is very important that the courts should not be prevented by a strict definition of what is the boundary of public law from extending supervision of the courts to bodies which otherwise would exercise uncontrolled power. Secondly, the decision is important because it lays down that generally (and I emphasise the word 'generally', as did Lord Diplock in his speech in *O'Reilly v Mackman*) if a case is appropriate for an application for judicial review then the application has to be made by way of judicial review since to do otherwise would be an abuse of the process of the court. Where I believe the critics of the decision of *O'Reilly v Mackman* are in error is that they regard the decision as in some way building an insurmountable wall between judicial review and private law proceedings which can prejudice litigants and result in very unattractive demarcation disputes between public law and private law proceedings. I do not believe that this is, or needs to be, the result of *O'Reilly v Mackman*.

---

[51] Ibid, vii.
[52] See Lord Goff's speech in the case involving *The State of Norway (No 2) Application* [1989] 2 WLR 458.

Sir William said:

> The rigid dichotomy which has been imposed . . . must be accounted a serious
> setback for administrative law. It has caused many cases which on their merits
> might have succeeded, to fail merely because of the wrong form of action. It is
> a step back to the times of the old forms of action which were so deservedly
> buried in 1852.[53]

With respect to Sir William, I am not aware of the 'many' cases which might
have succeeded where this unfortunate result has occurred. If a case should
have been brought by judicial review and is not but it is a case with merit,
then it is always open to the judge, as I have myself done, to give leave there
and then for the matter to proceed and to treat the pleadings which already
exist as being a sufficient compliance with the requirements of Order 53.[54]
If on the other hand the matter came before the court under Order 53 as
an application for judicial review but could more conveniently have been
dealt with as an action, the reverse procedure could have been adopted by
using a similar strategy or alternatively taking advantage of Order 53,
rule 9(5), to order that the proceedings should continue as if they had been
begun by writ. What, however, should not have been allowed in my view was
for a litigant to have been able deliberately to avoid the safeguards built into
an application for judicial review if he would not have been able to fulfil their
requirements. It should be emphasised that in *O'Reilly v Mackman* there
was no question of any mistake as to which procedure should be used. In Lord
Diplock's words it was a case of 'blatant attempts to avoid protection for
respondents for which Order 53 provides' and the case was so regarded by
Lord Wilberforce in *Davy v Spelthorne Borough Council*.[55] He said 'the
plaintiffs were improperly and flagrantly seeking to evade the protection
which the rule confers on public authorities'.[56] In addition to referring to
'a general rule', Lord Diplock was also careful to say no more than 'it may
normally be appropriate to apply . . . by the summary process of striking out
the action'.[57] He also pointed out that there may be exceptions and it is clear
that he was laying down the general rule so as to avoid public authorities
being put to the expense of contesting proceedings in order to establish that
they were without merit. It is the regrettable fact that in ordinary civil

---

[53] Wade, *Administrative Law*, n 25 above, 677.
[54] As explained earlier in this paper, Order 53 has been replaced with CPR Part 54.
[55] [1984] AC 262.
[56] Ibid, 278.
[57] Ibid, 285.

proceedings, the power to strike out proceedings is extremely limited and rarely successfully invoked.

The real issue was surely not whether the decision in *O'Reilly v Mackman* was right having regard to the provisions of Order 53, but whether Order 53 should have been amended so as to remove the safeguards which were the special features of its procedure. If the safeguards were to remain then cases which were obviously within Order 53 must have gone down that route. If, however, the safeguards were removed then there would have been no need to require litigants to adopt the procedure.

It is true that since *O'Reilly v Mackman* there have been a number of cases where it has been argued, sometimes successfully, that a claim could be dismissed because the wrong procedure had been adopted[58] and it remains the fact that if it had not been for the decision in *O'Reilly v Mackman* it may well be that the preliminary issue as to the appropriateness of the procedure which was being adopted would not have arisen. However, when there has been an advance in the law of this magnitude, it always takes a time for the extent of that development to be accurately appreciated and for pragmatic solutions to be worked out on a case-by-case basis.

There were also problems, which flowed from the special requirements contained in Order 53 and which had nothing to do with judicial review being

---

[58] The first of those cases was the case which immediately followed *O'Reilly v Mackman*, the case of *Cox v Thanet District Council* [1983] 2 AC 286. But that case has also been misunderstood. It should be noted that the issue was whether the proceedings could be properly brought in the County Court rather than the High Court. In *Cox* there would have to be two sets of proceedings in any event if Mr Cox was to recover damages because, as Lord Bridge made clear, if the decision to refuse to house Mr Cox was flawed the decision would have to be retaken and Mr Cox's right to damages would depend on the result of that reconsideration. Speaking for myself, I can see there is an argument for saying the matter could properly be dealt with in the County Court, or, better still, by a tribunal. Against that view it has to be recognised that the policy so far has been, and this policy has been generally accepted, that public law issues should be tried in the High Court and tried by the nominated judges who have the experience of the legislation in question. Another case which progressed to the House of Lords was *Davy v Spelthorne Borough Council* [1984] AC 262, in the year following *O'Reilly v Mackman*. In that case the House of Lords concluded that it was perfectly appropriate for the plaintiff not to have proceeded by way of Order 53, so it did not help to substantiate the criticisms which were advanced to *O'Reilly v Mackman*. It is also to be noted that quite distinct arguments were advanced by the defendants for saying the case was misconceived and it is therefore probable that the litigation in that case would have taken place irrespective of what had been the decision in *O'Reilly v Mackman*. (The alternative arguments relied on the specific statutory provisions applicable to the proceedings under the Town and Country Planning Act 1971.) The third case was *Wandsworth Borough Council v Winder* [1985] AC 461. In that case it was decided by the House of Lords that it was possible to rely upon a public law defence in proceedings brought against the defendant without making a separate application for judicial review. In this case as well, therefore, no problem should have been created by the decision of *O'Reilly v Mackman* and following the House of Lords decision, no problem should have arisen in the future.

an exclusive remedy but resulted from the discretionary nature of judicial review, arising from the decision of the House of Lords in *Wandsworth London Borough Council v Winder*.[59] You will recall that Mr Winder was a Council tenant who was sued by the Council in the County Court because he was in arrears with his rent. His defence was that the decision of the Council to increase council house tenants' rents by approximately 50 per cent was unreasonable and therefore invalid. If he was right this would affect many other tenants and the income of the Council. The Council failed in its application to strike out the defence on the basis that an allegation of this nature could only be raised on applications for judicial review. Because of the delay which had taken place, success on an application for judicial review would require an exercise of the Court's discretion in Mr Winder's favour. As he had been refused leave to apply for a judicial review we can assume that the Court would not have been prepared to exercise its discretion in his favour. Nonetheless the House of Lords decided that Mr Winder was entitled to rely upon the alleged invalidity of the resolution of the local authority to increase his rent not only as a defence to the local authority's claim to the arrears of rent but also as the basis of a counterclaim for a declaration that he was under no liability.

I am bound to say that, unlike the academics who apparently regarded the case as being a welcome exception to the *O'Reilly v Mackman* case, the decision left me in a state of confusion. I could see some sense in the question of the invalidity of the resolution to increase the rent being able to be raised as a defence rather than in separate proceedings. I would, however, have expected there to have been some indication by the House of Lords that the right to rely on the defence would be subject to the court exercising its discretion in the same way as it would on an application for judicial review, and therefore that it would be preferable for the case to be transferred to the High Court so that it could be heard by one of the nominated judges who would have heard the application for judicial review. I was, however, appalled that a situation should have been able to arise where Mr Winder would not succeed on an application for judicial review because the court would not exercise discretion in his favour but he could still succeed on the same facts as a defence and for the purposes of obtaining a declaration by way of counterclaim. It appeared that for no good reason we had as a result of the *Winder* case not only an understandable exception to the *O'Reilly v Mackman* principle

---

[59] Ibid.

but also had accepted that different standards would apply where the invalidity of a council decision was relied on as a defence from those which would apply when it was relied on as the grounds for an application for judicial review. However, Lord Fraser and the House of Lords were well aware of the arguments against the decision to which they came since they were set out clearly and succinctly in the court below by Ackner LJ in a dissenting judgment of considerable force. What, if I may say so, may have been overlooked is that while the public interest arises most frequently in public law proceedings it can also arise in private law proceedings. An application for an injunction against a union in relation to a proposed strike or the *Spycatcher* type of case are prime examples. Whether the proceedings are brought by a private individual or the Attorney-General, the court should be able to consider the public interest and make use of the expertise developed on applications for judicial review as to the grant of discretionary relief. There are therefore still anomalies which the courts will have to resolve between public and private law proceedings.

The problem may be related to the fact that the courts have yet to establish clearly the effect of a decision being void. Does it remain valid until the courts have ruled on its invalidity? While giving the lectures I was a party to the decision of the Divisional Court in the case of *Hazell v The London Borough of Hammersmith and Fulham*[60] which vividly highlights the problems without resolving them. This question is at the heart of my problems with the *Winder* case and it may be that the anomalies involved in the decision will be resolved in the process of finally and clearly deciding what is the effect of invalidity.[61]

I leave the debate as to whether the safeguards contained in Order 53 should have been retained and whether Order 53 should generally have been the required procedure for reviewing the activities of public bodies by emphasising that both questions have been related. I have also emphasised that the

---

[60] 1 November 1989, unreported.

[61] See *Hoffmann-La Roche & Co v Secretary of State for Trade and Industry* [1975] AC 295. In *Hoffmann*, the House of Lords held there is a presumption of validity in favour of a disputed order during the time that must elapse before the court can decide the question. In later decisions however, the House explained the limited effect of this case, which dealt only with the interim situation while the question of validity was in suspense, awaiting determination by the court. The presumption was 'an evidential matter at the interlocutory stage' and involved no 'sweeping proposition that subordinate legislation must be treated for all purposes as valid until set aside' (*R v Wicks* [1998] AC 92 at 116). Also, 'there is no rule that lends validity to invalid acts' (*Boddington v British Transport Police* [1999] 2 AC 143, 174).

answer adopted was likely to be of critical importance to the further development of administrative law since, as Lord Wilberforce pointed out in *Davy
v Spelthorne Borough Council*, 'English law fastens not on principles but
on remedies'.[62] The flexible nature of the remedy of judicial review, of which
the safeguards are the prime ingredient, have contributed to the rapid
development of judicial review and have enabled the further developments
which I have regarded as needed to take place. I identified these developments in my later lectures.

It was because I considered that it was essential to retain this flexibility
that I did not advocate the codification and enactment of the grounds for
judicial review as was advocated in the Justice All Souls Report.[63] I agreed
that the objective of clarifying the law to which the authors referred was a
desirable one but the inflexibility which could have resulted could have
been too high a price to pay. The Committee pointed out as a precedent the
Australian Administrative Decisions (Judicial Review) Act 1977, as amended,
which did set out in clear terms the grounds on which an application could
be made. However, in fact, the Australian experiment confirmed my fears of
what can follow from statutory intervention in this area. The August 1988
report published by the Australian Administrative Review Council pointed
out that 'significant areas of administrative action remain to which the
Act does not extend'. In consequence, resort is being had, in Australia, to
the old prerogative writ jurisdiction under section 39(b) of the Australian
Judiciary Act 1983. It is because of that writ jurisdiction that developments
can still take place in Australian law. In particular, reflecting similar progress
in this country, it is now established that decisions of the Governor General
which cannot be reviewed under the Act of 1977 are now capable of being
reviewed by use of the prerogative writs. In this area in Australia if it
were not for the fact that there was a second means of review the 1977 Act
would have frustrated the development of judicial review. Their legislation
required amendment to catch up with these changes. However, in this country if we were to codify the grounds of judicial review it would not have
been possible to by-pass, as did the Australians, the restrictive effect of the
code since the prerogative writs had already been subsumed into judicial
review.

---

[62] [1984] AC 262, 276.
[63] *Some Necessary Reforms*, n 44 above, para 6.34.

Conclusion

That brings me, with some relief, to the end of what I want to say about procedure. I apologise for taking so long and can only plead in mitigation that this is the base upon which I will build my later lectures and that I regard the safeguards as being critical to our system of judicial review. I believe that if the safeguards were impaired this would not only retard the future development of judicial review but would also destroy much of what already has been achieved to meet Lord Denning's challenge.

I regard the distinction, albeit blurred, between public law and private law as now being an essential feature at the heart of our administrative law system. I regard judicial review as primarily concerned with enforcing public duties on behalf of the public as a whole and as only concerned with vindicating the interests of the individual as part of the process of ensuring that public bodies do not act unlawfully and do perform their public duties. The procedure of judicial review therefore does have and should have safeguards which do not exist in other proceedings so as to reduce, as far as is consistent with the courts' role of reviewing administrative action, the interference to which public bodies are subject. This is not because I want to protect public bodies but because it is in the interest of the public as a whole.

In performing this task before the court grants relief it is required to ask itself the critical question of whether justice requires the decision or action of the administrative body to be quashed or otherwise interfered with by the courts. If looking at the situation as a whole—and I emphasise not looking at just one step in a complete process of adjudication—there has been unfairness then of course the court must interfere unless there is very good reason for not doing so. If on the other hand, there is or has been some procedural error but the result is not unjust or unfair then the court in its discretion should be ready to refuse relief. The discretion should be exercised with a strong bias to remedying injustice and against unnecessary intervention where there is no injustice. There are a multitude of considerations which will point in different directions in each case. The approach necessitates developing separate public law procedures and also separate public law principles. It also involves identifying the situations to which the separate proceedings and principles apply. This is what has been happening in the courts over the last 40 years and should continue. It involves a fundamental change from the traditional approach of English law, which in the past tended to equate the rights and duties of public bodies with those of private individuals. On the Continent, this new role of the courts has long been the approach. The pressures of contemporary society in this country have resulted in our producing our own solution designed to achieve the same result. I believe our procedure is working well, is capable of meeting Lord Denning's challenge, and that it is the base on which to build in the future. As our procedure is working well it would be a mistake to try and mend it by removing the safeguards which have been the explanation of the success so far.

2

Remedies

Abstract This paper provides an historical insight into the development of remedies that are available to litigants in the English legal system. It considers the declaratory judgment, damages, and injunctions, and explores how the courts have used them for the benefit of the public. While this paper supports the use of such remedies, it emphasises that it is not in favour of more judicial intervention into the activities of public bodies. Used efficiently and effectively, they can assist the court in maintaining a proper balance between protecting the public and allowing those who have the responsibility for governing us to govern.

At the beginning of the first of these lectures I cited the passage with which Lord Denning concluded the first Hamlyn Lecture 57 years ago. That passage ended with these words:

> Just as the pick and shovel is no longer suitable for the winning of coal, so also the procedure for mandamus, certiorari and actions on the case are not suitable for the winning of freedom in the new age. They must be replaced by new and up to date machinery, by declarations, injunctions and actions for negligence.[1]

Contrary to this advice, over the past 57 years we have not, except for the action on the case, retired the old remedies. Instead, they have been remodelled and given a new lease of life alongside Lord Denning's 'new and up to date machinery' of declarations and injunctions and, where there is a cause of action, damages.

---

* This paper was originally delivered as the second of four lectures in the forty-first series of the Hamlyn Lectures. See H Woolf, *Protection of the Public—A New Challenge* (Stevens & Sons, 1990), 37–66.

[1] 'Freedom Under the Law' (Hamlyn Lectures, 1949), 126.

The combining in this way of the remedies available was both in historic and practical terms dramatic. It halted what otherwise would have been the progressive decline of the prerogative remedies, but it also gave an opportunity to exploit the new machinery which would not have been possible but for the change in procedure. In this lecture, I want to examine the way in which the courts have taken advantage of this opportunity to use the 'new machinery' for the benefit of the public.

The Declaratory Judgment

I start off with the declaration not only because it was the first of the new machines referred to, but also because it is in relation to the use of the declaration that the courts have been most successful in developing and adopting an existing private law remedy to meet the new challenge. Prior to the introduction of Order 53,[2] litigants were with increasing frequency resorting to declaratory proceedings instead of applying for the prerogative writs in order to control the abuse of power by public authorities. There were good practical reasons for this. The prerogative orders were encrusted with technical rules and success normally depended upon establishing some error on the fact of the record or some jurisdictional defect. There was also the difficulty that usually discovery and cross-examination were not available.

Probably the greatest advantage of seeking a declaration instead of applying for what were conventionally regarded as being the public law remedies, the prerogative orders, was that it was possible to bypass the Divisional Court. By the 1960s, the Divisional Court was grossly overwhelmed with work. The Court only sat in one Division and it was almost invariably presided over by the Lord Chief Justice of the day so that he could ensure consistency. However, in addition to dealing with applications for the prerogative orders the Court had to deal with the appeals from magistrates and a host of statutory tribunals including the VAT Tribunal. The Divisional Court could only attempt to cope with the huge volume of cases which were coming before it by strictly limiting the argument and hearing an unconscionable number of cases each day. Even then, and despite all the efforts and expertise and outstanding ability of the Chief Justices of those times, a substantial backlog developed so that even urgent matters were having to wait for an unacceptable period to come before the Court.

---

[2] Now replaced with CPR Part 54.

An application for a declaration, usually made to the Chancery Division, was a very attractive alternative. The Chancery Division was staffed by judges of the highest quality who were not subject to the same overwhelming pressure. They had time to give cases which raised important issues the attention which they deserved. I can again turn to Lord Denning to describe the situation graphically:

> At one time there was a blackout on any development of administrative law. The curtains were drawn across to prevent the light coming in. The remedy of certiorari was hedged about with all sorts of technical limitations. While the darkness still prevailed we let in some light by means of a declaration.[3]

It was therefore no coincidence that of the three cases, which Lord Diplock identified in *O'Reilly v Mackman* as being the landmark cases which were the source of our system of administration law, two, namely *Ridge v Baldwin*[4] and *Anisminic v Foreign Compensation Commission*,[5] involved proceedings for a declaration, and it was only the third case, namely *Padfield v The Minister of Agriculture, Fisheries and Food*,[6] which appeared before the Divisional Court on an application for a prerogative order.

However, until the introduction of judicial review there were still problems in seeking declaratory relief because the declaration was a private law remedy, by which I mean a remedy for declaring private rights. This meant that the applicant for declaratory relief had to establish that he had the necessary *locus standi* to bring proceedings, that is to say that he had at least some personal interest which was adversely affected. He could not normally bring proceedings on behalf of the public. Nonetheless, it was not necessary for the applicant to have a course of action, as was decided in a case which we would now decide on judicial review, which in 1911 confirmed the potential of declaratory relief.[7] This meant in practice that although a cause of action was not needed, the applicant, in order to establish that a public right had been infringed, had either to obtain the assistance of the Attorney-General, so as to bring a relator action in his name, or he had to establish that his private law rights had been infringed or that a breach of statutory duty had resulted in his suffering special damage. This was made abundantly clear by the decision of the House of Lords in *Gouriet v The*

---

[3] In *O'Reilly v Mackman* [1983] 2 AC 237, 253.

[4] [1964] AC 40.

[5] [1969] 2 AC 147.

[6] [1968] AC 997.

[7] *Dyson v Attorney-General* [1912] 1 Ch 158.

Union of Post Office Workers.[8] The problem did not exist to the same degree in prerogative proceedings where it was sufficient to show that you had a real interest.

The introduction of the new Order 53 removed this limitation on the availability of declaratory relief on an application for judicial review. As a result the declaratory judgment was given an immense boost. The declaration proved to be the ideal remedy in public law proceedings. It was much more flexible than the prerogative orders, which could quash decisions, order decisions to be made or prohibit decisions being taken, but could not give specific guidance as to how these decisions should be reached. The declaration was very much in accord with the role and spirit of judicial review which was primarily but not exclusively concerned with the decision-making process rather than the merits of a particular decision. The declaration by careful drafting could be applied with considerable precision. This was attractive to courts because it enabled them to cut out the defective part of the decision without necessarily cutting down the whole of a decision, something which was quite impossible in the case of certiorari.

I have already stressed in the first lecture the importance of the existence of the safeguards in judicial review as giving the courts confidence to extend the scope of their jurisdiction to review the activities of public bodies. I have little doubt that the sophisticated nature of declaratory relief had a similar influence. In the case of *Inland Revenue Commissioners v National Federation of Self-Employed and Small Businesses Ltd,*[9] Lord Wilberforce indicated that although in Order 53, rule 3,[10] the same words were used to cover all the forms of remedy available on judicial review, other than damages, the rule did not mean the test was the same in all cases. Lord Wilberforce went on:

> . . . when Lord Parker CJ said that in cases of mandamus the test may be stricter . . . 'on a very strict basis' he was not stating a technical rule which can now be discarded but a rule of common sense reflecting the different character of the relief asked for. It would seem obvious enough that the interests of a

---

[8] [1978] AC 435. So far as an ordinary action is concerned the position is still the same today; see *Meadows Indemnity Co v Insurance Co of Ireland* [1989] 2 Lloyd's Rep 298, applied more recently by the Singapore Court of Appeal in *Karaha Bodas Co LLC v Pertamina Energy Trading Ltd* [2006] 4 LRC 86.

[9] [1982] AC 617.

[10] The rule which dealt with standing. Today, on standing, see s 31(3) of the Supreme Court Act 1981 and CPR Part 54. It is also to be noted that a claim for judicial review of a Convention right must be brought by a 'victim', for which the test is more restrictive than for 'standing' in judicial review. See *Amuur v France* (1996) 22 EHRR 533.

person seeking to compel an authority to carry out a duty is different from that of a person complaining that a judicial or administrative body has, to his detriment, exceeded its powers.[11]

Lord Wilberforce ended this part of his speech by saying 'it is hardly necessary to add that recognition of the value of guiding authorities does not mean the process of judicial review must stand still'.[12]

Indeed it has not stood still. The position has now been reached where it is virtually impossible to find a case in which declaratory relief is sought that would otherwise have succeeded on an application for judicial review where an applicant was deprived of relief because of, for example, lack of *locus standi*. This has in turn had a liberating effect on what were the prerogative remedies. Practitioners have ceased to take technical points as to the limits of mandamus, certiorari or prohibition since the court could in any event avoid the technical point by granting a declaration.[13]

The new attitude of the courts was reflected in Lord Diplock's speech in the *Self Employed* case:

> It would, in my view, be a grave lacuna in our system of public law if a pressure group, like the Federation or even a single public spirited taxpayer, were prevented by outdated technical rules of *locus standi* from bringing the matter to the attention of the court to vindicate the rule of law and get unlawful conduct stopped.[14]

Lord Diplock added that so far as the misdeeds of central government are concerned, the Attorney-General is of no assistance since in practice he never applies for prerogative orders against government departments. It is therefore important that the individual can do so since while government departments:

> ... are accountable to Parliament for what they do so far as regards efficiency and policy, and of that Parliament is the only judge; they are responsible to a court of justice for the lawfulness of what they do, and of that the court is the only judge.[15]

---

[11] *Self Employed*, n 9 above, 631.

[12] Ibid.

[13] Or 'mandatory, prohibiting or quashing orders' as they are now known. See the Civil Procedure (Modification of the Supreme Court Act 1981) Order 2004, which amends certain language within the Supreme Court Act 1981, s 31.

[14] *Self Employed*, n 9 above, 643.

[15] Ibid, 644.

Interestingly, having established this broad approach to *locus standi* in relation to declaratory relief on applications for judicial review,[16] the courts have also without argument adopted a similar approach to applications for declarations against public bodies where the application is not made by way of judicial review. When Mrs Gillick applied for her declarations against the Department of Health and Social Security, she did so in an ordinary action, but it is doubtful whether there was any prospect of her being within the test of *locus standi* laid down in the *Gouriet* case.[17] Likewise, in the *Royal College of Nursing* case a declaration was sought and it was refused not on any technical basis that the Royal College was not entitled to bring proceedings but because of the merits of their case.[18]

In the House of Lords, in the *Gillick* case Lord Bridge alone addressed this point.[19] He recognised that a great leap forward had been made, not so much as to the standing necessary to bring proceedings, but as to the nature of the subject matter which was amenable to judicial review. What was in issue in the *Gillick* case was not the exercise of some statutory discretion or power, but a mere departmental circular or advice which had no statutory or other legal authority. What Lord Bridge had to say was, however, also relevant to the right to bring proceedings[20] and he considered that the extended jurisdiction which he identified should be exercised with considerable care and caution. Lord Bridge had in mind the dangers involved in the courts intervening to control the activities of government beyond the permissible limits. Similar unease was expressed in a letter written to *The Times* by Sir William Wade about an application for judicial review in respect of the publication of a leaflet by the government as to the community charge or poll tax which was alleged to be misleading. However, the letter provoked an immediate response from other distinguished correspondents, indicating the dangers which could result

---

[16] The courts have extended this broad approach to include trade unions (see *R v Secretary of State for the Home Department, ex parte Fire Brigades Union & Others* [1995] 2 AC 513) and to groups protecting or campaigning for a particular public interest (see *R v DPP, ex parte Bull & Another* [1998] 2 All ER 755). More generally, see *R v Somerset County Council, ex parte Dixon* [1998] Env LR 111; *R (Bulger) v Secretary of State for the Home Department* [2001] 3 All ER 449; *R (Kides) v South Cambridgeshire District Council* [2002] EWCA Civ 1370, 4 PLR 66.

[17] [1978] AC 435.

[18] *Royal College of Nursing of the UK v Department of Health and Social Security* [1981] AC 800.

[19] *Gillick v West Norfolk and Wisbech Area Health Authority* [1986] AC 112, 191.

[20] *Gillick* but not the *Royal College of Nursing* case may be explained by the fact that some of their Lordships at any rate appeared to think that Mrs Gillick had a private right which was, if she was correct, infringed by the Department of Health's circular.

from there being no control over the use of the immensely powerful machinery of government to disseminate false information or the exercise of unbridled power by non-statutory bodies.

The solution to this dispute in my view was not to hold that the courts never have any power to intervene in an area which could be grossly abused, such as the dissemination of propaganda, but to regard that power as one to be exercised with considerable caution and discretion, bearing in mind both that it is no part of the role of the courts to be a critic or censor of governmental circulars, and Lord Bridge's advice in the *Gillick* case. In those rare cases where it is appropriate to intervene the court can only do so by declaration. A circular cannot be quashed and prohibition is too blunt an instrument for use in such circumstances.

The desire to avoid the exercise of considerable power which is not subject to the supervision of the courts also explains the decision in the case of *Datafin*,[21] which marked a further extension of the boundaries of the jurisdiction of the court on judicial review. In that case the Court of Appeal accepted that it had jurisdiction to supervise the activities of the Takeover Panel. The then Master of the Rolls was concerned about interfering with the operation of the City in the takeover area and it is clear that the decision might well have been different if it were not for the flexibility of the remedy of a declaration and the safeguards which are built into the judicial review procedure including the ability to provide relief with remarkable rapidity where this is necessary.[22] The Court indicated that except in the most exceptional circumstances it would intervene by declaring the law of the future rather than seeking to disturb the decision of a panel in a particular case. As the Master of the Rolls said:

> I wish to make it clear beyond peradventure that in the light of the special nature of the panel and its functions and the market in which it is operating, the timescales which are inherent in that market and the need to safeguard the position of third parties who may be numbered in thousands all of whom are entitled to continue to trade upon an assumption of the validity of the

---

[21] [1987] QB 815.

[22] The timescale bears repeating. On the same day as the application was first made it was considered by the single judge who refused leave and was then before the Court of Appeal. The Court of Appeal granted leave, continued with the hearing and announced its decision straight away but gave its reasons a few days later. The undesirable consequences of delay were therefore kept to a minimum. Lloyd LJ stated that the proceedings, as a matter of policy 'should be in the realm of public law rather than private law not only because they are quicker but also because the requirements of leave under Order 53 would exclude claims which are clearly unmeritorious'.

> panel's rules and decisions unless and until they are quashed by the Court,
> I should expect the relationship between the panel and the Court to be historic
> rather than contemporaneous. I should expect the Court to allow contempo-
> rary decisions to take their course, considering the complaint and intervening,
> if at all, later and in retrospect by declaratory orders which would enable the
> panel not to repeat any error and will relieve individuals of the disciplinary
> consequences of any erroneous finding of breach of the rules.[23]

Relief of the sort which the Master of the Rolls had in mind could only be granted in the form of a declaration. His use of the court's jurisdiction in this way was novel and important and provides a blueprint for the control of similar bodies in the future.

It is difficult to conceive how this extension of the role of the court would be possible if the declaration had remained a private law remedy. The normal consequence of a party succeeding in private law proceedings is that he only seeks and obtains relief which is immediately effective to further his private interests. There is no question of a court confining itself merely to giving guidance for the future. Indeed, the giving of guidance of this nature would, at one time, have been regarded as being wrong in principle since the courts had turned their face against giving decisions which were purely advisory. There are, however, procedural problems which will arise if the court is only prepared to give an advisory decision. Litigants will normally not be interested in making applications if they are not going to be granted relief which is of more immediate benefit to them. This could lead to the need, particularly in the area of administrative law, of an independent person to bring proceedings in the public interest.[24] It would be unfortunate if the lack of an applicant prevented the advisory role the Master of the Rolls had in mind being developed.

It could be a great advantage in this field if the courts were prepared to give declaratory judgments which clarified the legal position. Indeed, subject to not over-burdening the courts, it could be very much in the public interest for public bodies to avail themselves of the power of the courts to grant declarations when they are in doubt as to the legality of some important administration decision which they are about to take. At present, the approach of public bodies is no doubt to conscientiously

---

[23] *Datafin* [1987] QB 815, 842.

[24] The law has since been developed to allow trade unions and groups protecting or campaigning for a particular public interest to pursue judicial review. See the *Fire Brigades Union* and *ex parte Bull* cases, n 16 above.

come to their own decision as to whether the course which they are proposing to adopt is lawful and then to wait and see whether what they have done is challenged. Could there not be many situations where it would be more sensible to obtain an anticipatory ruling? Take, for example, a road enquiry where it is known that there is likely to be highly vociferous opposition. The Department wants to take steps to limit the access of the public, but does arrange for there to be an overflow meeting with audio visual communication with the main hall. The Department is, however, concerned as to whether it is entitled to hold an enquiry at more than one location and also wants to know whether if there is a disturbance at the meeting it can require all the public to attend the overflow meeting. The enquiry is likely to take up to a year and if the validity of the procedure is only challenged after the enquiry, the construction of the road could be delayed as the result of one objector who may or may not succeed. How much better in these sort of circumstances to obtain a guidance of the court prior to the enquiry?

At one time this would not have been possible because the application would be considered premature and academic. But a different attitude could well be adopted by the courts today. This is indicated by the case of *R v Her Majesty's Treasury, ex parte Smedley*.[25] In that case Mr Smedley sought a declaration that a draft Order in Council authorising the payment of funds to meet a supplementary budget of the EEC was unlawful, although the draft order, before it could be made in Council by Her Majesty, required, but had not received, the approval of both Houses of Parliament. One of the many arguments advanced against the granting of such declaratory relief was that it was premature and that it would be an interference with the sovereignty of Parliament for the courts to declare the draft order *ultra vires* before it had been considered by Parliament. However, the Court of Appeal, while accepting that there was not in existence any Order in Council to which Mr Smedley could object, rejected this argument because in the circumstances an expression of a view by the courts on a question of law, which could arise for decision if Parliament were to approve the draft, might be of service not only to the parties, but also to each House of Parliament itself. It was pointed out that this was exactly the course which was adopted

---

[25] [1985] 1 QB 657.

as long ago as 1923 in *R v Electricity Commissioners, ex parte London Electricity Joint Committee*.[26] In that case Younger LJ had said:

> The interference of the court in such a case as this and at this stage, so far from being a challenge to its supremacy even in the most diluted sense of the word, will be an assistance to Parliament.[27]

In fact, declaratory relief was not granted because Mr Smedley failed on the merits of his application. However, but for this it appears he would have succeeded—the court being equally unimpressed by arguments that Mr Smedley had no *locus standi* as a taxpayer to make the application.

However, the Court of Appeal did emphasise that the jurisdiction was one which had to be exercised with care. I would endorse this. Certainly, I would not want the courts to be saddled with a large number of unnecessary applications and I recognise there could be a danger of administrative bodies seeking to play safe by trying to obtain anticipatory rulings of the court. The power should be preserved for cases where there is a real risk of challenge, and where the challenge were it to occur, could cause delay in implementing a decision, contrary to the public interests. I doubt whether there would be abuse of such a power. The *Smedley* case has not been followed by a succession of similar cases and if, as I would expect, the initiative would normally have to come from the public body to initiate proceedings, such bodies can be expected to exercise a degree of caution about drawing attention to possible weaknesses in their proposals. However, subject to these qualifications the development of the practice of seeking advisory opinions from the courts would appear to me to be sensible and constructive. The *Conseil d'Etat* has a section which provides a similar service in France, and for the courts in this country to provide declaratory relief in these sort of circumstances may not only improve administrative efficiency but also make a contribution to improving the attitudes of administrators to judicial review. It could result in them being more ready to regard judicial review as being constructive and not solely destructive, as I fear is frequently their attitude at present.

The significant difference between what happened in the *Smedley* case and what I am suggesting is that it was not the Department that took the initiative of bringing proceedings in the *Smedley* case. Where the application is brought by a department of central government, the problem would

---

[26] [1924] 1 KB 171.
[27] Ibid, 213.

arise as to who should be the respondent. Constitutionally, as matters are at present and in the absence of any other appropriate body, this would have to be the Attorney-General. There has to be some party who can properly put before the court arguments against the proposal so as to make the decision binding thereafter. Wearing his hat as the guardian of the public interest the Attorney-General should be perfectly capable of ensuring all arguments are properly before the court. However, here again I do believe that it would be much better if there were to be some other representative who would act as the respondent on behalf of the public, called perhaps a Director of Civil Proceedings, rather than the officer responsible for advising the government on legal matters.

Returning to the *Datafin* case, another feature of that case which is likely to be of immense importance in the future is the decision of the Court that the Takeover Panel was the subject of judicial review, albeit that prior to the *Datafin* case there was considerable doubt as to whether a non-statutory, self-regulatory body could be subject to supervision by the courts. As the then Master of the Rolls, at the beginning of his judgment made clear, the Take-Over Panel is a most unusual body. He said:

> The panel on take-overs and mergers is a truly remarkable body. Perched on the twentieth floor of the Stock Exchange building in the City of London both literally and metaphysically it oversees and regulates a very important part of the United Kingdom financial market yet it performs this function without visible means of legal support.[28]

He went on, however, to point out that while the panel lacks 'any authority *de jure*' it exercises immense power *de facto* by devising, promulgating and interpreting the City code on takeovers and mergers by waiving or modifying the application of the code in particular circumstances, by investigating and reporting upon alleged breaches of the code, and by the application or threat of sanctions'.[29] An important reason for the court being able to come to the conclusion that the Panel was subject to judicial review was that it was performing a public function. Prior to the *Datafin* case, the question of amenability to judicial review tended to turn on the source of the body's authority. However, as Lloyd LJ said:

> I do not agree that the source of the power is the sole test of a body subject to judicial review ... of course the source of power will perhaps usually be decisive.

---

[28] *Datafin* [1987] QB 815, 824.
[29] Ibid, 825.

> If a source of power is statute or subordinate legislation under statute then clearly the body in question will be subject to judicial review. If, on the other end of the scale the source of power is contractual as in the case of private arbitration then clearly the arbitrator is not subject to judicial review . . . but in between these extremes there is an area in which it is helpful to look not just at the source of the power but at the nature of the power.[30]

As I said in a case referred to by Lloyd LJ, 'the application for judicial review is refined to reviewing *activities* of a public nature as opposed to those of a purely private or domestic character'.[31]

The ability to look at the activity performed by a body in order to decide whether it is subject to judicial review could be of real significance and importance to the public with regard to the privatisation policy of successive governments.[32] A particular activity which undoubtedly has been performed by a public body is just as likely to give rise to the need for judicial review if that body is privatised. In conjunction with privatisation, regulatory bodies have been established and those bodies wield great powers. They could use those powers in an oppressive manner and so judicial review is important in their case as well. The extent of the need is highlighted by the fact that in February 1988 plans were announced to reform the Civil Service by hiving off 70,000 jobs to new executive agencies.[33] These plans have become known as 'The Next Steps' following the report of Sir Robin Ibbs entitled 'Improving Management in Government—The Next Steps'.[34] These new agencies are subject to judicial review and the guidelines are given to such agencies by the department responsible for overseeing their activities. In exercising their supervisory role, the courts have to be careful not to frustrate the proper endeavours of the new agencies or to interfere unnecessarily with the relationship between the agencies and their departments. However, the existence of the agencies must not be allowed to interfere with the residual ability of courts to protect the public against abuse of power by the growing number of bodies exercising functions which were previously exercised by the more conventional organs of central or local government.

---

[30] Ibid, 847.

[31] *R v BBC, ex parte Lavelle* [1983] 1 WLR 23.

[32] On privatisation, see 'Droit Public—English style', Chapter 3 in this book.

[33] See R Baldwin [1988] 51 MLR 622.

[34] (HMSO, 1988).

The flexibility of declaratory relief will assist the courts to maintain the proper balance between not interfering unduly and protecting the interests of the public when it is necessary for the courts to grant relief. The *Datafin* case is a vivid example of what can be achieved. The courts have created a new creature—the prospective declaration.[35] The extent to which public bodies should be required to reopen decisions already taken as opposed to mending their ways in the future is now capable of being considered by the courts when granting relief. It has, however, to be the right case for this to be done and normally the litigant is entitled if he succeeds to have an ultra vires decision cast aside.[36]

There can be many considerations which make it undesirable to declare a decision retrospectively a nullity. In the *ICI* case the Court of Appeal, disagreeing with Woolf J, did not consider the possible prejudice to Shell, Esso and BP of setting aside the valuation previously adopted by the Inland Revenue in assessing their liability to what could be a vast amount of tax sufficient to justify only granting prospective relief. On the other hand, in the *Chief Constable of North Wales v Evans*,[37] the judge at first instance—I regret to say, Woolf J again—the Court of Appeal and House of Lords all agreed that the Chief Constable had acted in breach of the rules of natural justice in compelling a probationary constable to resign by threatening that otherwise he would be dismissed, but differed as to what form the relief should take. The judge at first instance was arrogantly of the opinion that his judgment gave the constable all that he could expect and did not grant any relief. The Court of Appeal granted the constable a declaration that the decision requiring the constable to resign was void, but did not spell out the consequences of this. Presumably it meant that he was still a probationary constable—the sole remedy the constable was really interested in—as he was determined if possible to pursue his career in the police force. The House of Lords, having found the question of what form of relief was appropriate, difficult, concluded that in the circumstances it would be wrong to require the reinstatement of a probationary constable whom the police force did not want and awarded a declaration that Evans had, as the result

---

[35] See C Lewis, 'Retrospective and Prospective Rulings in Administrative Law' [1988] PL 78.

[36] In *R v Attorney-General, ex parte Imperial Chemical Industries Plc* [1987] 1 CMLR 72, the Court of Appeal allowed an appeal against that part of the decision of the judge at first instance (Woolf J) granting prospective relief only in relation to a challenge by ICI as to the approach possibly adopted by the Inland Revenue in valuing ethane of ICI's competitors, Shell, Esso and BP, at their proposed plants.

[37] [1982] 1 WLR 1155.

of an unlawfully induced resignation, become entitled to all the rights and remedies short of reinstatement that he would have had if the Chief Constable had unlawfully dismissed him. By this, the House of Lords used the declaration with precision to protect the constable financially but not to put him retrospectively in the position he would have been in if not compelled to resign.

I mention this saga because it is an excellent illustration of the value of declaratory relief in public law proceedings. I had refused any relief because I shied away from inflicting on the Chief Constable an officer whom he did not want. The Court of Appeal adopted the private law approach and did not concern itself unduly with the consequences of its decision. The House of Lords, however, used the declaration in a way which recognised the constable's interests to the extent that was consistent with the interests of the public in there being an efficient police force. In *Ridge v Baldwin*[38] itself the House of Lords made it clear that there was no question of the Chief Constable being reinstated and the declaratory relief granted was also designed mainly to safeguard his financial situation.

The granting of only prospective declarations also fits in with the provisions of section 31(6) of the Supreme Court Act 1981. This subsection requires the court to take into account the effects of granting relief in cases where there has been undue delay which is likely to cause substantial hardship or substantial prejudice to third parties or be detrimental to good administration. A prospective declaration is less likely to have these undesirable consequences. Accordingly, it would be open to the court having regard to the language of section 31(6) to refuse retrospective relief but be prepared to grant prospective relief. As Clive Lewis points out in his article on prospective rulings in administrative law,[39] in tailoring the declaration to the needs of a particular situation, the English courts are following in the footsteps of the European Court.[40]

---

[38] [1964] AC 40.

[39] See n 35 above.

[40] He refers in particular to the *Snupat* case [1961] ECR 53 and the *Hoogovens* case [1962] ECR 253 and the first civil service salaries case 81/72 [1973] ECR 573 and shows how the European Court has been more explicit than English courts in dealing with the interaction of the principles of legality with the principles of legal certainty. In situations such as that which arose in the *ICI* case, n 36 above, the European Court will attach greater importance to the possible impact of declaring a decision void retrospectively on the activities of third parties who have relief in good faith on the decision and made their arrangements accordingly. Where a remedy is flexible this can be done and it is appropriate that it should be done in the public law area.

This is again a situation where a distinction can be drawn between the remedies available to a person who can claim that his private rights have been infringed, and who normally will have those rights protected automatically by the courts, and the person who claims that he has been adversely affected by the manner in which a public body has performed its public functions where there is not the same automatic right to redress. Although in both types of proceedings the motive of the applicant for resorting to the courts may be the same, in the case of the public law proceedings the applicant is doing no more than seeking to enforce a duty which is owed to the public in general. Whereas in private law proceedings he is seeking to enforce a right to which he is entitled. Of the remedies which are now available in public law proceedings the declaration has become the most beneficial because it enables the court to sculpture the relief which it grants so that it fits as closely as possible both the needs of the individual applicant and the public.[41]

Damages

I turn to damages, which Lord Denning also regarded as being part of his 'up to date machinery'. In drafting the new Order 53[42] and when providing the statutory backing in section 31 of the Supreme Court Act 1981, damages could have been made a public as well as a private law remedy. The contrasting treatments of damages on the one hand and declarations on the other make it clear that this course was deliberately rejected. The result is that the citizen's liability to obtain compensation for wrongful and arbitrary administrative action is extremely limited. He can obtain compensation in accordance with the normal principles of liability in cases of negligence,[43] where a statute expressly or by implication provides him with a remedy or

---

[41] It is to be noted that since the coming into force of the Human Rights Act 1998, s 4 of the Act has given the courts (any senior court, including the Administrative Court) the power to declare a 'provision of primary legislation' incompatible with a Convention right. Such a declaration does not have the effect of making primary legislation invalid, but the government may take remedial action to remove the incompatibility. For example, in *A v Secretary of State for the Home Department* [2005] 2 WLR 87, the House of Lords declared s 23 of the Anti-terrorism, Crime and Security Act 2001 (which gave the Secretary of State power to detain indefinitely, without charge or trial, non-British nationals whom he suspected of international terrorist activity, but whom he could not deport) incompatible with the Human Rights Act. Section 23 continued in force while the government considered means of amending it.

[42] As mentioned previously, this has been replaced by CPR Part 54.

[43] While a claimant may include a claim for damages in his claim for judicial review, breach of a public law right does not of itself give rise to financial compensation.

where he can show that the official in question has acted in bad faith.[44] However, there can be many circumstances where as the law at present exists he has no remedy. In this situation the Justice All Souls Committee recommended a radical change, namely that a remedy in the form of compensation should be available:

(a) When a person suffers a loss as a result of wrong administrative action not involving negligence;

(b) Where a loss is caused by excessive or unreasonable delay in reaching a decision.

The Committee thought that the law relating to negligence could be left to develop on a case-by-case basis and that the ordinary principles of causation, remoteness and measure of damage should apply. I have considerable sympathy for these recommendations but having regard to the width of their terms I cannot wholly endorse them.

That the proper protection of the citizen requires the court to have some new, wide power to award compensation I have, however, no doubt. Indeed, I am sure that it is in the interests of government, both central and local, that there should be such a power. The case of *Chief Constable of Wales v Evans*,[45] to which I have recently made reference, illustrates the need. What the House of Lords was struggling to do was to ensure that the probationary constable was compensated for the Chief Constable's breach of the rules of natural justice; that was the appropriate remedy.

In the case of loss caused by conduct which for a private body would create an estoppel, the public authority should be allowed only to pursue an alternative course dictated by the requirements of good administration if it is prepared to pay the appropriate compensation. Where a statutory scheme affects the public at large, in many situations it would be preferable if,

---

[44] The Court has been cautious in finding that a 'duty of care' exists (which has to be established from a claim in negligence) if the claim is in respect of the negligent breach of a public law duty. Where it can be shown that the decision-maker was not merely negligent, but acted with 'malice', a private law action for damages is possible for the tort of misfeasance in public office. For example, where an illegal entrant, with a record of violence known by the police, escaped deportation by offering information on criminal associates and later committed murder. See *Akenzua v Secretary of State for the Home Department and Metropolitan Police Commissioners* [2003] 1 WLR 741. Furthermore, s 8 of the Human Rights Act 1998 allows the Court to award damages where it finds that a public authority has acted incompatibly with a Convention right, where the Court is satisfied the award is necessary to afford 'just satisfaction'. The approach of the Court has so far been fairly cautious. See, for example, *R (Greenfield) v Secretary of State for the Home Department* [2005] 1 WLR 673.

[45] See n 37 above.

instead of using the blunt instrument of certiorari to quash the scheme, the court could compensate the few objectors and allow the scheme to proceed. In the case of delay, the court in its discretion might consider that justice would be done if damages were awarded instead of granting an order of certiorari or mandamus which would have been appropriate if there had not been delay. Damages or compensation could be the most valuable additional weapon in the armoury of the High Court judge exercising his discretionary powers of judicial review.

However, the proposal put forward by the Committee appeared to go much further than was necessary. First of all, if damages became a public law remedy, I could see that there could be public policy reasons for saying that the measure of damages should be different from those in a common law action. The applicant would be seeking compensation for the failure to comply with a duty or the failure to exercise properly a power which exists for the benefit of the public at large, not for the applicant alone, and this could be a material consideration in deciding what is the appropriate rate of compensation. The judicial restraint in the award of damages for loss of expectation of life provides a precedent for an entirely different scale of damages in the appropriate situation.

The Committee in making its recommendation took into account the risk of public bodies being inhibited from acting promptly or being encouraged to be overcautious in their approach in order to avoid the risk of their incurring liability. The Committee felt that this risk could be discounted. However, I am by no means sure that this was right. In particular, I do consider that there would be a considerable danger of the smaller public bodies being inhibited; certainly there have been dramatic stories in circulation about the consequences of making local authorities liable to pay damages for the negligence of their building inspectors. There is also the difficulty with the Committee's recommendations that they could result in the injured person's rights being greater if a particular injury is inflicted upon him by a public body than if exactly the same injury is imposed upon him in the same circumstances by a private body. This can hardly be a desirable result.

I argued that if there were to be reform, then I would advocate that a step by step approach should be adopted, albeit that this required legislation. As a start I advocated limiting the courts' power to grant compensation to those cases where the alternative remedies provided by judicial review were insufficient to secure substantial justice in the case and material hardship would have been caused to an applicant if compensation were not awarded in lieu of or in addition to other relief. There were many other formulae which could have achieved the sort of result that I had in mind and the innovation, since that is what it would have been, should have been regarded as being an experiment to be reviewed thereafter. However, during the period of experiment the powers of the Ombudsman to recommend *ex gratia* compensation in the case of maladministration should have been exercised so as not to result in greater compensation being granted than could be awarded by the courts. It was surely highly undesirable that the situation where the Ombudsman was able, in effect, to award compensation when the courts could not do so, should have continued, particularly bearing in mind that the Ombudsman was normally required to decline to exercise his jurisdiction where the person aggrieved could have had a remedy in any court of law.[46] An even more unattractive position could have arisen as a result of a litigant unsuccessfully exhausting his remedies in this country and then going to Strasbourg. In the Strasbourg proceedings he could have obtained compensation which is not available from the courts in his own country. I considered that the necessary reform, at least on the lines which I suggested, was most likely to be of value and I intended it primarily to apply in those cases which could have been broadly described as being cases of non-feasance on the part of the administrative body.

As to the category (b) situation identified by the Committee, where a person is caused loss by excessive or unreasonable delay, I have regarded it as a grave injustice that administrative delays can result in very real damage to the individual, but that this damage can only be compensated, if at all, by the intervention of the Ombudsman.

The Justice All Souls Report was not able to take into account the Privy Council decision in *Rowling v Takaro Properties Ltd*[47] which resulted in the decision of the High Court of New Zealand being reversed so that no compensation was recovered. If the outcome of the appeal had been known, I suspect that the Committee would not have been as confident about their recommendation to leave the law of negligence to develop on a case-by-case basis. The opinion of Lord Keith in that case strongly suggested that the distinction that Lord Wilberforce drew in *Anns v Merton*,[48] between policy or planning decisions and operational decisions was likely to be consigned to the same fate

---

[46] Parliamentary Commissioner Act 1967, s 5. In addition to the Ombudsman, there is a separate Welsh Administration Ombudsman who deals with complaints against the Welsh Assembly and certain bodies dealing with matters devolved to Wales, and a corresponding Scottish Public Services Ombudsman.

[47] [1988] 1 All ER 163.

[48] [1987] AC 728.

as the test Lord Wilberforce laid down in the same case for ascertaining whether a duty of care exists. This would have been unfortunate and, as Lord Keith was careful to indicate that their Lordships were not expressing any final conclusion, there still remained a prospect that my pessimism was unjustified. While I fully appreciated the dangers of administrators becoming overcautious if they were exposed to actions for damages, I expected the overcaution to manifest itself more in the policy area than in the operational area. An advantage of Lord Wilberforce's approach was therefore properly to exclude those cases where the development of the law was least desirable.

Lord Keith identified considerations which their Lordships felt 'militate against imposition of liability'.[49] I recognised that those considerations indicated the position was by no means easy, but I venture to suggest that there could be situations where delay could cause very substantial disadvantage to an applicant and that if he never had a remedy for delay he could suffer real injustice. In addition, I suggested that the possible liability to make compensation for undue delay could have a very salutary effect upon the speed of the decision-making process. Obviously, where there was no fixed period in which a decision had to be taken, there would be a degree of flexibility as to the date by which the decision was to be taken and it was only in those cases which went beyond the limits set by that degree of flexibility that the right to compensation would arise. If real damage was caused by the delay, and it should have been appreciated by the decision-maker that the delay would cause real damage, I was bound to say that this was the type of situation where I felt redress should have been available. It would have been necessary to show that there was a breach of duty which could be categorised as negligence and I appreciated, as Lord Keith pointed out, that this may have been no easy achievement. However, if negligence could have been established the difficulty of proof was not a reason for refusing relief. As the number of agencies grew that were responsible for taking decisions which could have a material effect on an applicant's livelihood, the ability to obtain compensation was surely going to become more valuable.

Finally, I drew attention to the existence of a limited route for possible progress which had the benefit of not requiring legislation. Frequently, in seeking to persuade the court to exercise its discretion to refuse relief the public body against whom an application for judicial review was made stressed the undesirable consequences which could flow from quashing a

---

[49] [1988] 1 All ER 163, 172–1/5.

decision. Returning to our proposed new motorway, years of work may have been wasted if as a result of the intervention of the courts a new enquiry had to be held. In such a case it could have been open to the court to say to the public body that if those who had been adversely affected were compensated then the court would not grant relief but otherwise the court would reluctantly be compelled to do so. I recognised this could be regarded as an unattractive way in which a public body would, in effect, be able to 'buy off' the normal consequences of having acted in abuse of its powers. It would, however, have been a pragmatic way of protecting the public as a whole from the full adverse effects of what frequently may have been no more than administrative incompetence. If justice could have been done to the applicant by the provision of compensation, then it may have been that the harmful effects of quashing a decision could have been avoided without causing injustice.

The Injunction

I turn now to the remaining feature of the new machinery of Lord Denning, the injunction.

The learned editor of the fourth edition of de Smith's *Judicial Review of Administrative Action*,[50] Professor Evans, compared the progress which had been made in the use of injunctions with declarations as a public law remedy. He said:

> Certainly its capacity for growth has not been fully exploited. The remarkable emergence of the declaratory order as a major public law remedy has been pointing for some years to the road ahead. For reasons not easy to identify with confidence, reasons connected, however, with its primary role as a private law remedy, the injunction has lagged behind.[51]

Those words are still true today.[52] The explanation which I would put forward for the lack of progress is that as a final order, prohibition is capable of achieving virtually the same result as an injunction.[53]

---

[50] S A de Smith, *Judicial Review of Administrative Action* (4th edn, 1980). For the latest edition, see S A de Smith, A Le Sueur, J L Jowell, H Woolf (9th edn, 2007).

[51] Ibid (4th edn, 1980), 474.

[52] Indeed, final injunctions continue to be a rarity in judicial review as, when dealing with public bodies, declaratory relief (particularly when coupled with a quashing order) will usually suffice.

[53] In the past prohibition may have been regarded as being primarily available against inferior courts and other tribunals but that is no longer true today.

Before the introduction of judicial review, the use of an injunction as a public law remedy was largely confined to situations where local and other authorities were proposing to act unlawfully or in aid of the criminal law, normally in proceedings commenced by the Attorney-General or with his authority. Except as an alternative to prohibition, that is still its role.[54]

Where, however, an injunction has great advantages over prohibition is that an injunction can provide interim relief. Although the procedure on an application for judicial review is expeditious, it is by no means rare for the court to have to hold the ring until it can permanently determine the legality of a proposed course of action. As a public law remedy the injunction has therefore come into its own as the prime method of obtaining interim relief. Indeed, it is the only way of obtaining interim relief save for the power contained in Order 53, rule 10,[55] which permitted the court when it granted leave to apply for judicial review in the form of an order of certiorari or prohibition to direct that the leave should operate as a stay of the proceedings impugned until the final determination of the application or the court otherwise ordered. Precisely what was meant by proceedings for this purpose is not clear.[56]

Before the introduction of judicial review, it was always accepted that it was not possible to obtain an injunction against the Crown. Until the late 1980s it was accepted that judicial review had not altered the situation and therefore it was not possible to obtain interim relief against the Crown[57] on an application for judicial review.[58] However, in 1987, Hodgson J in a carefully reasoned judgment[59] advanced arguments which I personally found

---

[54] It is noteworthy that the position in the United States is very different. In Federal administrative law the injunction is probably the most important judicial remedy.

[55] Again, this has been replaced by CPR Part 54.

[56] In *R (on the application of Ashworth Hospital Authority) v Mental Health Review Tribunal for West Midlands and Northwest Region* [2002] EWCA Civ 923, [2003] 1 WLR 127, the Court of Appeal explained that 'stay of proceedings' should be given a wide interpretation to enhance the effectiveness of the judicial review jurisdiction. It stated that the Court had jurisdiction to stay the decision of a tribunal that was subject to a judicial review challenge even when the decision had been fully implemented. However, it added that the jurisdiction to grant a stay in these circumstances should be exercised sparingly.

[57] This is no longer the case. Since the seminal decision of *M v Home Office* [1994] 1 AC 377 (injunction against the Secretary of State for the Home Department, in his professional rather than personal capacity) it is now clear the Court has power to grant injunctions against the Crown. However, parliamentary privilege still precludes the making of an injunction in relation to matters relating to the internal proceedings of Parliament. See *Bradlaugh v Gossett* (1884) 12 QBD 271. It is not clear to what extent this holds true for matters potentially in conflict with EU law.

[58] It has always been clear that an interim declaration was not available in this country as in Israel.

[59] See *R v Secretary of State for the Home Department, ex parte Herbage* [1987] QB 872.

compelling based on section 31 of the Supreme Court Act 1981 as to why on an application for judicial review the court has power to grant an injunction. That reasoning was followed by the majority of the Court of Appeal, of which I was a member.[60] However, in a decision given on 18 May 1989, the House of Lords rejected that reasoning and made it clear that there is no power to grant injunctions, interim or final, against the Crown.[61]

It must therefore be accepted that until Parliament intervenes, which it is most unlikely to do, the courts cannot grant interim or final injunctions against the Crown. I regret that this should be the position, notwithstanding the fact that in my experience the Crown is normally prepared to hold its hand where proceedings are pending before the court where if it did not do so irreversible damage would be done to the individual. My regret is primarily based upon the belief that it is not right that the protection of the individual should be entirely dependent upon the willingness of the Crown to hold its hand as a matter of grace. In the future, the Crown may not be so sensitive to the rights of the individual. I also regret that this should be the position because frequently the inability of the court to rule on the issue as to whether interim relief should be granted causes the Crown to abstain from taking action pending the outcome of proceedings when in fact if the court were able to rule it would not be prepared to grant interim relief. It is particularly unfortunate that this should be the position since the House of Lords, unlike the Supreme Court of Israel, has set its face against interim declarations which could be awarded against the Crown.[62]

However, the position may not be quite as unsatisfactory as it seems as a result of the House of Lords decision, since on a careful reading of Lord Bridge's speech, which was agreed by the other members of the House, it is clear that he made no mention of the power of the court to grant a stay. I feel this was no accident. I am, however, somewhat sceptical as to whether this possibility will prove to be more than a mirage since the reasoning of

---

[60] *R v Licensing Authority established under Medicines Act 1968, ex parte Smith Kline and French Laboratories Ltd (No 2)* [1989] 2 WLR 378.

[61] *R v Secretary of State for Transport, ex parte Factortame and Others* [1989] 2 WLR 997. I do not regard it as appropriate to defend my own reasoning against that of the House of Lords. However, I regret that the argument accepted by the House of Lords for rejecting 'in the light of history' my reasoning which would otherwise have had 'great force' was never advanced before the Court of Appeal since I consider there is at last a respectable argument for taking a different view from that of Lord Bridge (who gave the only speech) and that it would have been preferable if the arguments could have been considered by the Lords. Would a Director of Civil Proceedings' intervention in the House of Lords have helped?

[62] See *Gouriet v Attorney-General* [1978] AC 435.

Lord Bridge would appear to be as applicable to a stay as it is to an interim injunction. On the other hand, if Lord Bridge had formed the clear view that a stay could not be granted, I would have expected him to have said so even though his opinion would have been *obiter*.

Certainly, for the time being at any rate, the injunction as a public law remedy will continue to lag behind the declaration.[63]

Conclusion

It will be apparent from the views that I have expressed that I am in favour of more declarations, more injunctions and more damages or compensation on applications for judicial review. I would, however, make it clear that this does not mean that I am in favour of more judicial intervention into the activities of public bodies. It is my belief that if the changes which I would favour were to be implemented, they would result in more effective and efficient use of, but not more, judicial review, and would assist the court in maintaining a proper balance between protecting the public and allowing those who have the responsibility for governing us to govern. Unfortunately, the initiative and imagination displayed by the courts in relation to the declaration has not been shown in relation to the other remedies. The opportunity has been there but so far it has not been taken. I hope more attention will be paid to Lord Denning's words over the next 57 years.

---

[63] In addition to the areas covered in this lecture, it is to be noted there have been significant developments in the law on remedies which have influenced English law, two in particular are mentioned here: (1) EC state liability claims (see case C-9/90 *Francovich v Italian Republic* [1991] ECR I-5357, and Cases C-46 and C-48/93 *Brasserie du Pêcheur v Federal Republic of Germany* and *R v Secretary of State for Transport, ex parte Factortame Ltd and Others* [1996] ECR I-1029); and (2) actions for the tort of misfeasance in public office (see *Three Rivers DC v Bank of England (No 3)* [2003] 2 AC 1).

3

Droit Public—English Style

Abstract This paper discusses the growth of public law in England through a pragmatic approach in which the law has been developed on a case-by-case basis. It identifies distinct public law principles that are of general application, independent of private law and comparable to those in civil jurisdictions. Distinguishing between public and private law, it suggests an issue is subject to public law if the public have a legitimate concern as to its outcome and it is not an issue already satisfactorily protected by private law. The relationship between the courts and Parliament is examined, and it is suggested that both arms of government are partners in a common enterprise involving upholding the rule of law.

The English public law model is different from those which exist in civil jurisdictions, but it is not necessarily the worse for this. As has been pointed out by a distinguished commentator, in no two nations is the system of public law identical.[1] It is my thesis that we have now a developed set of distinct public law principles which are of general application, independent of private law and comparable to those in civil jurisdictions. While the principles are enforced by the High Court, with its extensive private law jurisdiction and not a separate supreme public or administrative law tribunal, the High Court when applying those principles is not exercising its normal jurisdiction.[2]

---

* Originally given as the Annual F A Mann Lecture at Lincoln's Inn on 5 November 1994. A revised version was published in *Public Law* ((1995) PL 57).

[1] See the Introduction to the *International Encyclopedia of Comparative Law*, Vol 2, per Prof Szladits, paras 25/57; *Re Norway's Application* [1990] 1 AC 723, 802–803.

[2] There is an Administrative Court, presently with 37 judges, including judges from the Chancery Division and Family Division, who act as additional judges of the Queen's Bench Division of the High Court, when dealing with cases in the Administrative Court List. The Administrative Court has jurisdiction in a number of varied areas, including judicial review of decisions of inferior courts and tribunals, public bodies and persons exercising a public function; criminal cases may arise from decisions of Magistrates' Courts or the Crown Court when it is acting in appellate capacity; and statutory appeals and applications.

It is exercising a quite separate jurisdiction: its inherent power to review administrative action.

As to this separate jurisdiction, there have been several events which are of importance to public law in this country. First of all, following in the footsteps of a third edition of Paul Craig's distinguished work *Administrative Law*,[3] the seventh edition of Professor Sir William Wade's *Administrative Law*[4] has been published. In it, Professor Wade gave an authoritative assessment of the many developments which have occurred in public law. The new Wade was in turn followed by the publication of the Law Commission's Report on Administrative Law and *Judicial Review and Statutory Appeals*.[5] It was, of course, the previous report of the Law Commission on *Remedies in Administrative Law*,[6] in 1976, which resulted in the modern procedure of judicial review. This proved to be a catalyst for the development of public law, so naturally everyone involved in public law was anxious to learn the extent to which the Law Commission would decide that further change was necessary. In the event, they recommended changes of detail rather than wholesale reform. This was an implicit general endorsement of the current satisfactory state of health of our public law. The Commission considered that there was no need to look at the substantive grounds for judicial review. Instead, these were to be 'the subject of judicial development'. Changes of detail can, however, have a significant collective impact and I was sure this would be the case with their recommendations.

The Growth of Public Law

Although the Law Commission did not consider that radical change was necessary, there can be no dispute as to the dramatic nature of the changes which have occurred in the principles or substance of public law since the introduction of the new procedure for judicial review. The changes have been accompanied and stimulated by developments in other jurisdictions, including many parts of the Commonwealth and the European Court of Human Rights in Strasbourg and the European Court of Justice in Luxembourg. They have also been influenced by the political situation at home. It is one of

---

[3] The latest edition, the fifth, was published in 2003.

[4] In conjunction with Dr Christopher Forsyth (now Professor Christopher Forsyth) (OUP, 1994). The latest edition, the ninth, was published in 2004.

[5] 1994, Law Com No 226.

[6] Law Com No 73, Cmnd 6407.

the strengths of the common law that it enables the courts to vary the extent of their intervention to reflect current needs, and by this means it helps to maintain the delicate balance of a democratic society. This can be compared with the frenetic activity of the Warren Court in the United States in the 1950s and 1960s and the interventionalist role of the Indian Supreme Court on behalf of the weakest sections of society in recent times.[7] Sir William Wade, who was not given to hyperbole, in the preface of his sixth edition, referred to a 'ferment' and the manner in which the judges 'in defiance of theoretical obstacles . . . have extended their empire' in relation to judicial review. In his seventh edition he referred to the fact that his book:

> . . . began life 33 years ago as a slim volume of fewer than 300 pages. Its growth through seven editions reflects the development of what is almost a new subject, rich now in principle and detail resulting from the work of adventurous judges and of a less adventurous but, nevertheless, supportive Parliament. Together they have established high standards of administrative justice, to such an extent that the defects are mainly those of an elaborate legal system – procedural judicial resources . . . on balance, the picture has become brighter with each successive edition.[8]

The shortcomings to which Sir William referred were of course the shortcomings of the civil justice system as a whole. They were shortcomings which I earnestly hoped, building on the Law Commission's report, I would be able to tackle effectively in the course of my Inquiry into Access to Justice on behalf of the Lord Chancellor.[9] The shortcomings apart, the picture described by Sir William was (and is) a positive one, which reflects well upon the qualities of vitality and flexibility of the common law.

It is not only in the sensational cases which attract the headlines that the judiciary has been busy. The immigrant, the disabled, investors, parents of children in the care of local authorities, corporations as large as ICI and the trade unions have all successfully resorted to judicial review when no other remedy was available. However, it is right to acknowledge that the picture would be less favourable if it had not been for the influence of what has been happening in the other jurisdictions to which I have referred. In many areas,

---

[7] S Sorabjee, 'Obliging Government to Control itself: Recent Developments in Indian Administrative Law,' [1994] PL 39.

[8] H W R Wade, *Administrative Law* (7th edn, 1994), v.

[9] H Woolf, *Access to Justice Final Report* (HMSO, 1996) does tackle these shortcomings, although, as I explain in the Introduction in this book, some of my recommendations are still to be implemented. An abstract of the Final Report Overview is included at Chapter 19 of this book.

the English judiciary has done no more than follow the path marked out by those who have gone before them in those jurisdictions. Fortunately, there have now been established very good lines of communication between the various jurisdictions both on a judicial and a professional level. What the judges do not learn for themselves in the course of judicial exchanges, has been taught by advocates, such as Lord Lester of Herne Hill, who have persevered, sometimes in the face of vigorous judicial opposition, in educating the judiciary as to the developments overseas.

Our system of public law does, however, have two obvious features which distinguish it from systems in other jurisdictions. Not only do we not have a written constitution or Bill of Rights, but until 2000, with the coming into effect of the Human Rights Act 1998, we did not allow our citizens to enforce directly in our courts the provisions of the European or any other international Convention on Human Rights. As a consequence, the legislative powers of Parliament in this country were less restricted than those in most other countries. The other distinctive feature of the English scene is the absence of any *Conseil d'Etat*. As I have pointed out, judicial review is under the control of the High Court. The control over the executive and the administration is in the hands of judges and not administrators, which is the position in those countries which have a *Conseil d'Etat*.

This last characteristic may have significance for the respective standing of judges and civil servants in this country. At the end of the first Anglo-French exchange between the administrators of the *Conseil d'Etat* and the English judiciary, Lord Scarman tried to explain the difference between our systems. He suggested that the success of the *Conseil d'Etat* was rooted in the fact that the French had greater trust in their administrators than their judges, whereas in England it was the judges and not the administrators who were trusted. This suggestion, as you would expect, went down well with an audience of English judges and French administrators. However, its validity was clouded in doubt when I tried it out on an audience of Italian academics. I was assured by them that in Italy the public trusted neither the judges nor the administrators. Surprisingly, they thought that in Italy it was the academics who were trusted.

It would also be wrong to be misled by the extent of the developments since 1977, following the introduction of the new procedure of judicial review, into thinking that England had no public law system long before that date. We tend to make the mistake of assimilating public law with judicial review. Public law may have been less developed then, but it can be clearly traced back into history. That history is intertwined with that of the prerogative writs. Back in the seventeenth and eighteenth centuries the prerogative writs were being used to supervise inferior bodies. In those days the prime targets for the prerogative writs were the justices of the peace. However, the significant feature to note is that the justices at that time had wide administrative functions as well as judicial so that it would be wrong, even then, to regard the High Court supervisory role as being limited to the judicial activities of inferior bodies. Although the progress since has been erratic it has been continuous. The procedural and structural changes which were introduced as part of the new procedure of judicial review under Order 53 accelerated the pace of that progress.[10] The changes improved access to the courts at a time when the public felt a greater need for protection from the abuse of administrative power. The result was a rapid increase in the number and also in the variety of public law applications to the court. In 1980 there were 525 applications; in 1991 2,089, a four-fold increase; since which time by 1994 there had been an increase of almost a further 50 per cent.[11] This growth would not have occurred if the new procedure had not been accompanied by the application by the courts of increasingly sophisticated principles of public law.

In Defence of the Public-Private Divide

An important consequence of the expansion in the number and nature of the applications for judicial review has been a new appreciation of the significance of the distinction between English public and private law. This was initially highlighted by the procedural divide between public and private law proceedings. This was treated as having been erected by the House of Lords in 1983 by its decision in *O'Reilly v Mackman*.[12] Like many of the other judges, if not all, who had the task of hearing applications for judicial review, I felt that although there is nothing in the rules which requires this, there had to be an exclusivity rule if the procedural safeguards for public bodies and the discretion of the court, which were an integral part of judicial review, were to be retained. If this was not the case, those safeguards could be bypassed.[13] As is well known, those safeguards include a requirement to obtain the leave of court to make an application, a short time in which to make the application,

---

[10] The procedure for judicial review in Order 53 has since been replaced with CPR Part 54.
[11] See Law Com (n 5 above) paras 212–213.
[12] [1983] 2 AC 237.
[13] Although subject to much academic criticism the Law Commission accepted that it was necessary to have an exclusivity rule. See n 5 above, para 315.

three months, which can be extended; and the discretionary nature of the remedies that the court provides on judicial review. The existence of the discretion is of the greatest importance since it means that even if the applicant succeeds in establishing a ground for relief, that relief can be refused if his application is unmeritorious. This gives the court considerable power to determine when it should and should not interfere with administrative decisions. This degree of discretion is appropriate in a public law but not a private law context and is usually not a feature of private law proceedings unless an equitable remedy is sought. The problem is that the different degree of discretion underlines the significance of the distinction between private and public law. This results in a significant number of unedifying disputes, which travel upwards through the court system, over the issue as to whether proceedings should be struck out as an abuse of the court for not being brought by the correct procedure. Such disputes have been encouraged because it is extraordinarily difficult at the margins to say with confidence whether a particular issue should be classified as public or private.

If all that was involved in these disputes was the question as to what was the correct procedure to adopt, then I would strongly endorse the critics of the exclusivity principle. However, cases which appear to involve a barren dispute as to procedure can involve a battle over a substantive issue of importance. This is because of the nature of the task which the courts are performing on an application for judicial review. That task is to ensure that bodies which perform public functions should do so in accordance with the requirements of the law. Many of those functions to differing degrees, affect a great many people. This gives rise to a need to avoid the uncertainty that the existence of proceedings can cause, so as to protect not only the workings of government and other public bodies, but also all those members of the public whom the decision affects. In addition, there is the need for there to be different, that is higher, standards to which public, but not private, bodies should be required to conform by the courts when performing public functions. I do believe that these features provide a solid foundation for the procedural divide.

On the other hand I, of course, endorsed the approach of the Law Commission. This was to recommend changes of procedure of a technical nature designed to minimise the inconvenience to which the divide could give rise. I did, however, recognise that even if the Commission's recommendations were implemented problems would remain. They would remain because of the difficulty already referred to of identifying those functions which are properly the legitimate subject matter of applications for judicial review. This is a difficulty which has not been confined to this country. The same principle arises in all other jurisdictions which have a distinct system for controlling public bodies. Their definition of what is a public body and what is a public function may differ from ours, but wherever the border is drawn its limits are likely to give rise to the same problem. For this reason, in some jurisdictions they actually have a separate court whose function is to adjudicate whether particular litigation is properly classified as involving public or private law.[14]

While acknowledging the difficulty, I emphasised that it is a difficulty which cannot be avoided. It will remain even if all proceedings are commenced in the same way and the courts, instead of the parties, are responsible for deciding in which list a case is heard. This is because the importance of the distinction between public and private law issues goes far beyond the correctness of the procedure by which a challenge to an activity should be brought. For example, it determines who can bring the proceedings. At one time it was thought that only those who are affected in some way that goes beyond the effect which the activity has on the public as a whole could bring proceedings, but now it is generally accepted that a much more generous approach to an issue as to standing needs to be adopted. This is necessary to ensure that there is never a situation where a public wrong can be committed without anyone having the right to seek redress. The courts should welcome the publicly interested litigant. I approve of the activities in different spheres of the Child Poverty Action Group and Greenpeace in bringing situations where there is a real issue which justifies the involvement of the courts to be determined.[15]

The division is also necessary because of the separate principles and standards which the courts will require of public as opposed to private bodies. The courts can and do require of those who perform public functions higher standards of behaviour than those which are required when what is being performed is a private activity. This is what public law is all about. What judicial review does is to provide a remedy, usually when no other remedy is available, to ensure that bodies adhere to those standards when performing public functions.

---

[14] In France, but not Belgium which has a very similar system, there exists a *Tribunal des conflits*; See further G Braibant, *Le Droit Administratif Francais* (Dalloz, 1992).

[15] The courts have adopted a more generous approach to standing to include, for example, trade unions (see *R v Secretary of State for the Home Department, ex parte Fire Brigades Union & Others* [1995] 2 AC 513) and groups protecting or campaigning for a particular public interest (see *R v DPP, ex parte Bull & Another* [1998] 2 All ER 755).

In some systems of public law the determining factor as to whether the issue involves public law is whether a body is or is not properly regarded as being a public body. This is the position in France. If a public body is involved, a dispute is considered to be public. Thus, disputes between a civil servant and the government in France are subject to public law whereas in England they are usually the subject of private law. In the case of English law, what I consider to be critical is the nature of the function which is being performed. Is the function properly classified as public or private?[16] Of course if it is a governmental activity, that is an act performed by the government, that will mean that activity is a strong candidate for being regarded as a public function.[17] However, as I have just indicated, even governments, never mind Members of Parliament, are recognised by English law, if not the media, as having the capacity to perform private activities. Against this there can be a body which has no links with the government, such as the Takeover Panel, which can perform public functions which will be subject to the scrutiny of the courts on an application for judicial review. The importance of this is underlined by the current fashion of privatisation. Increasingly, services which at one time were regarded as an essential part of government are being performed by private bodies. It is my belief that the fact that a body ceases to be a public body and becomes a private corporation does not mean that an activity which was previously subject to public law ceases to be subject

---

[16] This is very important today. If a body is a public authority, individuals have direct remedies for breach of s 6(1) of the Human Rights Act 1998, either by judicial review or for breach of the statutory duty under s 6 of the Human Rights Act to act in conformity with the Convention (unless there is a statutory excuse). The term 'public authority' is not defined positively in the Human Rights Act, except that the term includes a court or tribunal (s 6(3)(a)) and any person certain of whose functions are of a public nature in respect of the performance of those public functions (s 6(3)(b) and (5)), but does not include either House of Parliament (except the House of Lords when acting in a judicial capacity) or a person exercising functions in connection with proceedings in Parliament (s 6(3) and (4)).

[17] Government departments and ministers are now regarded as 'core public authorities', as are local authorities, NHS Trusts, coroners, police, prisons, bodies such as the Parole Board, Legal Services Commission, General Medical Council and Broadcasting Standards Commission. See *Aston Cantlow and Wilmcot with Billesley Parochial Church Council v Wallbank* [2003] UKHL 37, [2003] 1 AC 546. While the Human Rights Act defines public authorities broadly, the extent to which the definition includes private organisations performing public functions delegated by the state is controversial. The consequence is that privatised companies or bodies which undertake 'contracted out' work which would have otherwise been governmental activities, may not be subject to duties under the Human Rights Act. See *Donoghue v Poplar Housing* [2001] EWCA Civ 595, [2002] QB 48; *R (Heather) v Leonard Cheshire Foundation* [2002] EWCA Civ 366, [2002] 2 All ER 936; *R (Johnson) v Havering LBC* [2006] EWHC 1714. The government is considering legislative solutions to the problem. See Anne McGuire MP, Parliamentary Under-Secretary of State for Work and Pensions, *Hansard*, HC, col 1337, 21 November 2005.

to public law.[18] I can see no justification for the law allowing privatised bodies to adopt lower standards than those they were previously required to maintain. Parliament has recognised this by establishing regulatory bodies. When such bodies exist, judicial review pragmatically recognises that they, and not the courts, are the more appropriate means to achieve hands-on control. However, judicial review remains in the background to exercise control where necessary. This can be done by regulating the regulator or, if this is necessary, although it can create considerable difficulty, by controlling the privatised body directly, as has happened in New Zealand.[19]

We have the Monopolies and Mergers Commission[20] but there is a long history of the courts being prepared to control the exercise of monopolistic power. A common law principle that a monopoly supplier is not entitled to exploit his monopoly can be traced back to Hale's *Treatise de Portibus Maris*, written about 1670 but first published in 1787. Hale stated, in respect of a wharf licensed by the Queen or where there was no other wharf, 'there cannot be taken arbitrarily in excessive duties . . . but the duties must be reasonable and moderate . . . for now the wharf and crane . . . are affected with public interest, and they cease to be *juris private* only'.[21] My point was also made succinctly in 1877 in a United States case where Wate CJ, after citing Hale, said: 'When property is devoted to public use, it is subject to public regulation.'[22]

The same approach is illustrated by the New Zealand Bill of Rights 1990. New Zealand public law probably has the closest links to our own. Significantly, in addition to applying the Bill of Rights to various branches of government, section 3 goes on to provide that it also applies to the performance by '*any* person or body of any public *function*, power or duty, conferred or imposed pursuant to law'. I stress the reference to public function.

This is an approach which I find attractive. It seems to me that it should be the nature of the activity and not the nature of the body which should be decisive in deciding whether those who would be affected by the activity

---

[18] In addition to the above, it is thought that 'public' will cover the BBC, privatised utilities and the Jockey Club. See *R (Prolife Alliance) v BBC* [2002] 3 WLR 1080.

[19] See *Mercury Energy Ltd v Electricity Corp. of New Zealand* [1994] 1 WLR 521, *New Zealand Council v AG of New Zealand* [1994] 2 WLR 254, and M Taggart, 'Corporatisation, contracting and the courts' [1994] PL 351.

[20] Now the Competition Commission.

[21] See P Craig 'Constitutions, property and regulation' [1991] 1 PL 538; M Taggart, 'State Owned Enterprises and Social Responsibility: a Contradiction in Terms?' [1993] NZ Rec L Rev 343, and *Mercury Energy Ltd*, n 19 above.

[22] *Munn v Illinois* 94 US 113 (1877).

should have the protection of public law.[23] That protection goes beyond the protection of private law. If a citizen has a private action he may have no need for the remedies which public law provides over and above those available in a private law action. Where, however, activities of a public nature are being performed, the body performing those duties should be required to conform to standards which public law requires in the performance of those duties. As a matter of principle, the approach of the authorities to religious and sporting activities and 'private' ombudsmen has appeared questionable.[24] The controlling bodies of a sport and religious authorities can exercise monopolistic powers, and the Ombudsman is administering a system which provides an alternative method of resolving disputes to that provided by the courts. How then as a last resort can the courts be justifiably excluded? We are, however, at the edge of the divide, trying to clarify a boundary which is indistinct and evolving. In relation to public employment, I have myself tried in the Court of Appeal to draw attention to indicators which would penetrate the gloom but I do not suggest I have been wholly successful.[25]

---

[23] In *Aston Cantlow Parochial Church Council v Wallbank* [2003] UKHL 37, [2004] 1 AC 546, the House of Lords emphasised that the determining factor in deciding whether bodies come within the s 6(3)(b) Human Rights Act 'functional' public authority definition is whether the nature of the function they perform is public. This broad approach has not generally been reflected by the lower courts. It is unclear to what degree *Aston Cantlow* overrules previous cases as the House of Lords did not expressly correct the analysis of the lower courts. See, for example, *R (Heather) v Leonard Cheshire Foundation* [2002] EWCA Civ, [2002] 2 All ER 936. Several long-stay patients in a care home applied for judicial review of a decision to close the home. The Court of Appeal upheld the lower court's decision that the Foundation was not a public authority for the purposes of the Human Rights Act despite the fact it received public funding, was regulated by the State, and, if it had not provided care, such care would have to be provided by the State. The reasoning provided was that 'public' in s 6(3)(c) of the Human Rights Act was used in the sense of 'governmental'. The courts have not reflected the intention of the drafters of the Human Rights Act of a generous interpretation of 'public functions' and specifically that the Human Rights Act should be available to challenge decisions the substance of which was a public function, rather than matters which were strictly 'governmental'. During the passage of the Human Rights Bill, Jack Straw MP (then Home Secretary) stated: '. . . as we are dealing with public functions and with an evolving situation, we believe that the test must relate to the substance and nature of the act, not to the form and legal personality'. See *Hansard*, HC, cols 409–10, 17 June 1998.

[24] *R v Insurance Ombudsman, ex parte Aegon Life Ltd* [1994] COD 426 and the cases cited therein.

[25] See 'Public or Private? State Employees and Judicial Review' (1991) 107 LQR 298 and the cases there referred to including *McLaren v Home Office* [1990] IRLR 338. In general, employment law questions are questions of private law (see *R v East Berkshire Health Authority, ex parte Walsh* [1985] QB 152), but they may be questions of public law if they relate to policy questions (see *R v Crown Prosecution Service, ex parte Hogg* [1994] COD 237). An employee of a functional public authority cannot claim breach of s 6 of the Human Rights Act in an 'ordinary' employment situation, because the decisions which the functional public body took as an employer would be taken in its private capacity. But this might be different if the issue related to some question concerning public functions.

If there were to be an overriding test, I would wish it to have two primary requirements: an issue is subject to public law if (a) it is one about which the public has a legitimate concern as to its outcome; and (b) it is not an issue which is already satisfactorily protected by private law.

It is very easy to generalise about what should be the standards set by public law, but often it is a matter of fine judgement as to how they are to be applied in particular circumstances. The standards require that the functions should be performed in a manner which does not contravene any law, that is not illegally, not unfairly and not unreasonably performed. The fact that these standards are so broad explains why it has been possible for them to be developed by the courts as they have. Over the years, the attitudes of the judiciary have changed, but fortunately the attitudes of the judiciary have kept broadly in step with the attitudes of the public. What would be regarded as being tolerable or reasonable in one age can change if one puts aside the fiction that when the courts develop the common law they are merely discovering some hidden treasure which was always there waiting to be revealed.

The ability of the courts to demand those standards is, I believe, derived from the inherent jurisdiction of the High Court, of great antiquity, to review the activities of inferior bodies by the use of the ancient prerogative writs. It is now and always has been a jurisdiction which is confined to the High Court. It was continuously exercised down the centuries until the creation of the new procedure of judicial review. It was recognised when the new procedure was given statutory backing by section 31 of the Supreme Court Act 1981. When that section set out the new power of the High Court on judicial review, not only to grant one of the prerogative orders but also to make a declaration or grant an injunction, it linked the power to the situations where the prerogative orders could be granted, linked to when the High Court considers that they should be granted, having regard to, inter alia, 'the nature of the matters in respect in which relief may be granted by order of mandamus, prohibition or certiorari' or 'mandatory, prohibiting or quashing orders' as they are now known. The section also demonstrates this by providing that when the High Court is exercising this power it should have regard to 'the nature of persons and bodies against whom relief could be granted by such orders'. The section finally requires the court to have regard to 'all the circumstances of the case' and whether it would be 'just and convenient' for the relief to be granted. The breadth of the language happily reflects the width of the jurisdiction.

That judicial review is a jurisdiction of the High Court which supplements the private law and enables the High Court to review the performance of public functions is reflected in a dictum of Lord Templeman. He said: 'judicial review was a judicial invention to secure that decisions are made by the executive or a public body according to law even if the decision does not otherwise involve an actionable wrong'.[26] While it can be described as a judicial invention, as Sir Robin Cooke[27] once pointed out, it is 'of ancient lineage and no more and no less a judicial invention than any other part of common law or equity'.[28]

The Ultra Vires Rule: A Fairy Tale?

These statements lead me to the so-called doctrine of ultra vires[29] and the presumed intention of Parliament and its impact on public law. It has been suggested by those whose views command great respect[30] that this doctrine is the source of the court's jurisdiction on applications for judicial review. I have reservations as to whether this is correct. I am not happy about transferring into public law a Latin tag which has a clearly defined role in private, and in particular, company law. There are cases where ultra vires can readily be applied; for example, where an administrative body goes beyond its powers. But it cannot apply so readily to all situations in which judicial review is available. How for example can you apply the principle ultra vires when what is complained of is a non-exercise of power? There are also difficulties of using ultra vires in the case of non-statutory bodies such as the Take-Over Panel.

In addition, the doctrine of ultra vires does not for me sit comfortably with the ability of the court to refuse relief on discretionary grounds. If a decision was ultra vires, then it would normally follow that it was a nullity and that at any time it would be possible to challenge its validity and have it set aside. However, as public law has developed it has increasingly become apparent that unless and until a decision in public law is set aside, it remains fully effective and that the failure to challenge administrative action in time

---

[26] *Mercury Energy*, n 19 above, 388.

[27] Later, Lord Cooke.

[28] 'Has Administrative Law gone too far?', International Bar Association 25th Bi-annual Conference Melbourne, October 1994.

[29] The simple proposition that a public authority may not act outside its powers.

[30] Wade, n 8 above, 41. Approved in terms in *Boddington v British Transport Police* [1999] 2 AC 143, 171, but without consideration of the constitutional questions.

can mean that it is beyond challenge. In terms of good administration this can, as section 31 acknowledges, be highly desirable.

As we have been reminded,[31] it was many years ago that Lord Reid in his famous lecture about 'The Judge as a Lawmaker' made his remark that:

> There was a time when it was thought almost indecent to suggest that judges make law–they only declare it. Those with the taste for fairy tales seem to have thought that in some Aladdin's Cave there is hidden the common law in all its splendour and that on a judge's appointment there descends on him knowledge of the magic words 'Open Sesame!'. Bad decisions are given when the judge muddles the password and the wrong door opens–We do not believe in fairy tales any more.[32]

Are we in administrative law still to rely on fairy tales? It is possible to justify the courts demanding fairness and reasonableness in the performance of a public duty by reading into a statute which contains no such requirement, an implied requirement that any powers conferred by the statute are to be exercised fairly and reasonably and then to say if they are not so exercised the public body has exceeded unfairly or unreasonably. The statute may, however, although this was not appreciated at the time, unwittingly, by its express provision, achieve this result. Where this happens it is the duty of the court to remedy the defect in the statute by supplementing the statutory code.

I am far from sure whether in these circumstances the court is fulfilling an intention Parliament actually possessed or, by seeking to justify the need to achieve fairness on this basis, indulging in a fondness for fairy tales. However, if this gives the role of the court respectability, so be it. The technique was referred to with good effect by Lord Mustill in the House of Lords in the *Doody* case.[33] He imposed on the Home Secretary substantial additional procedural requirements, including that of giving reasons for his decision, which had no statutory source in the case of those prisoners sentenced to a mandatory life sentence. In doing so, Lord Mustill referred to the presumed intention of Parliament, but the language of his speech as a whole also strongly suggests that his primary concern was with establishing a regime which is fair.

---

[31] A Lester, 'English Judges as Lawmakers' [1993] PL 269.
[32] J Reid, 'The Judge as Lawmaker' [1972] J Soc Pub Teach L 22; and Lester, ibid.
[33] *Doody v Secretary of State for the Home Department* [1993] 3 All ER 92.

Parliamentary Sovereignty and the Rule of Law

But what happens if, taking advantage of *Pepper v Hart*,[34] the examination of *Hansard* discloses that the Minister was asked about these safeguards, but that he indicated that the Treasury considered the expense would be too great? Do the courts throw up their hands in despair and say there is nothing we can do? I would hope not.[35] If this was to be the consequence, it could be a result of that decision which may not have been succinctly considered.

The doctrine could be seen as providing a cloak of respectability where, as happened in the *Factortame*[36] case, there is a conflict between Community law and subsequent domestic legislation. Where two English statutes conflict, the purely domestic approach is that the later can be regarded as repealing the earlier insofar as they are inconsistent. In the case of a conflict between Community law and subsequent UK parliamentary legislation, Community law prevails. This can be explained by saying it was not Parliament's intention when passing the legislation in question to interfere with Community law. Thus, by writing down the express language of the later statute the court is doing no more than recognising the giving of effect to the true intent of Parliament, notwithstanding that in reality the court is at the lowest curtailing the language of the statute.

In both these situations the fairy tale is harmless, although in other jurisdictions the existence of a written constitution would be likely to make a more direct approach possible. But what happens if a party with a large majority in Parliament uses that majority to abolish the courts' entire power of judicial review in express terms? It is administratively expensive, absorbs far too large a proportion of the legal aid fund and results in the judiciary having misconceived notions of grandeur. Do the courts then accept that the legislation means what it says? I am sure this is, in practice, unthinkable. It will never happen. But if it did, for reasons I will now summarise, my own personal view is that they do not. This is despite the fact that Professor Mann, a number of years ago, probably felt compelled to concede that this may be the position. He did, however, cite Blackstone's comment that: 'Acts of Parliament that are impossible to be performed are of no validity; and if

---

[34] [1992] 3 WLR 1032. See also D Oliver, 'Comment: Pepper v Hart: A suitable case for reference to Hansard?' [1993] PL 5.

[35] Lord Lester (the successful advocate in the case) does not consider this should be the consequence: see 'Pepper v Hart Revisited' (1994) 15(1) Stat L Rev 21.

[36] *R v Secretary of State for Transport, ex parte Factortame (No 2)* [1990] 1 AC 603.

there arise out of them collaterally any absurd consequences, manifestly contradictory to common reason, they are, with regard to those collateral consequences, void.'[37] Furthermore, he made clear his unhappiness at the situation by asking a parallel question:

> Suppose Parliament enacts a statute depriving Jews of their British nationality, prohibits marriages between Christians and non-Christians, dissolving marriages between blacks and whites or vesting the property of all red haired women in the State. Is it really suggested that English judges would have to apply such a law? Do not evade the issue, do not avoid the legal test by asserting that, as we all hope and believe, no English Parliament would ever pass such a statute. Would the hypothetical question really have to be answered in the affirmative, while a similar German statute was condemned by four Law Lords as constituting 'so grave an infringement of human rights that the courts of this country ought to refuse to recognise it as a law at all'?[38]

Our parliamentary democracy is based on the rule of law. One of the twin principles upon which the rule of law depends is the supremacy of Parliament in its legislative capacity. The other principle is that the courts are the final arbiters as to the interpretation and application of the law. Both Parliament and the courts derive their authority from the rule of law, so both are subject to it and cannot act in a manner which involves its repudiation. The respective roles do not give rise to conflict because the courts and Parliament each respect the role of the other. For example, Parliament is meticulous in upholding the *sub judice* rule so as to avoid interfering with the role of the courts. Equally, the courts always respect the privileges of Parliament and will not become involved with the internal workings of Parliament. In addition, the courts will seek to give effect wherever possible to both primary and subordinate legislation. The courts will, for example, where there is a conflict between Community and domestic legislation uphold the domestic legislation as far as possible. The courts will also readily accept legislation which controls how it exercises its jurisdiction or which confers or modifies its existing statutory jurisdiction. I, however, see a distinction between such legislative action and that which seeks to undermine in a fundamental way the rule of law, on which our unwritten constitution depends, by removing or substantially impairing the entire reviewing role of the High Court on

---

[37] F A Mann, 3rd Blackstone Lecture (1978), 91.
[38] Ibid, citing *Oppenheimer v Cattermole* [1976] AC 249, 278.

judicial review. This role is as ancient as the common law and predates our present form of parliamentary democracy and the Bill of Rights of 1689.

My approach, which is a shadow reflection of a trail blazed by Sir Robin Cooke,[39] does involve dispensing with fairy tales once and for all, but I would suggest this is healthy. It involves a proper recognition of both pillars of the rule of law and the equal responsibility that Parliament and the courts are under a duty to respect the other's burdens and to play their proper part in upholding the rule of law. I see the courts and Parliament as being partners both engaged in a common enterprise involving the upholding of the rule of law. It is reflected in the way that frequently the House of Lords in its judicial capacity will stress the desirability of legislation when faced with the new problems that contemporary society can create rather than creating a solution itself.

There are however situations where already, in upholding the rule of law, the courts have had to take a stand. The example that springs to mind is the *Anisminic* case.[40] In that case, even the statement in an Act of Parliament that the Commission's decision 'shall not be called in question in any court of law', did not succeed in excluding the jurisdiction of the court. Since that case, Parliament has again mounted such a challenge to the reviewing power of the High Court.[41] There has been, and I am confident there will continue to be, mutual respect for each other's roles.

However, if Parliament did the unthinkable, then I would say that the courts would also be required to act in a manner which would be without precedent. Some judges might choose to do so by saying that it was an unrebuttable presumption that Parliament could never intend such a result. I myself would consider there were advantages in making it clear that ultimately there are even limits on the supremacy of Parliament which it is the courts' inalienable responsibility to identify and uphold. They are limits of the most modest dimensions, which I believe any democrat would accept. They are no more than are necessary to enable the rule of law to be preserved.

---

[39] Later Lord Cooke. See R Cooke, 'Fundamentals' [1988] NZLJ 158.

[40] [1969] 2 AC 147.

[41] See, for example, *A v Secretary of State for the Home Department* [2005] UKHL 56, [2006] 2 AC 68, where the lawfulness of the derogation from Art 5 ECHR in part 4 of the Anti-Terrorism, Crime and Security Act 2001 was successfully challenged in the House of Lords.

Droit Public English Style: Fairy Tale
or Fundamental Principles?

Is then the position of droit public English style satisfactory? Parliament is apparently content that it should continue to develop on a case-by-case basis. The courts are entitled to insist on fairness and reasonableness and compliance with the law. Parliament can provide a statutory context which will limit their effectiveness but does not attempt to exclude them entirely. While the courts usually make no distinction between the level or class of administrative action which is being reviewed, increasingly the role of interpretation and application of the law has involved the courts in identifying the fundamental principles underlying the common law. These principles are what enabled Lord Browne-Wilkinson to say in a lecture in 1992 that:

> It is now inconceivable that any court in this country would hold that, apart from statutory provision, individual freedoms of a private person are any less extensive than the basic human rights protected by the European Convention on Human Rights. Whenever the provisions of the European Convention on Human Rights have been raised before the courts, the judges have asserted that the Convention confers no greater rights than those protected by the common law.[42]

In the same lecture, Lord Browne-Wilkinson drew attention to the way in which, through our membership of the European Community, via Community law, there was incorporated into our domestic law part of the European Convention on Human Rights, even before it actually became implemented into our domestic law in 2000 when the Human Rights Act 1998 came into effect. Lord Browne-Wilkinson also drew attention to areas where the situation was still far from satisfactory, even though there were great advantages in a pragmatic approach in which the law was (and is) developed on a case-by-case basis.

I share these views. I would, however, hesitate long before changing the relationship between the courts and Parliament which has served our country well. On the other hand, I have always seen advantages in this country having a new Bill of Rights of its own. I have considered that it is unacceptable

---

[42] N Browne-Wilkinson, 'The Infiltration of a Bill of Rights' [1992] PL 405. It is to be noted that this was said before the European Convention on Human Rights was incorporated into the UK via the Human Rights Act 1998, which came into force in 2000.

that our citizens should have been able to obtain a remedy which the government would honour in the European Court of Human Rights, which they could not obtain from the courts in this country. The Human Rights Act 1998 avoids the difficulty which previously existed in protecting some of our basic rights. It enables us to play our part in the development of human rights jurisprudence internationally. Across the globe there is a comparative approach to human rights. The Privy Council has in deciding Commonwealth appeals with increasing frequency been able to play a part in the international development of those rights. However, until relatively recently, the European Court of Human Rights has been deprived of the full contribution which the courts in this country could and should have made.

But what about the sovereignty of Parliament? Some of those who were opposed to a Bill of Rights saw it as a threat to that sovereignty. There were, however, different forms that a Bill of Rights could take. I have referred earlier to the New Zealand Bill of Rights. That Bill seemed to me to provide an ideal precedent for a Bill of Rights in this country since it is in accord with our democratic and parliamentary traditions. It sets out in seven pages of simple prose the fundamental freedoms which we regard as an inherent part of our inheritance. But it does not make them entrenched provisions, something which may not in any event have been possible under our constitution. Instead it provides:

> Wherever an enactment can be given a meaning that is consistent with the rights and freedoms contained in this Bill of Rights that meaning shall be preferred to any other meaning.[43]

Subject to this, legislation is not affected. Parliament retains the right to state that it intends to exclude the fundamental rights, but if it fails to do this, those fundamental rights are part of any legislation passed by Parliament.[44] This seemed to be a satisfactory compromise to which all should have been able to subscribe. My New Zealand colleagues said it worked well. It has not been subject to the excesses of which some complain in the case of the

---

[43] New Zealand Bill of Rights 1990.

[44] In the UK, s 19 of the Human Rights Act 1998 requires a Minister of the Crown with conduct of any Bill, before its second reading, either to make and publish a 'statement of compatibility', or openly make a statement that he or she is unable to state that the legislation is compatible with the Convention rights. It is also to be noted that s 3 of the Human Rights Act requires generous and progressive interpretation of all legislation, primary and secondary, whenever enacted, in a way which is compatible with Convention rights whenever possible.

Canadian Charter of Rights. I have doubted if our Parliament would ever want to interfere expressly with our fundamental rights,[45] but have said it would avoid Parliament doing just that accidentally. Finally, I have argued, and it seems our Human Rights Act regime has shown, that such a system would and has enabled those who enjoy fairy tales to continue to do so. It has enabled me to be even more proud than I have been previously of droit public—English style.

---

[45] This is now questionable in view of recent case law where the courts have felt it necessary to use their power in s 4 of the Human Rights Act to declare particular legislation incompatible with the Human Rights Act. See, for example, *A v Secretary of State for the Home Department*, n 41 above.

4

The Education the Justice System Requires Today

Abstract This paper discusses the change of culture in legal education, with a greater emphasis being placed on policy and the social and economic consequences of developing the law, following the coming into effect of the new Civil Procedure Rules, the development of public law and the Human Rights Act 1998. It recognises that universities today have a much broader role than merely to provide a vocational course to lawyers wishing to move directly into practice. Universities must emphasise the importance of professional standards and inculcate an understanding of the responsibilities which lawyers owe to the courts if they are to prepare lawyers to enter the legal profession and wider world.

It is my pleasure to give this lecture at the invitation of Lord Templeman. When you become a Law Lord you move from the Strand to Westminster. You feel very much like a new boy who has changed school. A warm welcome by the senior boys is very much appreciated. On my arrival the second most senior boy was Sydney Templeman. Not only was he very kind at the time I arrived, but he continued to be a marvellous mentor until he retired. I particularly admired the manner in which he could distil the essence of what took me 20 pages to express into half a page of elegant prose. There are no doubt many reasons for the Association of Law Teachers selecting Lord Templeman to be their President, but I am sure one of the reasons was his qualities as a lawyer. The Association made a wise choice.

This lecture is of course named after the first President of the Association, Lord Upjohn. The fact that I received my invitation from Lord Templeman and the lecture is in memory of Lord Upjohn meant that Lord Templeman's invitation was not one I could refuse.

---

* Upjohn Lecture, orignially given on 14 June 2000 at the Inns of Court School of Law, London.

I have previously been the Upjohn Lecturer. It was back in 1986 when I had just become President of the Association. My previous lecture was my first engagement in public as President. By coincidence this is my fist public engagement as Chief Justice. I suppose I should offer you an apology. You were expecting to be addressed by the Master of the Rolls but instead you have a mere Chief Justice. Certainly while I was Master of the Rolls (my opinion may be changing) I always regarded the office of Master of the Rolls as much more distinguished than that of Chief Justice. Almost all jurisdictions have a Chief Justice. Even Gibraltar, where there are only two judges, has a Chief Justice and a Deputy Chief Justice. Furthermore, it is much simpler to make jokes about the office of Master of the Rolls than that of Chief Justice. In Paris, I was described as the 'maître de petit-pains' and in Japan, recalling a famous letter that Lord Denning received from someone in India who wished to be employed at the Rolls Royce factory, I introduced myself as Master of the Honda.

Prior to coming here this evening I looked up my previous Upjohn Lecture given some time ago. I had completely forgotten about the subject of my talk. Because of the anecdotes of which I have been told concerning Lord Upjohn I took as my title 'Civil Procedure—Time for Changes'. As this was over a decade prior to my Access to Justice Report it is interesting to speculate whether Lord MacKay, a former Lord Chancellor, who launched me on that project, was in the habit of reading 'The Law Teacher' in which the lecture was published.

If there is a connection, this is ironic because I commenced the earlier lecture by referring to the fact that Lord Upjohn was the only person of whom I have heard who regularly slept with a copy of the Supreme Court Practice by his bedside. It is interesting to speculate as to whether, if Lord Upjohn were still alive, he would now sleep with a copy of the Civil Procedure Rules by his bedside. If he would, I would like to know which is his better antidote for insomnia.

The changes to civil procedure are part of the explanation for my title. I do believe that civil procedure is a subject the importance of which has been grossly underestimated in the past by both academics and practitioners. With a small number of distinguished exceptions, the input to the subject from the universities has been modest. This probably explains why I have not heard of many students who picketed Parliament or even the European Court of Justice protesting about the lamentable state of our civil procedure. The Overriding Objectives in Part 1 of the Civil Procedure Rules have fundamentally changed what is involved in deciding cases justly. The law of evidence has been dramatically transformed by the Civil Procedure Rules. Full advantage has been taken of an apparently modest provision in the 1st Schedule to the Civil Procedure Act of 1997. The provision allows the new Rules to 'modify the rules of evidence as they apply to proceedings in any court within the scope of the Rules'. Relying on this provision, the Civil Procedure Rules virtually abolish the old technical rules of evidence.

Let me remind you of the terms of Part 32.1 of the Civil Procedure Rules. Rule 1 states:

(1) The court may control the evidence by giving directions as to—
    (a) the issues on which it requires evidence;
    (b) the nature of the evidence which it requires to decide those issues;
    (c) the way in which the evidence is to be placed before the court.
(2) The court may use its power under this Rule to exclude evidence that would otherwise be admissible.
(3) The court may limit cross-examination.

The changes are ones which I regard as being beneficial: I would say so wouldn't I! They release evidence from the bondage to which it has been subjected because of the supposed inability of the jury properly to evaluate evidence and their supposed inability to recognise the prejudicial as well as probative qualities of evidence. Except in limited circumstances, we no longer have any juries, but as Professor Jolowicz has pointed out, the ghost of the jury system was still controlling what evidence could be placed before a court prior to the introduction of the Civil Procedure Rules.

The Rules of Evidence together with Rules of Procedure play at least as important a role as the substantive law in the justice system. However, if some of the anecdotal information which I am given is correct, both subjects are at best given a minimal role during the academic stage of the training of the would-be lawyer. The new culture of the Civil Procedure Rules in redefining, as it does, what is involved in achieving justice, is not being given the scrutiny it deserves, in the academic as well as the vocational stage of training. It is after all quite fundamental to have jettisoned our traditional view that the public has no interest in how private law litigation is conducted. In addition, by lawyers, including a full appreciation of the contribution which can be made is no longer an optional extra for specialist lawyers. Dispute resolution is now a pre-litigation process.

Public Law is recognised as being one of the foundations of legal knowledge by the Bar Council. It is a required part of the academic stage of training for the Bar. However, both procedure and remedies have played a fundamental role in the development of our public law. The new procedure leading to the harmonisation of public and private law is likely to have as great an influence on the development of public law in the future as Order 53 had in the past. But I am not confident that the young are being taught the importance of this. The young lawyer needs to be aware that procedural law and the availability of remedies can have significant effects on substantive law.

The changes in civil procedure are only one of the fundamental changes which are taking place in our law and constitutional arrangements at the present time. We may not have a federal system which is equivalent to that in the United States, but devolution has fundamentally changed our constitutional arrangements.

Lord Justice Sedley is not only one of our most distinguished administrative law jurists, he was responsible for overseeing the judicial education which the Judicial Studies Board provided prior to the Human Rights Act 1998 coming into force. His invitation to this lecture provoked him to send me a letter he had written a year earlier to Professor Patterson, who was about to chair a meeting of the heads of UK law schools. The letter was copied to the heads of the law schools. In the letter to Professor Patterson, Lord Justice Sedley, in my view correctly, commented that if lawyers simply use the Human Rights Act and European Convention as a fall-back where no other argument is available 'they will rapidly lose credibility and the Act will become a dead letter. If, on the other hand, lawyers make intelligent and creative use of the new law, we can hope to develop a true judicial Human Rights culture.' Lord Justice Sedley went on to say that it is to:

> . . . the generation which now and in the coming years passes through law schools that we are going to have to look for educated help in making the Act and Convention work. This requires a re-casting of much of the law school curriculum. It is no good treating Human Rights as an optional extra to existing courses. The need is to rethink pretty well every area of law in a way which will make human rights an integral part of it.

Lord Justice Sedley, in his letter to me, said that the enquiries which he had made a year later suggested that relatively few teachers were changing what they taught. Human rights was typically still being offered as a bolt-on extra in university law courses, taught by a specialist lecturer. He speculated as to whether perhaps it was not the judiciary who needed a shake-up but the academics.

Like Lord Justice Sedley, I can only speculate as to the position within the law schools, but I do believe that now, human rights is increasingly being taught at most, if not all, law schools in this country. If, however, Lord Justice

Sedley's fears are still justified this would be unfortunate. If the Human Rights Act and the European Convention are to be the force for good that they should be, it is essential that the change of culture which they are intended to bring about is given a central role in the education of the next generation of lawyers.

Why it is so important that the Human Rights Act and European Convention should be given a central platform in the academic training of our lawyers is because of the value judgements which are required. Our substantive law has traditionally consisted of a spectrum of relatively sharply defined concepts. The European Convention is couched in general terms subject to broad qualifications. Ascertaining the law requires lawyers to be involved in a critically important task so far as society is concerned. That task is the making of value judgements between conflicting fundamental rights and values. In almost any situation, before you can ascertain the impact of the Human Rights Act and European Convention, a complex value judgement has to be made. The facts of a dispute have to be carefully assessed against the conflicting human values before the law can be ascertained. This is a task which is fundamentally different to that involved in seeking to make sense of badly drafted contracts or legislation.

The new approach is not confined to human rights. It applies across the whole tapestry of the law. In order to resolve legal issues, especially where the law is unclear, a more broadly based approach is required than in the past. Greater emphasis has to be placed on the social and economic consequences of developing the law. This is already apparent when deciding whether a duty of care exists to provide protection from economic loss. The threefold test laid down in *Caparo Industries Plc v Dickman*[1] involves as one of its requirements that it should be just and reasonable to impose the duty. The economic and social consequences of imposing a duty are highly relevant in determining what is just and reasonable. The considerations which are relevant are complex and the process involves new skills on the part of the lawyer. The European Court of Human Rights has been criticised for its decision in *Osman v UK*.[2] It has been suggested that they should not have become involved in a question which was an issue of

---

[1] [1990] 2 AC 605.

[2] (2000) 29 EHHR 245. While immunity accorded to police for negligence in investigation and suppression of crime, held a breach of Art 6(1) ECHR that there is a substantial facet to Art 6(1) has not since found favour. See, for example, *DP and JC v UK* (2003) 36 EHRR 14.

substantive law within this jurisdiction. However, the European Court saw the situation differently. They saw the issue as having a procedural dimension. The European Court considered that this was the type of issue which could not be determined as a preliminary issue on an application to strike out. The process of ascertaining substantive law has become much more policy-based than was the position hitherto.

Another illustration is provided by the decision of the Court of Appeal as to what is the appropriate level of damages for non-pecuniary loss.[3] Injuries, pain and suffering cannot be simply converted into currency terms. The Law Commission made a report suggesting a substantial adjustment was required. In coming to a conclusion that a more modest adjustment was required, the Court saw it as its task to ascertain a figure which reflected what was fair, just and reasonable to the different interests involved. The interests of the injured person, the interests of the defendant, and the interests of the wider community, had to be taken into account. The wider community interests had to be considered because it is the public which will ultimately have to bear the burden of the additional expense. This would be either in the form of higher insurance premiums or reduced health care in the case of claims against the health service.

Even the task of interpreting documents is now broader than hitherto. The matrix of relevant surrounding circumstances is continuing to expand. The process which plays such an important part in determining whether a liability exists under a contract is evolving. I do not know whether these developments are influencing the teaching of the law to the extent they should if the content of the law is to be understood properly.

The approach is becoming ever broader. The Senior Law Lord, Lord Bingham, when a Lord Justice, gave something of the flavour of the change. He said: 'Just as equity remedied the inadequacies of the common law, so has the law of torts filled gaps left by other causes of action where the interests of justice so required.'[4]

I appreciate that the universities today have a much broader role than merely to provide a vocational course to lawyers wishing to move directly into practice. I understand that more than ten thousand law graduates are provided by universities each year and more than half are not moving directly into practice. Instead, they move into post-graduate law courses and use their

---

[3] *Heil v Rankin* [2000] 3 All ER 138.
[4] *Simaan General Contracting Company v Pilkington Glass Limited (No 2)* [1998] QB 758, 782.

legal education in multifarious fields of endeavour, including insurance, banking, public service, welfare advice, and so on.[5] The interests of the non-practitioners must not be neglected. However, that broadening of the approach to education in the law which I am suggesting may be necessary is very much in the interests of both those who do and do not intend to practise. The universities must prepare lawyers to enter the profession and the wider world to which they are making an ever-growing contribution.

A few years ago, Judge Harry Edwards of the United States Court of Appeal for the District of Columbia Circuit delivered a damning indictment of the law schools in the United States, under the title 'The Growing Disjunction Between Legal Education and the Legal Profession'.[6] He first referred to the statement of Felix Frankfurter that 'in the last analysis, the law is what the lawyers are. And the law and the lawyers are what the law schools make them'.[7] Judge Edwards expressed the fear that American law schools and law firms were moving in opposite directions. He said:

> The schools should be training ethical practitioners and producing scholarships that judges, legislators, and practitioners can use. The Firm should be ensuring that associates and partners practice law in an ethical manner. But many law schools— especially so called 'elite' ones—have abandoned their proper place by emphasising abstract theory at the expense of practical scholarship and pedagogy. Many law firms have abandoned *their* place, by pursuing profit above all else. While schools are moving towards pure theory, the firms are moving towards pure commerce, and the middle ground—ethical practice—has been deserted by both. This disjunction calls into question our status as an honourable profession.[8]

Judge Edwards's criticisms of the American scene must be seen in the context of a system where there is not our division between the academic and vocational stage of legal education. However, even making that allowance, I would certainly not make the same criticisms as the judge makes of the law schools in our universities. I suspect that most members of our judiciary would regard the quality of contribution to academic journals as being extremely high and of significant relevance to the practice and development

---

[5] See Director of the Law Programme the Open University, G Slapper, 'Innovation in a Conservative Community: Teaching Law Off Campus in the UK', delivered at the University of Adelaide, 12 April 2000.

[6] (1992) 91(1) Mich L Rev 34.

[7] Ibid, 75.

[8] Ibid, 34.

of the law. Our problem is finding the time to keep abreast of the massive volume of extremely valuable academic writing which is available. Whereas at one time it could have been said that the divide between the academic and the practitioner was too broad and too deep, numerous bridges have since been built between those who are engaged in the teaching and the practice of the law. My concern, like that of Lord Justice Sedley, is whether law courses in the universities are always aware just how rapidly developments in the law are taking place. Those developments have to be taken into account in teaching the law. While the universities have to be responsive to the needs of those who will not be practising law, both future practitioners and non-practitioners have to develop during their academic training the hallmarks of the good lawyer. They must be able to analyse problems and having done so find the correct solutions. That requires not only the skills of a traditional black letter lawyer but also the ability to identify the broad principles which are involved in creating a just society subject to the rule of law.

Judge Edwards has also expressed concern about the need to inculcate the lawyer of the future with the correct ethical standards. Here he sees a very serious conflict between increasing commercialisation and the maintenance of professional standards. The same conflict exists in our jurisdiction. The pressures on the young lawyer today whether an academic, a solicitor or a barrister are growing contentiously more intense. Commercial activities, including arranging conferences and billable hours are becoming as important on this side of the Atlantic as they are in the United States. Competition is intensifying. The profession is having to adjust to conditional fees and the fact that lawyers have a stake in the outcome of the litigation and have to assess risk. Fresh temptations are being placed in the way of the lawyer to serve his own interests rather than those of the client's. The profession is becoming increasingly polarised according to the work which it does. Some types of work are generously, perhaps even over-generously, rewarded. It is regrettable but understandable that there should be talk by some lawyers of withdrawing their services because of the inadequacy of the rewards provided out of the public funds. The university law schools now have the heavy responsibility of emphasising the importance of our professional standards. An understanding of the responsibilities which lawyers owe to the courts has to be inculcated.

Fortunately, there is considerable evidence of young lawyers on both sides of the profession developing a greater recognition of their obligation to provide pro bono legal services and to provide part-time assistance at law centres and Citizens' Advice Bureaux. Splendid evidence of the value of their contribution is provided by the support which they are providing to the Citizens' Advice Bureau in the Royal Courts of Justice. The assistance is, however, far from confined to London.

A danger remains because of the contrasts in the fortunes of different parts of the profession. We are fortunate that in London the big city firms have provided exemplary support for pro bono schemes and law student activities. However, a recent development which causes me concern is the decision of eight of the most important city firms to establish their own legal practice course.[9] It must be for these firms to decide for themselves whether the existing training is satisfactory or not. However, it would certainly have been preferable if they could have influenced the existing providers to improve their standards rather than singling out three providers. I appreciate that the selected providers will not restrict their intake to the nominees of these large city firms, however, what was proposed has resulted in two standards. This is implicit from what has happened. The consortium created more demanding courses which provide trainees for the City with the enhanced abilities for which they are looking.

The distorting effect of what has happened should not be ignored. The same city firms have already recruited from the most able graduates of the universities. Their recruits are an elite. For the elite to go to a small percentage of the provider colleges and courses has adversely influenced the other providers. In any educational institution the less able students benefit from the contribution made by the more able. It is important the lawyers emerging into practice regard themselves as one profession. If their vocational training is divided, this is more difficult to achieve.

The city firms depend on recruiting the brightest lawyers to maintain their competitiveness within a global legal community. However, with candidates of the quality they attract, it should be possible to provide any enhanced training which they require after a Legal Practice Course which is common to the profession as a whole.

Having identified the challenge it only remains for me to acknowledge what I believe to be the case. The quality of our young lawyers is higher than it has ever been during my time in the law. The law teachers must be on the whole providing the education the lawyer of today requires. Nonetheless, it is always possible to do even better.

---

[9] Currently, some institutions have tailor-made legal practice courses for future trainees of leading law firms. Some law firms do not subscribe to such legal practice courses but do require their future trainees to complete particular elective subjects.

PART II

The Constitution and the Judiciary

5

Magna Carta: A Precedent for Recent Constitutional Change

Abstract This paper provides an historical account of the fundamental principles of the rule of law. Reference is made to the chapters at the heart of the Magna Carta of 1215 as containing many of the core features of societies that today adhere to the rule of law. Magna Carta principles are placed within a contemporary setting through a discussion of the UK's new constitutional arrangements that include the abolition of the old Office of Lord Chancellor and provision for a new Supreme Court. It explains that increased recognition of the rule of law is apparent from its impact upon the global economy and strident argument which has occurred over the recent flood of asylum seekers, the invasion over Iraq, and dispute over the legal status of detainees.

Introduction

790 years ago, John, the King of England was having a little local difficulty with his barons. His attempts to defend his extensive dominions across the Channel, including Normandy and a considerable proportion of western France, had been a disaster. This was despite the exorbitant demands that he had made of his subjects. The taxes he had imposed were extortionate. There had been ruthless reprisals against defectors. The administration of justice for which he was responsible could with generosity be described as capricious. Instead of depending on the traditional establishment for his advisers and confidants, John looked to 'new men', who wielded immense power. Today no doubt the media would describe them as 'John's cronies'. In the world of politics, little changes.

---

* Originally given at Royal Holloway, University of London, on 15 June 2005.

John's barons became increasingly disaffected. They knew John needed their support for his further military adventures in France. Not to lose an opportunity, in January 1215, the barons collectively decided upon industrial action. They insisted that, as a condition of their support, John execute a charter that recognised their liberties as a safeguard against further arbitrary behaviour on the part of the King.

In order to press home their cause, the barons took up arms against the King. In May 1215 they captured London. England was on the brink of being engulfed in civil war. Instead of allowing this to happen, both sides of the dispute behaved in an exemplary manner. If they had been litigants before our courts, they would have received my unqualified commendation for deciding to rely on Alternative Dispute Resolution, or as lawyers say today ADR, as an alternative to battle to the death.

On 10 June 1215, they met at Runnymede[1] and, in the meadow, compromised their differences and agreed terms which were outlined in the Articles of the Barons to which the King's great seal was attached on 15 June 1215. The immediate result was that the barons renewed their oath of allegiance and once more supported the King in his endeavours in France.

You can settle disputes but there is no guarantee the settlement will be honoured. In the past Pope Innocent III had his own disputes with John. John had refused to accept the Pope's candidate, Stephen Langton, as Archbishop of Canterbury when the previous archbishop died. Relations between the Pope and John broke down and John was for a time excommunicated by the Pope. However, John had by the time of the meeting with the Barons at Runnymede already settled his dispute with the Pope and had been rehabilitated. Langton had become Archbishop and had played a part in creating the Charter.

However, no sooner was the Charter sealed than Innocent III, encouraged by John, intervened. He condemned the Charter as exacted by extortion and declared it was of no validity whatsoever.

John needed no more encouragement not to observe the Charter into which he had freely entered. John reneged on his commitments to surrender castles, borrowed money to hire foreign troops, and rallied his forces to subdue the nobles. Fortunately for us and for history John was prevented by ill health from pursuing his plans and his early death in October 1216

---

[1] Runnymede is a water-meadow in Surrey, England, and is associated with the signing of the Magna Carta.

put an end to his double dealing. The Charter survived and this, for those times, was a remarkable outcome.

But this does not explain why we are gathered here today, precisely 790 years after the document which in due course became known as Magna Carta was sealed, or why we are due to reconvene annually over the next nine years until 2015, the 800th Anniversary of what happened in Runnymede in June 1215.

The Two Explanations for the Importance of the Charter

The Contents

In fact there are two better explanations for why we are here today. The first is that the *contents* of the charter fully justified its title, Magna Carta. It was by any standards a remarkable document for its time. The Charter goes far beyond what was needed to resolve the immediate dispute between John and his barons. While the Charter did address real, contemporary and practical problems of the time, it was not merely concerned with the immediate dispute. It was intended to govern the relations between successive kings and their most powerful subjects forever.

Confirmation of its importance in medieval times is provided by the fact that three new editions were produced, after John died, by his son Henry III. Henry had ascended the throne at nine years of age. He was in no position to renew the struggle with the Barons and the first new edition was created in 1216, just a month after John's death. It was followed by further editions in 1217 and 1225.

Then, in the next reign, on 28 March 1297, Edward I, the 'father of Parliament', signed letters patent containing the Charter which were entered on statute rolls so that, insofar as it has not been repealed, it binds the Crown even today.[2] Indeed, the first petition presented by the commons to the monarch at each new parliament is a request that the 'Great Charta' be kept.

The long title of the 1297 edition reflects the status Magna Carta had already achieved by that date. The title reads: 'the Great Charter of the Liberties of England, and the Liberties of the Forest; confirmed by King Edward, in the 25th year of his reign'. The contents of the Charter justified that title.

---

[2] *R (on the application of Bancourt) v Secretary of State for the Foreign and Commonwealth Office* [2001] 2 WLR 1219 and *Chagos Islanders v Attorney-General* [2004] EWCA (Civ) 997, [2004] All ER (D) 85 (Aug).

The first article, perhaps in view of the history to which I have referred disingenuously proclaims:

> We have granted to God and by this charter have confirmed for us and our heirs in perpetuity, that the English Church shall be free, and shall have its rights undiminished and its liberties unimpaired.

It added that 'we', that is John, before the present dispute confirmed the Church's elections and what is more caused it to be confirmed by Innocent III, and desired it to observed in good faith by his heirs in perpetuity.

John in the remainder of the Charter addresses 'all free men of our Kingdom' and grants them 'for us and our heirs forever, all the liberties written out below, to have and to keep for them and their heirs, of us and our heirs'. So while the settlement was made with the barons, the class which it purported to protect was much wider—not everyone, as this was still feudal England, but 'all freemen', which is as broad a category as was conceivable at that time.

The liberties are then listed. As you would expect in view of the background to the Charter, pride of place is given to restrictions on the King's ability to abuse his position by extracting extortionate taxes.

Some of the taxes have exotic medieval names, such as 'scutage', which was the obligation to provide money in lieu of men to fight for the King, and 'aids', which was an exceptional tax to meet an exceptional need which John had regularly demanded as a matter of course.

What was perhaps most surprising was the protection of heirs, especially those under age. While under age, heirs became the King's wards and their estates came under the King's control. John treated them as his own. They were to have their inheritance 'without relief or fine' when they came of age and should receive their land properly maintained and stocked.[3]

The medieval attitude to women is not that of which the founders of this great College, initially devoted to the education of women, would have approved. However, again, the Charter language is remarkably liberal in relation, for example, to widows—the practice had been to treat them as in the King's custody so that their lands would also come under the King's control. If the King was short of money he would auction widows off to the highest bidders.

In the case of one widow, Henry II had consigned her to the tower, no doubt because her lands were so considerable. Another noble lady who had already been widowed and married three times was prepared to pay the King's demand

---

[3] See Magna Carta, chs 3–5.

of £3,000 to escape being married a fourth time. In contrast with this treatment, the Charter provided that widows were to have their 'marriage portion and inheritance at once and without trouble'[4] and that no widow was to be compelled to marry 'as long as she wishes to remain without a husband'.[5]

Even if a widow did want to marry, the marriage could be a lonely one as has been recorded by the present Master of the Rolls (MR) in a previous speech.[6] King John expected his court to dance attendance upon him unencumbered by their wives. One wife, apparently frustrated by this practice, offered John 200 chickens to enable her husband to spend one night at Christmas with her. John accepted. I share Lord Phillips's hope that this was a worthwhile investment.

There is a provision contained in chapter 11 of the Magna Carta restricting the recovery of debts by Jews out of the estate of a debtor which certainly sounds racially discriminatory, but the sting of the provision is drawn by the concluding words of the chapter which provide: 'Debts owed to persons other than Jews are to be dealt with similarly.'

Other provisions that were to benefit the public were those that establish standard measures and weights throughout the Kingdom[7] and that the city of London and other cities, boroughs, towns and ports were to enjoy all their liberties and free customs. In addition, with certain exceptions, there was a general right to leave and return to the kingdom 'unharmed and without fear'.[8]

The provisions I have already cited, you may agree with me, are remarkable for a document negotiated 790 years ago, but they diminish into insignificance when compared to those chapters dealing with the individual's rights to justice. Here I will let the articles speak for themselves. I use their original chapter numbers:

20. For a trivial offence, a free man shall be fined only in proportion to the degree of his offence, and for a serious offence correspondingly, but not so heavily as to deprive him of his livelihood.

. . .

38. In future no official shall place a man on trial upon his own unsupported statement, without producing credible witness to the truth of it.

. . .

---

[4] Ibid, ch 7.
[5] Ibid, ch 8.
[6] Lord Phillips, former Master of the Rolls and Lord Chief Justice of England and Wales since October 2005. See N Phillips, National Society Magna Carta Dames and Barons, Magna Carta at Bury St Edmunds, on 13 June 2004.
[7] See Magna Carta, ch 35.
[8] Ibid, ch 42.

39. No free man shall be seized or imprisoned, or stripped of his rights or pos-
    sessions, or outlawed or exiled, or deprived of his standing in any other
    way, nor will we proceed with force against him, or send others to do so,
    except by the lawful judgement of his equals or by the law of the land.

    . . .

40. To no one will we sell, to no one deny or delay right or justice.

    . . .

45. We will appoint as justices, constable, sheriffs, or other officials, only men
    that know the law of the realm and are minded to keep it well.

These are the chapters at the heart of Magna Carta. They set out the sense
rather than the actual words of the original Latin but by themselves they
justify treating Magna Carta as a document of outstanding importance.
They contain many of the core features of a society that today adheres to
the rule of law.

They explain why Magna Carta captured the imagination of Rudyard
Kipling[9] and why Lord Denning, perhaps the judge who more than any other
placed a premium on personal liberty, loved at the slightest excuse to recite
from Kipling's homage to Magna Carta. Although I cannot hope to emulate
Lord Denning's delivery, let me jog your memory by citing part of 'Runnymede'.
It describes so accurately the place of Runnymede in this country's history.

> At Runnymede, at Runnymede,
> Oh, hear the reeds at Runnymede:
> 'You musn't sell, delay, deny,
> A freeman's right or liberty.
> It wakes the stubborn Englishry,
> We saw 'em roused at Runnymede!
>
> When through our ranks the Barons came,
> With little thought of praise or blame,
> But resolute to play the game,
> They lumbered up to Runnymede;
> And there they launched in solid line
> The first attack on Right Divine,
> The curt uncompromising "Sign!"
> They settled John at Runnymede.
>
> At Runnymede, at Runnymede,
> Your rights were won at Runnymede!
> No freeman shall be fined or bound,

---

[9] R Kipling (1865–1936).

Or dispossessed of freehold ground,
Except by lawful judgment found
And passed upon him by his peers.
Forget not, after all these years,
The Charter signed at Runnymede.

And still when mob or Monarch lays
Too rude a hand on English ways,
The whisper wakes, the shudder plays,
Across the reeds at Runnymede.
And Thames, that knows the moods of kings,
And crowds and priests and suchlike things,
Rolls deep and dreadful as he brings
Their warning down from Runnymede!

The Influence of Magna Carta

The second reason why Magna Carta is so important is because of the *influence* that it has had, not only in this country, but around the globe, in establishing the constitutional principles that today are generally accepted as governing any society committed to the rule of law. It is a constitutional instrument for which there was no precedent. Neither the Barons nor the King needed to reach such a wide-ranging and long-term agreement. Yet, they created a Charter that placed limits on the sovereign power of the King.

However, the full significance of Magna Carta could not have been recognised by its authors. For the Barons it was no more than an acknowledgement of their immediate grievances. For the King it was a useful short-term expedient to buy time. It provided practical remedies for actual wrongs. It was not based on any lofty ideals or philosophical theory and at least until after the last war it took its place with other events in the development of what Lord Bingham has described as our unentrenched constitution.[10]

For a time Magna Carta disappeared off the horizon, only to be resurrected at the time of a different conflict. This time the dispute was between King James I, and subsequently Charles I, and Parliament. Sir Edward Coke, in turn Attorney-General, Chief Justice of the Common Pleas and Lord Chief Justice claimed effectively, but inaccurately, that Magna Carta recorded the liberties and freedoms enjoyed since time immemorial by the people of England. It was therefore an antidote to the Stuarts' claims to unbridled

---

[10] T Bingham, 'Judging Today', the Ditchley Foundation Lecture (2003).

power based on the divine rights of kings. Coke's approach to Magna Carta was dramatically in contrast to that of Oliver Cromwell.

Once he became Protector he was contemptuous of Magna Carta to redress grievances. For Cromwell it was not Magna Carta but 'Magna Farta'.[11] Such a boorish dismissal of Magna Carta was even more unjustified than Coke's claims for it.

Fortunately, historians redressed the balance. However, the Charter still has not had the recognition that, in my view, it should have, as the first of a series of instruments that now are recognised as having a special constitutional status. They include the Habeas Corpus Act, the Petition of Right of 1627,[12] the Bill of Rights confirmed by the Crown and Recognition Act 1689 and the Act of Settlement 1700. The long title to the Act of Settlement makes clear its links with Magna Carta since it states that it is an Act for the further limitations of the Crown and securing the rights and liberties of the subject. Importantly it secured the independence of the judiciary. Previously the judiciary had been dependent on the goodwill of the monarch for remaining in office.

It is, however, Magna Carta that has played the most critical role in developing our form of democratic government subject to the rule of law.

Magna Carta has also had a huge influence on the constitutional developments of those countries that have conventional written entrenched constitutions. One of the earliest of these constitutions and the model for a great many that followed was the Constitution of the United States.

The links between the United States' Constitution and in particular their Bill of Rights and Magna Carta is widely acknowledged. This connection explains the response of Americans to the Lincoln Cathedral's copy of the Magna Carta being transported to the United States Library of Congress for safe-keeping in 1939. No less than 14 million people queued to see it for themselves. When at the end of the war it was returned to this country, the Minister receiving it on behalf of the Crown referred to its lineage which he regarded as being 'without equal in human history'. He also considered with justification that the preamble to the United Nation's Charter was the most recent of Magna Carta's 'authentic offspring'.

Magna Carta's influence has also spread throughout the Commonwealth. Attention was drawn to this by Lord Irvine of Lairg when, as Lord Chancellor,

---

[11] N Phillips, Magna Carta, n 6 above.
[12] Largely the work of Coke and very much influenced by Magna Carta.

he visited Australia and gave his authoritative lecture on 'The Spirit of Magna Carta Continues to Resonate in Modern Law'.[13]

As he stated: 'In many respects, the Magna Carta has transcended the distinction between law and politics and its legacy represents a joint commitment by Monarchs, Parliamentarians and the Courts to the rule of law.'[14] That Lord Irvine should be giving a lecture on Magna Carta, on the other side of the globe in Australia was far from surprising. Magna Carta has been accepted in many of the Australian jurisdictions by statute, in some it is still almost entirely in force notwithstanding the repeals in this country.

It is part of Australian Common Law and was described by Isaac J as 'the groundwork of all our constitutions'.[15] Undoubtedly, as Laws LJ has pointed out, the 'enduring significance' of Magna Carta is that it was a 'proclamation of the rule of law' and 'in this guise, it followed the English flag even to the Chagos Archipelago'.[16]

India's very distinguished Supreme Court has the task of upholding the rule of law in the largest democracy in the world. It is no surprise to find that Court deciding that the right for a citizen to have a passport is based on Magna Carta.[17]

The principles enshrined in Magna Carta have also, from time to time, surfaced in different parts of the world that have never been part of the British Empire or a common law legal system. The principles are universal. Thomas Paine's *Rights of Man* took them to the different legal systems on the continent. They played their part in the French Revolution of 1789.

After the last war, the world had learnt the painful lesson, that John and the Barons' method of settling a little local difficulty had advantages over resorting to warfare. The world decided to do better in future and the result was that, in addition to playing a role in establishing the principles set out in the United Nation's Charter, the provisions of Magna Carta were highly influential when it came to drawing up the European Convention on Human Rights. It is easy to draw a parallel between the broad rights of that Convention and the broad statements contained in Magna Carta. As this country played its part in drawing up that Convention, it is not surprising

---

[13] (2003) LQR 119.
[14] Ibid.
[15] *Ex parte Walsh & Johnson* (1925) 37 CLR 36, 79.
[16] *R (Bancoult) v Secretary of State for Foreign and Commonwealth Office* [2001] QB 1067.
[17] *Sawhney v Assistant Passport Officer, Government of India* (1967), The Times, 15 April 1967.

that a number of the articles of that Convention have a distinct Magna Carta resonance.

Surprisingly, however, the importance of Magna Carta has never had the recognition by the public at large in this country that it deserves. Magna Carta and the Act of Settlement have been at least as important in protecting the public of this country's liberties as great battles such as that of Trafalgar, whose bi-centenary was celebrated later in 2005. Rightly, there were great reviews of the fleet and fireworks to mark the bi-centenary. By way of contrast, the bi-centenary of the Act of Settlement went unnoticed here as far I am aware, but in Canada, there was a great conference at which the event was celebrated with judges attending from all round the world.

Surely the time has come to rectify this position. I have mentioned Royal Holloway. There is, however, a co-host of these lectures. It is the Magna Carta Trust, established in 1957 with a most distinguished membership. Its Chairmen, commencing with Lord Evershed, have been the Master of the Rolls for the time being.

The then Prime Minister Sir Anthony Eden wrote a letter marking the inaugural meeting of the Trust in these terms:

> The 15 June 1215 is rightly regarded as one of the most notable days in the history of the world. Those who were at Runnymede that day could not know the consequences that were to flow from their proceedings. The granting of Magna Carta marked the road to individual freedom, to parliamentary democracy and to the supremacy of the law. The principles of Magna Carta, developed over the centuries by the Common Law, are the heritage now, not only of those who live in these Islands, but in countless millions of all races and creeds throughout the world.

At least Runnymede is in safe custody in the hands of the National Trust. But, that said, the identification of the actual site of the historic events in 1215 depends not on an English initiative, but on the initiative of the American Bar Association, supported by the Trust and the Pilgrim Trust, who on land leased by what is now the Runnymede Borough Council erected a monument in 1957 to commemorate and dedicate themselves to the principles of Magna Carta. In 2000 the American Bar Association held a rededication ceremony at which US Justice Sandra Day O'Connor spoke.

Visits have been made to the site by Presidents of India and Hungary. The President of Hungary came to the site to mark its importance to the emerging democracies of Eastern Europe.

Many thousands of members of the public visit the site each year, but they leave with no information of the significance of Magna Carta. No national or heritage money is made available to the Magna Carta Trust but it strives to do its best with the resources that are available to it. There is an undoubted need for a visitor centre at the site. The treatment of Runnymede demonstrates an unfortunate tendency of this country to be unduly complacent about the freedoms of which Magna Carta is a symbol. We cannot afford to take our freedoms for granted.

The same complacency also contributed to the delay in making the European Convention, even though it is based on Magna Carta principles, part of our domestic law.

This had at least two disadvantages. First before October 2000, citizens in order to obtain the benefits of the European Convention on Human Rights had to go to Strasbourg; not a happy situation for the nation that had made such a significant contribution to establishing the importance of the rule of law. Secondly, until the Convention became part of our domestic law, our judiciary were not able to make the contribution they would have made otherwise, by their judgments, to the development of the European jurisprudence relating to human rights.

Today the courts recognise specially protected rights. They are the very same rights that Magna Carta protected. They are the rights which, in this country, whilst they do not override the sovereignty of Parliament, control and constrain how that sovereignty is exercised.

Now the courts have an additional role. They are under a duty both to ensure that legislation is interpreted, whenever possible, in accord with the European Convention and to ensure that public bodies do not contravene the Convention. This increased responsibility of the courts enhances the importance of access to the courts for the protection of human rights. Those rights would be illusory if members of the public who considered their rights had been infringed could not seek the appropriate protection from the courts. This is but one example in a contemporary setting of the relevance of Magna Carta principles.

When the public seek their protection, the courts have to be seen to be wholly free of the influence of the executive. There is a need for independent judges who treat all who come before them in the same manner. Again, these are among the constitutional necessities that Magna Carta recognised.

That our judges would demonstrate such independence had been taken for granted but two events were to draw attention to the need for constant vigilance. The first warning came with the decision of the Prime Minister, announced in a press release in June 2003, to abolish the office of the Lord Chancellor which was then occupied by Lord Irvine of Lairg. What was apparently not appreciated at the time was that, while one individual as Lord Chancellor could, for historic reasons, exercise all the responsibilities of Lord Chancellor, a Secretary of State could not. In particular, the judiciary considered it wholly inconsistent with their independence for a Secretary of State to exercise the Lord Chancellor's traditional role as head of the judiciary.

It is now my personal view that even if this announcement had not been made, the conflict between the Lord Chancellor's different roles would inevitably have made changes necessary. However, this announcement accelerated the process. Fortunately, it was recognised both by the government and by the judiciary that the respective responsibilities of the relevant minister and the judiciary had to be redefined. The time had come when responsibilities previously performed by the Lord Chancellor had to be performed by a body or an individual who was clearly seen to be independent from the executive. There needed to be greater clarity as to the separate roles of the government and the judges. While up until that time, the separation of powers had not been a part of the English constitutional scene, at least in relation to the judiciary, the role of both the executive and the legislature now had to be seen to be separate from that of the judiciary. The need for this separation had already been made clear by the European Court of Human Rights. Prior to the announcement, the European Court had by its decision in relation to the Bailiff of Guernsey, given warning that the Lord Chancellor's different roles might be in conflict with the European Convention.[18]

The judiciary were obviously the most directly affected by the proposed changes. There was a massive amount of legislation giving tasks to the Lord Chancellor as head of the judiciary which would have been more appropriately dealt with by a new head of the judiciary once the Lord Chancellor was disqualified from performing that role. There were other responsibilities which could appropriately be shared by the new Minister and the new head of the judiciary and there were yet other responsibilities which should be performed by someone independent of both the Executive and the judiciary.

To deal with this novel situation, a novel negotiation took place between the Executive, led by the Lord Chancellor and the judiciary which I led as Chief Justice. The setting for the negotiation was not exactly a riverside meadow, but the objective as in the case of Magna Carta was to reach a consensus for the future as to how these differing responsibilities should

---

[18] *McGonnell v United Kingdom* (2000) 30 EHRR 289.

be performed. I hope you detect an echo with the process that took place on Runnymede 790 years ago. The parallel is, of course, not exact. To begin with, the process took far longer. In addition, both the King and the nobles produced that remarkable document notwithstanding that they were motivated by their own self-interest. I hope you will accept, that from the start both the judiciary and the Lord Chancellor were acting solely in the long-term constitutional interests of the country. We were seeking to identify the proper boundaries between the roles of the executive and the judiciary and Parliament.

It was remarkable that as a result of these negotiations a consensual document was agreed which defines the respective roles of the parties and came to be known as the Concordat. Even more remarkably, the Concordat was universally acceptable to the judiciary, the executive and the different political parties in Parliament.

There were differences of opinion between the different parties as to whether the office of Lord Chancellor should be abolished and as to whether, if the office was not abolished, which of his other roles should be affected. There were also the disputes as to whether, in future, the Lord Chancellor had to be a lawyer and a member of the House of Lords, but these disputes did not conflict with the terms of the Concordat.

The same is true of the issue as to whether the House of Lords should remain the final court of appeal for the whole of the UK or whether there should be a new Supreme Court. Here, there was hotly contested debate in Parliament but, miraculously, before the General Election on 5 May 2005, the Constitutional Reform Act was passed giving effect to the Concordat and Parliament's decision on the contested issues.

This required great parliamentary statesmanship on all sides. The Act now protects the judiciary by making clear their responsibilities and those of the executive. It is a new constitutional settlement giving effect to the rule of law. This is a further step in the process commenced 790 years ago.

The other development to which I referred was also of great importance. Dealing with a flood of asylum seekers was creating problems for the government. The process for determining claims for asylum and removing those whose claims failed was not effective. The system had too many tiers of appeal. The process was so protracted that by the time it had finished, the unsuccessful applicant could say that there had been a sufficient change of circumstances to justify the process being restarted. Many attempts were made to modify the system to make it more efficient with limited success.

The government, therefore, decided that a much more radical change was needed. They opted for a single tier with no right of access to the courts. They drafted legislation which it was intended would exclude the courts in their entirety. Over the years, since the last war, attempts have been made to do this in a number of contexts but they have always failed. The courts are not prepared to accept that Parliament intends to exclude their residual jurisdiction to prevent the individual being treated unlawfully contrary to Magna Carta. However, the proposed clause was intended to make it impossible for the courts to say that, if the legislation was passed, it was not the intention of Parliament to remove any residual jurisdiction of the courts, however great the injustice that might result.

Fortunately, before the clause was debated in the Lords, the government was persuaded to think again. The fact that they did so avoided the risk of a confrontation between the courts, the government and Parliament. It is my belief that, for the future, the recognition by the government of the need to take account of the requirements of the rule of law enshrined in Magna Carta is more significant than the misguided attempt to exclude access to the courts in the search for an expedient way of handling a difficult situation.

Increased recognition of the rule of law is also apparent in the strident argument which has taken place over the invasion in Iraq. The requirements of international law in relation to the invasion are, like most other areas of the international law, highly debatable at least at the fringes. However, it is commendable that the argument is to whether the invasion was lawful or unlawful. The argument is focussing upon the legality of what was done. It is not as might have been the case in the past on what is in the strategic interests of this country. In other words, the issue is, has the government acted in accordance with the rule of law?

The same is true over the dispute as to the legal status of the detainees both at Guantanamo Bay and Belmarsh Prison, which rightly have concerned the Supreme Court of the United States and the Appellate Committee of the House of Lords. The final illustration of the importance today of the rule of law and consequently its source, Magna Carta, is their impact upon the global economy. It is now accepted that the improvements in the standard of living are adversely affected by the absence of an established legal system which can ensure observance of the rule of law. There can be extreme reluctance to invest in a jurisdiction if there is a lack of confidence that disputes will be impartially resolved by an independent court system which is free from corruption and capable of upholding the rule of law. For the same reason, the European Union has insisted that the legal institutions of the countries applying for membership of the Union should be of acceptable standards before entry.

Conclusion

What I have said enables me to bring to a conclusion the first of the ten lectures on the relevance of Magna Carta today.

In 2004, all around the world in both the civil and common law jurisdictions, including this country, celebrations were held to mark the bi-centenary of the *Code Civil*. The *Code Civil* is the procedural code which has served civil jurisdictions so well for 200 years. In the common law world, there is nothing comparable to the *Code Civil*. Even if there had been, it is doubtful whether we would have celebrated it in the same way as was done in France. The French rightly saw the *Code Civil* as part of France's contribution to the legal systems of the world.

Hitherto, we have not sufficiently promoted the contribution of this country to the establishment of a world governed by the rule of law. The common law has spread and provided a contribution to justice, day in and day out, to about one-third of the population of the world. It has influenced other systems of justice. There is no code to which we can draw attention. However, Magna Carta is a symbol for the values of the common law. Magna Carta is also remarkable because it is such a historic statement of the fundamental principles of the rule of law.

The solution to a little local difficulty 790 years ago has become more important today than it has ever been. It is important that its eighth centenary should be celebrated in a manner that is worthy of what was achieved in Runnymede on 15 June 1215. While I do not congratulate the Trust and Royal Holloway on their choice of the first speaker, I do commend their efforts to ensure the eighth Centenary will mark the important contributions of this country to establishing the rule of law which I have attempted to identify.

6

The Rule of Law and a Change
in the Constitution

Abstract This paper provides an account of the new constitutional reforms provided by the Constitutional Reform Act 2005 and discusses how they came about. It suggests that the traditional constitutional arrangements, including the role of the Lord Chancellor, have successfully protected the rule of law, evolving as the needs of society have changed, without a need for a written constitution. We have benefited from a tradition of mutual respect, restraint and cooperation between the three arms of government. There have been times of tension, but with good sense and good will on all sides they have been successfully managed. It asks whether as part of the process of change we are paying sufficient attention to retaining or replacing the checks upon which, in the past, the delicate balance of our constitution has depended.

Any worthwhile society requires an efficient and effective legal system. A healthy legal system requires great law libraries. This is particularly true of common law legal systems. It is as true today as it has been in the past. Great law libraries are the treasuries of a legal system. They are the warehouse where we find the law. They are also where we collate, catalogue, index and digest the sources of our, and other, systems of law.

Our ability to obtain access to those sources is being transformed by technology. The forward march of technology has not, however, reduced the importance of law libraries. It has instead dramatically increased the quantity and quality of information which is now regarded as indispensable in order to educate and train the lawyers who will be responsible for teaching, drafting, practising, interpreting and applying the law.

---

* Originally given as the Squire Centenary Lecture, University of Cambridge, on 3 March 2004. Published in its original form in the *Cambridge Law Journal* ((2004) 63 CLJ 317).

It is a cause for celebration that the Squire has already been transformed. It celebrates its centenary in the new Sir Norman Foster Law Faculty Building that provides a magnificent contemporary setting in which to meet the challenges it now faces. I did not know the Cockerell Building before it was gloriously refurbished by its new owners, but I must confess I was surprised when an eminent lawyer and politician who is a graduate of this University assured me that in his day it was not called the Squire but the Squalor. I suspect this disrespect for a venerable building was an attempt to justify the fact that he had failed to benefit to the extent that he would or should have if he had spent more time in the Squire.

Certainly there can be no excuse for not regarding the new quarters as an ideal space for supporting research and teaching. It is a centre of excellence. I have to admit there is one respect in which it undoubtedly puts the Bar Library at the Royal Courts of Justice in the shade. The librarian there describes how members of the public and tourists regularly traipse up the grand staircase leading to the Bar Library only to be disappointed when they arrive to find no liquid refreshments. I am assured by my judicial assistant that excellence at the Squire extends to Nadia's in the basement where the lemon drizzle cakes and florentines are worthy of a detour.

Libraries have to evolve to meet the needs of their readers. Constitutions have to evolve to meet the needs of their citizens. A virtue of our being one of the three developed nations that does not have a written constitution, is that our constitution has always been capable of evolving as the needs of society change. The evolution can be incremental in a way which would be difficult if we had a written constitution. But flexibility comes at a price. We have never had the protection that a written constitution can provide for institutions that have a fundamental role to play in society. One of those institutions is a legal system that is effective, efficient and independent. A democratic society, pledged to the rule of law, would be deeply flawed without such a legal system.

So far we have coped successfully without a written constitution. That we entered the 21st century without there being more of a clamour for our constitutional arrangements to be reduced into writing is a situation in which we can take genuine pride. It reflects our national culture. It suggests we have benefited from a tradition of mutual respect, restraint and coopera-tion between the three arms of government. Of course there have been times of tension, but with good sense and good will on all sides they have been successfully managed. This was made easier not because of the separa-tion of powers, but because of the absence of the separation of powers.

The time may have been long past when Lord Chief Justices were, like Mansfield and Ellenborough, members of the cabinet, but still strong links continue to exist between the different arms of government. Key examples have been the dual role of the Law Lords as judges and parliamentarians and the unique position of the old Office of Chancellor as a member of the executive and head of the judiciary. There was also the long tradition of combining a successful career at the Bar with an equally successful political career and then both careers culminating in a career as a judge. Good relations between Parliament, the executive, and the judiciary were enhanced because judges had extensive experience, and therefore an understanding, of politics, Parliament and, not infrequently, government.

Such a background is not available to the English and Welsh judiciary today. But the advantages that come from such experience are not yet lost entirely. Lord Rodger of Earlsferry, a former head of the judiciary of Scotland, has experience of all these areas and combines this with a career as an academic; all achieved at an astonishingly early age.

The scale of recent change is illustrated by the fact that in 1960, 25 per cent of the members of the Commons were barristers and in 2001 the percentage was 5.2 per cent. Despite this fall, the Bar is still well-represented in government.

I mentioned that our ability to cope without a written constitution has depended on our tradition of mutual respect, restraint and cooperation. Many examples of self-restraint can be given, but it will probably suffice if I give one. It is Parliament's responsibility to legislate. The task of the court is to interpret that legislation. Interpretation is given an extended and novel meaning by the Human Rights Act 1998. By enacting section 3 Parliament has placed judges under a duty to interpret legislation in a manner that is, as far as possible, Convention compliant. But the courts should not treat section 3 as a licence to intrude into Parliament's role. As Lord Hope said: 'the rule is only a rule of interpretation. It does not entitle the judges to act as legislators.'[1]

Our ability to manage very well, thank you, without one of those written constitutions which we so generously drafted for our former colonies, was probably also assisted by the fact that, as Dr Robert Stevens points out; with the exception of the 17th century: 'Traditionally the growth of the English

---

[1] *R v A (No 2)* [2002] 1 AC 45, [108].

Constitution has been organic, the rate of change glacial.'[2] By contrast, during the lifetime of the Labour government, prior to 12 June 2003, there had been already a torrent of constitutional changes. Let me remind you; the removal of the hereditary peers from the House of Lords, devolution, the incorporation into domestic law of the European Convention on Human Rights and the creation of a unified courts administration.

This is by no means the whole story. There is hardly an institution performing functions of a public nature which has not been the subject of change. The changes have had an impact on the way in which our constitution operates. They have been introduced in separate legislation, but little attention has been paid to their cumulative effect.

It is against that background that the changes announced by the government on 12 June 2003 and provided for by the Constitutional Reform Act 2005, have to be considered. The question that has to be asked is whether as part of the process of change we are paying sufficient attention to retaining or replacing the checks upon which, in the past, the delicate balance of our constitution has depended. Initially, the announcement may not have been seen as being of great significance. Certainly, the government did not appreciate its significance because, if they had, it would have been announced in a different way. It was apparently seen by government as a reform capable of being achieved by a press release.

During the last administration, the office of Lord Chancellor has accumulated greater power than at any time in its history—apart from, possibly, the time of Cardinal Wolsey. So much so, that it was felt no longer appropriate for the old department to be under the control of a member of the House of Lords rather than the Commons. An indication of the scale of the department is given by the fact that in 2004 its annual budget was around £3.5 billion.

What had been seriously underestimated was the significance of the removal of the Lord Chancellor. It had not been appreciated sufficiently that the Lord Chancellor played a pivotal role in coordinating the three arms of government. Nor had sufficient attention been paid to the fact that, because of his membership of the Cabinet, the Lord Chancellor was able to act as a lightening conductor at times of high tension between the executive and the judiciary.

However, if this was not appreciated in June 2003, I accept that it is appreciated now. In the Constitutional Reform Bill introduced in the House of

---

[2] R Stevens, *The English Judges: Their Role in the Changing Constitution* (Oxford: 2002), xiii.

Lords on 24 February 2004, the government sought to put in place mechanisms to redress the deficit that could result from the proposed changes. The Bill was remarkable, in my experience, in that it consisted of 212 pages, relatively modest by today's standards, of which the Schedules took up all but 37 pages. An examination of their provisions demonstrated just how extensive were the tendrils of the Lord Chancellor's powers and the scale of the redistribution of those powers that would be necessary if the office was abolished. It also demonstrated the scale of the task that had to be performed within a very short time.

Apart from the scale of the change, what was the importance of the proposals, which have since been enacted in the Constitutional Reform Act 2005? To a non-lawyer they may not seem to be of particular significance. What is the difference between a Lord Chancellor and a Secretary of State, the man on the Clapham Omnibus could, with reason, ask. After all, that engagingly friendly and cheerful chappie, the former Lord Chancellor, Lord Falconer, seemed to be quite happy playing both roles.

Over recent years, recognition of the importance of the rule of law and the significance of the independence of the judiciary has increased dramatically. One of the most important of the judiciary's responsibilities is to uphold the rule of law, since it is the rule of law which prevents the government of the day from abusing its powers. Ultimately, it is the rule of law which stops a democracy descending into an elected dictatorship. To perform its task, the judiciary has to be, and seen to be, independent of government. Unless the public accepts that the judiciary are independent, they will have no confidence in the honesty and fairness of the decisions of the courts.

How successfully the Lord Chancellor performed the task of protecting the judiciary is controversial. What is not controversial is that the judiciary were content that he should have this role until 12 June 2003, because, by convention, he was Head of the Judiciary and accepted the responsibility of being the protector of the judiciary. Personally, I was on record as being in favour of the retention of the office. I set out my views in these terms five years ago:

> As a member of the Cabinet, he [the Lord Chancellor] can act as an advocate on behalf of the courts and the justice system. He can explain to his colleagues in the Cabinet the proper significance of a decision which they regard as being distasteful in consequence of an application for judicial review. He can, as a member of the Government, ensure that the courts are properly resourced. On the other hand, on behalf of the Government, he can explain to the judiciary the realities of the political situation and the constraints on the resources

which they must inevitably accept . . . As long as the Lord Chancellor is punctilious in keeping his separate roles distinct, the separation of powers is not undermined and the justice system benefits immeasurably. The justice system is better served by having the head of the judiciary at the centre of Government than it would be by having its interests represented by a Minister of Justice who would lack these other roles.[3]

I would add that having a Lord Chancellor was very comfortable for the judiciary. They could avoid the chore of having to shoulder all the administrative tasks that were performed by the Lord Chancellor and his department on their behalf. Since the office has been changed a great burden of administration has descended on the Lord Chief Justice in particular and the judiciary in general. What is more, when things go wrong the Lord Chancellor, with his reduced roles, will no longer be there to take the blame.

However, since 12 June 2003, I personally, with reluctance, joined those who said the Lord Chancellor could no longer play his traditional role as Head of the Judiciary unless his responsibilities were significantly reduced. The reasons for my conversion included:

1. The scale of the Lord Chancellor's responsibilities as a spending Minister meant the office had become increasingly politically charged.
2. His involvement in criminal justice, tribunals and asylum were at times inconsistent with his role as Head of the Judiciary.
3. There were an increasing number of occasions on which there were conflicts between his ministerial interests and those of the judiciary.
4. The Department had three Ministers in addition to the Lord Chancellor and two Permanent Secretaries. The junior ministers did not see themselves as mini-Lord Chancellors or as being subject to the restraints that, by convention, applied to this role. They were, and saw themselves as being, ministers having main-line departmental responsibilities.
5. The system of appointments was, in any event, in need of fundamental reform. Not because it was not appointing excellent judges; that it did so, was not in dispute. But the system was finding it almost impossible to appoint judges and, in particular, silks in a manner which met the existing Judicial Appointments Commission's standards of objectivity. The paper trails were unsatisfactory. The process was insufficiently based on verifiable criteria.

---

[3] See 'Judicial Review—The Tensions Between the Executive and the Judiciary', Chapter 7 in this book.

6. Finally, I had reservations as to whether there was any way of putting the clock back once you have had a Secretary of State and a Lord Chancellor; a combination of roles that I regarded as being wholly inconsistent one with the other. I also doubted whether it would have been possible to restore the special culture that needed to exist if the Lord Chancellor was to successfully combine his different and conflicting responsibilities.

It is becoming increasing clear that the independence of the judiciary requires increased statutory protection. The Act of Settlement, whose third centenary was a cause for celebration was, until section 3 of the Constitutional Reform Act 2005, the guarantee of 'continued judicial independence', came into force, still the principal statutory protection. The remainder of the protection was dependent upon insecure conventions and understandings. For example, a letter passing between myself and the former Lord Chancellor Lord Irvine recording the need for my consent, was the only brake on the Lord Chancellor's power to discipline judges. There were many ways in which, consciously or unconsciously, his Department could give directions to Court Service staff which resulted in the courts becoming a tool of government policy. In the setting of targets for the courts, pressure could be placed on the Court Service to meet certain policy objectives—perhaps giving early hearings for street crimes—at the expense of other waiting cases. The only impediment to this sort of interference was the clear acknowledgement that 'listing' was a judicial function even if, in practice, listing is performed by civil servants.

The first event that made the need for more statutory protection clear was an attempt to transfer, without consultation, responsibility for the Court Service from the Lord Chancellor's Department to the Home Office as part of a government reshuffle. The attempt was only frustrated at the last minute with the help of the judiciary. It was disturbing that—at that time—it was not appreciated within government that it was inappropriate for the department that most frequently had to defend proceedings for judicial review in the courts and that had lead responsibility for criminal justice policy to be in charge of what should be seen as an impartial Court Service.

Then there was the announcement of 12 June 2003 which clearly indicated an extraordinary lack of appreciation of the significance of what was being proposed. This was followed, shortly after 12 June and, again, without consultation, by the transfer of the Court Service from the Lord Chancellor to the Secretary of State for Constitutional Affairs. This last action could well have been due to oversight, but it demonstrates there is a lack of appreciation of the significance of the independence of the judiciary in the corridors of government.

Having been confronted with the 12 June proposals, the reaction of the judiciary was that, whether the proposals were implemented or not, the judiciary should strive for a new constitutional settlement, recorded in legislation, that would protect as many interests of the judiciary as possible. In our response to the consultation papers we drew attention to the need for a public debate.

Irrespective of whether there is a Lord Chancellor and an impressive new Supreme Court (if possible, purpose-built to the quality of the Squire), the position of the judiciary has been demonstrated to be far too exposed.

I am relieved that the former Lord Chancellor and I achieved a concordat and that this is now in the public domain, a document recording our agreement having been lodged, earlier in 2004, in the libraries of both Houses of Parliament. I believe the concordat provided an appropriate constitutional framework for the future relationship between the government and the judiciary. It will ensure that the judiciary comes of age and takes on responsibility for those features of the relationship that are critical to its future well-being. It is important to emphasise that the judiciary's concern with protecting its independence is so that it can fulfil its responsibility to the public. The concordat that was agreed was not designed to exclude the legislature and the executive from having any responsibility for the justice system. On the contrary, it will be seen that many of its provisions involve shared responsibility. Implemented, the legislation will, however, require a radical overhaul of the manner in which the judiciary organises itself. The implementation of the concordat will be the type of consensual constitutional evolution that could, for the time being, postpone the need to resort to the less flexible alternative of a written constitution.

Subject to some amendments which the Lord Chancellor had already agreed to make, the Constitutional Reform Act reflects the concordat. The judiciary, as a whole, were satisfied that, if the concordat were to be implemented, the judiciary's independence would be protected. It would not be protected in the same way as it was in the past by a Lord Chancellor, but it is my judgement that the protection of the 'package' as a whole will mean that there need be no concern that the new arrangements threaten the future independence of the judiciary. The package also sought to ensure the accountability of the judiciary, since accountability must accompany independence.

There are new bodies with primary responsibility for appointments and discipline. In both there is, for the first time, a role for non-lawyers.

The Secretary of State, or Minister of Justice as the position is now known,[4] still has a role, but his role is limited to acting upon the recommendations of the two bodies. Unlike the old Lord Chancellor, he is no longer in charge, but he does have sufficient responsibility to enable him to answer for the bodies to Parliament.

In some jurisdictions, the judiciary are provided with the resources to run the courts. It may be argued that it is only where this happens that true independence of the court system is possible. However, our judiciary have not, as yet, the experience to enable them to run a court system. Accordingly, the Minister of Justice is to be under a statutory duty to ensure that there are efficient and effective systems to support the business of the courts in England and Wales. But the concordat provides for the judiciary to be represented in decision-making as to the resourcing of the Unified Court Agency and the Department by way of representation on the Boards of both bodies. In this way, the judiciary will, for the first time, have an early input into the preparation of funding bids and the allocation of resources that will enable them to have a genuine influence on the outcome. The partnership that has developed over the last 20 years or so between the judiciary and administrators is not only being maintained, but developed. Thus, the Minister of Justice's responsibility for the efficient and effective administration of the court system is now exercised in consultation with the Lord Chief Justice. Within the framework of the court system, it is the Lord Chief Justice who is responsible for the posting and roles of individual judges.

While the Chief Justice is the recipient named in the Act for many functions previously performed by the Lord Chancellor, he is in a position to delegate those powers. The Lord Chief Justice must continue to function as a judge, so there will be a number of other judges of different levels of seniority who will provide leadership. Their appointment will fall to the Lord Chief Justice, but he will act either with the concurrence or in the consultation with the Minister of Justice depending on the nature of the post.

The Minister of Justice will have the responsibility for determining the framework governing the appointment of judges to the numerous committees, boards and similar bodies on which they now sit, but it will be the Chief Justice who determines which individual judges should be appointed to those bodies. Usually rules will be made by the relevant rule committee, with the Minister of Justice having the power to approve or

---

[4] From May 2007 the Department for Constitutional Affairs became the Ministry of Justice.

disallow those rules. Where no rule committee exists, the Chief Justice will make the rules with the concurrence of the Minister of Justice. Appointments of the non-judicial members of the rules committees will be made by the Minister of Justice, in consultation with the Lord Chief Justice, while judicial members will be appointed by the Lord Chief Justice, after consultation with the Minister of Justice.

Practice directions will be made by the Lord Chief Justice with the concurrence of the Minister of Justice. The education and training of the judiciary will be the responsibility of the Lord Chief Justice, but the Minister of Justice will be responsible for providing the resources.

If you were to undertake the laborious task—I would not recommend you to do so—of studying in detail the schedules to the Act, you would find that the 700 or so statutory provisions which name the Lord Chancellor have been divided between the Minister of Justice and Lord Chief Justice in a manner which reflects the divisions of responsibility to which I have just referred.

So far, I have said nothing about the proposal which has probably attracted most attention from the public. That is, the proposal for a new Supreme Court separate and independent from the House of Lords. On this subject, the judiciary has not spoken with one voice in the same way as they have on the reforms made necessary by the abolition of the old Office of the Lord Chancellor.

It is intended that the new court shall have very much the same jurisdiction as the Appellate Committee of the House of Lords has at present, save that it will also deal with the devolution issues which are, at present, primarily dealt with by the Law Lords in the Privy Council. This means that, though called a Supreme Court, it will not, in fact, be a supreme court. Except in relation to Community Law and in respect of devolution issues, the new court will be subordinate to the will of Parliament as expressed in legislation and will have no jurisdiction to hear Scottish criminal appeals. Among the Supreme Courts of the world, our Supreme Court will, because of its more limited role, be a poor relation. We will be exchanging a first class Final Court of Appeal for a second class Supreme Court.

The reason for having a Final Court of Appeal separate from the House of Lords is largely symbolic. However, symbols can have unexpected results. Separating the House of Lords in its legislative capacity from its activities as the Final Court of Appeal, could act as a catalyst causing the new court to be more proactive than its predecessor. This could lead to tensions. Although the Law Lords' involvement in the legislative chamber is limited, the very fact that they are members of the legislature does provide them with an insight and understanding of the workings of Parliament to a greater extent than will be possible if they are no longer part of the House of Lords. The Scots are nervous about the change proposed and not supportive of it. We should pay particular attention to their concerns, in view of the proposal that the Supreme Court should deal with devolution issues.

There is also the question of the resources that will be required to establish and run the new Court. I have been particularly unhappy about the suggestion that running costs would be recouped by imposing a surcharge on court fees. Those fees are, in my judgement, high enough already. In addition, I want to know the extent, if at all, that court fees in Scotland and Northern Ireland will contribute to the new Court.

These worries did not cause me to be wholly hostile to the idea of a new Supreme Court. However, if I had had a vote on the subject, I would have been in favour of deferring a decision, until I knew, first of all, the building which it was intended the Supreme Court should occupy[5] and, secondly, the method by which the other (non-judicial) members of the House of Lords were to be appointed. If they were all to be elected, then it is unlikely that the Law Lords could remain part of the membership.[6] This would have resolved the issue for me. Certainly, it would have made the presence of a Chief Justice as a member of the House incongruous. The Appellate Committee's accommodation and support had improved since I was a full-time Lord of Appeal in Ordinary. Certainly, I saw no reason to rush into establishing the Supreme Court before its new home had been decided upon. To push ahead then, despite the many reservations which have been expressed, would, it seemed to me, have been inconsistent with the desirability of achieving constitutional change by consensus.

We cannot take the continued individual, or collective, independence of the judiciary for granted. Fairly recent events have caused me to still have real concerns for the future. The government made no secret of the fact that in the future it would be likely the Minister of Justice would be a member of the Commons, as indeed he is now, and could well be a non-lawyer. Particularly because of a perceived need for a joined-up approach to criminal justice, I was worried about the Ministry of Justice becoming a subsidiary of the

---

[5] This is now known to be a renovated Middlesex Guildhall, with an expected move date of 1 October 2009.

[6] Note that the Law Lords will be disqualified from voting and sitting in the House of Lords when the new Supreme Court comes into existence. See Constitutional Reform Act 2005, s 137(3).

Home Office or unable to compete with the dominance of the Home Office. The result could have been the Home Office being in a position to dictate the agenda for the courts which would not have accorded with the need for independence. Perhaps I was unduly worried since I was conscious that one of my predecessors, Lord Hewitt, had similar fears in the 1920s. I hope my fears have been unjustified, but it is worrying when changes are advocated without apparent appreciation of their significance.

Another cause of the same concern has been the Asylum and Immigration (Treatment of Claimants etc) Act 2004. The Act seeks to establish a single tier of appeal against Home Office decisions in relation to asylum and immigration matters to replace the two tiers which previously existed.

However, it is not this aspect of the Act, worrying though it is, upon which I wish to focus now. What I want to focus upon is clause 11 of the Bill as it was. This clause was undoubtedly unique in the lengths to which it went in order to prevent the courts from adjudicating on whether the new appeal tribunal had acted in accordance with the law. As the House of Commons Constitutional Affairs Committee stated in its report of 26 February 2004:

> An ouster clause as extensive as the one suggested in the Bill is without precedent. As a matter of constitutional principle some form of higher judicial oversight of lower tribunals and executive decisions should be retained. This is particularly true when life and liberty may be at stake.[7]

The provision had to be read to appreciate the lengths to which the government had gone to try and exclude the possibility of intervention by the courts. Extensive consultation took place with myself and other members of the judiciary before the Bill was introduced. We recognised that there was a problem of abuse to be tackled. However, our advice was that a clause of the nature included in the Bill was fundamentally in conflict with the rule of law and should not be contemplated by any government if it had respect for the rule of law.

We advised that the clause was unlikely to be effective and identified why. The result was that clause 11 was initially extended to close the loopholes we had identified, instead of being abandoned as we had argued. The only concession that appeared to have been made to our representations was to give the complainant the right to ask for an internal review. In addition, we argued that ouster was not necessary and that action could be taken

---

[7] Constitutional Affairs Committee, *Asylum and Immigration Appeals*, Second Report, 2004, para 70.

which was more likely to be effective than a clause of this nature. Importantly, we pointed out that the danger of the proposed ouster clause was that it could bring the judiciary, the executive and the legislature into conflict. Apparently this was of little concern.

Once the Bill was introduced, the clause was criticised by distinguished constitutional lawyers and by Lord Mackay, the former Lord Chancellor. What made the provision even more objectionable, was that the Nationality, Immigration and Asylum Act 2002 introduced a form of statutory review by the High Court on the papers which was extremely expeditious (taking a few weeks rather than months) and which gave every indication of being successful. The judiciary recommended this new procedure and cooperated in its introduction to prevent abuse of the protection afforded by the courts. Because the process was so speedy, there was no great advantage to be gained from making abusive applications and this was one of the reasons why the number of statutory reviews had been relatively modest.

The Constitutional Affairs Committee recommend that 'no change should be made until there had been more experience of the impact' of this initiative. I agreed. In discussions which took place between the judiciary and the government, there were attempts to justify the clause, but these were specious and unsatisfactory. It is particularly regrettable that the Lord Chancellor and Secretary of State at the time found it acceptable to have responsibility for promoting this clause.

I understand that the then Lord Chancellor said the clause was not intended to exclude habeas corpus. In view of the language of the clause this surprised me. It also surprised me because, if the clause did not exclude habeas corpus, then I would have thought it inevitable that it would, in practice, lead to an increase in delay. This is because the right to apply for habeas corpus does not involve the safeguard of a requirement as to leave. It also surprised me that the government did not see it as inconsistent to promote a clause designed to exclude the courts from performing their basic role of protecting the rule of law at the same time that it introduced the present constitutional reforms. Their actions were totally inconsistent and I urged the government to think again as the cross-party Constitutional Affairs Committee recommended. There was still time. The implementation of the clause would have been a blot on the reputation of the government and would have undermined its attempts to be a champion of the rule of law overseas. Happily, the clause was withdrawn by the government. Notwithstanding this, the attempt to include it in legislation could have resulted in a loss of confidence in the commitment of the government to the rule of law.

I have not over-dramatised the position, but if this clause had become law, it would have been so inconsistent with the spirit of mutual respect between the different arms of government that it could have been the catalyst for a campaign for a written constitution. Immigration and asylum involve basic human rights. What areas of government decision-making would be next to be removed from the scrutiny of the courts? What is the use of courts if you cannot access them? It was for this reason that a prison governor was found to be in contempt for interfering with a prisoner's access to the courts.[8] Professor Sir William Wade described the right of access to the courts as 'the critical right' in the great textbook he edited with Dr Christopher Forsyth (now Professor Christopher Forsyth), *Administrative Law*. The response of the government and the House of Lords to the chorus of criticism of clause 11 produced the answer to the question of whether our freedoms could be left in their hands under an unwritten constitution.

The judiciary are facing change on an unprecedented scale. These changes are not confined to the proposed constitutional reforms which have been the prime subject in this paper. They include judges taking on a much more central role in the management of civil, family and criminal litigation. A spirit of partnership between the judiciary, the legislature and the executive is essential if the judiciary are to meet the changing needs of society. Nothing can be more important than that spirit should not be damaged. Our judiciary today are not only as well-qualified as they have ever been to meet the challenges that confront them, they are also now better organised than they have been in the past. I am confident that the judiciary will continue to seek to uphold the rule of law to the best of their ability. They hope for the support of the government and Parliament in their efforts.

That brings me to the end of the comments I wish to make. You are fortunate that I am recovering from a cold otherwise I would have treated you to a fine rendition of Happy Birthday to the Squire Library. As it is, I will confine myself to saying 'Many Happy Returns Squire on a centenary of great achievements. We look forward with confidence to your next century.'

---

[8] *Raymond v Honey* [1983] 1 AC 1.

7

Judicial Review—The Tensions Between the Executive and the Judiciary

Abstract This paper discusses the delicate relationship between the courts, the legislature and the executive. It supports the accretion of law on a case-by-case basis and suggests this has helped develop administrative law principles and maintain the necessary balance between the interests of the public and administrators. The tensions created between the courts and the government by judicial review proceedings are acceptable; such proceedings ensure government actions comply with the law. It discusses how the courts have assisted the efficient working of government by reducing judicial review waiting times and wherever possible, clarifying the principles upon which they will intervene. In reviewing the actions of public authorities, the judiciary, it concludes, are doing no more than their duty to uphold the rule of law.

The doctrine of the separation of powers was adopted by the convention of 1787 not to promote efficiency but to preclude the exercise of arbitrary power. The purpose was not to avoid friction, but, by means of the inevitable friction incident to the distribution of the governmental powers among three departments, to save the people from autocracy.[1]

The Role of the Judge and Judicial Review

Judges spend the majority of their time deciding individual cases. Those cases establish the precedent which collectively constitute a solid proportion of our law. Nowhere is this more true than in the case of administrative law.

---

* Originally given as the inaugural Neill Lecture at the University of Oxford on 6 November 1997. A revised version was later published in the *Law Quarterly Review* ((1998) 114 LQR 579).

[1] In *Myers v US*, 272 US, at 293 (1926), per Brandeis J.

Here, the involvement of legislation has been confined to matters of procedure and practice. The accretion to the law has been confined to matters of procedure and practice. The accretion to the law on a case-by-case basis has proved to be an ideal manner in which to establish principles of administrative law. It has helped to maintain the necessary delicate balance between the interests of the public and administrators.

However, the approach does have disadvantages. One is that, if the judge concentrates on the trees, he can lose sight of the horizon of the landscape in which they grow. The advantage of a judge being invited to give a lecture or write an article is that it causes him to raise his sights and view the subject from a wider perspective than when deciding individual cases. It is on this wider perspective that I will concentrate. In doing so, I will approach my subject by what may appear to be a cautious route.

I have no doubt that there is and has been, particularly in recent times, tension between the judiciary and the executive, and that the tension has from time to time increased as a result of the decisions of judges on application for judicial review. I, however, do not regard this as a matter of concern. It is no more than an indication that judicial review has been working well during a period when the other restraints on the executive were not as great as ideally they should be. Until recently it was a period during which both local government and the opposition to the executive in Parliament was weak and when power had become increasingly centralised. It was also a period of frenetic activity by the government of the day. The government was taking policy decision after decision, which had significant implications for the justice system and the vulnerable sections of the community whose only source of protection is the courts. Examples are provided by the decisions adversely affecting prisoners[2] and asylum seekers.[3]

As I can remember vividly, this is not the first time this has happened. A similar situation existed for different reasons during the period when we last had a Labour government and Lord Denning was the Master of the Rolls. At that time I was the Treasury Junior. I recall leaving court after my leader, the Attorney-General, Sam Silkin, had suffered another bruising encounter with the Master of the Rolls being told by him prophetically that

---

[2] *R v Secretary of State for the Home Department, ex parte Doody* [1994] 1 AC 531; *R v Secretary of State for the Home Department, ex parte Duggan* [1994] 3 All ER 277; *R v Secretary of State for the Home Department, ex parte Venables* [1998] AC 407.

[3] *R v Secretary of State for Social Security, ex parte Joint Council for the Welfare of Immigrants* [1997] 1 WLR 275.

this would postpone our adoption of the European Convention as part of our domestic law for at least a decade.[4]

The tension created by judicial review is acceptable because it demonstrates that the courts are performing their role of ensuring that the actions of the government of the day are being taken in accordance with the law. The tension is a necessary consequence of maintaining the balance of power between the legislature, the executive and the judiciary upon which our constitution depends. The tension is no more than that created by the unseen chains which, in the absence of a written constitution, hold the three spheres of government in position. If one chain slackens, then another needs to take the strain. However, so long as there is no danger of the chains breaking, the fact that this happens is not a manifestation of weakness but of strength.

The Other Roles of the Judiciary

In assessing whether there is any danger of the chain between the judiciary and the executive breaking, it is constructive to look beyond judicial review to the other relationships which the judiciary have and seeing how they fare. There is the role of the judiciary and the legislature. There is the judiciary's role outside the courts in conducting inquiries, delivering papers and giving lectures and, most importantly of all, there is the role in jointly running the justice system with the executive. The last point is a matter of particular importance at times of reform of the justice system such as those which we are going through at the moment. Without close cooperation between the executive and the judiciary, such programmes of reform will not be effective.

Parliament

The relationship between the courts and Parliament is clearly defined and today creates no significant difficulty for the courts. The Bill of Rights of 1689 makes it clear that the court should not encroach upon the exclusive province of proceedings in the Houses of Parliament and the courts accept the sovereignty of Parliament.

There are, however, principles of the highest constitutional importance in play in the area. The sovereignty of Parliament is but an important aspect of the rule of law. There are other principles which are part of the rule

---

[4] *Gouri et v Union of Post Office Workers* [1977] QB 729; in House of Lords [1978] AC 435.

of law, for example, that the public are entitled to have resort to the courts; that the courts are for the resolution of their disputes; that it is the courts' responsibility to protect the public against the unlawful activities of others including the executive; and that it is the responsibility of the courts to determine the proper interpretation of the law.

Just as the courts respect Parliament's sovereignty, so the courts are entitled to assume that, absent very clear language to the contrary, Parliament, having passed legislation, does not intend to interfere with the responsibilities of the courts under the rule of law. Accordingly, when interpreting and applying the legislation, the courts assume Parliament does not intend to interfere with the court's role in upholding the rule of law.[5]

The position was elegantly expressed by Sedley J in a case which appeared before the Court of Appeal. Sedley J described the position as being a 'mutuality of respect between two constitutional sovereignties'.[6] In that case the Court of Appeal upheld the decision of Sedley J and refused Mr Al Fayed's application for leave to apply for judicial review of a report prepared by the Parliamentary Commissioner for Public Standards in respect of an alleged bribe said to have been received by the then Home Secretary, Jack Straw. On behalf of Mr Al Fayed it was argued that the position of the Parliamentary Commissioner for Public Standards was no different from that of the Parliamentary Commissioner for Administration, who is in appropriate circumstances subject to judicial review.[7] We disagreed in the case of the activities in issue. The Parliamentary Commissioner for Administration, the Ombudsman, is concerned with the activities of administrative bodies because of the effect which they have on those outside Parliament—that is, the public. The Parliamentary Commissioner for Public Standards is concerned with the activities of members of Parliament because of the effect which they have inside Parliament—that is to say, on the workings of Parliament.[8]

Confusion can also be caused to those not familiar with our traditions in this country because members of the Appellate Committee of the House of Lords are members of Parliament. The fact that they should take part in debates in the House of Lords on legal subjects is not controversial. By that

---

[5] *R v Secretary of State for the Home Department, ex parte Fayed* [1998] 1 WLR 763.
[6] *R v Parliamentary Commissioner for Standards, ex parte Fayed* [1997] COD 376, 377, [1998] 1 WLR 669 at 670.
[7] *R v Parliamentary Commissioner for Administration, ex parte Balchin* [1997] COD 146.
[8] See *ex parte Fayed*, n 6 above, 377.

```
            MS BRAEMAR
          MORNING LIGHT BAR
115 NITI

CHK 2500    02JAN13 12:47

  1 OLD SPECKLED HEN        3.15
    SUBTOTAL                3.15
    TOTAL PAID          3 . 1 5
    6077
    XXXN130102124737N
    MANUAL ENTRY
    Cabin/Acc:6077
    Mr Geoffrey Lloyd
    CABIN CHARGE            3.15
-----115 CLOSED 02JAN 12:47


CABIN #:_____

PRINT NAME:_____

SIGNATURE:_____
```

I mean that it has not been a part of the House of Lords' constitution which is a candidate for reform.[9]

The Lord Chancellor and his Department

The position of the Lord Chancellor has, however, been the subject of comment and indeed treated as being unsatisfactory in a lecture of great distinction given by Lord Steyn.[10] The cause of the concern was the fact that the Lord Chancellor combined his role of head of the judiciary with that of being a senior member of the government and having to preside in the House of Lords. The remarkable combination of these three roles could be, and often was, not surprisingly, suggested to be inconsistent with the separation of powers. However, I was not sure this was necessarily correct so long as the Lord Chancellor could be relied on to remember which of his three hats he was wearing at any particular time. While accepting that no one would today give the Lord Chancellor such huge responsibilities, I would suggest the retention of those roles until recently is as important today as it was in the past. While no one drafting a constitution would place such heavy responsibilities on one man, in practice their combination did have huge practical benefits. In particular, in relation to my subject, the Lord Chancellor of the day could and still can act as a safety valve avoiding undue tension between the judiciary and the government and possibly between the judiciary and Parliament as well.

As a member of the Cabinet, he could act as an advocate on behalf of the courts and the justice system. He could explain to his colleagues in the

---

[9] By the end of the 1990s all but 92 hereditary peers were excluded from membership of the House of Lords. It is also to be noted that the Lords of Appeal in Ordinary will soon become Justices of a new Supreme Court and will cease to be entitled to sit, and therefore to speak, in the House of Lords and any of its committees. The disqualification in the Constitutional Reform Act 2005, s 137(3) extends to voting as well as sitting. The disqualification will come into effect when the Supreme Court comes into existence on 1 October 2009, subject to completion of renovations to Middlesex Guildhall in time for the move from the House of Lords to have been achieved by that date.

[10] J Steyn, 'The Weakest and Least Dangerous Department of Government' [1997] PL 84. Following recent reforms resonating from the Constitutional Reform Act 2005, the old Office of Lord Chancellor has been abolished. From May 2007, the Lord Chancellor became the Head of a Ministry of Justice. Other changes to the Lord Chancellor's role include: his role in judicial appointments has become limited to saying 'no' to one candidate recommended by the independent Judicial Appointments Commission; there is a new system for dealing with complaints; the Lord Chief Justice is now Head of the Judiciary; and the Lord Chancellor is no longer a member of the House of Lords. What follows in this paper is of historical value on the old Office of Lord Chancellor and should be considered in light of the recent reforms.

Cabinet the proper significance of a decision which they regarded as being distasteful in consequence of an application for judicial review. He could, as a member of the government, ensure that the courts were properly resourced. On the other hand, on behalf of the government he could explain to the judiciary the realities of the political situation and the constraints on resources which they must inevitably accept. As long as the Lord Chancellor was punctilious in keeping his separate roles distinct, the separation of powers was not undermined and the justice system benefited immeasurably. The justice system was well served by having the head of the judiciary at the centre of government.

There were of course real risks of the roles becoming confused and not understood, but the risks should not have been exaggerated since the Lord Chancellor's fellow judges and fellow politicians subjected his actions to the closest scrutiny—the politicians in case he was acting in the interests of the judiciary when he should have been acting as a politician and his fellow judges in case he was acting as a politician when he should have been acting as a judge. The risks involved were worthwhile because they reduced the danger of relations between the judiciary and the government being subjected to excessive strain.

In referring to the old position of Lord Chancellor, I have not forgotten that at one time it was not unknown for the Master of the Rolls to be a member of the House of Commons and even Speaker. One such Master of the Rolls was Sir John Trevor, who it is said owed the fact that he combined both roles in the 17th century to his cousin being Judge Jeffreys.[11] It was because of what was described as his unblushing rapacity, participating in the corruption which was then prevalent, that resulted in his losing the office of Speaker. This, however, did not prevent his continuing as Master of the Rolls for 22 years, and causing the wits to remark that in his case 'justice was blind but bribery only squinted'!

Running the Courts

I turn next to consider the important subject of the running of the courts. If the courts do not function efficiently, then no matter the quality of the judiciary, justice will suffer.

---

[11] Judge Jeffreys, also known as the 'Hanging Judge', became notable during the Reign of King James II, rising to the position of Lord Chancellor.

In 1969 the Beeching Commission reported.[12] Dr Beeching, having reformed our railways, had turned his attention to the way in which the courts were administered or, as he thought, not administered. He made far reaching recommendations designed to transform the way in which the judiciary and the courts were organised. Many of its recommendations were implemented by the Courts Act 1971. A centrally administered court system was created. Courts of Assize and Quarter Sessions were abolished. The control which judges had previously exercised over their own work was substantially reduced. The High Court judge on circuit was to be no longer in virtually exclusive control of the administration of justice at the Assize Court which he was visiting. The Chairman of the County Sessions and the Recorder of the Borough Sessions were no longer in charge of Quarter Sessions. They were abolished.

Now the Supreme Court[13] consisted of the Court of Appeal and the High Court together with the Crown Court. The Lord Chancellor became responsible for the administration of the Supreme Court. This was made clear by section 27 of the Courts Act 1971 which gave the Lord Chancellor the power to:

> appoint such officers and other staff of the Supreme Court and county courts
> as appear to him necessary for—
> (a) setting up a unified administrative court services; and
> (b) discharging any functions in those courts . . .; and
> (c) generally for carrying out the administrative work of those courts.

The new Court Service which the Courts Act set up was intended to be virtually in the exclusive control of the executive, that was the Lord Chancellor's Department. The only recognition of the involvement of the judiciary was in relation to the presiding judges, who had ill-defined responsibilities for overseeing what occurred on each circuit.

Initially, the judiciary were content that the administration of the courts should be in the hands of the executive. This abdication of responsibility took place at a time when in other common law jurisdictions the movement was in the opposite direction. In those jurisdictions the judiciary were striving to achieve greater control of the running of the courts, including the control of their own budget.

---

[12] Cmnd 4153 (1969).

[13] Not to be confused with the provisions in the Constitutional Reform Act 2005 for a new Supreme Court that will replace the Appellate Committee of the House of Lords in October 2009.

Fortunately, within a few years of the new Court Service being established it was accepted both by the old Lord Chancellor's Department and the judiciary that the judiciary needed once more to be involved in the management of the justice system. The result is that today the courts are managed by the Court Service in partnership with the judiciary. The Court Service fully accepts that one of its principle functions is to perform its responsibilities in a way which supports the judiciary and assists them to perform their role. Without friction or confrontation with the Court Service, the judiciary have become more involved and responsible for the administration of justice than at any time since the 19th century. The working relationship between the judiciary and the Court Service is now usually entirely harmonious. The judiciary have at the same time remained fiercely independent. Their status and role in achieving justice has not been diminished. On the contrary, it has been enhanced.

Furthermore, the present and previous Lord Chancellors, on behalf of their respective governments, have accepted that the judges should take on new responsibilities in managing civil litigation. Since 1971 the number of judges has increased dramatically. The increase has been in each tier of the judiciary. It is only among the Lords of Appeal in Ordinary that the increase has been other than substantial. Numerous new courts have been built. The size of the Lord Chancellor's Department mushroomed at least proportionately. New offices have been created for members of the judiciary. There is now, as well as Presiding Judges responsible for a circuit, a Senior Presiding Judge who is responsible for the well-being of both civil and criminal justice outside London. We have had a Deputy Chief Justice and we now have a Vice-President of the Queen's Bench and Court of Appeal Criminal Division. A judge is Chairman of the Law Commission, another is Chairman of the Judicial Studies Board. Judges are the Chairmen of the Criminal and Civil Justice Councils. There is a Judges' Council presided over by the Lord Chief Justice and a Council of Circuit Judges and an Association of District Judges. The judiciary is now better organised to look after its own interests and the interests of justice than ever before. These changes have taken place with the complete support of and finance provided by the government. Successive Lord Chancellors have used their clout within government to ensure the system has been properly resourced.

Meetings have taken place regularly between the Lord Chancellor and the Heads of Division. In general, the consultation between the judiciary and the old Lord Chancellor's Department and the Court Service was excellent. Normally there was remarkably little tension between the judiciary and the Department and the Court Service as to the running of the very large court system which now exists.

I do not forget that there was a period of confrontation between some of the judiciary and the former Lord Chancellor, Lord MacKay, but that was primarily concerned with reforms relating to the professions, including rights of audience for solicitors, and not the role of the judiciary in the administration of the courts. There was also the concern over the shortage of judges in 1994/95. However, after powerful and frank speeches by the then Lord Chief Justice and Master of the Rolls, a much-needed injection of additional judges was provided. The former Lord Chancellor, Lord Irvine of Lairg also proposed far-reaching changes to the rights of audience, but these were not met with the same hostility.

This degree of cooperation between the judiciary and the executive I believe was made possible because of two of the old Lord Chancellor's roles to which I have referred: the fact that he was the head of the judiciary and at the same time one of the most senior members of the government of the UK. If he was not head of the judiciary, it seemed the partnership between his department and the judiciary to which I have referred would be much more difficult, if not impossible.[14]

That Lord Chancellors were able to keep their balance on the tightrope meant that the judiciary came to perform their role in relation to judicial review on a strong foundation of cooperation between the judiciary and what became one of the largest government departments. It should be remembered that the members of the judiciary who determine cases of judicial review were appointed by the Queen on the advice of the Lord Chancellor after extensive consultation and in particular close consultation with the senior judiciary. The senior judiciary were themselves appointed on the recommendation of the Prime Minister. Their quality is confirmation that usually the collaboration worked well. The judiciary have certainly retained their independence. Ability, fearlessness and objectivity are characteristics which are essential qualities of a judge who hears applications for judicial review. Under different constitutional arrangements it would be more difficult for the judiciary to be closely involved in appointments. For example, in the case of the Supreme Court of the United States the justices are not formally consulted as to the selection for appointment of a new member.

---

[14] Speech of the former Lord Chancellor, Lord Irvine, to the Citizenship Foundation, 'Parliament and the Judges: a Constitutional Challenge?', 8 July 1996 (reported in (1997) 63 Arbitration 94).

Judicial Inquiries

Judicial inquiries have also been undertaken with increasing frequency over the period I have discussed. They are an extra-curricular burden shouldered at the request of the government. The government recognises that the undoubted independence of the judiciary gives their findings and recommendations a credibility that a governmental or other internal inquiry could not match. The fact that the judiciary are prepared to take on this task is another aspect of the culture of cooperation between the judiciary and the government which we tend to take for granted. That they should do this is often convenient for the government, but the appointments are accepted irrespective of this as a form of public duty. Again, the position can be contrasted with that in the United States, where it has been suggested that even Chief Justice Warren Burger was in error in accepting the invitation to conduct the inquiry into the death of President Kennedy.

The framework against which the judiciary hears applications for judicial review is therefore one where they have close and, on the whole, totally amicable relations with the other arms of government when performing a number of different roles. The situation is not one where the relations between the judiciary and the executive are so distant that it is easy for each to misunderstand the other because of lack of communication. In the past it was a strength of the judiciary that they had among their number judges who had previously held high office in government and had long experience of government. Today the absence of that experience is partially compensated for by the involvement of the judiciary with the executive in the administration of the courts. The involvement does not reduce the independence of the judiciary. On the contrary, it is increased and protected by their involvement in the administration of the courts. Their involvement in administration includes ensuring that the process of judicial review operates effectively. Both the government and the public would have cause to complain if the process of judicial review did not work as effectively as it does.

Judicial Review

Any legal proceedings against the government by way of judicial review which succeed are bound to reflect adversely on the activities of the executive. However, what can be said with confidence is that, despite the remarkable growth in the number of applications for judicial review, the frustrating effects of those applications has been significantly less than it would have been if the procedure was less efficient than it is. The increase in applications has been remarkable: 491 in 1980 and 3,901 in 1996.[15] There have been increases in every year except two, and an increase of over 34 per cent in a single year. They are, of course, not all against the government, but a substantial proportion are.

Whereas in 1981 they were dealt with at first instance by four Queen's Bench judges nominated by the Lord Chief Justice, in 1997 they were dealt with by 24 judges including two judges of the Chancery Division.[16] A Lord Justice, Lord Justice Simon Brown,[17] had judicial oversight and control of the list. Whereas at one time an application could take as long as two years to be resolved, today the waiting time has been reduced to six or seven months except for those applications which are the subject of expedition and the waiting time can then be a matter of days rather than months. The courts fully accept their responsibility to the public and to the government to ensure that the delay does not unnecessarily add to the problems of the government.

The courts have also assisted the efficient working of government by, wherever possible, clarifying the principles upon which they will intervene. In a common law system the limits to the application of the principles can never be precisely defined. It would be a great mistake to do so as a new situation will inevitably arise which has not been anticipated. However, while administrators will not necessarily share my view, I believe that we have reached the position where Ministers should be able to be guided with reasonable confidence in the majority of situations as to whether their actions will be accepted by the 'Judge Over Your Shoulder'.

That there will be tensions resulting from applications for judicial review is inevitable. Government plans and timetables can be thwarted. The publicity when a case is lost by the government unfairly often depicts the Minister as being found with his hand in the till. The word 'unlawful' can have different meanings and however carefully the judgment is framed it is rarely made clear that nothing more heinous has occurred than that the

---

[15] By 2005, the number of applications had increased to 5,382.

[16] Today, judges of the High Court are nominated by the Lord Chief Justice to hear cases in the Administrative Court List, the Administrative Court being established as part of the Queen's Bench Division in 2000. There are presently 37 judges, including judges of the Chancery Division and Family Division, who act as additional judges of the Queen's Bench Division when dealing with cases in the Administrative Court List.

[17] Now Lord Brown, a Lord of Appeal in Ordinary.

Minister has interpreted obscurely worded legislation differently from the judge. A finding that there has been unreasonableness is even more difficult for the media to report fairly. In Parliament, unfair political capital can be made of an adverse finding.

If the judiciary seeks to provide a press release which sets out the position fairly, that in itself will be viewed with suspicion. By contrast, cases that a Minister wins are ignored.

Judicial Review is Executive-Friendly

What I would like to see is the government take the offensive and say that they welcome judicial guidance, since if they have gone wrong they wish to know so that they can rectify the position, possibly by paying compensation. However, a change of this sort is probably expecting too much.[18] No one likes to be on the receiving end of litigation. The government could, however, launch applications themselves where the legal position is unclear and seek advisory declarations. In addition, it must be remembered that the judiciary shield the executive by treating judicial review as being not available where an alternative remedy exists which is at least equally effective.

If tensions must be accepted then the interests of the executive on an application for judicial review are protected in a way in which litigants in private law proceedings are not. This is by the need to obtain leave to make the application and the fact that the relief is discretionary. The special needs of the executive to be able to govern are recognised. Nowhere is this more apparent than in the requirement that the application has to be made promptly and the provision in section 31(6) of the Supreme Court Act 1981 that where there has been delay the court must refuse leave or, if leave has already been given, any relief sought on the application, if it considers that the granting of the relief would be 'detrimental to good administration'.

The protection provided for the executive in this way has had some consequences which have been a long-standing source, not of tension, but of amicable disagreement between Sir Patrick Neill[19] and myself as to whether the divide between public and private law procedures is desirable.[20]

---

[18] But see the speech of the former Prime Minister, John Major, in 1996 cited by B Alexander, *The Voice of the People: a Constitution for Tomorrow* (Weidenfeld & Nicolson, 1997), 49.

[19] Now Lord Neill QC.

[20] See P Neill, *Some Necessary Reforms* (Oxford: Clarendon Press, 1988).

Sir Patrick saw the divide as a snake down which the potential litigant could slide for no good reason, whereas I see it as a ladder which could enable the judiciary to approach judicial review from a higher threshold; a threshold where the courts could be satisfied that if they were going to be involved, there would be good reason to do so.

Sir Patrick was, however, worried about those cases where the litigant would find that he had to start again because of the adoption of the wrong procedure. In relation to the executive, it is normally but not invariably clear whether judicial review is the appropriate procedure. There can, however, be real problems in relation to other public bodies and I recognise that even in relation to the executive there is a problem to be resolved. Fortunately, my reforms in relation to civil justice, the new civil procedures, have helped bridge the divide. I am reasonably confident that the rejection of proceedings on the basis of the wrong choice of procedure is now a problem of the past.[21]

The disappearance of the procedural divide does not mean that there is no substantive divide. Some of the public law principles still differ from those in private law. However, here I hope that in future there will be a process of harmonisation between public and private law, and in relation to this process the European Convention has acted as a catalyst.

The Enlargement of the Scope of Judicial Review

If the procedure for judicial review is executive-friendly, what are the aspects of the development of judicial review which are less friendly?

Here I have supposed the prime target must be the enlargement of the scope of judicial review. Unlike the position in relation to the proceedings of Parliament, in respect of the workings of government we have now reached, rightly, the stage where the courts have accepted jurisdiction over virtually all the activities of government.

It is generally accepted that the fact that the source of the power which is being exercised is the prerogative rather than statute does not prevent the exercise of the power being scrutinised on an application for judicial review. Even in the area of national security, in the *GCHQ* case Lord Fraser of Tullybelton considered the government was 'under an obligation to

---

[21] See *Access to Justice Final Report* (HMSO, 1996), 256.

produce evidence that the decision was in fact based on grounds of national security'.[22]

In another *Fayed* case,[23] the Court of Appeal considered that even a decision to refuse citizenship was capable of examination on an application for judicial review. A refusal of citizenship was quashed because of unfairness by the Secretary of State even though the statute specifically said he was not required to give reasons. In the *Pergau Dam* case, judicial review was granted although foreign relations were involved.[24]

The Differing Intensity of Review

How the courts intervene is dependent upon the subject matter of the particular case. In other words, the scope of judicial review is not limited, but the degree of scrutiny exercised and therefore the depth of the review varies according to the subject matter. In addition, issues can be non-justiciable. This is the position as to the exercise of the prerogative of mercy. In many areas the courts will readily accept that they are not qualified to intervene and will not do so. Thus, setting the norm of local government expenditure is a matter of national economic policy depending essentially upon political judgement where the courts will rarely be willing to be involved. This is made abundantly clear by Lord Bridge's speech in *Nottinghamshire County Council v Secretary of State for the Environment.*[25] The result of the approach was, however, not that the courts could never intervene but that they would only intervene in exceptional situations where, for example, it could be shown that there was bad faith.[26]

At the other end of the scale are situations where what are at stake are fundamentally rights of the individual. In such cases the courts will find no difficulty in concluding that the issue is justiciable and examine the decision strictly. If, for example, a claim for asylum is involved, where the claimant's life can be at stake, careful scrutiny is obviously justified. Similarly, even the Home Secretary's power to make regulations will be strictly construed if its effect will be to prejudice rights conferred on asylum seekers to claim refugee status by depriving them of the means of survival while their claims

---

[22] *CCSU v Minister of State for the Civil Service* [1985] AC 374, 402.

[23] See n 5 above.

[24] *R v Secretary of State for Foreign Affairs, ex parte World Development Movement Ltd* [1995] 1 WLR 386: see also P Cane, 'Standing Up for the Public' [1995] PL 276.

[25] [1986] AC 240.

[26] See, for example, *Porter v Magill* [2002] 2 AC 357.

are being considered. This is what happened in the case of *R v Secretary of State for Social Security, ex parte Joint Council for the Welfare of Immigrants.*[27] The impact on asylum seekers of what the Minister was seeking to do was so grave it required primary legislation. The result in that case was reversed by primary legislation. Of course, the courts could not go behind that legislation. However, the courts in a subsequent case did construe its language strictly, and as it did not expressly refer to national assistance, it was held that a local authority would still be under an obligation to consider whether asylum seekers should receive help under the National Assistance Act even though this was brought about by their statutory exclusion from other benefits.[28]

In relation to access to the courts, the courts will be alert to prevent a citizen's right of access being abrogated. So, the rules as to standing have been extended to the position where a claim with merit is most unlikely to fail for lack of standing. Again, when the former Lord Chancellor changed the provisions as to court fees in a way which did not take into account the position of those who lacked means but would be ineligible for legal aid, the regulations so far as they had this effect were declared unlawful. This was the result in the case of *R v Lord Chancellor, ex parte Witham.*[29] The regulations were quashed even though they were made with the concurrence of the Heads of Divisions including, I am ashamed to say, myself.

The cases to which I have referred are cases where the facts are striking. They are cases where I would hope that the Minister responsible would recognise that there had been a departure from the appropriate standards of good administration. There are many other cases of a similar nature concerning prisoners, concerning criminal injury compensation, where one can see the courts daily adopting the same approach. The other side of the picture is that many more cases can be found where the courts do not intervene and the applications are dismissed. They do not attract the attention of the press.

The Absence of Other Constitutional Safeguards

However, even making due allowance for this and the growth of judicial review generally, it is right to acknowledge that the number of situations where the courts have felt it right to intervene is surprisingly high and suggests

---

[27] [1997] 1 WLR 275.
[28] *R v Hammersmith & Fulham LBC, ex parte M* [1996] TLR 31.
[29] [1998] QB 575.

a reluctance of the executive on occasions to adopt proper standards of good administration. It is possible to look at the pattern of the cases decided and see a line being clearly drawn by the courts as to what is acceptable and what is not. The number of cases crossing onto the wrong side of that line, perhaps, can also be attributed to a period when the other checks on government were not operating as effectively as they usually do. This resulted in forceful and energetic Ministers being tempted to cross the line when good administration would have suggested a more circumspect approach. A good example of this is the attempt to impose a new non-statutory scheme for criminal injuries compensation when there was already a statutory scheme waiting to be brought into force by the Minister.[30] The tension placed on the relationship between the government and the judiciary has increased, I would urge not because of any defaults on the part of the judiciary. However, there was never a risk of the chain being broken. The courts' decisions were observed and implemented and there was no confrontation. In the case of *M v Home Office*,[31] the courts had made it clear that even in relation to government they are not without sanctions to enforce their remedies.

The Effect of Constitutional Change

The picture that I have painted so far is not one of a judiciary striving to exercise greater powers than it has hitherto. The judiciary are doing no more than their duty to uphold the rule of law. The nature of that duty changes as our constitution evolves. We have now embarked on a period of constitutional change of the greatest importance. Devolution has given to our highest court heavy additional responsibilities. It is not only in a European Community context that legislation does now have to be struck down.

The Human Rights Act 1998, bringing home the European Convention on Human Rights, came into force in 2000. The courts had already discovered that most of the principles enshrined in the Convention were part of the common law. However, that Act has changed the focus of our law. It has given each member of the public the right to seek the help of the courts to protect his or her human rights. The courts now investigate whether infringement of those rights can be justified. The courts have had to develop new skills. I had no doubt as to their ability to do so. However, personally I am

---

[30] *R v Secretary of State for the Home Department, ex parte Fire Brigades Union* [1995] 2 AC 513.

[31] [1994] 1 AC 377.

pleased that the Act restricts the courts' power to declare that an Act of Parliament is inconsistent with a provision of the Convention and does not give the courts power to strike down or otherwise to affect the validity of an Act of Parliament. In this the Act reflects the views of the vast majority of, if not possibly all, the senior judiciary. The judiciary have regarded this as being far more desirable than an Act which would have enabled the judiciary to strike down legislation. There have been a few cases where the courts have been unable to construe legislation in accordance with the Convention.[32] Where they cannot, it is right that Parliament should decide how the situation should be rectified. A political decision of this sort is not an appropriate task for the courts.

My main concern about the Act, which on the whole has been warmly welcomed, is its very narrow requirement as to standing. It has been only a 'victim' who can rely on the Convention before our courts. If we had not been careful, we could have had a new divide with two parties making the same complaint, one able to rely on both traditional judicial review grounds and the Convention, and the other only being able to rely on traditional judicial review grounds.

The Act has been loyally applied by the courts. In applying the Act, the courts have been adopting the role which they traditionally clearly identified when hearing applications for judicial review. That role involves upholding the law. If the judiciary are doing no more than that, the tension which is necessary to uphold our constitution should never be subject to excessive strain. This is the position, even though the enactment of the Act has undoubtedly increased the responsibilities of the courts.

Conclusion

For the purpose of this lecture I took down from the shelf my copy of Sir Patrick Neill's All Souls Justice Report and noted his personal endorsement thanking me for 'friendly advice and some even friendlier criticism'. I have acknowledged, at least as to the 'divide', that criticism was not deserved. I also note that some of the recommendations, for which I have only praise, still await implementation, such as a general public law requirement

---

[32] See, for example, *R (Anderson) v Secretary of State for the Home Department* [2003] 1 AC 837; *Bellinger v Bellinger* [2003] UKHL 21, [2003] 2 AC 467; *A v Secretary of State for the Home Department* [2004] UKHL 56, [2005] 2 AC 68; and *R (Hooper) v Secretary of State for Work and Pensions* [2005] UKHL 29, [2005] 1 WLR 1681.

to give reasons[33] and pay compensation.[34] These recommendations deserve reconsideration. If as a result they were to be implemented, they would complement the Act and could make not only for an era of better administration but also an era, much to be desired, of unprecedented cooperation between the courts and the executive.

---

[33] *R v Secretary of State for Transport, ex parte Factortame (No. 2)* [1991] 1 AC 603.
[34] *R v Secretary of State for the Home Department, ex parte Doody* [1993] 3 All ER 92.

8

Should the Media and the Judiciary be on Speaking Terms?

Abstract This paper discusses the complex issue of reconciling the requirement in a parliamentary democracy of a free and independent judiciary with the need for a free and independent media. It supports the distinct roles played by the courts and the media to act as independent checks on the government that with a substantial parliamentary majority, and left unchecked, could yield immense power. It advises that the judiciary must not forfeit its independence in its dealings with the media; to do so could be extremely damaging to the public's confidence in the legal system. It is in the interests of both the courts and media that they continue to be on speaking terms.

It is a pleasure and a privilege to be with you tonight. A pleasure because Dublin is indeed a fair city, and a privilege because of the prestigious nature of the lecture.

Among those who have previously given this lecture there are many that I admire and in whose footsteps I regard it as an honour to follow. One of my distinguished predecessors was Lord Irvine, whose great and ancient office of Lord High Chancellor of Great Britain and Northern Ireland has been changed by his successor. Lord Irvine drew attention to the distinction of University College Dublin. I am a graduate of University College London.[1] The two colleges have Jeremy Bentham in common and I am able to assure the audience that his mummified body is still mummified and regularly meets lawyers at UCL.

---

* Originally given as the English RTÉ/UCD Law Faculty Lecture at University College Dublin, on 22 October 2003.

[1] Hereafter, 'UCL'.

I turn to the title of my talk and the question it poses. When I gave the title to the organisers, it was intended to be smart and snappy and designed to avoid the speech being delivered to an empty hall. At least I am not addressing an empty hall. I must admit that when I came to ask myself whether the media and the judiciary should be on speaking terms, the answer was painfully obvious. It was the single word 'yes'. However, as often happens, what appears an obvious answer proves, on further examination, to mask a complex and difficult issue of some importance. That, I believe, is the position here.

Parliamentary democracy depends upon the existence of a free and independent media and a free and independent judiciary. What is more, it is possible that a free media depends upon the existence of a free judiciary, and a free judiciary depends in turn upon a free and independent media. While this may be true, the judiciary must be independent of the media and the media must be independent of the judiciary. What I am about to do is to try to explain how this paradox comes about.

Today, governments can exercise an immense amount of power. The extent of that power in a parliamentary democracy depends on the popularity of the party in power. Ironically, if the popularity of the party means that it has a substantial parliamentary majority then that majority can enable the government, though freely elected, to become impatient of interference and criticism. If it does so, it can lose its sensitivity to the importance of a free and independent media and judiciary. In such a situation, checks on the power of government are particularly important. They are provided by the media and by the courts. Independently, they can together ensure that a government does not abuse its power. The roles of the media and the judiciary are different. The media exposes and the judiciary determines illegality. The part played by the media is the more subtle. By making known to the public the activities of the government, it acts as a cleansing agent. A government that is engaged in abusing its powers cannot afford to have this exposed to the public gaze. In this way, the media can and does hold the government to account.

This explains why written constitutions invariably contain provisions that protect freedom of information. The Westminster Constitution, which many former colonies inherited on obtaining their independence, provides such protection. The constitution of Ireland (Bunreácht na hEireann Article 40.6.1) includes protection for the right of the citizens to 'express freely their convictions and opinions'. But interestingly, the Article recognises that the media can also abuse its power by adding words that will be familiar to my audience, but that came as somewhat of a surprise to me:

> The education of public opinion being, however, a matter of such grave import to the common good, the State shall endeavour to ensure that organs of public opinion, such as the radio, the press, the cinema, while preserving their rightful liberty of expression, including criticism of Government policy, shall not be used to undermine public order or morality or the authority of the State.

Although Article 40.6.1 refers to 'opinion', that includes facts, Article 40 does not stand alone. Our sponsors RTÉ are also, by statute, under an obligation of impartiality and objectivity in relation to matters of public controversy or political debate.

Although in the UK we do not have the advantage of a written constitution, we now have as part of our domestic law the European Convention on Human Rights. Article 10 of the Convention is also qualified and recognises that the media should be subject to control. Article 10 provides:

1. Everyone has the right to freedom of expression. The right shall include freedom to hold opinions and to receive and impart information and ideas without interference by public authority regardless of frontiers. This article shall not prevent States from requiring the licensing of broadcasting, television or cinema enterprises.
2. The exercise of these freedoms, since it carries with it duties and responsibilities, may be subject to such formalities, conditions, restrictions or penalties as are prescribed by law and are necessary within a democratic society, in the interests of national security, territorial integrity or public safety, for the prevention of disorder or crime, for the protection of health or morals, for the protection of the reputation or rights of others, for preventing the disclosure of information received in confidence, or for maintaining the authority and impartiality of the judiciary.

Neither of these provisions provide as extensive protection as the first and fourteenth amendments of the US Constitution. Still, the protection that they do provide for the media is sufficient to enable the media to play its critical role in protecting a free and democratic society.

The independence of the courts is equally important. The courts have the task of upholding, in Ireland, the Constitution and, in mine, the European Convention. More simply, it is the job of the courts to ensure that governments observe the law. As Michael Addo of the University of Exeter has said: 'The judiciary is a uniquely different organ of government whose effective functioning depends critically on its independence.'[2] Mrs Justice Denham also expressed it well when she chose the title 'The Diamond in a Democracy: An independent, accountable judiciary', for an admirable address she gave in Australia.[3]

An independent and accountable judiciary is the diamond in a democracy. Yet this is not what the European Convention expressly says. Instead, Article 6 of the Convention contains no more than an indirect requirement that there should be an independent judiciary. Article 6 of the Convention provides: 'In the determination of his civil rights and obligations or of any criminal charge against him, everyone is entitled to a fair and public hearing within a reasonable time by an independent and impartial tribunal established by law.' It is to members of the public that Article 6 gives the entitlement to a hearing before an independent tribunal, that is, a judge. The creation of the right in this way makes the important point that independence of the judiciary is not the privilege of the judiciary, but a requirement that exists for the benefit of the citizen.

In this respect the Irish constitution does better than the European Convention. Article 35 of Bunreácht na hEireann makes the trenchant statement: 'All judges shall be independent in the exercise of their judicial functions and subject only to this Constitution and the law.' The right to freedom of expression is also not the property of any sectional interest. The right to inform and be informed by the press is, in the language of Article 10, the right of everyone.

In neither of our countries is the right to freedom of expression an absolute right. However, our respective independent courts have, particularly in the last ten years, been extremely sensitive about interfering with this right. Any interference has to be necessary and so proportionate. As the constitutional provisions indicate, the courts have to draw a balance between the rights of the media to free expression and the rights of the individual, including an individual's right to privacy. The Hutton Inquiry, the Report of which was published in 2004, has demonstrated most impressively the importance of both an open and patently fair judicial investigation and the extensive reporting of the process so that the public can be involved and form their own conclusions.

---

[2] M Addo, *Freedom of Expression and the Criticism of Judges* (Ashgate, 2000).
[3] A keynote address to the Annual Conference of the Australian Institute of Judicial Administration, Darwin, North Territory, Australia, 14–16 July 2000.

I know the media will not agree that the judiciary has always come to the right conclusion when deciding on where the balance lies. What is more important, the privacy of a football player or the desire of a newspaper to tell its readers the sordid details of his sexual activities? How do you value the right of the media to publish the account by a former member of the secret service of what he considers to be the iniquities of MI5 as against the need for MI5 not to leak like a sieve? When should the courts decide that what has been published should be regarded as amounting to contempt? Views can differ as to where the balance falls. In relation to contempt, there have been times when the Irish approach has been more relaxed than the English though, as far as I can ascertain from his judgments, the Irish Chief Justice's conclusions on this subject and mine are likely to coincide today. However, I hope the media of both our jurisdictions would accept that, in general, at least in my judicial lifetime, the judiciary have been conscious of the dangers involved in even 'chilling' freedom of expression. They have not allowed the laws of defamation or contempt to be used as means of suppressing the right of the media to play their role in keeping the public informed. Above all, unlike some jurisdictions the courts have not been used to intimidate the media into docility.

So the media has reason to be at least moderately grateful for the judiciary's appreciation of the importance of freedom of expression. But this is not a lecture on the law as to prior restraint, defamation, or contempt. So I content myself by saying that at least the courts of both our jurisdictions are aware of the importance of getting the balance right and seek to achieve this. It involves weighing conflicting interests since, in the words of Article 10 of the European Convention, freedom of expression carries with it 'duties and responsibilities'.

By contrast, although this may not be so obvious, it is also my belief that the judiciary have reason to be grateful to the media. The media can be among the staunchest protectors of the independence of the judiciary. They do not wish to see an executive not subject to any control. If a government is intent on destroying the independence of the judiciary the next candidate is likely to be the media. A regime intent on undermining democracy will quickly find, as Hitler and Stalin did and more recently Mugabe has, that a free and independent judiciary and media are an inconvenience that needs to be dealt with.

Media also plays another important role in relation to the judiciary. As with the media, the judiciary's independence carries with it responsibilities. The fact that, unless the interests of justice make this impossible, courts sit in public means the media can be relied upon to reveal any inappropriate judicial behaviour. The protection against a judgment that is wrong is an appeal. A protection against inappropriate behaviour on the part of a judge can be exposure in the media. Such behaviour is not to be tolerated and, as long as the criticism is responsible, it is to be welcome. I have described the media as 'protection' since, although an aspect of judicial independence is security of tenure, the judiciary are subject to disciplinary processes to deal with inappropriate conduct. These disciplinary processes include, as a last resort for serious misbehaviour, removal. A power that I am relieved to be able to say has not been used in my jurisdiction in recent times.

'In recent times?' Well, you may have seen on ITV there has been a drama featuring Henry VIII.[4] As you would expect, the programme paid more attention to the fate of Henry's wives than the fact that he executed his Lord Chancellors almost as frequently as his wives, and his Lord Chief Justices fared little better. Well what can you expect of a king who took advantage of the break with Rome to require the Irish Parliament to declare him King of Ireland in 1541?

The judiciary also have an interest in achieving a public awareness of what is happening in the courts. Public confidence in the judicial system is of critical importance to the well-being of a modern nation. Few have the first-hand experience that comes from actual engagement in litigation. Reporting by the media therefore provides the majority of the public with information about what is happening. Even if the reporting sometimes leaves a lot to be desired, at least the public have a prospect of learning of the sentence that is meant to deter, which the public need to know about if they are to be deterred. Many cases have wide implications for society and can be controversial. Again, the public need to know and the media usually provides the most satisfactory means of bringing them to the public's attention. In this company, I add that academic writing can also play a part.

Here in England, and I am sure the same is true in Ireland, we have the considerable benefit of first-class law reporters. The fact that both countries now place their judgments on the same website—the British and Irish Legal Information Institute (BAILII)—adds to the benefit of this. We also have excellent legal correspondents in all sections of the media including the BBC. Here RTÉ's sponsorship of these lectures shows RTÉ's healthy interest in legal issues.

---

[4] In 2003, when this paper was originally given, the television company ITV released a popular programme by Peter Morgan, *Henry VIII and His Wives*.

However, there are issues on which I have quite failed to have a rational discussion with the media, in particular issues that involve sentencing. It is sad that, in order to protect the young men who killed the Bulger baby, our courts have had to develop a lifetime injunction against disclosure of the young men's identity; even though they have both served their sentence and, as far as I know, are trying to re-establish themselves as decent members of society.

Then there is the fact that our Court System like every public service is short of resources. The media are rightly interested in the quality of public services. In part, the justice system is the weakest arm of government because, in England, it is totally dependent on the executive for its resources. In relation to this issue, the media has from time to time provided valuable assistance to the justice system. A sympathetic article or programme can certainly encourage greater generosity on the part of the government.

Pausing to take stock; the position is that the judiciary are dependent, at least in part, on the media. But so are the media dependent upon the judiciary not using their powers to restrict inappropriately the media's powers of free expression.

The judiciary and the media therefore have interests in common and they should certainly be on speaking terms. But alas, the position is still not straightforward. The involvement of the judiciary in making rulings on the ability of the media to perform its basic activity of publishing news does at least sound warning bells as to the possible dangers of too close a relationship between the judiciary and the media. The judiciary must not forfeit its independence in its dealings with the media. The media has its own agenda.

Conflict between different arms of government provides good red meat for a media that has an insatiable appetite for news. As the judiciary is regularly required to adjudicate on issues involving the media, the judiciary must be circumspect about having a relationship with the media that will raise questions as to the judiciary's impartiality. Obviously there is no difficulty in the media speaking to judges, the problem is judges speaking to the media. A litigant is entitled to have his case decided not only by a judge who is impartial, but by a judge in relation to whom there are no reasonable grounds for saying that he might be impartial.

A judge who has publicly expressed his opinions too vigorously may not be seen as impartial if he is required to adjudicate upon the issues about which he has commented to the media. Certainly, a judge should not have any communication with the media which suggests that he or she covets the approval of the media. All too often, judges are required to make unpopular decisions in order to perform their duty. To hesitate in that duty would be a derogation of that duty. A judge must avoid any situation that could even give a hint that being popular with the media or the public was more important to the judge than coming to a just decision.

It is when the judge has to make unpopular decisions that his independence and integrity are most important. Here I have antecedents. One of the first times I came to the notice of the press was when I was called upon to decide a case in which a man claimed damages for a personality change caused by an accident. The medical evidence supported his claim that the personality change had resulted in him committing rape. I awarded him damages, aware that he was being sued by his victim and that she would be the ultimate recipient of a large proportion of the compensation he received. This subtlety was lost on the press, who greeted my decision with uproar. My wife was door-stepped, I believe that is the technical term, and was asked for a reaction to my judgment. She replied, 'I can't say a word—my husband will kill me'. Her remarks were not reported. The term 'the gentlemen of the press' is not entirely archaic.

I have said that with the judiciary's independence comes responsibility. This is also true of the media. I have to be frank. They do not always show the responsibility they should. I cite sentencing. Not because some elements of the English press have referred to me as 'Chief Justice let-em-off—so wet he leaks', rather, because the inaccuracy of the reporting of this issue is preventing an open debate. An open public debate is a pre-condition for sensible sentencing.

In these circumstances, it is not surprising that our judiciary has been, and still is, provided with guidance as to what its relationship with the media should be. At one time, our judiciary's position was governed by what were called the Kilmuir Rules. Rules based on a letter, by the then Lord Chancellor, Lord Kilmuir, of 12 December 1955 to the Director General of the BBC. The letter made clear that 'as a general rule it is undesirable for members of the judiciary to broadcast on the wireless or to appear on television'.

The letter was written in the context of a proposal by the BBC that there should be a series of lectures on the third programme about great judges of the past and the BBC wanted to have the assessment of the qualities of eminent judges of the past from an existing member of the judiciary. Hardly a matter of intense controversy. However, Lord Kilmuir, having consulted the then holder of my office and the other Heads of Division, was of the opinion that, and again I quote, 'the importance of keeping the judiciary insulated from the controversies of the day' meant that it was preferable that judges did not take part. As Lord Kilmuir explained, 'so long as a judge keeps silent his reputation for wisdom and impartiality remains unassailable: but every utterance which he makes in public except in the course of the actual performance of his judicial duties, must necessarily bring him within the focus of criticism'. He added, therefore, it would 'be inappropriate for the judiciary to be associated with any series of talks or anything which can be fairly interpreted as entertainment'. The letter went on to make it clear that before engaging in public discussion, which would include discussion with the media, the judiciary should obtain the consent of the Lord Chancellor.

This was the cosy situation when I became a judge. It made life easy for the judiciary. If approached by a reporter, no matter how interesting the subject, they had a simple answer, 'not allowed to contribute without the Lord Chancellor's consent' and the media was well aware the consent was unlikely to be forthcoming in practice so this was the end of the discussion.

However, when Lord MacKay became Lord Chancellor in 1987 during his first interview with the press he took a different view. He stated that the rules laid down by Lord Kilmuir, were, and I quote, 'difficult to reconcile with the independence of the judiciary'. He therefore stated that he would no longer require judges to seek his consent to their contributing to public discussion. He added: 'I believe that those who have been given Her Majesty's commission for the discharge of judicial office should have the judgment to decide such matters for themselves'.[5] The change which he made was to place the responsibility to decide whether to contribute to public discussion on the shoulders of the judge concerned. He added that judges 'must avoid public statements either on general issues or particular cases which cast any doubt on their complete impartiality, and above all, they should avoid any involvement, either direct or indirect, in issues which are or might become politically controversial'.[6]

On the other hand, Lord Mackay recognised that there were cases in which the media might 'in a spirit of enquiry, wish to explore matters effecting the legal system . . . where the value of such programmes may be enhanced by the participation of a judge'.[7] This, however, still left a vacuum of which one circuit judge who had a penchant for self publicity was not slow to take advantage. I remember being consulted as to whether being engaged in a programme that was undoubtedly entertainment was misconduct.

---

[5] The remark was made in November 1987 and was subsequently repeated in Lord MacKay's Hamlyn Lecture, 'The Administration of Justice' (1994), 26.

[6] Ibid.

[7] Ibid.

Fortunately, the judge was a novelty of which the public soon tired and so the position, given time, resolved itself. With this exception however, our judiciary has behaved with great discretion. The positive side of the relationship has gone well. That is, members of the judiciary have gone on numerous programmes that did not involve political controversy. The media have been pleased they have done so and treated them fairly.

The position of the Lord Chief Justice and the senior judiciary has been recognised to be different. In a short 'Guide for Judges' issued by the former Lord Chancellor Lord Irvine in July 2000, he stated: 'It has long been accepted that the Lord Chief Justice and the senior judges may speak out in the House of Lords and elsewhere on behalf of the judiciary on matters affecting the administration of justice, such as mandatory life sentences for murder.'[8] The example given makes clear I was the Chief Justice at the time. The Manual also accurately reports the fact that public scrutiny of the justice system has increased in recent years and that the number of column inches and broadcast time devoted to it has grown accordingly. The causes are probably a combination of the growth of judicial review, the Human Rights Act 1998, and the fact that, for long periods of time, we have until recently had a parliamentary situation where the government has had a substantial majority and first one, and then the other, main opposition party has been in disarray.

With the increased reporting of our activities has come more misreporting, especially in relation to sentencing, which by now you will have realised is my hobby horse. The misreporting is often innocent, but a problem is created for the judiciary. Once there is an inaccurate report, the misreporting tends to be repeated again and again and can be extremely damaging to the public's confidence in the legal system. This is what has happened in relation to sentencing guidelines for burglary. It has been reported that I do not consider burglars should be sent to prison. Repeated sufficiently, the misquotation has become an accepted fact. That it is nonsense the press have now accepted. We therefore try by letter to obtain retractions and, above all, a correction of the archives. We also are better in assisting the press not to make mistakes. Summaries of complicated judgments are handed down; sentencing remarks are reduced to writing and we have at many courts a judge or other official who can provide an accurate account of what actually happened in court.

---

[8] *The Media: A Guide for Judges* (Lord Chancellor's Department, July 2000).

We were greatly helped in the past by the old Lord Chancellor's Press Office, and the judiciary now has a press office of its own, the Judicial Communications Office. Not, I emphasise, to spin, but to provide the media with the basic facts they need. It is to be hoped we can, in this way, proceed without again having to rely on the law of contempt to protect the dignity of our judges; though this is becoming more difficult. I remember well Lord Denning expressing the view that judges are not personally affected by what they have to read about themselves in the media. I am not sure. His remarks were in the days before the door-stepping of judges and what can be intense and unpleasant media pressure. As the Strasbourg Court has recognised, proceedings for contempt can be justified.

The relationship between the judiciary and the press is an evolving saga. It is not even possible to speculate how matters will develop. I can only express the hope that the media and the judiciary will continue to be on speaking terms. It is in the interests of both that this continues to be the position. In any event, I am most grateful to RTÉ and University College Dublin for giving me the opportunity to speak to you tonight.

9

Judicial Independence Not Judicial Isolation

Abstract This paper argues that the judiciary should be both independent and involved. It should not be isolated. In any jurisdiction the
existence of a judiciary which is both individually and institutionally
independent is critical to the rule of law. Recent constitutional upheavals
are fundamentally altering the relationship between the judiciary
and the other arms of government. This paper expresses concern that
while some of the changes will, as is intended, increase the protection of
independence for the judiciary, others will undermine the checks and
balances which have contributed to that independence. Increasing the
separation of the judiciary from the other arms of government risks
isolation which can itself damage the administration of justice.

Introduction

I congratulate Clifford Chance for sponsoring this series of lectures. Clifford
Chance is a prestigious and highly successful law firm. I find it reassuring
that they are also hugely supportive of Academic Institutions, regularly
sponsoring series of lectures such as this. It demonstrates that contrary to
suggestions lawyers are not generous when it comes to charity, there are law
firms which recognise that with success comes responsibility. For example,
the responsibility for supporting universities like Essex who help to provide
the young lawyers upon whom Clifford Chance's and other legal firms' continued success depends. Having recently returned from the US and visited
two US University law schools, I recognise how important such generosity is.
The law schools in the States are endowed on a scale that is unknown in this

---

* Originally delivered as the Clifford Chance Lecture at the University of Essex, on 26 April 2007.

country and this is all too evident in the difference between our and their facilities that are available for law students.

Professor Maurice Sunkin, whose empirical research I have admired for very many years, invited me to give this lecture. He told me I could choose my own topic, but that my subject should be of 'key contemporary importance designed to attract the interest of opinion-formers from both within and beyond the legal profession'.

When I look round the audience, I am bound to say you look to me as though you could be 'opinion-formers', though I defer to your own opinion as to whether you are or not. I have to confess I am not sure what an audience of opinion-formers looks like.

The Title

The title of my talk is intended to suggest that our judiciary should be both independent and involved. Our judiciary should not be isolated. In any jurisdiction the existence of a judiciary which is both individually and institutionally independent is critical to the rule of law. So my subject is one of importance. Furthermore, as to the requirement that the issue should also be 'contemporary', it is the recent constitutional upheavals (the last of which has been announced and now partly implemented) which are fundamentally altering the relationship between the judiciary and the other arms of government that have highlighted the problem. This also explains why I have chosen this subject. It is because I am concerned that while some of the changes will, as is intended, increase the protection for the independence of the judiciary, others will undermine the checks and balances which hitherto have contributed to that independence. This danger arises because the additional protection has been achieved by increasing the separation of the judiciary from the other arms of government. However, increased separation brings with it the risk of isolation which I will seek to demonstrate can, in our system of government, itself damage the administration of justice.

The Effect of the Human Rights Act 1998 on the Role of the Judiciary

That risk has to be taken seriously because this is a particularly sensitive time for the judiciary. The full significance of the Human Rights Act 1998 is only now beginning to be appreciated. Incorporating the European Convention has given the judiciary important increased responsibilities. In their judgments, the judiciary are now regularly required to balance the rights of the individual under the Convention against the interests of the State. This can involve determining whether legislation passed by Parliament conforms to the Convention and if it cannot be interpreted so that it conforms, declaring it incompatible to the Convention. This is a novel task for judges in a parliamentary democracy in which Parliament has always been considered to be sovereign. These tasks can be made even more difficult because, in cases involving suspected terrorists, the rights which have to be balanced are on the one hand the rights of those suspects and on the other, the perceived need for the government to protect the safety of the public.

It is beyond dispute that the judiciary cannot step aside from these responsibilities without breaching their fundamental obligation to uphold the rule of law. Happily, it is clear from their decisions that the courts from the House of Lords downwards have not shirked their duty. However, the existence of this responsibility undoubtedly strengthens the case for the separation of powers. It also creates pressures which, if not confronted, will damage the relationship between the judiciary and the other arms of government.

Separation of Powers and the Lord Chancellor

Many countries take the view that you cannot have an independent judiciary unless it is accompanied by the separation of powers. By the separation of powers, I mean separation between the legislature, the executive and the judiciary. The separation is said to be necessary so that one arm of government cannot interfere with other arms of government. In particular, it is critical that the executive is not in a position to dictate to the judiciary as to how they should decide the cases that come before them. This can and does happen still in some parts of the world. An example of what should not happen is provided by what the late Lord Desmond Ackner, christened 'telephone judges'—a telephone judge being a judge who, in some jurisdictions after he has heard a case, rings up the authorities for instructions as to how he should decide the case. It is obvious that such a practice is totally incompatible with the rule of law and the necessary independence which has two dimensions: first, independence as an individual judge and secondly, corporate independence as part of the judiciary as a whole. Independence in both senses is essential if justice is not only to be done, but also seen to be done. It is, however, corporate independence upon which I will be primarily focussing, since we are indeed fortunate in this country that in recent history the independence of our judges can be taken for granted. No one, not even a

Chief Justice, would be foolish enough to try to influence how an individual judge decides a case.

In this country there is probably a consensus as to the constitutional importance of there being a degree of separation of power between the three arms of government but there is no consensus as to the extent of the separation that is desirable. In almost all other countries, following the precedent set by the US that created its constitution 270 years ago, the separation of powers is an entrenched constitutional principle. By contrast our un-entrenched constitution has evolved over a millennium to what it is today. It started with a sovereign monarch with unlimited power. He or she was the executive, the legislator and the source of justice all in one. However, over the last decade we have been subject to unprecedented change and nearly every aspect of our constitutional arrangements has been the subject of a radical process of change, including the extent to which the judiciary are now separate from the other arms of government.

Some distinguished commentators have traced the seeds of the separation of powers of this country to the 13th Century. They include F W Maitland.[1] Viscount Bolingbroke (1678–1751) in *Remarks on the History of England* argued that the protection of liberty within a State involved achieving equilibrium between the Crown, parliament and the people. He propounded that 'in a constitution like ours, the safety of the whole depended on the balance of the parts'.

One of the chief proponents of the separation of powers was Baron Montesquieu (1689–1755). He lived in England for four years from 1729–1731. He was much impressed by what he thought he observed. He stressed the importance of the independence of the judiciary in *De l'Esperit des Lois* (1748) in terms of the separation of powers. His views were highly influential in relation to the United States Constitution. He stated:

> When the legislature and executive powers are united in the same person or in the same body of magistrates there can be no liberty . . . There would be an end to everything if the same men, or the same body, whether of the nobles or the people, were to exercise those three powers, that of enacting laws, that of executing public affairs, and that of trying crimes or individual causes.

So far as these remarks were based on his observations of the English scene, they were misconceived. The separation of powers was not then part of our constitutional tradition. Bolingbroke was more accurate in his description.

---

[1] (1908), 20.

What at that time was already illustrated by the English un-entrenched constitution was the virtue of checks and balances. Blackstone was a disciple of Montesquieu but he reworked his central idea. While it was of crucial importance to Blackstone that 'there should be sufficient separation of power to avoid tyranny' for him a partial separation is sufficient to achieve a mixed and balanced constitution.

However, even a limited separation of powers was hardly consistent with the existence of the great office of Lord Chancellor that has continued to evolve from 1068, when he was the King's secretary, to the present day. As the office evolved it became a living testament to the limited nature of separation of powers under our constitution. The Lord Chancellor's three principal roles, as part of the legislature, as Speaker of the House of Lords, as a member of the Executive holding a senior cabinet office and as head of the judiciary were, by the 21st Century, a remarkable and unique confrontation of the doctrine of the separation of powers. He was the most senior judge. Yet his selection for appointment is solely in the hands of the Prime Minister of the day. On appointment, he becomes one of the most senior members of his cabinet. But like any other member of the cabinet, his hold on his office is dependent on his party remaining in power and the Prime Minister's continued support. He has no security of tenure. By international standards the Lord Chancellor was entirely unsuited to be a judge but he was, until 2006, head of the English judiciary.

Yet far from the Lord Chancellor's triple roles being 'the end of everything', they were an important part of the answer to tyranny; they were part of the adhesive that held our un-entrenched constitution together. Not all holders of the office were equally effective and in recent times the office has placed huge demands upon its holder. Yet in practice the office, in addition to its other advantages, was capable of being and was seen by the judiciary as being an important part of their protection against outside interference. In addition, the Lord Chancellor was extremely influential in achieving the resources the judiciary needed to administer justice. The judiciary had their spokesman on the top table.

The Lord Chancellor's triple role was also extremely important from the point of view of the government of the day. He ensured judicial and government policy usually coincided. If there were differences he was the lightning conducted that prevented them from getting out of hand. His office was also partly the explanation as to why the judiciary, in addition to deciding cases, have come to play a critical role in the running of this country's justice system—a subject which I should now briefly deal with.

The Lord Chancellor's task of administering the courts has grown dramatically since the Courts Act 1972. That Act centralised the administration of a system that until then had been largely a fragmented cottage industry which was substantially administered locally. The magistrates' courts which provided local justice were under the umbrella of the Home Office. There were independent Borough and County Quarter Sessions administered by Recorders and the Chairman of County Quarter Sessions, as well as the different circuit Assizes, largely administered by the High Court judges visiting the circuit at any particular time. The cottage industry ran on a shoestring. Insofar as there was anything central, it consisted of the Lord Chancellor and a handful of officials who were predominantly lawyers.

The Courts Act 1970 implemented a highly critical report of an industrialist, Dr Beeching, 'the axe of the rail network'. His reforms resulted in the creation of a centralised structure with the Lord Chancellor at its pinnacle. Quarter Sessions and Assizes disappeared and were replaced by the Crown Courts, which were administered through officials exercising firm managerial control from Circuit Offices with a civil servant, a Circuit Administrator overseeing court administrators in charge of each Court.[2]

Initially, the judiciary withdrew almost completely from playing any part in the administration of the courts leaving, with relief, the responsibility for the administration to the ever-increasing number of civil servants employed by the Lord Chancellor. A similar process occurred in relation to legal aid, which had previously been run locally by the professions under the overall control of the Law Society. By 2000, the Lord Chancellor's Department had become a large and complex enterprise employing an appropriately large number of staff.

However, the clear lesson of those years was that the court system could only function through judges and officials working closely together throughout the system. Judges know about the workings of their courts better than anyone else. Administrators, however conscientious they are, lack this knowledge. To achieve the necessary harmonious working relations, a recommendation of the Beeching Report was implemented. The recommendation was for the appointment of a senior member of the judiciary who would have a general responsibility for Circuit matters and a particular responsibility for all matters affecting the judiciary serving there.

---

[2] *The Royal Commission on the Courts* (1996–1999) (Cmnd 4156), para 256.

This is what happened. The judge became the presiding judge of the circuit around whom developed a hierarchy of judges on each circuit matching the official of similar status in what became, in 1995, HM's Courts Service, an Executive Agency, reporting to the Lord Chancellor. Ten years later, in 2005, the administration of Magistrates' Courts were transferred to the Service as well, so that the Service was responsible in cooperation with the judiciary for administering all the courts in England and Wales.

With the passage of time, the Court Service developed its own ethos. This recognised that the Service's role in relation to the Courts meant its staff had to be conscious of the special nature and responsibility of their work for the courts and the judiciary involving, as it did, the need to preserve the independence of the judiciary. The involvement of the Lord Chancellor made the development of this special relationship far easier to achieve because the same individual was head of the judiciary and head of the department to which the Court Service reported. In my experience the relationship certainly worked well, with both sides cooperating closely to make the justice system effective. Such cooperation makes a significant contribution to the administration of justice.

This situation was assisted by the fact that as the office of Lord Chancellor evolved so did that of the Lord Chief Justice. By 2000, when I took office, the Lord Chief Justice was already the professional, although not the constitutional head of all the judiciary, with considerable administrative responsibilities. He was supported by a group of senior judges, including outstanding Senior Presiding Judges and subsequently, a Deputy Chief Justice who relieved the Chief Justice of some of the burden. Together with the other Heads of Division, he was in regular consultation with the Lord Chancellor. Although the Lord Chancellor had the last word, a multitude of decisions were being taken on a consensual basis in close consultation with the senior judiciary. In his negotiations with the Lord Chancellor, the Chief Justice could pray in aid the support of the Judges' Council, a council which could, with increasing justification, claim that it was the voice of the whole of the judiciary.

While the Lord Chancellor continued in his traditional role, I could be forgiven for believing that judicial independence was safe without the need for the separation of powers. Both the Lord Chancellor's Department and Parliament fully recognised the need to protect that independence and usually this was scrupulously observed.

Reform of the Office of Lord Chancellor

However, by the time I took office there was a question mark over the period that the office of Lord Chancellor could survive without being fundamentally overhauled. By the 21st century he had become an anachronistic figure. By international standards, his role appeared inconsistent with at least the appearance of judicial independence. In addition, it has to be admitted that at least in the case of the last two, and probably the last three, holders of the office the reality was very different from what the pomp and circumstance would lead you to believe: under the black and gold robes and wig, the Lord Chancellor was increasingly becoming a political figure, chairing cabinet committees and a close political ally of the Prime Minister. So much so, that when Lord Irvine compared himself to Cardinal Wolsey, the all powerful figure in the reign of Henry VIII, at first no one was sure whether he was joking.

When he was shadow Lord Chancellor, Lord Irvine had committed his party to support the introduction of the European Convention of Human Rights[3] into English domestic law. He prophesised that this could mean his appointment as Lord Chancellor would only be for the time it took to abolish the office. He recognised that the Court of Human Rights was firmly committed to ensuring the independence of the judiciary by insisting on the separation of powers.

There are now 46 countries in Europe to which the Convention applies. Many of the countries have no tradition of having an independent judiciary. It is therefore not surprising that European Court of Human Rights jurisprudence was more demanding than English law as to the formalities required to protect judicial independence. Under ECHR jurisprudence, it was doubtful whether the Lord Chancellor could meet the standards required by Article 6.[4] Despite these reservations, when the change occurred, it came unexpectedly out of the blue. The abolition of the office was announced as a part of a government ministerial reshuffle, in a press release. In fact it was impossible to abolish the office in this way and the office has survived, becoming held together with the office of Secretary of State for Constitutional Affairs.[5] The House of Lords is also to be replaced as our

---

[3] Hereafter, 'ECHR'.

[4] Article 6 ECHR provides the right of individuals to a fair and public hearing within a reasonable time by an independent and impartial tribunal.

[5] Now the Secretary of State for Justice.

final court of appeal by a separate Supreme Court. The Chief Justice has become the Head of the Judiciary.

The consultation that should have taken place earlier then took place between me, on behalf of the judiciary, and Lord Falconer, Lord Chancellor and Secretary of State. The result of the negotiations was a document known as the Concordat. The Concordat, applying agreed principles relating to the separation of powers, identifies what are the responsibilities for the judiciary that the Lord Chancellor retains, the responsibilities that are the Lord Chief Justice's and the responsibilities that are shared. The principles that were applied in drawing up the Concordat were later reflected in the Constitutional Reform Act 2005.

The agreeing of the Concordat was an example of the cooperation between Lord Chancellor and myself working together, which we were both anxious to preserve into the future. In the same spirit, a powerful judicial team, ably led by Lady Justice Arden and the Department's team were able to reach agreement over a mass of detailed provisions for dividing and sharing the former role of the Lord Chancellor. The agreement reached was a good omen for the future and, in due course, there was agreement as to the resources and staff that had to be transferred to the Lord Chief Justice to enable him to perform his responsibilities. The consensual nature of the operation should not disguise its scale. While there is no clear blue water between the judiciary and the executive and the judiciary and the legislature, the judiciary is now primarily dependent on the executive for resources and staff. The judges, while serving on the Supreme Court and the senior judges, who would have been Law Lords, will no longer be members of the House of Lords. There is a new independent appointment system for judges, in relation to which the Lord Chancellor's role is now limited to saying 'no' to one candidate recommended by the independent commission, over which he has no control. There is also a new system for dealing with complaints. This requires the agreement of the Lord Chancellor and the Chief Justice before action is taken.

It is true that in the normal way the judiciary should be in control of its own resources because otherwise in theory their independence could be undermined. However, although as we will see the resources provided, especially for civil litigation, need to be more generous, in practice resources have never to my knowledge been used as a lever to interfere with the judiciary's independence. In addition, during its passage through Parliament, useful provisions were added to the Act placing Ministers and, in particular the Lord Chancellor, under express duties to protect their independence.

The first section of the Constitutional Reform Act provides:

> This Act does not adversely affect:—
> (a) the existing constitutional principle of the rule of law; or,
> (b) the Lord Chancellor's existing constitutional role in relation to that principle.

Section 3 provides:

> (1) The Lord Chancellor, other Ministers of the Crown and all with responsibility for matters relating to the judiciary or otherwise to the administration of justice must uphold the continued independence of the judiciary ...
> (5) The Lord Chancellor and Ministers of the Crown must not seek to influence particular judicial decisions through any special access to the judiciary.
> (6) The Lord Chancellor must have regard to:—
> (a) the need to defend that independence;
> (b) the need for the judiciary to have the support necessary to enable them to exercise their functions;
> (c) the need for the public interest in regard to matters relating to the judiciary or otherwise to the administration of justice to be properly represented.

The 2005 Act already imposed an express duty on the Lord Chancellor to ensure that the courts receive the resources that the judges need to exercise their functions. Despite this, in a lecture Lord Phillips, the Lord Chief justice, gave earlier in 2007 to the Judicial Studies Board, he stated he had real concerns as to resources.[6] He was right to be worried. Reports that he had been receiving from all over the country show that these economies imposed because of financial stringency are damaging the administration of justice. They have led Judge Paul Collins to protest publicly at the problems that resource restrictions are having on the functioning of civil justice in Central London.

Speaking on Radio 4 he said:

> I believe that the civil justice system is currently in crisis and it seems to me that the effect of the cuts this year together with further cuts looming throughout the life of the next comprehensive spending review will if visited upon the County Courts, run the risk of bringing about a real collapse in the service that we are able to give to litigants.

---

[6] N Phillips, 'Constitutional Reform One Year On', the Judicial Studies Board Annual Lecture, Inner Temple, on 22 March 2007.

The Magistrates Association was led to write to the Prime Minister protest-ing, I quote, that 'the extent of the financial cuts that have been made in recent years makes it impossible for the system to perform adequately'. This is a serious situation, but it does not relate to the separation of powers or the independence of the judiciary. It demonstrates a failure of the government to attach sufficient importance to the needs of the justice system and certainly a failure of Lord Falconer's formidable advocacy on behalf of the courts.

A Ministry of Justice

In March 2007 the Prime Minister again surprised us, although this time there was some advance notice of what was proposed. From May, the Lord Chancellor became the head of a Ministry of Justice. Such a Ministry should not directly adversely affect the position of the judiciary, and clearly it has benefits in bringing all the agencies other than the police, immigration and anti-terrorism under one departmental roof. However, this may be one proposal where the devil is in the detail. In addition, it may merely be an example of passing on an unattractive parcel from a department 'not fit for purpose'.

In recent years there has been crisis after crisis involving the Home Office. The Home Office has a massive portfolio of responsibilities, many of which are of high sensitivity. Some of the most highly charged of these responsibilities have been transferred to the new Ministry of Justice. They include the continually controversial subjects of Criminal Justice Policy, Prisons and Probation. The additional burdens are bound to divert the atten-tion of the Lord Chancellor from his existing responsibilities. In addition, unless resources are ring-fenced, there is likely to be an enhanced risk of resources being diverted from the courts, aggravating the situation to which I have already referred. Also, Jack Straw MP, is Lord Falconer's successor in the Commons *and* is a lawyer. Despite the new Department's title, there is a real danger that justice will become a backwater so far as the Department is concerned.

When the 2005 Act was proceeding through Parliament all sides, while accepting the need for change, wished to preserve, so far as possible, the unique features of the office of Lord Chancellor that has preserved our adherence to the rule of law. The scale of this most recent further change in our constitutional arrangements makes preservation so much more difficult that the change should have been subject to detailed public scrutiny, but this has not happened.

My concerns are enhanced by the fact that during my period of office, as is already in the public domain, with senior colleagues I had exercised my traditional right to see the Prime Minister because of a threatened transfer of responsibilities in the opposite direction, from the Lord Chancellor to the Home Office. We felt constitutionally this was highly undesirable, not least because of the volume of litigation in which the Home Office is involved. The Prime Minister, in deference to our concerns, did not proceed with this proposal for which my colleagues and I were grateful. Much of the litigation hitherto will now be against the new Department and so raises the same concerns. I appreciate that it will be said there are many countries that have a Ministry of Justice that have the same responsibilities put in place in this jurisdiction. However, the difference is that those countries have entrenched constitutional protection of their liberties that we do not possess. Instead, we rely on checks and balances that have evolved over the centuries, which were personified in the former role of the Lord Chancellor.

The Attorney-General

The office of Attorney-General has a long and distinguished history similar to that of the Lord Chancellor. He also has in his wardrobe a selection of headgear to be worn when he performs his different roles. He is responsible for advising the government on legal issues, he is the guardian and the advocate of the public interest, which gives him a special role in relation to the courts.

Our penal policy is certainly in need of courageous and urgent reform. The numbers are increasing, remorselessly soaking up more and more money to little, if any, effect. Regrettably, we seem bent on following the policies that have been so unsuccessful in the States.

Two areas of policy that have been retained by the Home Office are responsibility for terrorism and asylum. These are areas that have been responsible for a number of decisions by the courts that have been extremely unpopular with the government. For example, the House of Lords have made decisions that overturned the detention of suspected terrorists who, it was thought, could not be tried in the normal way.[7] There was at least

---

[7] See, for example, *A v Secretary of State for the Home Department* [2004] UKHL 56, [2005] 2 AC 68.

a procedure by which the detainees could test the lawfulness of their detention but this, as was appreciated, did not conform to Article 5 of the ECHR and so the government had attempted to exercise their right to derogate from that Article. Although the government no doubt did their best to balance the needs of security and the detainees, they found as a result of the House of Lords' decision that their policy was in disarray. The government then came up with control orders under which detainees were detained in their homes instead of in prison. However, this form of detention was also condemned by the courts.

Charles Clarke, who was the then Home Secretary, was at a loss as to what else he could do. He was convinced the detainees were a danger, but he felt the courts were making his task of protecting the public impossible. He therefore wanted to meet the Law Lords informally to ascertain whether it was possible to find a solution that was acceptable to them. His invitation was refused. He was incensed by this and although he ceased to be Home Secretary prematurely, he was still very angry and expressed his view trenchantly to the media.

During my period as Chief Justice, I arranged for senior judges to be represented on the various coordinating committees that exist as part of the partnership to which I have referred. In addition, I had numerous personal meetings with the former Home Secretary as well as the previous Lord Chancellor. However, these were issues relating to the working of the courts, not to discuss matters that relate to issues involving the government that could come before the courts for decision. As to the issues that come before the courts for decision, there can be no question of the judiciary giving one party, even the government, access—formal or informal—to the Judiciary relating to disputes that they have to resolve. The one area where judicial independence requires total separation—yes, isolation—is in respect of the decision-making process.

While that must be clear, I understand and have some sympathy for Mr Clark's problem. Based on his experience, he had to go to considerable pains, advised by his lawyers, to put in place for the public's benefit a system for dealing with potential terrorists which he considered conformed to the law, only to have it struck down by the courts. He needed greater certainty as to the law and he needed it before, not after, he had gone to considerable expense and time to produce the system on which the courts would inevitably pronounce.

As much as certainty of the law is desirable, it cannot be obtained by backdoor access to judges. However, especially in areas such as counter terrorism, the courts must be sympathetic to requests to give guidance in their judgments. In France the *Conseil d'Etat* has a system which enables guidance to be given as to the merits of proposed legislation. However, in practice there are difficulties in achieving this in a common law system. Having thought about the problem for some time, I believe we could and should develop a procedure in situations where there are issues of great national importance to resolve.

Courts never like expressing views as to hypothetical situations. They need to use their time to resolve real disputes. We do, however, have a developing declaratory jurisdiction in England and, in appropriate circumstances this could be developed into providing a solution. It would be necessary to have proper interested parties to bring and defend the proceedings. However, the proceedings in England could be brought against the Attorney-General representing the State and there would be no shortage of public interest bodies which could represent the claimants. The Court would have total discretion over when and how proceedings are brought, but in the appropriate circumstances I believe they could be of great benefit.

The proceedings would also be a further example of close cooperation between two arms of government that should dispel any image of the judiciary being cloistered in isolation in some ivory tower.

10

The Needs of a 21st Century Judge

Abstract This paper suggests the judiciary has coped extraordinary well with changes imposed upon them in recent times. It attributes this success in part to the role played by the Judicial Studies Board. It would have been very difficult to successfully introduce the civil justice reforms, or implement the Human Rights Act 1998, without the training which the JSB provided. There is a discussion on the qualities required of being a judge and the role judges have to play in modern society. New demands are being placed upon judges. Referring, by way of example, to the civil justice reforms which have significantly extended the discretion of the judiciary as to case management decisions, it emphasises that the judiciary require skills which they currently lack. More resources are required to meet the long-term needs of the judiciary if it is to meet the needs of society in the 21st century.

For the last few years the justice system in this country has been subjected to unprecedented change. I sometimes think that the only thing that has not either changed, or is in the process of change, or the subject of a proposal for change, is the robes we wear. The system has stood up to the process extraordinarily well. The judiciary has also coped extraordinarily well with the changes imposed upon them. Remarkably, they have taken in their stride a fundamentally different approach to family law, civil procedure, and an ever more complex process of sentencing. They have also absorbed an entirely new tier of the judiciary. It is early days yet but the omens are encouraging to say that the domesticating of human rights has been achieved astonishingly smoothly.

That this has been possible is undoubtedly in part due to the Judicial Studies Board,[1] an institution which some feared and others regarded as unnecessary

---

* This lecture was originally given at the Judicial Studies Board, London, on 22 March 2001.

[1] Hereafter, 'the JSB'.

when it was established, but which is now recognised as being an immense success. It is an institution which is already of fundamental importance to the judiciary at all levels. Its beneficial influence has been considerable.

It was established, thanks to a recommendation contained in a report of Lord Justice Bridge,[2] in 1979, the year I was appointed a judge. The initial remit was confined to the full and part-time judiciary of the Crown Court and it made no impact on a newly appointed High Court Judge such as myself. Even when it was recreated in 1985 to provide Family and Civil training, it was not directly concerned with the senior judiciary. If you were appointed to the High Court bench, it was assumed that the fact that you had been meant that you must know how to perform your responsibilities.

When Lord Lloyd was appointed High Court Judge in 1978, I remember how his fellow junior judges admired his courage when he confronted the then Chief Justice, Lord Widgery. Lord Widgery was a forbidding figure. He looked the image of the brigadier that he had been during the war. The newly appointed Lloyd J told the Chief he was not prepared to travel forthwith to Liverpool to try a murder case. He pointed out, I thought not unreasonably, that it just would not do for his first experience of having to address a jury, or witness a jury trial, to be as the trial judge in a murder trial. On reflection, the Lord Chief Justice did not disagree and Lloyd J was allowed to spend three or four days at the Bailey before he presided over his first jury trial. I believe that this incident would never happen today. This is because the judge would almost inevitably have been a recorder or part-time judge and would have attended at least one residential JSB course.[3]

The JSB has become, so far as its present role is concerned, a centre of excellence. Its remit has been continuously expanded. It now includes Crown, Family, and Civil Court induction and continuation courses for full and part-time judges. It also covers ticketed family judges, stipendiary judges and tribunals. In the year 2000, it included among its participants High Court, District and Deputy Judges.[4] It does not purport to be a law school but

---

[2] Now, the late Lord Bridge, a former Lord of Appeal in Ordinary.

[3] Consider the position in Australia, where newly appointed judges attend a week-long orientation programme run by the Australian Institute of Judicial Administration. Similar programmes are run in America by the Federal Judicial Center and in New Zealand by the Institute of Judicial Studies which was established in 1998 to assist professional development, promote judicial excellence and foster awareness of judicial administration, developments in the law and social and community issues.

[4] This was still the case in 2007.

it in fact provides excellent publications which have a huge influence on the way the judiciary works. It does all this with an administrative staff of 26 and just one virtually full-time Circuit Judge Director (previously two) operating under a Board chaired by a Lord Justice and respective committees.[5] The cost in 2000 was a modest £5m,[6] a sum far exceeded by the savings it helped to generate through reduced numbers of appeals and more efficient conduct of trials.

I have no doubt that all who have been involved, particularly the successive judicial chairmen and directors, deserve our unqualified gratitude. I welcome this opportunity to publicly offer my congratulations to them for this immense contribution, which they have made to our legal system. It would have been impossible to successfully introduce the civil justice reforms without the training which the JSB provided, under the wise stewardship of Lord Justice Henry, or implement the Human Rights Act 1998 without the equally constructive contribution of the JSB under Lord Justice Waller, and their respective Directors of Studies, Christopher Sumner, Paul Collins, Christopher Pitchers and David Pearl.

However, it was my thesis that the time had come for the role of the JSB to be significantly expanded.[7] I regarded this not as an option; it was essential. Its role did not include valuable features that similar institutions in other common law and civil jurisdictions were providing. This had to be remedied. However, my contention was more fundamental. This was that the JSB was still the most obvious body to perform a vital role—which I will explain—which was and is not performed elsewhere.

Part of the reason the JSB is a success story is the fact that it is based on judges training judges. Until recently, we lacked any institution that acts as a think tank. The type of issues we have needed judges to consider have included:

(1) the qualities we should be seeking in the judges we appoint and promote;

(2) how we appoint judges;

(3) their terms of appointment;

(4) their deployment;

(5) their career development;

---

[5] The latest figures available from the JSB Annual Report 2006–2007 reveal that there are now 59 permanent members of staff and the Secretariat's headcount ceiling is 65.

[6] For 2006–2007, this figure had increased to £8.1m. Ibid.

[7] The role of the JSB has expanded considerably since this paper was originally given. See Postscript below.

(6) management of judges;

(7) the support which the contemporary judge requires; and

(8) the role of the judiciary in promoting mediation.

These were all subjects of interest to the old Lord Chancellor's Department[8] but the judiciary's contribution had been entirely reactive; it should have been proactive. The fact that it was reactive meant that many of the subjects did not receive the consideration they should. This resulted in decisions which were neither in the interest of the judiciary nor the public and decisions not being taken which would be in the interests of both.

The judiciary has grown in size but the senior judiciary, with notable and distinguished exceptions, have until recently been recruited by very much the same process and from the same section of the practising profession as when I became a judge in 1979. Furthermore, at least to the casual onlooker, the way in which the judiciary performs its role has not altered since when I became a judge. The Queen's Bench judges still travel on circuit in much the same way as they did. We still have the distinction between the Divisions. Non-Chancery practitioners are appointed to the Chancery Division.

There are new court buildings but the courts in those buildings are contemporary reproductions of the courts in the old buildings. The furniture may be lighter but the layout is basically unaltered. Are the designs still correct? Should they be based on the United States concept of the multi-door court so as to reflect the new responsibility of the judiciary to support Alternative Dispute Resolution?

So far I have been talking of the past. But the dimension of the changes which the judiciary has had to absorb up to now diminishes dramatically when compared with the scale of change with which it is faced in the foreseeable future. The scale of this change is daunting but it should be welcomed. I have repeatedly said that although this may not be as widely accepted as it should be, we have the finest judiciary in the world. However, if we are going to maintain this position, it is essential that the judiciary itself presses energetically for the resources which it needs if it is to perform its role effectively in the future.

Why do I believe the changes are going to be so dramatic? Well, first of all, there is the impact that Information Technology[9] is having and will continue

---

[8] This is now the responsibility of the Secretary of State for Justice and the Judicial Appointments Commission.

[9] Hereafter, 'IT'.

to have on the way in which the justice system works. If any confirmation of this is required, it is provided by the consultation paper issued by the old Lord Chancellor's Department in January 2001 under the title *Modernising the Civil Courts*[10] as part of the Modernising Government Programme. The former Lord Chancellor's Parliamentary Secretary, in launching the report, said this:

> The way we run our courts has not in essence changed for 150 years. Almost every court still operates as both a hearing centre and administering the cases under its control. Whilst other services in the public and private sector have centralised administration and gain tangible benefits from IT to benefit their services, investment in the civil courts has been very limited ...
>
> It is not necessarily right to run our civil courts in the 21st century using the systems developed in the 19th century. Just as banking, insurance and many public services have modernised so our courts can and must take advantage of new technology and new ways of working and deliver the benefits to those who use the courts ...
>
> Modern technology allows the front office to leap beyond the doors of the court on to the personal computer and the digital TV and to develop partnerships with solicitors and advice agencies so that everyone has the opportunity to benefit from the new ways of working. This is an exciting concept.

I wholly agree.

MCC was an inspirational and visionary document. It was only a consultation paper but it made a serious attempt to demonstrate what should be the long-term objectives for the civil courts. A document of this sort is essential if the modernisation of the civil court is to be efficiently programmed. I am pleased that it acknowledged that the 'support to the judiciary is central to the success of MCC and to the purpose and objectives of the Court Service'. I am also delighted that Lord Justice Brooke was a member of the Programme Board charged with the task of taking forward the initiative. The work of the Board was also supported by a judicial working group led by Cresswell J, which had among its members judges who were highly experienced in judicial work at different levels. The programme did not deal with the modernising of the judiciary but it made clear that the manner in which the judiciary worked would be transformed.

I am immensely grateful to the members of the judiciary who contributed to its thinking. It took forward what was recommended in my civil justice report and reflected the thinking of Richard Susskind, who was the

---

[10] Lord Chancellor's Department (HMSO, January 2001). Hereafter, 'the MCC'.

consultant to the report and has been both Tom Bingham's[11] and my IT adviser. However, neither I nor any other of the Heads of Division or their deputies could have taken on the task of providing the substantial judicial input required which meant that the needs of the modern judge are properly reflected in what was recommended. Instead, a group of judges under Cresswell J who had the necessary knowledge ensured that the needs of the modern judge were properly taken into account. Judges made this contribution, involving many hours work, in addition to their normal judicial duty.[12] We know there have been hiccups: the IT of clerks has not been compatible with that of their judges; training has not been properly focussed, but we are making progress thanks to the help of judicial volunteers. But in the public interest, this is not the way that we should be looking at what the modern judge needs. It is obvious that we have to do better. To help bridge the gap, Brooke LJ took on yet another task: he was the Judge in Charge of Modernisation.

So far as the criminal justice system is concerned, the government produced proposals in its paper 'Criminal Justice—The Way Ahead'.[13] It was intended to be a blueprint for the modernisation of the criminal justice system. Like the MCC, it deserved careful study. It should, however, be regarded as being subject to a warning: 'subject to revision in the light of the Auld report'. Nevertheless, it was a radical document.

Sir Andrew Leggatt's report on the tribunal system was equally far reaching in its impact as the reports to which I have already referred. The Crown Prosecution Service has been through a process of change as a result of the report of Sir Iain Glidewell. There is also the report on modernisation of the Commercial Court.[14] This by no means exhaustive list of consultation documents provides compelling support for my conclusion as to the scale of change that lies ahead. They also confirm the amount of thought that continues to be given to the changes that have been needed to the justice system. However, the area on which the reports are silent was the strategic changes which may need to take place in the judiciary if we are to have

---

[11] Lord Bingham, Senior Law Lord.

[12] The introduction of IT to the judiciary has developed further. For example, the LINK project is bringing an IT infrastructure to all the judiciary and to court staff. It aims to provide desktop IT facilities and email access within the criminal and civil justice systems to facilitate better communication between the judiciary and staff with the public, colleagues and other Government Agencies.

[13] Secretary of State for the Home Department (HMSO, February 2001).

[14] More recently, for example, HM Courts Service announced, in 2006, the construction of a new Business Court in London.

a modern judiciary capable of performing their role in a manner which inspires public confidence.

The explanation for the inactivity in this area was probably a laudable desire to protect the independence of the judiciary. However, it was my belief that an in-depth examination of the way we use our judiciary was overdue. The judiciary would have had to be fully involved in any such review but it would have been assisted if the contribution it made was masterminded by a properly resourced think tank, constituting part of the JSB.

Fortunately the JSB was not oblivious to this need. In March 2001, it decided to conduct an analysis of the training needs of the senior judiciary. The first part of that review, namely the self-completion of a questionnaire distributed to all members of the senior judiciary, revealed interesting information as to the relationship between the judges' current work and their previous experience in practice. The survey indicated that there was, in the case of some judges, a substantial distinction between their previous expertise and the work which they now performed as judges (48 per cent). It also indicated that most judges would welcome having regular feedback on their performance. The survey also identified the tasks the judiciary found most difficult and how they thought their skills could be developed. I have no doubt that it provided useful guidance to the JSB as to the additional tasks that they should have been performing and for which they should have had the necessary resources.

The JSB survey was a most valuable start. It was supported by a questionnaire which I asked all High Court Judges to complete indicating their areas of interest and the categories of work which they would prefer to do, the period which they would like to spend on circuit and so on. This was a useful start. We were remarkably slow in seeking to find out the individual views of our judiciary.

However, a great deal more needed to be known before decisions could be taken. Let me give one example. In 2001, the whole judicial system was dependent upon the contribution of the part-time judiciary.[15] Our use of part-time judges in the UK is far greater than any other jurisdiction of which I am aware. I am in favour of a part-time judiciary because of the contribution which it makes to the selection and training of the permanent judiciary. However, the use of such a part-time judiciary far exceeds what is

---

[15] As at 1 February 2001, there were 2,379 part-time members of the judiciary. This figure comprised 1,344 Recorders, 764 Deputy District Judges and 171 Deputy District Judges (Magistrates Court).

required for this purpose. The Cause Lists indicate that deputy judges have sat as full-time judges. We have considered giving the deputies security of tenure. Is this desirable?

We were not aware of the reaction of the parties to having a deputy rather than a full-time judge. However, I strongly suspected the impression was adverse. The fact is that the volume of work which has attached to it the label 'High Court' and so gives the impression that it will be heard by High Court Judges is far in excess of that which High Court Judges can hear. A solution is to appoint a great many more High Court Judges. I would not favour this approach because of the potentially detrimental effect that it may have upon the calibre of the High Court Judge. The quality of our High Court judiciary is critical and I would not wish to see it watered down. The only alternative is to accept that a great deal of the work which is now labelled as being suitable for a High Court Judge should in fact be relabelled in some cases as 'Circuit Judge' work and possibly in other cases as 'Circuit Judge unless a High Court Judge is available'. The fact is that there are a great many more cases in the system now than previously which are extremely complex and raise very difficult issues. It is to the determination of these cases that High Court Judges should be confined. There is a need for greater selectivity in the allocation of cases.

The need for the reassessment of how we use High Court Judges is not confined to the Royal Courts of Justice. Nor is it confined to civil work. In 2001, Queen's Bench judges travelled to circuit centres for set periods of time. Attempts were made to match those periods of time to anticipated need but it was predominantly a time, rather than a work, dominated system. I had no doubt that it would be preferable if we could move to a system where the visits are matched to cases that really require a High Court judge to try them.

Grading cases by predetermined criteria is almost impossible. It requires sophisticated consideration. But an in-depth examination of the subject would be most valuable. The old Lord Chancellor's Department could commence the work but judicial input was essential. After all, the judiciary was (and is) best qualified to identify the manner in which scarce High Court Judge resources should best be deployed. Especially if we have the ability to use the advance video conferencing facilities which have recently come on stream, it may well be desirable for High Court judges to spend less time on circuit. Whether this is right or not will, however, depend on a careful survey of the work actually performed by High Court Judges on circuit at the present time. It is my belief that we need to perform a careful analysis of the potential of our different tiers of judges. The use of High Court Judges should however only be dictated by the complexity and importance of the cases waiting to be tried.

There are undoubted benefits of judges travelling out of London to different parts of the country quite apart from the number of cases which require determination. The visits play a very important role in maintaining collegiate judicial relations and standards. However, if it is recognised that this is the primary purpose of a visit, rather than the case work, then the visit can be tailored to meet this parochial agenda. A reassessment of the requirements of High Court Judges on circuit would not mean that any less work remained to be done. The shortfall between the work presently performed by the High Court Judges on circuit and that which would be performed in the future would fall to be dealt with by Circuit Judges. However, the success achieved by District Judges suggests that it would be very useful to reassess the relationships between the three tiers of the judiciary, at least as to civil work.

As to criminal work, there is the complication of the use of juries. It is, however, at least open to consideration that there is scope for raising the level of work done by Circuit Judges, or at least certain Circuit Judges, to cover much of the High Court work and for elements of their existing work to be performed by District Judges. The proposals already on the table of having larger court centres supported by satellite small courts have been supportive of this approach. The contemplated IT has also been supportive.

We are provided with the vision of paperless courts: documents entering the court system electronically and being distributed around the court system electronically. A system with an electronic basis of this nature can reassess the needs for judges to travel. Electronic files can be opened wherever the judge is for the time being and can revolutionise case management. They can also affect Listing. These are all subjects which have required in-depth analysis.

At the present time we have not obtained anything like the benefit that we should from case management. The primary reason has been that we have not been able to coordinate sittings with pre-reading time required by the judge. In the High Court, it has not been uncommon for a judge to commence a hearing and then be forced to adjourn for a period of time in order to complete the reading. The parties are entitled to expect that they come before a judge who is fully prepared to hear their case. In return, the court is entitled to expect the parties to provide the judge with the material required in sufficient time to allow him to carry out this preparation.

What happens at the beginning of a case is mirrored by what happens after the case is completed. The ideal time to write a judgment is immediately following the conclusion of a case. However, the manner in which we work means that unless the individual judge is prepared to insist upon time being made available at the end of the case for judgment writing, in the interest of the system as a whole he moves on to the next case before he is able to do more than scribble a few notes as to his views.

What has been needed, then, is a study as to the minimum time requirements of judges if they are to work efficiently and effectively. Judges practices and needs of course differ but there are basic minimum needs which should be clearly defined and set out as guidelines for those who are responsible for listing. A modernised court system must be one in which a judge is provided with the time to work efficiently.

The inroads on the judge's time are not only caused by the judge's court work. At all levels there are burdens of administration. The appointment of silks and the appointment of the part-time and full-time judiciary has only been as effective as they have been because of judicial input. The Court Service only works as effectively as it does because of judicial input. Judges have to take on increasingly administrative roles. The process of change is dependent upon judicial input. You do not need to perform my old job to know that unless the judiciary are prepared to make these contributions, the system would not work, or at least work as well as it does.

The partnership which developed between the old Lord Chancellor's Department and the Court Service on the one hand and the judiciary on the other was happily based on a satisfactory working relationship. However, the judicial contribution has been more necessary than ever before. It is no reflection on the Court Service or the old Lord Chancellor's Department that many of its senior posts have been staffed by officials who have not grown up within the court system. They have therefore had less instinctive understanding of what is or is not appropriate in the performance of judicial functions. This does not mean that I have disapproved of their involvement. On the contrary, I have been an enthusiastic convert to the need to have those with broader and varying experiences and backgrounds. However, if the talents which they bring are to be constructively used, they have to be supported by judicial input, in particular, input from those who have the background experience which they lack. To make their contribution, the judiciary in turn needs skills which they currently lack. They need to learn about management, they need to know about administration. We need to be able to quantify the amount and complexity of the work involved and the staff and training support that is needed to complete that work.

Our judiciary must not operate in isolation and in ignorance of what is happening in other parts of the world.[16] We do have a limited number of very successful judicial exchanges at a high level. However, seminars in other jurisdictions can make a substantial contribution to the career development of our judges. The former Lord Chancellor, Lord Irvine, announced an important initiative to assist the overseas judiciary and arrange visits to this country. Our senior judiciary have strongly supported this initiative. However this is an area where our contribution has depended entirely upon invitations extended by the judiciary of overseas jurisdictions to particular members of our judiciary who it is thought can assist the development of that overseas legal system. I would like to see, on a systematic basis as part of the career development of the judge, more encouragement to attend seminars organised by the JSB in both this country and abroad. It should be part of a judge's professional entitlement.[17] We have been parsimonious in our willingness to release our judges because of short-term need to staff our courts. We have to be prepared to spend time to save time. A judge who has been intellectually refreshed by attending a seminar or, dare I use the words, taking a sabbatical, could make a contribution on a different level than if he is ground down by unremitting toil at the coalface.

What about our terms of service? The Senior Salaries Review Body undertook an in-depth review once again in 2001. With the valuable help of the Vice-Chancellor and the Senior Presiding Judge, I did my best to ensure the judiciary's concerns were properly represented. Regrettably, our role has again been reactive. We have not had the resources to be proactive. The Lord Chancellor has certainly in his contribution taken our interests into

---

[16] Cf France. The National School for the Judiciary maintains links with a large number of foreign States through its International Sub-Division, which, between 1960 and 2001, trained 3,600 judges and prosecutors from around 100 countries.

[17] Consider, for example, the model of Mauritius, where although no formal institution comparable to the JSB exists, judges attend specialised conferences and seminars on a rotational basis, usually outside the jurisdiction. On average, a judge may attend such conferences twice yearly, spending two to four days per visit. Expenses are met by the government or the sponsors of the Conference. Another useful model is provided by the Family Court of Australia, which has conducted four-day National Conferences every three years. These Conferences have been attended by Judges, court staff and international speakers. In addition, the Court has organised training in gender and indigenous issues, family violence and from 2001, has offered a week-long intensive revision programme to one-third of all Family Court judges annually.

account but he also has to consider the interests of the government, which may not be identical. We need to be able to mount our own researched and well-documented contribution. It has been, for example, interesting to know how judges felt about our pension provisions, which are proportionately small by comparison with comparable jurisdictions.

All that I have said so far has emphasised the importance of a broader role for the JSB, including as a 'think tank' for the judiciary. The sort of issues which I have identified should be part of its agenda but the JSB has to be properly resourced to perform this task. We need a long-term strategy for the judiciary to match the strategy being provided for the courts and the civil and criminal justice systems. The judiciary must play a leading role in the creation of such a strategy. If the government is serious about modernising the justice system, as I am sure it is, then it should provide the resources to the JSB to enable it to play the role which is increasingly necessary.

We cannot, however, be complacent. The public has the right to demand not only a highly professional judiciary but also a judiciary that is more representative of the population than it is at present. The changing needs of society which have enhanced our role makes this justified. It is essential that we take steps to ensure that criticism is not justified. We have to recognise when appointing and promoting judges that their skills should not be confined to those traditionally thought necessary to preside at trials. The need for judicial administration and management skills must be acknowledged and taken into account when recruiting and appointing judges. We need to pay greater attention to management and career development issues. We have placed too much reliance upon the small group of our most senior judges to express the views of the judiciary as a whole to the Lord Chancellor and his department. As a judiciary, we have until recently neglected to develop a voice which can authoritatively speak for us all. The Judges Council could play this role but until recently it had not developed as it should. This has been hardly its fault. It had no resources, no dedicated staff or any terms of reference. Equivalent bodies in other jurisdictions have proper public status and issue annual reports. They have a programme of work.[18]

---

[18] Compare the Canadian Judicial Council which is accorded properly acknowledged public status and terms of reference and publishes an annual report providing a public statement of the activities of the Council in promoting the status of the Canadian federal judiciary. The Council also has responsibility for setting policies for judicial training (for example, it has launched a

We have needed to build lines of communication between the Judges Council and the JSB. The Judges Council must be able to speak for the judiciary as a whole. The judiciary must support the Judges Council as its spokesman so that it carries conviction when it speaks to the public at large. It has needed to become a proactive body. It has required terms of reference which clearly identify its responsibilities. By 2001, the Judges Council had recruited a senior representative of the Council of Circuit Judges and the Association of District Judges. This was a step in the right direction. However, this was also the time for it to expand its role so that it became the voice-piece of the judiciary. It needed to have the ability to set up committees and working parties. It needs to be a driving force spearheading the modernisation of the judiciary.

The Judges Council must not, however, become a voice of conservatism with a small 'c'. It must not see itself as seeking to protect the status quo. Instead it should be encouraging judicial evolution. It should be exploring the issues which face the judiciary as part of the modernisation programme. It should be closely involved in an enhanced JSB.

The Judges Council should also be taking the lead by embracing the requirement for performance appraisal. One of the interesting facts which emerged from the JSB survey was that the majority of members of the judiciary would welcome feedback on their performance. I can well understand this. It is extremely lonely sitting as a single judge. Even when sitting with colleagues, judges are remarkably circumspect about commenting on each other's performance. Of course, except for the House of Lords, our decisions are subject to the appraisal of an appeal court. Even in the case of the House of Lords, the speeches of their Lords are subject to the most critical academic scrutiny. At least in crime, the marking of their speeches by a professor with the initials 'JS' suggest that even the most sympathetic admirer might not be surprised if the judges' overall marks indicated room for improvement. But there is more to being a judge than giving a decision that is 'appeal proof'. What needs to be assessed in addition to our decisions is our interpersonal skills, our listening skills, and our skills in expressing ourselves orally. We all need a totally honest mentor to comment on our performance. The problem is that once we are appointed, we acquire bad habits of which we are not aware. Even if we start off as the model judge, it is easy to allow our standards to slide and to be unaware that this has occurred.

---

programme of social context education for judges) which a dedicated judicial training institution then implements.

I see no reason why we should not be prepared to subject our efficiency as judges to scrutiny by judges. A judge who is taking demonstrably longer than others to progress his work is a matter of concern. Without in any way subjecting him to criticism, he might need help and support. For a colleague who has the necessary skills and experience to talk the issue through with the judge in question can only be helpful for the individual judge and the system as a whole.

One of the consequences of the civil justice reforms is to significantly extend the discretion of the judiciary as to case management decisions. This creates new demands and new techniques but it also requires a degree of consistency and the use of training and discussion to promote consistency is clearly extremely important.

We should also be prepared to measure our performance against the standard of throughput, efficiency, and costs in other jurisdictions. My pride in our judiciary does not mean that we cannot learn from others.

I would eschew any idea of annual appraisal of judges even by colleagues. However, I have not been adverse to a culture developing where each member of the judiciary has the expectation that a more senior colleague would, once a year, discuss what can be done by way of training or otherwise to promote greater effectiveness and job satisfaction. Certainly while Chief Justice, my foray on circuit, where I sat at first instance, brought home to me how difficult it is to be a judge today and engendered within me an enthusiasm for the safety of the Court of Appeal Criminal Division!

While I regard this limited form of appraisal as justified in its own right, I do not lose sight of the fact that public perception is also important. In a world where appraisal in almost every activity is a matter of course, it does not necessarily help to win friends and increase trust and confidence of the public if the judiciary regard any form of appraisal as an anathema. Certainly I do not believe that what I have proposed would interfere with the independence of the judiciary.

I am afraid that we must be concerned about our image. Anything which helps this is important. You know of my enthusiasm for the schools programme. It has also been suggested that we establish a judicial website. The Lord Chancellor devised his website, so too did the JSB. There was merit in the judiciary, under the umbrella of the Judicial Council, having its own website as a means of promoting the image of the judiciary.[19]

---

[19] The judiciary now has its own website. See <http://www.judiciary.gov.uk>.

Finally, I come to the question of personal support for the judiciary. Seminars organised by the JSB have been a critical part of that support. So is the correct IT. But in addition, judges, particularly those who have an administrative and managerial role, are badly served by secretarial and other support. In the Court of Appeal, we have judicial assistants. I am sure they should be available to High Court Judges as well. High Court Judges have their clerks. Their role has not been appreciated as it should. Most judges are full of praise for their clerks. However, the character of the clerk is changing. They are becoming younger. There are many more women. Appointment is no longer at the end of an individual's career path. Their present role is well known to us all and I need not repeat it. The question is, should it be different? I believe that this question deserves careful examination.

As an example of what clerks can achieve, I cite a former clerk of mine who, with the support of the Court Service, aspired to qualify as a Fellow of the Institute of Legal Executives. In addition to her ordinary duties as my clerk, she had the responsibility of providing leadership to all the other judges' clerks. In 2001, this involved a commitment to 144 clerks. I would like to see all the judges' clerks having the opportunity to train to be Legal Executives or to complete an NVQ course designed by ILEX to meet their needs. With this qualification, they could be entrusted with more responsibility in relation to the management of their judge's work than at present. They could become an all-round assistant to their judge. With the introduction of the IT that we have been promised, clerks would be able to monitor the case load of their judge. They could play a more proactive role in discussing cases with the parties. Any in-depth examination of the future role of the judiciary must include the role of the judge's clerk. As the judicial role evolves, so should that of the clerk. The services of a clerk are after all guaranteed by statute.

By comparison to the High Court Judge, Circuit and District Judges are very badly served in terms of support, particularly where they have an additional administrative role, such as that of Resident Judge. Assessment of their needs and methods of adequately fulfilling this need has been long overdue.

This may appear to have been an over ambitious shopping list. But it has been in fact no more than a plea for an enhanced role for both the JSB and the Judges Council to enable the issues I have raised to be more fully explored. My comments are but the thoughts of a single judge. My expectations are limited to persuading my audience, who may otherwise not have had to endure this talk, that in this jurisdiction we have not, until recently, devoted sufficient time and resources to the long-term needs of our judiciary. Recently, improvements have been made, but more can and must be done. If this situation is not rectified adequately it is the public and the reputation of our legal system at home and abroad which will be the losers.

Postscript

Since this paper was given in 2001, there have been considerable developments in the roles of both the Judges Council and JSB, some of which address the challenges I discussed above.

In 2002, the Judges Council adopted a written constitution and has subsequently widened its membership to include representatives from all areas of the judiciary including the House of Lords, the Circuit and District Benches, the Magistrates Association and Tribunals. In March 2006, the Council further revised its constitution and membership following the coming into effect of the Constitutional Reform Act 2005. This Act and the Concordat vest in the Lord Chief Justice very considerable responsibilities in respect of the judiciary and of the business of the courts of England and Wales. The Lord Chief Justice exercises these responsibilities through the Judges' Council and the Judicial Executive Board.

The primary function of the present Judges' Council is now to be a body broadly representative of the judiciary as a whole which will inform and advise the Lord Chief Justice on matters as requested from time to time. At present these include:

(1) the maintenance of judicial independence;
(2) maintaining and developing a Judicial Code of Conduct;
(3) developing general policy for the welfare and guidance of the judiciary, including policy on career development and diversity;
(4) considering and making recommendations on the spending review priorities, targets and plans as they affect the judiciary and the financing and resources for the court system;
(5) considering and making representations as to the terms and conditions of Judges' employment, including pay and pensions;
(6) responding to consultation papers on policy and law reform;
(7) developing and making recommendations on IT policy through a standing committee, the Judicial Technology Board; and

(8) liaising with the Judicial Appointments Commission and the Judicial Studies Board.

The Judges' Council is also consulted to obtain a wide perspective on matters which concern more than one discrete judicial grouping. It considers and conveys views, ideas or concerns of the wider judicial family; provides detailed analysis and consideration of specific matters on which judicial views are sought and develops policy in matters within its areas of functional responsibility.

The present Council meets at least six times a year and is chaired by the Lord Chief Justice. With the exception of the Senior Presiding Judge, the other 16 members are selected by the Judicial Group or constituency which that member represents. Detailed work is now carried out through standing committees and working groups.

The Council is assigned the function of meeting with the Chief Executive of Her Majesty's Court Service to provide judicial input on resources. It has also recently selected three judicial members of the Judicial Appointments Commission. The Council is supported by its own independent Secretariat, publishes regular Newsletters to the judiciary and an annual report. Finally, it responds to government proposals on issues which have a direct impact on the running of the courts. The role of the Judges Council has vastly improved since 2001.

The constitutional changes implemented in April 2006, as the result of which responsibility for the judiciary moved from the Lord Chancellor to the Lord Chief Justice, prompted a review of the JSB's corporate governance arrangements. Since April 2006, part of the Lord Chief Justice's new responsibilities has been the provision and sponsorship of judicial training, within the resources provided by the Lord Chancellor. The Lord Chief Justice exercises his executive responsibilities for oversight of the JSB through the Judicial Executive Board—a permanent body with responsibility for the leadership, organisation and management of the judiciary of England and Wales—and it is through that body that the Chairman of the JSB advises the Lord Chief Justice on training issues, and raises particular issues for consideration, as appropriate.

From April 2007, the way in which the business of the JSB is handled internally changed through the establishment of an Advisory Council, an Executive Board and a series of governance principles. The broad intention behind this reorganisation was to provide for effective decision-making and clear lines of accountability.

In recent years the JSB has faced very demanding challenges. Its work is constantly expanding, with greater responsibility for the training of magistrates and tribunal members. It has also had to reflect changes in the system of judicial appointments. The increased emphasis on recruiting from more diverse backgrounds means that some of those being trained are likely to have less courtroom experience than has traditionally been the case. The JSB has also proactively sought to discover, via discussion groups and questionnaires, what judges need by way of training and what they feel is not currently being provided.

The Judges Council and JSB both provide invaluable support for the courts and judiciary in this country. It is to be hoped that their enhanced roles in recent times will further improve access to justice in the English legal system.

11

Current Challenges in Judging

Abstract Just as the common law has evolved to meet the changing requirements of society, so should the role of the common law judge. Unless the judicial role evolves in this way, the judiciary will be unable to fulfil the expectations of the public whom they serve. Whether it does so will depend on the calibre, commitment, organisation and training of the judiciary. It will also depend upon the executive and legislature providing the judiciary with the support they require. This paper discusses the new contemporary role of the judge—ranging from balancing the rights of individuals and the state, to assisting the judiciary of other jurisdictions, to providing knowledge about the legal system to school-children. The challenge is to preserve the best in our system as it has evolved over the centuries while at the same time making the changes necessary to ensure the judiciary are capable of meeting contemporary challenges.

The landscape in which judges have to perform their craft has been transformed. New responsibilities have been imposed upon the judiciary and those responsibilities have created new challenges for judges. They are both domestic and international. It is on the domestic challenges and how to meet them that I am going to concentrate upon here. I start with responsibilities.

It is my theme that, just as the common law has evolved to meet the changing requirements of society, so should the role of the common law judge. It is of critical importance to society that the judicial role evolves in this way. Unless it does so, the judiciary will be unable to fulfil the expectations of the public whom we serve. Whether it does so, will depend on the calibre

* Originally delivered at the 5th Worldwide Common Law Judiciary Conference, Sydney, Australia, on 10 April 2003.

and commitment and organisation and training of the judiciary. It will also depend upon the executive and legislature providing the judiciary with the support the judiciary require.

Traditional Responsibilities

I emphasise that, while our new responsibilities are of very considerable importance, this does not mean that the judiciary's traditional responsibilities have lost any of their significance. The standard of justice in a particular jurisdiction, and certainly in mine, continues to depend primarily upon the quality of its judges and their ability to find the facts so as to decide where the truth lies or, in a jury trial, to control the trial and sum up the issues in a way which assists the jury to perform their role. In addition, in common law jurisdictions like ours, the ability of the judges to develop the substantive law is of great significance.

At one time, our courts would not give advisory declarations. The previous rules of procedure referred to declarations of rights. The words 'of rights' have been dropped from the current procedure rules. However, before that amendment was made, there were circumstances in which the courts were already granting advisory declarations as long as there was a genuine dispute. Of course, there will be situations where it is appropriate to do this, but others where it is not appropriate. If the meaning of legislation is not clear and substantial expense will be incurred if either the government or a member of the public takes action the legality of which is disputed, it makes good sense to resolve the dispute as to the legality of what is proposed. On the other hand, prior to the beginning of the Iraqi war, the Divisional Court, presided over by Lord Justice Simon Brown,[1] in my view properly refused to grant a declaration as to the legality of what might or might not happen in the future in that conflict.

A more recent development is for the government to consult the judiciary on proposed legislation, which will affect the judiciary if implemented. At the present time, this is particularly true in relation to criminal legislation. To legislate as to the conduct of trial or as to sentencing without consulting the judiciary is unhelpful. Almost any legislation in relation to criminal justice has resource implications, which the judiciary are in the best position to assess. In addition, the judiciary are best equipped by experience to speak

---

[1] Now Lord Brown, Lord of Appeal in Ordinary.

with authority on legislation. In the case of legislation which arguably infringes the rights of individuals, the judiciary can at times identify a means of mitigating the consequences of what is proposed.

Let me give an important example. When the establishment of our Special Immigration Appeals Commission[2] was proposed, the legislation described it as a court of record. In response, the judiciary proposed and the government accepted that Court of Appeal and High Court Judges should be seconded to SIAC. We were content that, stiffened in this way, it was appropriate to designate SIAC as a court of record.

Access to Justice

At the forefront of the new challenges facing the judiciary, I place the obligation of the judge to help those who need the assistance of courts, to obtain access to justice. This involves managing the justice process. There are, of course, litigants who need no assistance. Those who can afford to employ competent lawyers can usually, but not always, look after themselves. However, outside the commercial field, there are fewer and fewer litigants who are in this privileged position in civil proceedings. If the great majority of litigants are to receive justice, the judiciary must no longer be passive but be prepared to promote the resolution of disputes. They have to be proactive in directing litigants to the correct forum in which to resolve their dispute. This is not, by any means, necessarily the courts. Where an alternative method of dispute resolution is better suited to the task, the courts should have the responsibility of pointing the litigant in the correct direction. Whether to follow that signpost is a matter for the litigant. Where litigation in the courts is unavoidable, then the judges need to be proactive in promoting settlement, the control of costs and the expeditious resolution of the dispute. There is an obligation upon us to strive continuously to reduce complexity, to simplify our procedures and make the law readily accessible.

As a symbol of what was required I urged, as part of our reforms, the abolition of Latin and the adoption of simple English when rewriting our Rules of Procedure and, indeed, in our courts. A recommendation which was singularly ill-received. How, it was complained, were you to make an *ex parte* interlocutory application *in terroram* for an interim order of

---

[2] Hereafter, 'SIAC'.

certiorari when the court needs to be assisted by an amicus curiae if there is no guardian *ad litem* or any pro bono representative? While no one takes it too seriously, we are making progress. On 21 March 2003, I received a letter from the Chairman of the venerable City of London Magistrates, saying that from then on they were not going to *adjourn sine die* but *adjourn without date*. I had suggested *adjourn generally*. I did hold a competition for the best substitute for 'pro bono'. Despite protests from a number of colleagues, the competition was a great success. I was, though, extremely worried for a time because I had offered a magnum of champagne to the winner and it looked as though the winning selection was going to be the choice of about a dozen different competitors which would have set me back a sizeable sum. Fortunately, however, I ended up only having to provide three magnums for 'law for free'.

The fact that the new rules are in understandable English may not be a seismic change. But it is a significant change because it is a signpost to the new contemporary role of the judge. This involves the judge taking a hold of litigation and determining its shape and the timetable according to which it is to be resolved. It necessitates judges being given and exercising greater discretion. Discretion to determine: in what order to resolve the issues; the evidence which shall be called; how issues are to be proved and the costs which it is appropriate to incur in resolving the dispute. Giving judges greater discretion involves trusting the judges to exercise their discretion properly. The exercise of discretion should not be readily interfered with on appeal. Appellate Courts must exercise self-restraint.

When preparing my interim report, I decided that we should start by identifying the overriding objective of a civil justice system in accordance with which the judge should exercise his discretion. This was novel, but important, because it identified what should motivate a civil justice system. Part I of the new procedure rules identifies the overriding objective as enabling the court to deal with cases justly. Because this rule epitomises the philosophy of our civil justice system it is worth setting out in detail. Part I states that dealing with a case justly includes, so far as is practicable:

    (a) ensuring the parties are on an equal footing;

    (b) saving expense;

    (c) dealing with the case in ways which are proportionate—

        (i) to the amount of money involved;

        (ii) to the importance of the case;

        (iii) to the complexity of the issues;

        (iv) to the financial position of each party;

(d) ensuring that it is dealt with expeditiously and fairly; and

(e) allotting to each case an appropriate share of the courts resources whilst taking into account the need to allow resources to other cases.

The general view of the new rules is that they have improved procedure but, for reasons that I have not time to explain, they have not yet tackled the problem of costs. Interestingly, what has been most successful in opening up 'access to justice' has been the small claims procedure. This is designed to be accessible to the litigant acting in person. The court fees were reduced. There is usually no order as to costs. The procedure from beginning to end is intended not to last, and does not last, more than a couple of months. Expert evidence is curtailed. The success of the procedure is illustrated by the number of claims made—in 2002 there were just over 55,000. The fact that, on the whole, claims do not settle indicates that litigants do not feel that they are compelled to settle. They can afford to litigate. This is surely what justice is about.

What is true of civil justice is also true of criminal justice. In the case of crime the State invariably picks up the bill but this does not reduce the need to control expense. The need to promote the simplification of procedure and the substantive law is equally important. However, the challenges are greater in achieving this in a criminal trial because of the consequences which can result from a wrong conviction and the fact that sanctions can be applied to a defendant facing a criminal trial. Furthermore, a defendant to a criminal charge must have a greater say as to how his trial is conducted. Administrative convenience cannot interfere with the need for a criminal offence to be strictly proved. Subject to these considerations, however, there is no reason why criminal justice should not be efficient and effective as in the civil justice system. In criminal as well as civil proceedings, the judge has a responsibility to ensure the cooperation of the advocates in achieving proportionate justice. Legislation proceeded through our Parliament and resulted in the establishment of a new Criminal Procedure Rule Committee and Sentencing Guidelines Council. We hoped there would be a Code of Evidence, but the government, for reasons I have difficulty understanding, found this unacceptable. A Code of Criminal Law would be of great value. This is something that the Law Commission has long advocated and, in relation to which, they have done an immense amount of preparatory work. If these codes are established, they will make a huge contribution to making law accessible. Codes are essentially a civil law concept and are an example of how one system can help another to promote justice.

The incorporation of the European Convention of Human Rights into our domestic law has added a new dimension to the task of achieving justice in the UK. Prior to this happening the judiciary had taken pride in the development of their administrative law. They were entitled to do so because there had been a remarkable change. The scale of the change in England is reflected in the fact that as late as 1967 Sir William Wade was complaining that there was 'an extraordinary reluctance to recognise administrative law as a body of general principles, indeed to recognise it as a subject at all'.[3] Yet in the Preface to the 8th edition, published in 2000, of *Administrative Law*, he stated:

> The judges whose adventurous policies were a theme of a our last edition, have established judicial review as an almost boundless jurisdiction over almost every kind of government activity. Ministerial decisions of policy have been strictly scrutinized and sometimes condemned, in fields such as foreign affairs, prison government, sentencing, immigration and criminal injury. The expanding jurisdiction is often linked with the decline of Parliament as a check on the Executive—a role now played more effectively by the upper than the lower House. It is said that, 'the person on the Clapham Omnibus might well conclude that judges were aggressively moving into the political vacuum and that they have been more–much more activist in their interpretation of statutes'. The same passenger may feel that we are moving into a period of 'government by judges', especially as some very eminent judges have suggested that the courts can claim entrenched constitutional status independent of Parliament.

He went on to say:

> As the Human Rights Act takes effect and judges are seen to be endowed with yet wider powers, there are likely to be more attacks upon them as unelected and devoid of legitimacy. Their achievement on the other hand, has been to set standards of fairness, reasonableness and legality which have greatly improved public administration.

Sir William added that:

> The next few years will be a time of great interest as the courts adjust themselves to their new powers and responsibilities. Above all they must defend the frontier between law and politics and so falsify the pessimistic forecast that a Bill of Rights would politicise judicial appointments in the way which is familiar in the

---

[3] H W R Wade, *Administrative Law* (2nd edn, OUP, 1967).

United States. At the heart of all the new developments is the need to bring more fairness along with justice into the law.

Sir William was clearly in favour of the expansion, but feared the risk of the judiciary being politicised. Our experience is that Sir William's fear has to an extent proved justified but not in a way which is doing more than create ripples in the relations between the executive and judges.

The task of a judge, on an application for judicial review, involves the exercise of discretion because the remedies which the court would grant if an application was successful were the old prerogative remedies without their Latin tags. Where a court is applying a convention of human rights, such as those contained in the European Convention, the court is given an additional responsibility in the case of most of the rights. The right to life and the right not to be subjected to cruel and unusual punishment are absolute rights, but the majority are qualified so as to preserve the needs of a democratic society. An example is provided by Article 8, which establishes the right to respect for an individual's private and family life, his home and correspondence. The right is subject to an exception in Article 8(2) in respect of interference which is:

> ... in accordance with the law and is necessary in a democratic society, in the interests of national security, public safety or the economic well-being of a country for the prevention of disorder or crime, for the protection of health or morals or for the protection of the rights and freedoms of others.

A balance has therefore to be drawn between the State and the individual and a judge is responsible for determining where the balance lies. This is a task new to the English judiciary, but a task of which the judiciary in many commonwealth jurisdictions have long experience. How the balancing act is done is extremely important. To be too favourable to the citizen can frustrate the ability of the government to govern and to be too favourable to the government can devalue the rights. To assist the English judges to strike the balance correctly, we have developed a doctrine of deference which they extend both to the legislature and the Executive when appropriate. On matters of national security, for example, a high degree of deference is shown. Similarly, in relation to matters of economic policy. There will be situations, however, in which the public body whose actions are being challenged is no better qualified to determine the issue than a judge. The position of the individual making the challenge also has to be taken into account. Such is the scale of the change involved in moving from a jurisdiction where the courts enforce public duties to one where the courts are required to enforce public rights, that a degree of conservatism is a virtue. Insofar as this is possible, the objective should be to convince the Legislature and the Executive that the supervision of the courts is wholly constructive. It results in better administration, better government and better legislation.

Standing

I now turn to the question of standing—you will note I do not use the term *locus standi*. It was on applications for judicial review that the traditional restrictive approach of the courts on standing melted away and was replaced by a broad and flexible approach. Today our procedure requires the leave of court to commence proceedings or there is a power in the court to strike out proceedings which have no prospect of success. There is, therefore, no reason to have a restricted rule as to standing; if an action has no merit, it will not get past the starting gate. There was not even any risk of a defendant being inappropriately embarrassed by proceedings because there is no requirement for a defendant to appear or make representations on the preliminary hearing to see whether permission should be granted. The generosity of the requirements of standing has allowed a much broader range of issues to be brought before the court than was the situation in the past. In particular, the jurisdiction of the court to grant a declaration has expanded as rapidly as the rules as to standing have been relaxed. This change of approach has resulted in the most difficult situations which a court has to determine coming before the courts for decision.

In particular, the medical profession has sought guidance as to the legality of a proposed course of conduct in the most harrowing of situations. To take as examples: whether it is right to turn off the life-support machines in the case of someone who is 'brain dead' and what action should be taken in relation to conjoined twins if an operation to separate them would almost certainly result in the death of one twin, but a failure to operate would result in the death of both within a relatively short time. A case being heard by the then Master of the Rolls, Lord Phillips,[4] immediately before I left England to come to this conference, was brought by a concerned member of the public challenging the right of our Human Fertilisation and Embryology Authority to permit the mother of a four-year-old boy with beta thalassaemia to go through IVF treatment. The child, Zaine, suffered from a genetic condition that stripped his body of the ability to make red blood cells.

---

[4] Lord Chief Justice of England and Wales since October 2005.

His mother wanted to go through a process of combining IVF with genetic diagnosis of the embryo to ensure that the embryo which was implanted would produce a child with matching tissue. If this could be achieved, the umbilical cord blood could be used to treat Zaine. Without this treatment, the probability was that Zaine would die. However, the difficulty arose because the prospects of getting an embryo which would serve the purpose were no more than 1 in 12. This meant that the IVF treatment of the mother would almost certainly result in embryos being destroyed. The person who initiated the proceedings was a member of a secular organisation that opposed the destruction of embryos. She contended that the process of producing what the media describes as a 'designer baby' was unlawful and that the Authority was not entitled to authorise what was proposed. The objector was successful before the judge and the Authority appealed. Not unreasonably, the mother regarded the life of her child as hanging on the decision of the court.

Issues of this sort naturally involve human rights, not least the right to life. The objector is concerned with the right to life of the embryos, the mother with that of her child. The court will have to decide where the law stands. In some of these cases, although the consequences can be highly emotional and heart-wrenching, they have to be resolved purely as a matter of interpretation. Others have to be resolved by a matter of deduction from first principles. In determining the cases, the courts have to show that they fully appreciate the scale of the issues involved and why they have come to the conclusion they did. The fact that these cases are difficult is demonstrated by the number of times a decision at first instance is reversed on an appeal. The full extent of the legal problems sometimes does not manifest itself until the appellate hearing.

I have already indicated that the Human Rights Act 1998 has a role to play in these cases and there is a provision in this Act which caused the judiciary some concerns, but in relation to which our concerns were not heeded. It states in section 7 that a person who claims that a public authority has acted in a way which is made unlawful by section 6 of the Act can bring proceedings against the Authority but, and these are the important words, 'only if he is [or would be] a victim of the unlawful Act'. It was pointed out by the judiciary that this was a much narrower test than now is applicable on an application for judicial review. However, in practice, if an applicant is not seeking compensation, section 7 appears to be causing little difficulty. The argument appears to run thus. If the court itself is a public authority, it would be unlawful for the court to contravene the

European Convention. And if the court came to a result which was inconsistent with the Convention, it would be acting contrary to the Convention. As to this complaint, the litigant would be a victim of the court's breach.

The Partnership and Management of the System

As is happening in most other jurisdictions, there is now a realisation in England and Wales that the managerial role of the courts should not be restricted to managing litigation. The court system requires management. In our jurisdiction, the Court Service is responsible for providing and running the courts. This does not, however, mean that the judiciary do not have a role to play. On the contrary, it is now accepted that the court system will only be effective if it is run by partnership between the independent judiciary and the government agency, the Court Service. The role of the Court Service is to support the judiciary and ensure that the judiciary are in a position to provide the standard of justice which the public require. To achieve this there are, at every level of the judiciary, judges who, in partnership with the civil servant of an equivalent seniority, have responsibility for the overall delivery of justice, either in a particular court or in part of the country or in the jurisdiction as a whole. Judges are not trained administrators, a subject which I will touch upon later, but they have a much greater practical insight into the workings of courts than it is possible for bureaucrats to have. Part of the court system is of course the judiciary serving within it and the judge who is responsible for working within the partnership can also provide administrative leadership in relation to his or her judicial colleagues.

Consultation as to Legislation

As I have mentioned, the judiciary in England and Wales are playing a greater role in advising on what should be included in prospective legislation and as to the interpretation and effect of existing legislation. Consultation is not necessary in relation to all legislation, but is very important in respect of legislation that has a direct impact on the justice system. The government is apt to forget that legislation can affect the courts even if it is not directly concerned with the courts. It will give rise to litigation. We try now to tell the government department promoting the legislation what we anticipate to be the cost implications for the courts and ask who will provide the resources. If the necessary resources are not provided, there will be a negative impact on the provision of justice. Cooperation as to how legislation is to be implemented can also assist. Our Law Commission is traditionally chaired by a High Court Judge. The Commission makes a very significant contribution to improving the quality of our substantive law by its reports which often include draft legislation.

In assisting in the way that I have indicated, the courts take good care not to become involved in party political issues. Their sole concern is to achieve the best results for the administration of justice. In cooperating in this way, members of the judiciary do not sacrifice their independence. They do no more than make recommendations. It is possible to have cooperation between the different arms of government where there is a community of interests. Both in the case of civil and criminal justice, there is now cooperation to achieve the best results for the government, the judiciary and the public. With reform of the system taking place with the frequency that it does at present, it is essential that the different arms of government work together to make a success of those reforms.

Judges in England and Wales also give evidence before Parliamentary Committees from time to time. I believe I was one of the first judges to do so. We now have agreed guidelines for judges who are considering attending.

Providing Judicial Training

Reforms result in a need for judicial training and that must be retained in judicial control. The training must be independent of any suggestion of political bias and the training of judges by judges ensures this. With independence of the judiciary comes responsibility and we are slowly moving forward to the adoption of performance appraisal for the judiciary. Again, this process must be in the hands of the judiciary. Naturally, there are healthy concerns and with experience we will learn how it can be done in a way which supports the judiciary and certainly does not interfere with their independence. Because of the increased administrative responsibility of judges, the training which is made available should include training in management.

The Welfare of the Judiciary

The senior judiciary should be especially concerned about the welfare of their more junior colleagues. The stresses to which the judiciary are subjected while performing their responsibilities under the glaring scrutiny of the media are of a different order from those in the past. Judges can need support.

Certainly in England, it is being increasingly realised that new judges may need mentors. The lonely responsibility of a judge sitting alone doing justice can at times become unbearable. It is difficult to impose upon busy colleagues. I believe there could be great value in another judge being identified as the person responsible for giving you support. Similarly, the performance appraisal process I mentioned earlier can give judges valuable reassurance and tactful guidance as to how they can improve. Another form of assistance we have recently provided for our judicial colleagues is the provision of a helpline to which they can refer if they have problems in relation to which they need counselling.

Our concerns as to standards should not be limited to judicial performance. An effective legal profession is critical to the health of the justice system. The judiciary should be playing an important role in promoting and assisting in academic and vocational training for those who are seeking to enter the profession and in the continuing education programmes which are today so much part of maintaining appropriate professional standards. The reforms which have been made and are yet to take place within the English judicial system are elevating the responsibility of the legal profession for the administration of justice to a higher level than has existed in the past. It is not easy, in the contemporary world, for members of the legal profession to maintain a sufficient degree of independence from their clients to be able to perform their duty to the court.

Conduct of Inquiries

A responsibility which we place upon the judiciary, which in some jurisdictions would be thought to be at least questionable, relates to inquiries into matters that cause deep public concern. I regard it as being part of the responsibility of today's judiciary, at the request of the government, to conduct such inquiries as long as they are likely to fulfil a need for public reassurance. A good example of a successful inquiry is that conducted into the spread of 'mad cow' disease. Considering the importance and difficulty of the subject, the then Master of the Rolls, Lord Phillips, conducted that inquiry with a care and expedition which was admired on all sides. It involved his going on a teach-in as to the science. It resulted in recommendations which I hope will avoid a further disaster occurring in the future. It would be invidious to mention all the other inquiries that have successfully taken place but I will mention two. One is into the multiple murders which Dr Shipman was able to commit. That was completed in 2005. The merits of the Saville Inquiry into the shootings in

Londonderry on Bloody Sunday are more debatable. That inquiry has already been operating for nine years and a report is expected to be published at the end of 2007 or possibly early 2008.

The Saville Inquiry is an example of international judicial cooperation because, as you probably know, although the inquiry is chaired by a British judge, he has the benefit of the assistance of the Honourable William L Hoyt, former Chief Justice of New Brunswick, Canada, and the Honourable John L Toohey, a former Justice of the High Court of Australia. The cost of this exercise is astronomical even with the most advanced technology that could be devised for any tribunal. As of the end of October 2002, Northern Ireland Office funding of the Inquiry totalled £71m. The current estimated cost of the Inquiry to the Northern Ireland Office is £400m. Is it all worthwhile? Well opinions differ and I do not feel that I should comment further.

Complaints Against the Judiciary

In addition to helping with inquiries of that sort, one of the improvements we have recently achieved, merely by a matter of contract, is the establishment of a clearly defined procedure covering the investigation of complaints against a member of the judiciary. Both the member of the judiciary and the public need protection. If a complaint is of any merit and might cause a consideration of action being taken, it is important that the facts are objectively ascertained. For this purpose, as Chief Justice I had the responsibility of appointing a judge to carry out an investigation. Under the agreement made with the former Lord Chancellor, my consent was required before he took any disciplinary action. This is an important provision, which recognises the constitutional position of the Lord Chancellor who, in relation to judges below the High Court, can remove a judge for misconduct while protecting the independence of the judiciary.[5]

---

[5] Today, the Judicial Appointments and Conduct Ombudsman may make recommendations to the Lord Chancellor and the Judicial Appointment Commission about what steps should be taken in relation to a complaint which has been upheld.

Providing Knowledge about the Legal System

The rather solemn responsibility of protecting the judiciary is matched by a responsibility, which I believe we have, to promote the next generation's understanding of the rule of the law. For this purpose we now have, I am glad to say, a successful programme of visits by judges to schools and by schoolchildren to the courts. I am sure we are not exceptional in this, but it is not a task which the distinguished judges who were in office when I became a barrister would have readily or comfortably undertaken. I take great satisfaction from the enthusiasm with which my current generation of colleagues have taken up the cause—a project now supported by an admirable website.[6]

Assisting the Judiciary of Other Jurisdictions

Another new responsibility of great importance is the judiciary's responsibility to work with and where appropriate, support the judiciaries of other countries. This is one of the greatest importance in the global society in which we now exist. The judiciary of the older democracies are fortunately to be spared the pressures to which some of the new democracies are subjected. The older judiciary, based on their experience, are peculiarly well placed to provide independent and impartial advice and assistance to jurisdictions where this is needed.

Promoting Confidence in Our Own Systems

If the judiciary are to shoulder these many responsibilities, it is critical that the public have confidence in the integrity and quality of their judiciary. It is because of this that I am concerned, deeply concerned, as to the corrosive reporting of the tabloid press. Today reporting is ignored which in the past would have been regarded as amounting to contempt. It would be wholly undesirable, however, to use the blunderbuss of contempt to restrain the media. The provision of press notices and identified press liaison officers can help. The main defence of the judiciary has to be the fact that at all times their conduct is beyond reproach. In addition, the judiciary must seek to avoid unnecessary controversy and take care to explain their decisions in their judgments with as much clarity as possible. Although I worry about the

---

[6] See <http://www.judiciary.gov.uk>.

effect of the media, I am reassured by the fact that when there is a matter of real concern to the public it is usually to the judiciary that both the public and the government turn to ensure that there is an impartial and thorough investigation into the causes of the concern.

Judges' Council

A recent response of the judiciary to the greater challenges with which we are faced is the reform and revitalisation of our Judges' Council. This semi-moribund body has now been refurbished so that it is in a position to speak for our judiciary as a whole. Already we are reaping the benefits. Issues such as judicial pensions and the publication of a first advisory code of ethics are on its agenda. I have no doubt that in the times that lie ahead, the voice of the Judges' Council will need to be heard if we are to achieve what must be our target for the future.[7]

That target is to preserve the best in our system as it has evolved over the centuries while at the same time making the changes necessary to ensure that our judiciary continue to be capable of meeting contemporary challenges. What we are doing is providing a contemporary service. The nature of that service is evolving and continues to evolve. However, we must make clear that, if we are to continue to maintain the quality, the service we provide must be properly resourced.

I am conscious that the account I have given of what is happening in my jurisdiction may be excessively parochial. I hope this is not critical. What is critical is, first, that the common law judiciary today is proactive, not reactive, in their response to the challenges that they face in administering justice. Secondly, that the fundamental role of the judiciary in promoting a just society is respected by the other arms of government and, thirdly, that we, the judiciary, deserve that respect.

---

[7] For a recent account of the reform of the Judges Counsel, see Postscript in 'The Needs of a 21st Century Judge', Chapter 10 in this book.

12

The Impact of Human Rights

Abstract If England is to be true to its heritage, a commitment to the rule of law, it has to be, and has to be seen to be, a champion of human rights. This paper discusses the incorporation of the European Convention on Human Rights into English law via the Human Rights Act 1998. It suggests the Act has strengthened our democracy by giving each member of the public his or her human rights in a manner that was not previously available. It discusses the position in English law prior to the Human Rights Act, where a member of the public could not go before the English courts and secure a remedy based on a human right, but instead had to complain that a public body had failed to comply with some legal duty or otherwise acted unlawfully. There has been a considerable change of culture in the role of judges and additional tension has arisen between the courts and the executive. It calls for the different arms of government to work in partnership together and play a full role in promoting the observance of human rights around the globe.

I am delighted to be sharing this Athenian Garden with you this evening. I am an enthusiast for the Lyceum initiative because of its international dimension. I know it is not solely concerned with lawyers or the law and certainly its primary interest is not the judiciary. You may, therefore, wonder why I have chosen a title which focusses on human rights. At first sight, viewed with the lofty objectives of the Lyceum, my subject may seem parochial. I hope to try and persuade you that it is not. I also hope to persuade you that, if this country is to be true to its heritage, it has to be, and has to be seen to be, a champion of human rights.

It is increasingly recognised around the world that the observance of the rule of law is the key to progress in the developing world. The problems

---

* Originally given at the Oxford Lyceum, on 6 March 2003.

confronting the different nations in Africa, Asia, and the new democracies are far from identical. However, it is generally accepted that, if progress is to be achieved, it is necessary to improve the observance of the rule of law in every part of the globe. This requires an effective system of justice. Assisting countries to establish effective systems of justice is very much a responsibility of the developed nations, including the judiciary of these nations. It is also very much in the interests of the developed nations that such systems should be established. They would make a permanent contribution to the fight against terrorism. It is where the rule of law has broken down that terrorism takes root. There is also no need for citizens of countries which observe the rule of law to seek asylum; an ever-increasing problem in the developed world.

Last month I attended an *All Africa Conference on Law, Justice and Development* in Abuja, Nigeria. Kofi Annan, former Secretary General of the United Nations and James Wolfensohn, former President of the World Bank, were both due to attend. Not surprisingly, in view of what was happening in other areas of the world, they did not do so, but papers were delivered on their behalf. Both recognised the importance of establishing effective justice systems in the developing world. I was particularly impressed by comments of James Wolfensohn. Amongst other things, he said:

> [What] we know is absolutely critical—absolutely critical—is that there should exist a legal and judicial system which functions equitably, transparently and honestly. If these forms of legal and judicial systems do not exist in Africa, there is no way that you can have equitable development.

He also stated:

> A steady neglect or decline in the rule of law in most countries in Africa has been a major reason for the decline in the development prospects for the continent.

He went on to illustrate his point by saying:

> Over 14 countries have faced one form of conflict or another on the continent in the last decade. Many of Africa's wars, armed conflicts and civil disturbances emanate directly from the hopelessness of people trying to find in their countries a suitable framework to have access to power, to exercise their political rights or to share in the equitable distribution of the national revenue; when citizens have difficulty understanding and seeing how governments use and sometimes abuse national resources, it makes it even more difficult for many African governments to raise fiscal revenues. Corruption at several levels permeates the political and economic life in many countries.

Trust of people that governments would redistribute revenues equally, is very low, breeding situations of non-payment of taxes by the citizenry.

He added:

Take the steady flight of capital out of the continent and the slow inflow of foreign and direct investment because both domestic and foreign investors alike have lost faith in the ability of the legal and judicial systems to ensure the protection of property rights or to adjudicate disputes timely and in a fair and predictable manner without undue or improper influences.

And finally he stated that, 'Africa needs strong, well-established rule of law regimes to enable it to trade itself into prosperity and out of poverty.' It is because this country recognises the importance of the rule of law to the developing world that a substantial proportion of our overseas aid goes to helping the nations concerned to develop their systems. Part of this aid is a steady flow of judges and practitioners overseas and visits to this country of judges and practitioners from overseas.

The European Union makes it clear to countries seeking to join the Union that they will need to have achieved systems of justice that adhere to the rule of law in order to qualify for membership. Similarly, the World Bank uses the leverage provided by its loans to encourage such improvements. They are not easy to achieve, particularly if corruption is endemic and the resources available modest. Although it may not be easy, it is without doubt worthwhile.

In what I have said so far I have been focussing on the rule of law, but the rule of law is intimately linked with the observance of human rights. I was in China in 2001. When I finished giving a talk, a member of the audience asked me whether there was any distinction between what I had said about the importance of being governed in accordance with the 'rule of law' and being 'ruled by law'. 'Ruled by law' being the expression the authorities in China were in the habit of using. There is a fundamental distinction between the two approaches. Both require compliance with the law irrespective of its content, but the rule of law also requires that the laws should accord with the democratic values which are reflected in a code of human rights such as the European Convention.

In China there is no tradition of government in accordance with either rule by law or rule of law. But their present government is committed, and I believe genuinely committed, at least to achieving a situation where the country is ruled by law and, probably, observing the rule of law as well. They are certainly anxious to learn and that is why I made my visit as head of a small British delegation of jurists, practitioners and academics. A country the size of China is confronted by an enormous task, but they are making very rapid progress indeed. I made a visit 15 years earlier and the contrast in the legal scene between my two visits was striking.

What is true of China is also true of Russia. Shortly after my visit to China, I was asked to attend a conference being organised in St Petersburg. Like the conference in Abuja, the conference in St Petersburg was intended to promote the rule of law. Again, I detected a great enthusiasm for change.

An example of the importance of a country at least being ruled by law is provided by South Africa. The transition of that country from an apartheid regime to its present status as a country governed in accordance with human rights under a comprehensive constitution and a distinguished constitutional court, would not have been so remarkably uneventful if it had not already had a judiciary and a legal system which fairly applied the laws of that country, however obnoxious those laws were prior to the period of transition. Confirmation of this is provided by the fact that the white Chief Justice at the time of the transition was encouraged to postpone his date of retirement by President Nelson Mandela.

Because of its colonial history, this country is in a particularly strong position to promote human rights in the developing world. It is looked upon as the mother, not only of Parliament, but of the common law system of justice. It is important that we remember this because, if do not adhere to our traditional standards of democracy and justice, those who are not well-disposed to democracy or justice will use our failures as a licence for theirs. As will already be clear, it is very much part of the responsibility of the senior judiciary now to have close relations with the judiciary of other countries. I attach particular importance to links between the judiciary of this country and other common law jurisdictions. I also believe that our growing connections with civil jurisdictions in Europe are important. They mean that we are peculiarly well placed to act as a bridge between the common law and civil justice systems.

However, in relation to the common law world, we are still the beneficiaries of a huge reservoir of respect and goodwill because we were the source of their present legal systems. Why this is so is brought home vividly if you visit the High Court in Bombay or the Supreme Court in Abuja. In the Bombay High Court there is a magnificent gothic hall reminiscent of the hall to the Royal Courts in London. Around the walls are portraits of the successive Chief Justices in their robes. It is not possible by looking at the portraits to identify when independence took place. In the Abuja Supreme Court, in a magnificent modern building, the walls are decorated by photographs of judges wearing robes and wigs which are the same as those worn in London. Of course robes are only symbolic; what is perhaps more important is that in 2003, 14 of the 18 Supreme Court judges of Nigeria were members of our Inns of Court. The links of both the new and the old commonwealth with the legal system of this country are still very strong indeed.

The regard for the legal system of this country is not confined to the common law world. It is true also of the civil systems in Europe. There has been a process of harmonisation taking place, but of course there are still significant differences between our respective approaches. However, the quality of our judicial decisions are recognised throughout Europe. Although it is only in recent times that the Human Rights Act 1998 came into force and the European Convention became part of our law, this country, despite its rather unhappy record at Strasbourg, is still regarded as a country which champions the rights of the individual and the rule of law. It was in part because I was conscious that, prior to the Human Rights Act coming into force, the judiciary in this country could not play its proper role in the development of human rights, that I welcomed the implementation of the Act.

Since the Human Rights Act has been in force, I have recognised that the fact that human rights could not be directly enforced as part of English law in the past meant that our form of democratic government was more vulnerable than it is now to the contravention of those rights. As Lord Hoffman has explained, the Human Rights Act was intended to strengthen the rule of law without inaugurating the rule of lawyers.[1] The Act has strengthened our democracy by giving each member of the public the right to seek the help of the courts to protect his or her human rights in a manner that was not previously available.

In the case of almost all the articles of the European Convention, the values equivalent to human rights were recognised as part of English law prior to the Human Rights Act coming into force. It was part of the long-established culture of this country that what could loosely be regarded as human rights values were observed both by government and Parliament. Furthermore, human rights were recognised by the courts as part of the common law, 'the birthright of the people' and part of the compact between the monarch and Parliament.[2]

---

[1] See (2001) 151 NLJ 713.

[2] See *Halsbury's Laws of England* (4th edn) Vol 8(2), para 101 and, eg, *Derbyshire County Council v Times Newspapers Ltd* [1993] AC 534.

The articles that have probably been the subject of most litigation since the Human Rights Act came into force are Article 6, the right to a fair procedure, and Article 10, freedom of speech, but both rights were long recognised by the courts prior to the Human Rights Act. As was pointed out in a letter to *The Times* from Francis Bennion on the 28 February 2003:

> Exactly 200 years ago the English town of Eastbourne occasioned the laying down of the definitive law on this point. In the case of *Rex v The Inhabitants of Eastbourne* (1803) the Chief Justice, Lord Ellenborough, ruled that our law required relief to be afforded to all starving paupers, whether statutorily entitled or not, who were found wandering abroad and lodging in the open air in the Duke of Devonshire's salubrious town of Eastbourne. Lord Ellenborough said: the law of humanity, which is anterior to all positive laws, obliges us to afford them relief, to save them from starving. What he meant was that in this respect, as in many others, the common law of England embraces the natural law and serves humanity.

Despite this, in more recent years it had become increasingly apparent that the citizens in this country, by comparison with their European neighbours, were at a significant disadvantage in having to rely primarily on the self-restraint of the government of the day for the protection of human rights values.

Prior to the Human Rights Act, a member of the public could not go before the courts and secure a remedy based on a human right. Prior to the Act you could not, as you can now, go before the courts and say my right to life is threatened: it is the State's duty and the Court's duty to protect me. Instead, a member of the public had to complain that a public body had failed to comply with some legal duty or otherwise acted unlawfully. Then, if the complaint was established, the courts, usually on an application for judicial review, would take the necessary action to ensure that a public body complied with the law. Otherwise, the only recourse was to make a complaint to the European Court of Human Rights at Strasbourg and possibly obtain a remedy of damages from that Court that our own courts could not provide. This was the consequence of this country not having a document which could appropriately be described as a written constitution or any other legislation which provided protection for its citizens' human rights. This change from enforcing public duties to protecting the public rights of an individual, constituted a dramatic change in the role of the courts. It meant the focus of the courts moved 180 degrees from the public body to the individual.

Some would no doubt say that, if we have managed without a written constitution for hundreds of years, why now do we need a statute which contains the fundamental rights that would appear in a written constitution?

This argument ignores the fact that the needs of society are continuously evolving. The only two other developed countries which did not have a written constitution, namely New Zealand and Israel, now have basic law provisions protecting human rights.

It is interesting to remember that, while it is possible to find cases like the *Eastbourne* case[3] to which we can look back with pride for the manner in which they uphold human rights values, there have been periods of our history in which the record has been more fragile. During the last war, for example, it was Lord Atkin alone who spoke up in *Liversidge v Anderson*[4] for the rights of the individual.

While there was considerable nervousness in the UK prior to the implementation of the Human Rights Act, the informed view is that making the European Convention part of our domestic law has proved to be a great success. Furthermore, that process of implementation has gone extremely smoothly. There are at least five reasons why, notwithstanding the scale of the change involved, the smooth transition has been achieved:

(1) The first reason is one to which I have already referred. Perhaps it is the most important. It is that the values to which the European Convention on Human Rights gives effect are very much the same values that have been recognised by the common law for hundreds of years. Although, prior to the present administration, no government of the UK had been prepared to give its citizens the right to enforce human rights directly, it was wrongly assumed that UK citizens were just as well off under the common law as if they had such a right. This assumption was surprising since, while those rights were not expressly conferred on our citizens, when former colonies were about to become independent from Britain it was thought that their citizens did need such rights. Thus, many of the nations which now make up the British Commonwealth were given, on independence, a written constitution containing such rights. Furthermore, while our citizens, if they wished to enforce their human rights, had to go to Strasbourg to enforce them, for many years the new independent members of the British Commonwealth still had to come to a UK court, the Privy Council, in order to have their rights finally adjudicated upon. This was fortunate because it meant that our most senior

---

[3] *Rex v The Inhabitants of Eastbourne* (1803) 4 East 107.
[4] [1942] AC 206.

judiciary were very familiar with the different techniques which a final court of appeal has to employ in order to give effect to human rights.

(2) This brings me to the second reason. Every judge from the Magistrate to the Law Lord has now to apply the European Convention. While the Privy Council had given the most senior judges a taste of what is involved in applying human rights, for the great majority of the judiciary this was a totally new experience. For this reason, before the Human Rights Act was brought into force, there was a breathing space of two years during which intensive training took place. Preparation for legislation on this scale was unprecedented in the UK. The training for the judiciary was accompanied by public bodies conducting an audit of their activities with the intention of identifying any practices which were not human rights compatible so that they could be changed before the Act came into force. This preparation in itself was very worthwhile since it meant not only judges, but also officials, Ministers, and advocates were immersed in a human rights culture. Change of culture is the most important aspect of the introduction of the Human Rights Act.

(3) Thirdly, the process of change was facilitated by the fact that English lawyers and our judiciary, as common lawyers, felt instinctively at home with the manner in which the Strasbourg jurisprudence had been developed. On the framework provided by the Articles of the Convention, the judges of the Strasbourg Court have developed their jurisprudence in very much a common law manner: developing the law by giving pragmatic decisions on the facts of the cases that came before them.

(4) Fourthly, the fact that the UK had already for many years been a member of the European Union, applying the Luxembourg jurisprudence, also assisted.

(5) Finally, the very sophisticated approach adopted by the legislature when making the European Convention part of our domestic law assisted. The legislature, instead of giving the UK courts power to strike down domestic legislation, limited the court's power to declaring that the legislation was incompatible with the Convention. The Act then provided a fast track enabling Parliament to remedy the situation.

Despite these advantages, the scale of the change should not be underestimated. The values to which the European Convention gives effect are, as I have indicated, shared by all Western democracies. However, for a country which has a long tradition of regarding the sovereignty of the democratic Parliament as being the cornerstone of its constitution, the fact that the

Convention is enforceable in our own courts has created additional tension. Administrators and Ministers are used to our judges reviewing their actions, but under the Human Rights Act the scrutiny can be more intense. It is entirely novel for our courts to have the power to grant a declaration of incompatibility.

In practice, the occasions on which the courts have had to resort to making a declaration of incompatibility have been limited. Even then the declaration has been set aside on appeal.[5] The reason the number of cases has been so small is partly due to section 3 of the Human Rights Act which is one of the most important provisions of the Act. Legislation, whenever it was enacted, becomes subject to the duty of the judiciary to read and give effect to it so that it accords rather than conflicts with Convention rights. If you consider that interference with human rights should be restricted, then surely section 3 is a thoroughly desirable, if novel, provision. It involves a new approach to the interpretation of statutes. I emphasise interpretation because as I have made clear in a judgment which benefits from the endorsement of Lord Hope, interpretation does not include legislation.[6]

I believe strongly that it is important that the different arms of government work in partnership together. The application of section 3 can be an example of that partnership in action. Section 19 requires the minister in charge of a Bill before Parliament to make a statement as to the compatibility of the Bill with Convention rights. Where a positive statement of compatibility is made, it can be assumed that Parliament intended the legislation to comply with the Convention. If it does not do so on a literal interpretation, then using section 3 to achieve a compatible interpretation is indeed fulfilling Parliament's intentions.

In addition, the courts are required to take into account, though not necessarily follow, the decisions of the Strasbourg Court. A happy consequence

---

[5] See, for example, *R (Anderson) v Secretary of State for the Home Department* [2003] 1 AC 837 (the Secretary of State's power to alter the tariff of life-sentenced prisoners); *Bellinger v Bellinger* [2003] 2 AC 467 (about the rights of a male to female post-operative transsexual); *R (Hooper) v Secretary of State for Work and Pensions* [2005] UKHL 29, [2005] 1 WLR 1681 (provisions of the Social Security (Contributions and Benefits) Act 1992 relating to 'widows' could not be read under s 3 Human Rights Act to include 'widowers'); and *A v Secretary of State for the Home Department* [2005] 2 AC 68 (where the detention of non-British nationals was held to be discriminatory).

[6] *Poplar Housing and Regeneration Community Association Ltd v Donoghue* [2001] 3 WLR 183; *Donoghue v Poplar Housing and Regeneration Community Association Ltd* (2001); and *Ghaidan v Godin-Mendoza* [2004] UKHL 30, [2004] 2 AC 557.

of this is that, while previously a few experts in the UK were aware of the rich jurisprudence of this Court, now that jurisprudence is familiar to every judge and competent lawyer in the country. In the cases that I hear, it is rare for a decision from Strasbourg not to be cited at some stage of the hearing. The remarkable thing is that although the Strasbourg cases are persuasive and not binding authority, I cannot recall it being suggested that our courts should not follow a Strasbourg precedent because it did not accurately reflect the law. Without exception, practitioners regard the Strasbourg decisions as being of the highest authority. The Strasbourg jurisprudence, however, is a base and should not be regarded as creating a cap on our recognition of human rights in the English courts.

A reason for this acceptance of the Strasbourg jurisprudence is the fact that that Court has wisely developed the practice of allowing the Signatory States a margin of appreciation as to how they give effect to the Convention rights. This practice is not directly transposable to the domestic situation. This is because domestic courts do not have to determine the relationship between an international body and a national body. Domestic courts are concerned with the different relationship, the relationship between the national court and the national authorities.

Fortunately, although this is controversial, the British courts have developed a parallel doctrine to the margin of appreciation to deal with the relations between the domestic courts and our Parliament and our executive. This in many situations avoids an overt clash between our courts and Parliament and the executive.

The parallel doctrine that has been developed is the doctrine of deference, or as I prefer to say the doctrine of respect. This requires the UK courts to recognise that there are situations where the national legislature or the executive are better placed to make the difficult choices between competing considerations than the national courts.

The courts recognise an area within which the judiciary defer on democratic grounds to the considered opinion of the elected body or person whose actual decision is said to be incompatible with the Convention. Such an area of deference is more readily found where the Convention requires a balance to be struck, or where the case raises issues of social and economic policy. It is less likely to be applied in situations where the Convention right is unqualified or where the rights are of a nature which the domestic courts are well placed to assess.

In addition, in general the courts have exercised the additional responsibilities which the Human Rights Act has given to them conservatively.

This has meant that vocal criticism of the manner in which the judiciary are exercising their new jurisdiction under the Act has been confined to a limited number of cases. The fact that, despite these criticisms, the judiciary have also been criticised for not being sufficiently proactive, perhaps indicates that usually the judges have got the balance right.

In relation to the criticism, what is overlooked is that judges are only doing what they have to swear to do on appointment and that is to give a judgment according to law. That law now includes the Human Rights Act. By upholding the Human Rights Act the courts are not interfering with the will of Parliament. On the contrary, when they interfere, the judges are protecting the public by ensuring that the government complies with the laws made by Parliament. The courts are therefore acting in support of Parliament and not otherwise.

It is of the greatest importance to make clear that, by recognising the need for deference when scrutinising the actions of public bodies, the judges are not slipping backward and reverting to their pre-Human Rights Act approach, the *Wednesbury* approach.[7]

I accept that the Convention cannot be described as a contemporary document. It is not drafted in the terms which would be used in a document created for the first time today. For example, unlike the South African constitution it does not deal with language, cultural, religious, social and economic rights. Importantly it also does not deal with environmental rights. Here it is to be noted that the Indian Constitution does not either, but this has not prevented the Indian Supreme Court extending the constitutional protection of the right to life so as to do so. However, half a loaf is better than no loaf and in recent times there has been little political support for a more far-reaching replacement in this jurisdiction.

But while the European Convention has the shortcomings to be expected of a 50-year-old Convention, it has already been subject during its life to considerable development by the Court at Strasbourg. It is a living instrument. The Court in accordance with the best common law traditions has extended the reach of the articles so that they make a significant contribution to achieving a society which is more just and more tolerant than it would be if we did not have the Convention.

---

[7] In English law, the 'Wednesbury approach' or 'Wednesbury unreasonableness' is unreasonableness of an administrative decision that is so extreme that courts may intervene to correct it. See *Associated Provincial Picture Houses v Wednesbury Corporation* [1948] 1 KB 223; *Council of Civil Service Unions v Minister for the Civil Service* [1985] AC 374.

Now our courts can take up the baton and make their contribution to international human rights jurisprudence. To give an example at random: Article 2, which protects the right to life, has been used as a justification for granting a lifelong injunction to protect the identity of Thompson and Venables[8] once they had served their punishment for their terrible crime; the same article has also been used to improve coroners' inquests. Again, Article 8 and the protection it provides for privacy and the right to family life is being used to ensure that mothers who are in prison are not, when this is practical, parted from their young babies.

After September 11, 2001 the UK passed the Anti-Terrorism, Crime and Security Act 2001. In order to bring the legislation into force, the UK government felt compelled to enter into a formal derogation from Article 5(1) of the Convention.[9] It has been pointed out that, despite the international nature of the present war on terrorism, the UK stood alone among European states in deeming it necessary to derogate from the terms of the Convention. I have been a member of a court that had to hear an appeal under that Act. I do not intend to detain you by referring to my judgment. While we did not uphold the challenge and did recognise the situation was one where respect was required to be appropriately extended to the government, we made clear that the manner in which the issues had been considered by the Court was wholly different as a consequence of the European Convention being part of our domestic law. We did not apply the *Wednesbury* test.

The problem with emergency legislation is that it is inevitably amongst the most controversial legislation from the point of view of human rights. It is usually passed into law with a great urgency at a time when Parliament has least time to consider dispassionately its intrusive effect on individual citizens. A distinguished American professor, Bruce Ackerman, has suggested, and I agree with him, that we should devise our emergency legislation at a time when we are not as a nation subject to pressure of an emergency, though he fears that breathing spaces between emergencies are going to be of increasingly reduced duration. This should avoid the danger that might otherwise arise, that, because legislation has not been the subject of mature deliberation,

---

[8] Robert Thompson and Jon Venables spent eight years in secure accommodation for the murder of two-year-old James Bulger in 1993. They were freed on life sentences in 2001.
[9] The lawfulness of the derogation was successfully challenged in the House of Lords in *A v Secretary of State for the Home Department* [2004] UKHL 56, [2006] 2 AC 221. As a result, Part 4 of the Anti-Terrorism, Crime and Security Act 2001 was repealed by the Prevention of Terrorism Act 2005, with effect from 14 March 2005, and the Human Rights Act 1998 (Amendment) Order 2005 (SI 2005/1071) reflected the withdrawal of this derogation from Art 5 ECHR in response to this.

it creates the impression that we are not, when an emergency exists, attaching the significance to human rights that we expect of other countries.

So far as human rights are concerned we can never afford to be complacent. A salutary consequence of human rights becoming enforceable is that the risk of us scoring an 'own goal' is substantially reduced. Thanks to the Human Rights Act we are now in a position to play a full role in promoting the observance of human rights around the globe. At the beginning of this talk I attempted to explain why I regarded this role as being important. I believe it can make a small contribution to making this a safer world. As to whether this is in fact possible, I can only recite Aristotle, with whom the Lyceum is associated, 'a likely impossibility is always preferable to an unconvincing possibility'.[10]

---

[10] Politics 24/1460.

13

Human Rights and Minorities

Abstract Our justice systems today have to be judged according to how they protect the rights of the individual. The role of the courts is not to legislate, not to determine policy, but to ensure access to the courts and to apply the law fearlessly. This paper discusses how the law in England has been used to protect the rights of minorities both prior to and after incorporation of the European Convention on Human Rights into English Law via the Human Rights Act 1998. If Parliament does not strike the right balance between the rights of society as a whole and the rights of the individual, the courts, with their power to declare legislation incompatible with the European Convention, will make the difficult decisions involved in upholding the rule of law to ensure individuals and minorities are not subject to discrimination.

Introduction

Despite the geographical gulf between us, Australia and the UK have more in common than divides us. One of the treasures we like to claim we have in common is Sir Zelman Cowen. He was, of course, a most distinguished Governor General of Australia. He has, however, spent a great deal of time in the UK. Both Sir Zelman and Lady Cowen are held in the highest esteem in the UK even though we do not see them as often as we would like. Indeed, so fond are we of Sir Zelman Cowen, I have little doubt that if the Queen usually resided in Australia and not in England, Sir Zelman Cowen would have been the Governor General of Great Britain. However, not being able to make Sir Zelman Governor General, we made him Provost of one of the most attractive colleges in Oxford and Oxford had also the good sense to make him Pro-Vice Chancellor of the University.

---

* This lecture was originally delivered at the B'nai B'rith Anti-Defamation Commission Inc, Melbourne, Australia, on 13 April 2003.

If there is one quality I associate with Sir Zelman, it is good judgement. However, I have to say that, in the invitation he extended to me for this evening, that judgement appears to have lapsed. The consequences are likely to be as painful for you as they are for me. Painful for you because you have to listen to me. Painful for me because I am following in a line of very distinguished orators. According to the *Concise Oxford Dictionary*—in Sir Zelman's company, I could not refer to any other dictionary—oratory consists of 'rhetoric, highly coloured presentation of facts; eloquent or exaggerating language'. I have never, with good reason, claimed to be an orator, but, having regard to that definition, I now know that I was right not to do so.

Fortunately, there are others who are orators. One such was Martin Luther King Jr. He eloquently summed up his view of the role of law in relation to discrimination when he said: 'A law will not make a man love me but it will stop him lynching me and that is certainly an improvement I value.' That is, in part, how I see the role of law in relation to discrimination. I believe that laws can affect behaviour even though they cannot control an individual's mind. Speed limits on the road provide a simple example.

A further statement made by Martin Luther King Jr, and one which reveals his skill in the use of language, is that: 'The test of a man is not where he stands in time of peace and ease, but where he stands in time of turmoil and difficulty.' The same can be true of a nation and the statement has a special resonance at the present time. Both our countries are engaged, not only in war, but in protecting our citizens against the malevolent intent of terrorists who are prepared to kill themselves if they can and kill and maim others.

I would also like to quote a second orator, one of the greatest political orators, Winston Churchill. When a young Home Secretary in 1911, Churchill made one of the most enlightened remarks about prison conditions that any politician has made. I refer, of course, to his statement to the House of Commons that: 'The mood and temper of the public with regard to the treatment of crime and criminals is one of the unfailing tests of the civilisation of a country.' Those eloquent words, I believe, could today be applied, not only to prisoners, but equally to immigrants, asylum seekers, and even those detained as suspected terrorists; in fact, to any minority that is reviled by the general public and so is in danger of being subject to discrimination.

These are difficult times for both our countries. Both are engaged in a war and, at the same time, are faced with very substantial moral problems. Problems which lead to forceful political debate. At times like this, it is critical that there should be laws which set the standards that we should observe. We have the advantage of our shared heritage, our shared tradition of tolerance and fairness, the fact that both countries have inherited the value of common law and that both are virile democracies. But, it is at times like the present that history teaches us that we have to be on our guard. Such times test not only our citizens but also our laws and courts. So far as our citizens are concerned, it is critically important that we have bodies like the B'nai B'rith Anti-Defamation Commission to combat racism and anti-semitism and promote cooperation between different communities. I congratulate the Commission on the very important work it is doing. So too, our justice systems have to be judged in these times by how they protect the rights of the individual. The role of the courts is not to legislate, not to determine policy, but to ensure access to the courts and to apply the law fearlessly.

It is no accident that it was after the end of the Second World War that the European Convention of Human Rights and other international human rights conventions were born. These conventions were born to meet a need. A need not only to tackle the wilful discrimination of totalitarian regimes, but to combat the discrimination against women, religious and racial groups which was then the accepted norm in most democracies, including our own.

Fortunately we have progressed. It is now generally accepted, at least amongst the citizens of developed countries that to observe the rule of law, that the observance of human rights values is a critical constituent of the rule of law and that the observance of the rule of law, and therefore human rights, is an essential part of the democratic process. It is appreciated that the observance of human rights values is a hallmark of a democratic society, because it demonstrates that the society values each member as an individual. Just as it is the essence of democracy that every individual has an equal right to vote, so each individual has the right to expect that a democratically elected government will regard it as its responsibility to protect each of its citizen's human rights. Human rights come with true democracy whether the government wants them or not. However, this liberal approach is of remarkably recent origin and therefore has to be regarded as fragile and never taken for granted. We have to see how it will stand up to the forces which the 21st century has already set loose.

Until 2000, when the Human Rights Act 1998 came into force in the UK, both our countries had in common the fact that we were among the few nations which did not have an entrenched Bill of Rights. Australia, unlike the UK, did have a constitution that protected certain civil rights, including freedom of religion. In addition, the Australian High Court has held that the Australian constitution contains implied freedoms of political communication, from detention of a penal or punitive character and a requirement of due process. I am aware that, as recently as 1985, Australia rejected incorporating the International Covenant on Civil and Political Rights into domestic law. I am confident that, if the UK had been asked in 1985 to do the same thing in respect of the European Convention of Human Rights, the initiative would have ended in the same way. Furthermore, at that time, a British Parliamentary Committee would have been likely to have made a similar assertion to that made by the New South Wales Parliamentary Committee which, I believe, indicated that, not only did Australia not need a Bill of Rights, but that to introduce one would positively harm the ability of government to govern.

The reason for that response would have been not that our respective societies did not value human rights, but that we were satisfied that those rights were sufficiently protected by the common law and the laws passed by our respective parliaments and, in the case of Australia, by its written constitution. Indeed, in the period during which I have been a judge, it is quite remarkable the extent to which both our judiciaries have found, buried in the common law, principles such as 'equality before the law' and the 'right of all persons to be treated uniformly by the state, unless there is valid reason to treat them differently' to accompany the traditional right to do anything you like unless there is some law restricting that right.

However, although we, probably complacently, regarded the UK as a bastion of civil liberties, it was extraordinary how often the European Court of Human Rights found that, in fact, we were not protecting the rights of our citizens as we should and so were in contravention of the European Convention of Human Rights. That this should be the position was not the fault of the courts. Over the previous 20 years there had been the most remarkable development in judicial review. There is now hardly any activity of a public body which could not be scrutinised by the courts on an application for judicial review. Yet, the courts were at a serious disadvantage in that they could not enforce a citizen's human rights directly. Instead, the courts could only enforce a public body's legal duties. Because the European Convention was not part of our domestic law, if our citizens wished to enforce their human rights directly they had to apply to the Court at Strasbourg alleging that the British government had breached rights to which they were entitled. Prior to the Human Rights Act coming into force, we were not entitled to claim that we were continuing, as in the past, to set an example to other nations as to human rights values. With the coming into force of the Human Rights Act in October 2000, the European Convention became part of our domestic law. It is now possible for an application to be made directly to the UK courts for the protection of fundamental rights enshrined in the Convention.

In England, prior to the first Race Relations Act in 1965 and the development of a full doctrine of judicial review, there was no common law rule, policy or principle outlawing racial or other forms of illegitimate discrimination.[1] There were instead, a few isolated areas in which specific non-discrimination principles had developed. When I think with pride of our past, I think of an 1803 case concerning the liability of an English parish to maintain a foreigner in which Lord Ellenborough referred to a common law of humanity 'which is anterior to all positive laws, [and] obliges us to afford [foreigners] relief to save them from starving'.[2] I also remember that the common law had imposed, at the same time, a duty on common carriers, innkeepers and some monopoly enterprises such as ports and harbours to accept, and I emphasise, all travellers without discrimination.[3]

These isolated instances apart, the common law was often a source of discrimination. The courts conceived of themselves as guardians of the principle of absolute freedom of contract as it applied to all types of dealing, including employment and the provision of basic public services. A necessary corollary of this absolute freedom of contract was the absolute freedom of employers and service-providers to discriminate against women, religious and racial groups, and other minorities. As a result, it was not only employers who were guilty of discrimination. For some time, even into the 20th century, our courts consistently held that the word 'person' did not cover women. This obstructed the extension of women's rights to attend university,[4] vote,[5] and enter the professions.[6]

The first anti-discrimination legislation properly so called was passed in the late 19th century in the form of statutes entitling married women to retain property and, later, their wages. After the First World War, the Sex Disqualification (Removal) Act 1919 was passed providing that 'a person shall not be disqualified by sex or marriage from the exercise of any

---

[1] J A G Griffith *et al*, 'English law has very little to say about discrimination' in *Coloured Immigrants in Britain* (OUP, 1960), 171.

[2] *R v Inhabitants of Eastbourne* (1803) 4 East 103.

[3] 'The Unreasonable Exercise of Power' in S A de Smith, H Woolf and J L Jowell, *Judicial Review of Administrative Action* (Sweet & Maxwell, 1995), 13-040.

[4] *Jex Blake v Edinburgh University* (1873) 11 M 784.

[5] *Nairn v St Andrews and Edinburgh University Courts* 1909 SC 10.

[6] *Bebb v Law Society* [1914] 1 Ch 286.

public function' including any civil or judicial office or from entering any civil profession or vocation.

In the second half of the 20th century, Britain, like Australia, passed a series of Acts of Parliament which prohibited racial, gender and disability discrimination. The resulting patchwork of anti-discrimination legislation has subsequently been overlaid by statutory codes of practice, providing guidance to employers and service providers on how to avoid discrimination and promote equality of opportunity. The codes are not binding in law and a failure to comply with them does not, of itself, give rise to liability. They are, however, admissible in evidence where a person claims that unlawful discrimination has taken place and the legislation and the codes have influenced what is the accepted practice and the attitudes of British society for the better.

However, we relied on a patchwork of statutes and codes which have justifiably been described as incoherent. By July 2000, there were in the UK no fewer than 30 Acts, 38 statutory instruments, 11 codes of practice and 12 EC directives and recommendations concerned with discrimination.[7] More have been forthcoming since.[8] In addition, as in Australia,[9] the British courts developed the common law so that it provided better protection for fundamental human rights. Notwithstanding this and the volume of the legislation, many rights acknowledged as fundamental human rights in the European Convention remained unprotected in English domestic law.

English law did not, for instance, prior to the Human Rights Act, recognise a positive right to freedom of thought and religion. Some, but not all, religious groups had been able to avail themselves of protection under the Race Relations legislation, but this had been because the act of religious discrimination complained of was also discriminatory on grounds of 'colour, race, nationality or ethnic or national origins' and not because the law protected the sanctity of religious belief. Thus, in 1983, a court held that the refusal to admit a Sikh pupil because it would be contrary to school rules for him to wear a turban constituted indirect racial discrimination on the grounds that Sikhs are a community recognisable by ethnic origins.[10] In that case, the House of Lords found that for a community to be recognisable

---

[7] B Hepple, M Coussey and T Choudhury, 'Equality: A New Framework', Report for the Independent Review of the Enforcement of UK Anti-Discrimination Legislation (Hart, 2000).

[8] *Hansard*, House of Lords Official Report, vol 645, no 54, col 2 (28 February 2003), 528.

[9] I have in mind, in particular, *Ah Hin Teoh* (1995) 128 ALR 353.

[10] *Mandla (Sewa Singh) v Dowell Lee* [1983] 2 AC 548.

by ethnic origins, it was essential that the group had a 'long shared history' and a 'cultural tradition of its own'.[11]

So Jews are also treated as a racial group within the meaning of the Race Relations Act 1976. In a 1987 case, the Court of Appeal held that questions to a Jewish job applicant about the nature of his faith, which discouraged him from continuing with an application for employment in the Middle East, were capable of amounting to discrimination under the 1976 Act.[12] However, Muslims do not constitute a racial group and an employer's refusal to allow Muslim employees time off work to celebrate a religious festival has been held in the UK to justify an award of compensation on the basis that it constitutes indirect racial and not religious discrimination.[13]

This improvised method of protecting religious groups was better than nothing at all. While, for example, a 'No Hindus' or 'No Jews' rule would be unlawful under the Race Relations provisions, a 'No Catholics' rule would not. New religious groups were also left without any protection as, by definition, they cannot have 'a long shared history' and 'cultural tradition'. Hence, it was held that Rastafarians did not constitute a racial group; they have existed for only 60 years.[14]

There was no legal right on the part of an individual to his or her own sexual preferences or his or her own sexual identity. Sexual orientation discrimination did not come within the scope of the Sex Discrimination Act 1975, and this meant that homosexuals and transsexuals who suffered verbal abuse or were otherwise discriminated against had no legal protection.[15]

Since the European Convention of Human Rights became part of our domestic law, the legal position in the UK has and is continuing to be transformed. Initially, it appeared that the effects would be limited, but it is becoming increasingly obvious that its influence is going to be greater than anticipated. It would be fair to say that human rights values have immersed the whole of our law.

Since coming into force, the Human Rights Act has been applied to enhance the rights of religious minorities. In one case, parents won the right to have their religious beliefs taken into account when applications on

---

[11] Ibid, 562.

[12] *Simon v Brinham Associates* [1987] ICR 596.

[13] *JH Walker Ltd v Hussain* [1996] ICR 291.

[14] *Crown Suppliers (Property Services Agency) v Dawkins* [1993] IRLR 284.

[15] Today, it is unlawful to discriminate against workers because of sexual orientation. See the Employment Equality (Sexual Orientation) Regulations 2003 and the Equality Act 2006, Part 3.

their child's behalf to particular schools were considered by their local council.[16]

Article 8 of the Convention, which guarantees respect for private and family life, has been held to confer a right on an individual to assert his sexual identity. Significantly, since the Human Rights Act, the Court of Appeal in the *Mendoza* case granted same-sex couples the right not to be discriminated against in important housing legislation by virtue of the Human Rights Act.[17] The Court agreed that the words 'husband' and 'wife' are in their natural meaning limited to persons who are party to a lawful marriage but, in the words of Lord Justice Buxton, 'Parliament having swallowed the camel of including unmarried partners within the protection given to married couples, it is not for this court to strain at the gnat of including such partners who are of the same sex as each other.'[18] This decision has had an impact upon a range of areas, such as pensions, social security and housing benefit, where homosexual couples have been discriminated against.

There have also been very significant developments, spurred by the European Convention, towards equality for the 5,000-strong minority of transsexuals in the UK. Following decisions of the European Court which found the UK government's policy on transsexuals to breach Article 8 and Article 12, the right to marry, the government committed itself to introducing a Bill to formally recognise a transsexual's acquired gender including the right to marry in the acquired gender.[19] The fact that this can only be achieved by legislation has been emphasised by a decision in recent times in the House of Lords.[20]

---

[16] *R v Newham London Borough Council, ex parte K*, 9 February 2002. More recently, see *R (Ullah) v Special Adjudicator* [2004] UKHL 26, [2004] 2 AC 232, where the House of Lords suggested that a positive obligation not to deport could arise under Art 9 ECHR, where the consequence of deportation would be the complete denial or nullification of the right to have or manifest a religion. See also, *R (SB) v Governors of Denbigh High School* [2006] UKHL 15, [2006] 2 WLR 719, where a Muslim schoolgirl was not permitted by her school to wear a 'jilbab', a long-coat garment which was considered to represent stricter adherence to the tenets of the Muslim faith. The House of Lords accepted that Art 9(1) ECHR was engaged as wearing the jilbab was a sincere manifestation of the schoolgirl's religious belief, but they went on to find that Art 9(1) did not require that people should be allowed to manifest their religion at any time and place of their choosing. The refusal to allow the claimant to attend school wearing a jilbab did not amount to an interference with her right to manifest her religious beliefs in practice or observance.

[17] *Mendoza v Ghaidan* [2002] EWCA Civ 1533.

[18] Ibid, [35].

[19] *Goodwin v UK* (11 July 2002). This Bill became the Gender Recognition Act 2004, which allows transsexual people to change their legal gender. See also the Civil Partnership Act 2004, which allows civil partnerships between same-sex people.

[20] *Bellinger v Bellinger* [2003] UKHL 21, [2003] 2 AC 467.

Other areas where there have been significant changes brought about as a consequence of the combined effect of the decisions at Strasbourg and the change in our domestic law are in relation to prisoners and asylum seekers.

There has been a rash of cases in relation to prison conditions and Winston Churchill would, I think, approve of the outcomes. I give one example. No doubt for reasons of good administration, the prison service had a series of blanket policies which they applied to particular circumstances. One such policy laid down how many weeks a mother who gave birth to a child in prison could keep that child with her. The Court of Appeal held that greater flexibility was required in applying the policy so as to ensure minimal interference with each baby's welfare. An individually based approach which accords with human rights was required.

In relation to mental health patients seeking release, the Human Rights Act has resulted in the reconsideration of policies as to the burden of proof and the speed with which applicants for release are heard.

Gypsies, a minority group regularly subject to discrimination, have also benefited from the Human Rights Act. The House of Lords has held that a planning inspector was prohibited under Articles 8 and 14 from taking into account a gypsy's refusal of an offer of conventional housing as a reason for refusing planning permission for a caravan on a different site. The council needed to consider in full the personal and surrounding circumstances, including the gypsies' attitudes to conventional housing and the role of their cultural background in precipitating those attitudes, and weigh these against the planning considerations in coming to a determination.[21]

On the other hand, in *R v Home Secretary, ex parte Farrakhan*,[22] a challenge to the Home Secretary's refusal to lift an exclusion order on the leader of the Nation of Islam who was alleged to have made malevolently anti-semitic remarks, based on his free expression rights under Article 10 of the Convention was rejected. The High Court found that the Home Secretary's decision struck a fair balance between freedom of expression and the legitimate aim of the prevention of public disorder.

It is, however, in the immigration and asylum field that decisions have been given by our courts which have caused the most concern to the executive, despite the fact that many of the decisions have been in the government's favour. The sensitivity is due to the fact that, in these cases, the courts in

---

[21] *Clarke v Environment Secretary* [2002] EWCA Civ 819. See also *R (Margaret Price) v Carmarthenshire County Council* [2003] EWHC 42, [2003] NPC 9.

[22] [2002] 2 WLR 481.

England and Wales have had to balance the human rights of the immigrant or asylum seeker with the government's policies designed to control the flow of immigrants into England or to detain those who are regarded a threat to National Security; policies which are strongly supported by substantial sections of the public urged on by the tabloid media. Here, Article 5 of the Convention which limits the circumstances in which an individual can be detained is relevant. The European Court of Human Rights at Strasbourg has recognised that it should extend a degree of latitude to member states, called a margin of appreciation, in this area. Our courts likewise extend a degree of deference or respect to the position of the government, but this latitude is not always enough to ensure the legality of the government's actions.

The September 11 2001, attacks closely followed by the bomb in Bali rightly attracted worldwide outrage and sympathy for the victims. One consequence was the passage of the Anti-Terrorist, Crime and Security Act 2001 through the British Parliament. The most controversial part of the Act has given the Home Secretary power to issue, in relation to an alien, a certificate as to the Home Secretary's reasonable belief that an individual's presence in the UK is a threat to national security and that the individual is, therefore, a suspected terrorist. Under the Act, such a person may be detained and deported. However, because of Article 3 of the European Convention, some of the aliens so suspected cannot be deported because, if they were, they would be subject to torture in the country to which they would be sent. The new legislation enables the alien in these circumstances to be detained indefinitely without trial. This legislation is not without its echoes of internment during the Second World War. The Home Secretary recognised that in order to implement such a measure he would have to derogate from Article 5 of the Human Rights Act and the British government did so.

The Act certainly contains draconian measures which should never be tolerated in peacetime. However, it was subject to detailed parliamentary scrutiny by the Joint Human Rights Committee and it has safeguards. The detainee can apply to a tribunal, the Special Immigration and Appeals Commission,[23] one member of which must have held high judicial office, and which has the power to discharge the certificate. In addition the powers of detention have to be renewed annually by Parliament.

---

[23] Hereafter, 'SIAC'.

In a case called *A, X, Y & Ors v Secretary of State for the Home Department*,[24] SIAC annulled the certificate of three aliens on the grounds that, since the Act applied only to aliens and not to nationals, it was discriminatory. It was argued that, since there could be equally dangerous British terrorists in the UK, there was no justification for singling out aliens. The Home Secretary appealed and the Court of Appeal, of which I was a member, allowed the appeal and upheld the validity of the legislation. The Court decided that there was, and always had been, a clear distinction between the position of aliens and nationals. The aliens could have been deported if the government had not held its hand to protect them from torture and, in these circumstances, it was reasonable to detain them until such time as they were prepared to leave the country.[25]

There has also been a series of cases in the UK where the Home Secretary's policy of depriving asylum seekers of financial and other support to deter them from coming to the UK has been challenged in the courts. The legislation could leave individuals destitute and naturally the courts have scrutinised it with great care. First, it was held that such a draconian measure could not be implemented by subordinate legislation. Then, it was successfully argued that while the newly introduced primary legislation operated to exclude one right to benefit, it did not exclude another, namely national assistance—the benefit of last resort. Recent legislation has deprived asylum seekers of all support if they do not claim asylum immediately on arrival in the UK. Again, this legislation has run into trouble, because it was being applied unreasonably. It was suggested that this was an example of the Human Rights Act preventing the government from governing and of the courts interfering with the will of Parliament. In fact, the courts intervened because the legislation was being inadequately administered. I emphasise that our courts were not interfering because they disapproved of the policy, they did so, because it is the courts' duty to ensure that, particularly in the case of legislation which renders people destitute, the executive is strictly complying with the legal requirements.

While there has been a seismic change in the manner and degree of protection for minorities in the UK, the limitations of Article 14 of the

---

[24] [2002] EWCA Civ 1502, [2004] QB 335. It is to be noted that the lawfulness of the derogation from Art 5 ECHR in this case was successfully challenged in the House of Lords in *A v Secretary of State for the Home Department* [2004] UKHL 56, [2006] 2 AC 221.

[25] I am aware of the Australian Legislation Amendment (Terrorism) Act 2002, but I believe that Act goes further than the UK legislation.

European Convention, which deals with discrimination, are noteworthy. The Article only prohibits discrimination by the State where the complainant can show that he has been discriminated against in relation to those rights and freedoms contained elsewhere in the Convention. Unlike the Bill of Rights of Canada, New Zealand, or South Africa, there has until recently been no general right in the UK not to be discriminated against on unjustifiable grounds.[26]

In the UK Parliament, Lord Lester, following considerable consultation and research, introduced the Equality Bill which, when passed, introduced a free standing right not to be discriminated against and a single framework for the protection and promotion of that right. It also established an Equality Commission for Great Britain.

This has been a way of rationalising anti-discrimination law. The issue for debate was whether this would be best achieved by legislation drafted to address specific areas of discrimination in detail or by the introduction of more general non-discrimination provisions, which the courts could apply and develop on a case-by-case basis. From my position, it may not surprise you to learn that I personally favoured the latter approach. I did so not out of ambition for increased power for the courts, but because our experience in the UK has been that specific legislation has the potential to generate a raft of litigation over the details of individual provisions with some odd results. Consequently, I believe that, in countries which have the benefit of a well-established and mature judiciary, the objectives of such rights-based legislation are better achieved where the legislation is based on general rights, which can subsequently be overlaid with more detailed, persuasive but non-binding codes as to the application of those rights.

I also consider that a dedicated Human Rights and Equality Commission, effective models for which can be found here in Australia as well as in India and Northern Ireland, is a valuable addition to our culture of equality and respect for the rights of individuals and minorities in the UK.[27]

---

[26] Hence, Protocol 12 to the European Convention was introduced to create a strong and free-standing anti-discrimination provision. See G Moon, *The Draft Discrimination Protocol to the ECHR: A Progress Report* [2000] EHRHR 49.

[27] I understand that, since its inception in the 1980s, the informed view is that Australia's national Human Rights and Equal Opportunities Commission has brought a number of advantages. Making one body responsible for the promotion of human rights has ensured a consistent and cost-effective approach and, as a result of its endeavours, the Commission has established a respected reputation nationally and on the world stage for the advocacy of human rights inside and outside Australia. See, for instance, S Beckett and I Clyde, *A Human Rights Commission for the United Kingdom: the Australian Experience* [2000] 2131 EHRLR.

The Commission will contribute substantially to the momentum with which the UK's human rights culture is developing. Bringing our various anti-discrimination commissions under one umbrella will mean their efforts and expertise will be combined.

There is no doubt that the Human Rights Act provides solid foundations for the protection of our vulnerable minorities. That said, it is acknowledged that the introduction of the European Convention on Human Rights in domestic law provides a 'floor not a ceiling' for the protection of human rights. It is of crucial importance that we continue to build upwards.

The advantages to be derived from the greater focus on human rights values far exceed the disadvantages. Just as the development of judicial review in the final quarter of the last century in England and Australia has improved administration in our increasingly complex societies, so will the existence of the Human Rights Act protect, in Britain, our individual interests, which are so easily lost sight of in meeting the demands of the global economy. The real test of the Human Rights Act arises when individuals or minorities attract the antagonism of the majority of the public; for example, when the tabloids are in full cry. Then, the courts must, without regard for their own interests, make the difficult decisions that ensure that those under attack have the benefit of the rule of law. At the heart of the Human Rights Act is the need to respect the dignity of every individual by ensuring he or she is not subject to discrimination.

Today we are confronted by dangers that may be as great or even greater than those which threatened our countries in 1939 when we offered succour to those fleeing from Nazism. There are now pressures posed by the need to protect the public from crime; pressures created by an unprecedented number of asylum seekers which can cause us to forget the extent to which the UK has benefited from immigration. As *The Independent* newspaper pointed out on 10 October 2002, 'historically this nation has been enriched by generations of asylum seekers from the Huguenots in the 17th century to the Jews in the 20th'. This, I suspect, is even more true of Australia, but on the other hand there are pressures created by the need to protect both our countries from merciless acts of international terrorists. These pressures will test our countries' national fibre and, in the UK, this will test the Human Rights Act. But the Human Rights Act is not a suicide pact, it does not require the UK to tie its hands behind its back in the face of aggression, terrorism or violent crime. It does, however, reduce the risk of our committing an 'own goal' In defending democracy, we must not forget the need to observe the values which make democracy worth defending.

We must also remember there are other nations watching how we respond and perhaps all too ready to follow our example if we let our standards fall.

It is our respective Parliaments and governments that have primary responsibility for defending both our democracies and their shared values. Nevertheless, if Parliament or the government does not strike the correct balance between the rights of society as a whole and the rights of the individual, it is important in the UK that the courts, as they could not before the Human Rights Act, act as a longstop; not by striking down legislation, but by declaring it incompatible with the European Convention. In doing so, as is their duty and as the law requires, the judiciary will make the difficult decisions involved in upholding the rule of law. Sometimes the judicial role will be unwelcome. If initiatives which have popular appeal are interfered with by the judiciary because of their adverse effect on the human rights of a minority, the judiciary will not be popular. But the temporary unpopularity of the judiciary is a price well worth paying if it ensures that Britain remains a democracy committed to the rule of law—a democracy which is therefore well worth defending.

What then would Martin Luther King and Winston Churchill say if they were alive today and able to call on their powers of oratory. I am sure that they would think that there are a great many ways in which our laws are influencing our societies' behaviour towards minorities for the better. Winston Churchill might, however, worry that, in Britain at any rate, the sunshine of fairness, tolerance and liberty was at risk of being obscured. Not by a gathering storm, but by no more than gathering clouds warning of possible storms ahead. We must at all times remain on our guard to protect the values for which our two countries have always stood.

PART III

Crime and Penal Reform

14

The Strangeways Prison Report: Overview

Abstract This overview identifies the main signposts which the Strangeways Inquiry considered the Prison Service should follow to remove the features of the prison system which resulted in instability and led to the prison riots in April 1990. Among its recommendations were proposals for the establishment of a Criminal Justice Council, more visible leadership, compacts, proposals for a national system of accredited standards and improved standards of justice.

Introduction

The first 25 days of April 1990 saw the worst series of prison riots in the history of the British penal system. The Home Secretary set up an Inquiry. This is the Report of that Inquiry. The Report attempts to provide the answers to four questions connected with those riots. They are:

(1) What happened during the six most serious riots?
(2) Were those six riots properly handled?
(3) What were the causes of those riots?
(4) What should be done to prevent riots of this type happening again?

The Inquiry was conducted in two parts. Part I concentrated primarily on questions (1) and (2). It examined the six most serious riots. They were at Manchester (Strangeways), Glen Parva, Dartmoor, Cardiff, Bristol and Pucklechurch. Part II of the Inquiry dealt with the answers to questions (3) and (4). This Report is also divided into Part I and Part II in order to reflect the way in which the Inquiry was conducted.

---

* Originally published in H Woolf and S Tumin, *Prison Disturbances, April 1990: Report of an Inquiry* (HMSO, 1991).

There are two more questions which I should mention. They are:

(1) Why did the riots not happen earlier?
(2) Why were the consequences of those riots not even more serious?

The answer to these two questions is clear. It is that the members of the Prison Service as a whole, against heavy odds, have managed over a number of years to contain an almost impossible situation by showing immense dedication, courage and professionalism.

I wanted to draw attention to the answer to those two questions at the outset of this Report because the Report contains a number of critical comments about the Prison Service. It is important that those comments do not obscure or detract from the fact that the public have every reason to be extremely grateful to the members of the Prison Service. They have coped, usually successfully, with what could have been very many explosive situations. Despite all the stresses to which the members of the Prison Service have been subjected, the vast majority have remained steadfastly loyal to the Prison Service and have continued to show a remarkable degree of professionalism.

Ironically, when the riots struck in April 1990, the Prison Service had already started to tackle some of the worst features of the prison system which had been in existence for many years. Long term problems were, for the first time, being confronted. However, as often happens at times of change, the improvements which were being introduced brought with them periods of increased instability which made the prison system particularly vulnerable to disturbances. The riots interrupted that process of improvement.

During the period in which this Inquiry was being conducted, the Prison Service resumed its programme of change. It is a programme designed to improve the prison system. The Prison Service is, however, well aware that there still remain a great many problems which need to be addressed. In providing answers to the foregoing four questions, the Inquiry's aim has been to assist the Prison Service to continue its programme for the reform of the prison system.

To help achieve this objective, the Report will erect a series of signposts identifying the route which the Inquiry believes the Prison Service should follow. The journey will take some time. There is a great deal of ground to be made up because of neglect in the past. However, if the members of the Prison Service have the confidence in themselves which I believe they should have, and if they receive the support that they deserve, then this country will have a prison system of which it can be proud. This would be a very different situation from that which exists at present.

The Inquiry has received an extraordinary volume of evidence. In addition to the 170 witnesses who gave evidence orally at the formal hearings, the Inquiry has had numerous meetings with staff and prisoners, individuals and organisations, both in this country and abroad. To the 1,730 letters from prisoners and prison staff which the Inquiry has received, there needs to be added the numerous letters from former members of staff, ex-prisoners, the public and organisations. The Inquiry received written expert evidence in abundance from organisations and individuals. The quality of the evidence naturally differed, but it was all of value. Some items of evidence were of value because they gave an insight into some small aspect of the conditions in a particular prison. Others were of value because they helped to create the global picture of the working of the prison system which the Inquiry needed in order to answer the four questions to which I have referred.

Part I of the Report examines what happened during the six riots. The Inquiry has had to consider both the detail and the general effect of this evidence. The detail has enabled the Inquiry to draw attention to events which occurred during each riot which call in some cases for commendation and in other cases criticism. The evidence as a whole has enabled the Inquiry to identify underlying problems which exist throughout the Prison Service and which, if they are to be tackled, require action to be taken which relates not only to individual prisons but to the whole of the prison system.

It will be noted that I make no reference to the names of prisoners. This is to avoid prejudicing them in any event of a prosecution or their being still in prison. It would be most unfortunate if their identities should be disclosed by the media. I appreciate that it may be possible for those who already know the identities of the prisoners to whom I refer to make the connection. However, if this is the case, I urge them not to publish the names which I have omitted.

The Inquiry deals with the underlying problems and the remedies which they require in Part II of this Report. Part II is in five sections. The five sections are headed: Imprisonment, Buildings, Management, Staff and Prisoners. Each section concentrates on more than one of the underlying problems and sets out recommendations or proposals for remedying them. The scale of the problems and the full significance of each recommendation or proposal can only be appreciated, however, if they are considered collectively. A number of the recommendations and proposals are dependent upon the implementation of others. In other words, the picture must be looked at as a whole.

For this purpose, it is essential to have an overview of the whole Report. It is that overview which this section of the Report seeks to provide.

The overview is divided into three parts. The first part is the thumbnail sketch of each of the six disturbances. This should provide a backcloth of what happened during the disturbances against which the remainder of the overview can be considered.

The second part of this section draws attention to the central problems of the Prison Service. These problems explain the instability which results in the prison system being disrupted by disturbances, of which the April 1990 riots are so far the most serious.

The third part of this section identifies the principle changes which are needed if the Prison Service is to be able to tackle its underlying problems. Twelve recommendations are made. But no reference is made here to the proposals which are set out in the succeeding sections of this Report. They are summarised with the recommendations in Section 15. The distinction which the Inquiry has drawn between its recommendations and its proposals is that, while both are important, the recommendations identify the major changes which the Inquiry would like to see made. The proposals identify the detailed improvements which the Inquiry regards as necessary. The recommendations are the signposts to which I referred earlier. The proposals are the steps which, over a period of time, the Prison Service should take in order to follow those signposts.

The Central Problems of the Prison Service

The riots which the Inquiry investigated were not isolated incidents. Other lesser, but still serious disturbances occurred in April 1990. They stem from a long history of violent disturbances in the prison system. On the evidence, prison riots cannot be dismissed as one-off events, or as local disasters, or a run of bad luck. They are symptomatic of a series of serious underlying difficulties in the prison system. They will only be brought to an end if these difficulties are addressed.

There was a considerable degree of consensus among those who provided evidence as to the causes of these successive disturbances. Differences tended to be ones of degree. The emphasis frequently depended on the perspective of the person providing the evidence. If it was a prisoner or a pressure group, the focus would usually be on: (i) the insanitary and overcrowded physical conditions to which prisoners were subjected; (ii) the negative and unconstructive nature of the regime; (iii) the lack of respect with which the prisoners were treated; (iv) the destructive effects of prison on the prisoner's family ties and the inadequacy of visits; and (v) the lack of any form of independent redress for grievances.

If the evidence was from uniformed staff, it would recognise a need to improve the conditions for prisoners, but would stress additional causes which staff felt were frustrating them in performing their duties. The evidence would draw attention to the lack of staff, lack of training, a sense of being undervalued, isolation from other staff and the divide between different grades and classes of staff. It would refer also to a lack of leadership within the Service.

Evidence from governors would agree that all the causes so far identified required attention. It would also draw attention to a lack of support and assistance from headquarters. Governors lacked confidence in headquarters. They felt powerless to implement the changes which they knew were needed within their establishments.

Some witnesses drew attention to a further problem. They identified a lack of coordination between the different parts of the Criminal Justice System. As the system operated at present, there was no link or established means of communication between the judges who were responsible for sending prisoners to prison, and the Prison Service which was responsible for holding them there. Some of those giving evidence suggested that the result of this breach in the chain of communication was chronic overcrowding. Unless a link were established, overcrowding would continue. Overcrowding led to an inherently instable prison system and resulted in disruption and riot.

I accept that these lists identify the majority, but not all, of the possible underlying causes of the riots. Each of these causes contributed to the present problems of the Prison Service. In the Report, there are recommendations of proposals which directly relate to them. They are dealt with under the respective headings of the sections in Part II of this Report.

It is possible, however, to identify one principal thread which links these causes and complaints and which draws together all our proposals and recommendations. It is that the Prison Service must set security, control and justice in prisons at the right level and it must provide the right balance between them. The stability of the prison system depends on the Prison Service doing so.

Security here refers to the need to prevent prisoners escaping. Control refers to the obligation, ultimately, to prevent prisoners causing a disturbance. Justice encapsulates the obligation on the Prison Service to treat prisoners with humanity and fairness and to act in concert with its responsibilities as part of the Criminal Justice System.

The April riots occurred because these three elements were out of balance. There were failures in the maintenance of control. There were failures to achieve the necessary standards of justice. There could easily have been a collapse in security.

These factors are each dependent on the other. If there is an absence of justice, prisoners will be aggrieved; control and security will be threatened. This is part of what happened in April. The scale of each of the riots indicates that in each establishment there was a substantial number of prisoners who were prepared to turn what otherwise could have been a limited disturbance into a full scale riot. This was, at least in part, because of the conditions in which they were held and the way in which they were treated. If a proper level of justice is provided in prisons, then it is less likely that prisoners will behave in this way. Justice, therefore, contributes to the maintenance of security and control.

Lapses in control affect both security and justice. Prisoners did not escape during the April disturbances. But they might easily have done so. They were very close to achieving this at Long Lartin prison on 2 April 1990. The April disturbances also clearly demonstrated that, with a breakdown in control, prisoners suffer as well as the Prison Service. No one can claim that the prisoners attacked in Strangeways, and intimidated in Cardiff, Pucklechurch and Dartmoor were at that time being treated in prison with justice. The breakdown in control led in many senses to a breakdown in justice in prisons.

Security, control and justice will not be set at the right level, and will not be held in balance, unless there are changes in the way the Prison Service structures its relations, both between management and staff, and between staff and prisoners. There is a fundamental lack of respect and a failure to give and require responsibility at all levels in the prison system. These shortcomings must be tackled if the Prison Service is to maintain a stable system.

The evidence from Part I of the Inquiry makes this clear. Industrial relations at Dartmoor were notoriously poor. The handling of the disturbance was hampered as a result. The senses of hostility by inmates at Pucklechurch was very marked. There were failures in communication among management and with headquarters which affected the handling of and which probably prolonged the Strangeways siege.

A central objective in our proposals and recommendations, therefore, is to ensure that relations within the prison system are based upon respect and responsibility. To do this we have addressed the structures and procedures which operate in the Prison Service. We have considered the nature and standard of provision for prisoners and for those who work in the Prison Service. If, through the operation of these structures, management show that they respect their staff and are ready to give them greater responsibility for their own work, then staff are more likely to treat prisoners in the same way. At the same time, prisoners will not respect staff if they know that staff have no respect for or confidence in their managers. Headquarters must give a lead, but it has a right also to expect that leadership to be followed.

These then should be the fundamental objectives of the Prison Service. If they are to be achieved, the Prison Service will need to be an integral part of a Criminal Justice System which cooperates to meet the objectives of all parts of that system. The recommendations and proposals in this Report are directed to these ends.

What Should Be Done to Prevent Repetition of the Riots?

The Prison Service is well aware of a need to improve the present situation in its prisons. Over recent years, the Prison Service has instituted a series of fundamental changes within the Service of the greatest importance.

First, there has been a vast rebuilding and refurbishment programme which was long overdue. In 1990/91, roughly £300m is to be spent on new prisons and almost £150m is to be spent on refurbishment. That programme necessarily takes time. It will transform the physical conditions within the prisons. This will both increase stability within prisons and improve relations between prisoners and staff and staff and management.

The Inquiry has had two aims in relation to the building and refurbishment programme. The first is to stress the importance of ensuring that the progress is as fast as is practicable. The second is to ensure that, where it is not already too late, the programme takes fully into account the lessons which are to be learnt from the recent disturbances and the principles which should apply for the future. The most important of these principles are that prisoners should be accompanied in small units and in community prisons.

Secondly, the Prison Service has introduced, since 1987, two different and radical managerial reforms. The first was a package designed to reform the organisation of staff and management within prison establishments. It was sorely needed. There were undoubtedly deeply embedded work practices within the Prison Service which were grossly inefficient and which needed to be addressed. There were structural difficulties which needed attention.

There were organisational problems which required change. 'Fresh Start' was an attempt to achieve the necessary changes.

Under 'Fresh Start', the excessive periods of overtime which prison officers were working, and were having to work in order to earn a reasonable wage, were to be phased out. The uniformed grades of staff and the governor grades were to be unified. The tasks within each prison establishment were to be grouped and were to be performed by teams of management and staff. These were all important changes for the better.

The manner in which the changes have been implemented, however, has meant that 'Fresh Start' has not succeeded in improving relations in many prisons. Staff feel that they were misled as to what was involved in the 'Fresh Start' package. They do not believe that the Prison Service has delivered what it promised. The objectives of the 'Fresh Start' package have been imperilled by a widely held belief that it has resulted in still more inadequate staffing levels.

Whether this last belief is justified or not can only be ascertained if some way is found of objectively ascertaining what is the proper staffing level within each prison establishment. The Prison Service is at present carrying out a process to enable this to be done. The merits of that process were in dispute before the Inquiry. The Prison Officers' Association at the present time are not prepared to be associated with the process. This is a reflection of the unhappy state of industrial relations between the Prison Officers' Association and the Prison Service. While the present approach for determining staffing levels may not be perfect, no better method of achieving the objective has been suggested to the Inquiry. If undertaken properly, the present exercise cannot but improve the position. It is for this reason that the Report urges the Prison Officers' Association to rethink their attitude to it.

The second managerial reform was implemented in September 1990. It involved the reorganisation of management above establishment level. There are aspects of this reorganisation which have been strongly criticised by governors and other staff. However, the reorganisation has been implemented. The Inquiry took the view that, this having been done, it should have an opportunity of proving its worth before its merits were assessed. The Inquiry has assumed, therefore, that, for the time being at any rate, this structure of management above establishment level will remain.

The changes which the Prison Service has already attempted and is attempting to bring about are important. However, they are primarily directed to the physical conditions within the prison system, and to the management of that system. There needs to be greater attention paid to the way in which prisoners and staff are treated. The way prisoners are treated can often be a reflection of the way staff themselves feel they are treated by management. An important lesson of the riots is that they would either not have taken place, or, if they had, they would have been on a different scale, if a substantial body of inmates had not been prepared to support those who instigated the initial disturbance which developed into a riot at each establishment. What is now required is a planned programme of change which will address the substantial problems which remain.

The planned programme should address the lack of stability and the unsatisfactory state of relations within the prison system. The programme has to take into account the need for a balance between security, control and justice. In Part II of this Report, together with His Honour Judge Tumin, I identify such a programme.

Our programme is based on 12 central recommendations. These are that there should be:

(1) closer cooperation between the different parts of the Criminal Justice System. For this purpose a national forum and local committees should be established;

(2) more visible leadership of the Prison Service by a Director General who is and is seen to be the operational head and in day-to-day charge of the Service. To achieve this there should be a published 'compact' or 'contract' given by Ministers to the Director General of the Prison Service, who should be responsible for the performance of that 'contract' and publicly answerable for the day-to-day operations of the Prison Service;

(3) increased delegation of responsibility to Governors of establishments;

(4) an enhanced role for prison officers;

(5) a 'compact' or 'contract' for each prisoner setting out the prisoner's expectations and responsibilities in the prison in which he or she is held;

(6) a national system of Accredited Standards, with which, in time, each prison establishment would be required to comply;

(7) a new Prison Rule that no establishment should hold more prisoners than is provided for in its certified normal level of accommodation, with provisions for Parliament to be informed if exceptionally there is to be a material departure from that rule;

(8) a public commitment from Ministers setting a timetable to provide access to sanitation for all inmates at the earliest practicable date not later than February 1996;

(9) better prospects for prisoners to maintain their links with families and the community through more visits and home leaves and through being located in community prisons as near to their homes as possible;

(10) a division of prison establishments into small and more manageable and secure units;

(11) a separate statement of purpose, separate conditions and generally a lower security categorisation for remand prisoners;

(12) improved standards of justice within prisons involving the giving of reasons to a prisoner for any decision which materially and adversely affects him; a grievance procedure and disciplinary proceedings which ensure that the Governor deals with most matters under his present powers; relieving Boards of Visitors of their adjudicatory role; and providing for final access to an Independent Complaints Adjudicator.

In the following paragraphs and in the remainder of the Report we describe these recommendations more fully. They are central to resolving the problems which have been identified from the April disturbances. They are also a package. They need to be considered together and moved forward together if the necessary balance in our prison system is to be achieved.

The Structures for Consultation Across the Criminal Justice System

The Prison Service must coordinate its activities with those of the other sections of the Criminal Justice System. In the course of this Report we identify many areas which require cooperation, coordination and consultation between the various parts of the Criminal Justice System. At the present time, there is no body in existence in which all those responsible for the different sections of the Criminal Justice System can consult together so as to perform more effectively their role in the system.

There are special conferences which make a contribution. There are trilateral meetings between the Lord Chancellor, the Home Secretary and the Attorney-General, complemented by regular meetings among officials. However, there is no body in which all the important interests are represented. In the Inquiry's judgement, there is a need for a forum in which information of mutual interest to the different sections of the Criminal Justice System can be exchanged and proposals for improvement can be considered. There is clearly room for debate as to what form this committee or forum should take, who should be involved and what its terms of reference should be. However, that a forum is needed, this Inquiry does not doubt. It therefore recommends that a national forum for this purpose should be created.

It is for those who would have the responsibility for setting up the forum to determine its precise nature. A possible model which the Inquiry would favour would involve creating a forum composed of a very senior Judge to represent the Lord Chief Justice, and possibly the permanent heads of the Home Office, the Lord Chancellor's Department, and the Head of the Crown Prosecution Service, together with a distinguished policeman and probation officer, who would be likely to command the respect of their colleagues. The Council Director General of the Prison Service would also be a member. The Council would co-opt other members when the business made this necessary. For example, the permanent head of the Department of Health would attend if there were a problem with regard to mentally disordered offenders. The forum might be called the Criminal Justice Consultative Council.

In addition to the national forum, there should be Local Committees reflecting similar interests and responsible for achieving similar objectives at a local level. Again, there is room for debate about the level at which the Local Committee should be pitched and as to what its precise terms of reference should be. We consider, however, that a local Judge should sit on each Committee. The Committees which exist in some parts of the country at present do not involve Judges. The experience of these Committees, however, shows clearly the value of a Committee of this sort. We consider that value can be increased by broadening their membership and scope, and by bringing them within the ambit of the national forum. It should be the responsibility of the national forum to determine what would be the preferable model of Local Committee, to set up the appropriate organisation for the Local Committees and to supervise them.

The Head of the Prison Service

During the April disturbances, and in particular during the disturbance at Strangeways, there was a widely held sense of a lack of visible leadership of the Prison Service. This was substantially due to the structure at the top of the Prison Service at that time. There was then, as now, a Director General who, subject to Ministers, was in overall charge of the Service. There was also a Deputy Director General. The Deputy Director General was in charge of the operational side of the Prison Service. The way the Director and Deputy

Director General divided their responsibilities resulted in the Deputy Director being in overall charge of the handling of the disturbances.

The consequence of this division in responsibility was that the Director General adopted a low profile during the disturbances. He hardly featured in the evidence during Part I of the Inquiry, while the Deputy Director General's role was examined in detail.

One of the changes made by the recent reorganisation has been to remove the office of Deputy Director General. The Inquiry regards this as a move in the right direction. But this, by itself, is not enough. The Director General must be and be seen to be the visible operational head in day-to-day charge of the Prison Service. He must also give the leadership which is expected of the head of an operational service.

In the course of the evidence, it was suggested that this objective could best be achieved by making the Prison Service a separate agency. However, the Inquiry does not consider it necessary to take a position on that issue. The necessary role and responsibilities can be given to the Director General within the present structure (as they could within an agency structure). Ministers have special responsibilities in relation to the Prison Service because of its role of having to keep in custody those sent to prison by the courts. Whatever the structure or status of the Prison Service, the Inquiry appreciates that Ministers are likely to want to ensure that their responsibilities are adequately reflected.

The necessary relationship between Ministers and the Director General should be marked by Ministers giving annually to the Director General a 'compact' or 'contract'. This would identify the resources which were to be provided to the Prison service. It would establish the priorities for the Prison Service during the period covered by the 'contract'. The 'contract' would be published so that the responsibilities of the Director General were known. Its performance would be supervised by Ministers and at any time they would be entitled to vary or add to its terms. But it would be seen that it was the obligation of the Director General as the operational head of the Service to ensure that the Prison Service fulfilled the published objectives set out in the 'contract'. He would expect to explain in public the Prison Service's performance in meeting those objectives. He would continue to fulfil his other role as advisor to Ministers on Prison Service issues. He would also seek to develop the necessary cooperation with other parts of the Criminal Justice System.

I use the word 'contract' to describe this document because that is a word which is in current use within the Prison Service to describe the document between an Area Manager and the Governor of a prison setting out the annual objectives for each person. However, neither document would be legally enforceable. A 'compact' may be a preferable name for these documents and the equivalent documents which we suggest should be provided for staff in prison and for prisoners.

The Relationship Between Headquarters and Establishments

If a prison is to operate to maximum efficiency, then the governor must be given the responsibility which he needs to run the establishment. There is a need for increased delegation. The Headquarters of the Prison Service must see its primary role as being to set out the policy and objectives to be achieved by the prison and then to support and monitor the efforts of those working in prisons to give effect to that policy and achieve those objectives. The role of Headquarters should be an enabling one: enabling Governors to govern and providing support for staff. This will involve a substantial change in the attitude of Headquarters.

The Enhanced Status of Prison Officers

The quality of the prison system ultimately depends on the quality of the performance of the prison officers who have to day-to-day responsibility for dealing with prisoners. The status of prison officers needs to be raised. They should be better trained with better prospects of promotion and they should generally only be deployed on duties appropriate to their status. In order to attract candidates of the appropriate calibre, the Inquiry approves opportunities for accelerated promotion. The promotion of uniformed staff through the ranks to senior managerial posts will make a substantial contribution to improving relations between different levels of staff.

If prison officers are to be able to perform their enhanced role, then other staff will have to take over responsibility for those tasks which can no longer be sensibly performed by prison officers. To unify the Service, the increased opportunities for uniformed staff need to be matched by a reassessment of the role of non-uniformed staff which was not sufficiently considered in 'Fresh Start'.

Prison staff, including prison officers, should receive from the Governor a 'contract' which sets out what the establishment will provide for the member of staff and the duties he has to fulfil in return.

Relations With Prisoners

As an extension of the 'contractual' arrangements which we recommend should exist between Ministers and the Prison Service, and which already exists between Area Managers and prisons, the prisoner should receive a 'compact' or 'contract' from the prison at which he is held. It would be provided to both remand and sentenced prisoners. It should identify what the prison expects to provide for the prisoner, and it should set out what the prison requires from the prisoner in return. The 'contract' would be discussed with the prisoner. It would include details relating to the features of the prison regime which are important to the prisoner. If the prisoner were still in the same prison after 12 months, the 'contract' would be reviewed with him then.

If the prisoner's expectations were not fulfilled, he would be entitled to enlist the aid of the Board of Visitors or to invoke the grievance procedures to ensure that the prison did not unreasonably depart from the 'contract'. As a last resort, the 'contract' could provide a platform for judicial review. If the prisoner misbehaves then, as a result of disciplinary proceedings, he could be deprived of certain of his expectations under the 'contract'.

The 'contract' would be a recognition of the respect to which the prisoner is entitled and the responsibility which is required from him in return. In due course, as sentence planning for all prisoners develops, the 'contract' would, in the case of a prisoner serving more than 12 months, be coordinated with his or her sentence plan. The provisions in the 'contract' would change as the prisoner progresses through his sentence.

Standards Within Prisons

In order to achieve justice within prisons there must be required standards of conditions and regime with prisons. After proper consultation, the Home Secretary should establish as series of national Accredited Standards applicable to all prisons. It would then be the responsibility of every prison establishment to reach at least that standard. Area Managers, by encouragement and using the 'contract' which they have with individual prisons, would be responsible for ensuring that, over a period of time, each prison in their area fulfils all the national Accredited Standards.

The Area Manager would certify when a prison had reached a required standard. When it fulfilled all the standards, it would be granted Accreditation

Status by the Home Secretary, on the recommendation of HM Chief Inspector of Prisons (HMCIP). For the time being, the national standards would have to be aspirational. Once they are achieved, that would be the time to consider whether it was necessary to make them legally enforceable. We would, however, expect that at that stage they would be incorporated in the Prison Rules and so would be legally enforceable by judicial review.

The Control on the Number of Prisoners Within a Prison

Each prison has a certified number of prisoners it can hold without overcrowding. That provides each prisoner's level of Certified Normal Accommodation (CNA). The validity of the CNA formula as a measure for establishing the point at which overcrowding starts is disputed. However, it has the great advantage that it is a formula already in use. While its shortcomings are recognised, the Inquiry considers that, for the time being, it should be the formula which is used to indicate the maximum number of prisoners who should be accommodated at any one time in a prison. As it is unlikely that all cells within a prison will be capable of being used at any particular time, even at the CNA figure, there may be a degree of overcrowding. Sensibly, therefore, a prison should normally be occupied under its CNA. That should also follow for some capacity to deal with variations in the size of the population week by week.

The Inquiry has noted that, by the end of 1992, the Prison Service expects the total prison population to equal the total prison accommodation available. If properly managed, overcrowding should then become a thing of the past. But this needs to be regularly and closely monitored and controlled if overcrowding is not again to become endemic. That system of control needs to make some formal provision for any occasion when, because of circumstances which cannot be anticipated, it might be necessary for a prison to exceed the CNA figure.

It is therefore recommended that there should be a new Prison Rule. The Rule should come into effect at the end of 1992, if by then the system is in equilibrium. The new Rule should provide that no establishment should hold prisoners in excess of CNA. It should be possible, however, for an establishment to exceed its CNA by no more than 3 per cent for no longer than seven days in any three months. Where there are exceptional circumstances in which such a saving is not sufficient to accommodate the prison population, the Secretary of State should be required to issue a certificate specifying the precise requirement and the reasons. The certificate would last up to three months and be renewable. The Secretary of State would be required to lay a copy of the certificate before both Houses of Parliament.

This recommendation would not by itself abolish overcrowding in prisons, but it should substantially inhibit that overcrowding and would require Parliament to be informed of the situation.

Sanitation

After overcrowding, the most destructive feature of the prison system at the present time is the lack of sanitation and the degrading process of slopping out which is its consequence. It destroys the morale of prisoners and staff. It is uncivilised and a symptom of an archaic prison system. The Prison Service accepts that slopping out has to be eradicated, but as yet there is no public commitment to a date on which this practice is to end and all prisoners are to have integral sanitation.

Ministers should announce the date by which such sanitation can be provided. It should be the earliest practicable date. It should not be later than that already recommended by HMCIP—February 1996. Such an announcement could send the clearest signal possible that the Prison Service is to be committed to bringing the prison system up to acceptable and just standards.

Links With the Community

As conditions within prisons improve, the Inquiry would like to see greater emphasis being placed throughout a prisoner's sentence on his eventual return to the community. If the destructive effects of imprisonment are to be reduced so that the prospects of the prisoner not reoffending can be improved, it is critical that, where this is possible, the prisoner's links with his family and the community should be maintained. The Report, therefore, recommends more extensive provision for visits and leave. Most prisoners attach the greatest importance to visits and leave and the opportunity to have them is a significant incentive to responsible behaviour.

It is also highly desirable for the stable running of a prison and for the prospects for the prisoner leading a law abiding life after release that, whenever practicable, he should be accommodated as near to his home and community as possible. The problem of holding prisoners remote from their homes and visitors was a very evident factor during the disturbances. So was the number of prisoners transferred from other prisons which were nearer to their homes.

We therefore recommend a system of community prisons. These would be either prisons near to the main centres of population, as many local prisons are now, with the facilities and accommodation capable of holding most prisoners throughout most of their sentence. Or they could be arranged in clusters of separate prisons within a locality through which the prisoner could progress. We recognise also that this is a recommendation which cannot be implemented in full immediately. It is a signpost which the Prison Service should follow and which should influence its management and use of its existing and new buildings.

Small Units

The implementation of the last recommendation would be facilitated if prisoners were to be accommodated in small units. Small units would also assist in the security and management of prisoners. A lesson of the April disturbances is that, within a large prison establishment, there need to be 'firebreaks' which can be readily secured by prison staff so as to prevent prisoners overwhelming the whole prison.

It is preferable, therefore, for prisoners to be accommodated and managed in units containing about 50–70 prisoners. Larger wings in existing and new prisons should be divided so as to hold approximately the desired number of prisoners. The ability to incorporate this approach into an existing prison is clearly demonstrated by the plans which the Prison Service has drawn up for the refurbishment of the main prison at Manchester.

It is also desirable that the number of prisoners treated as being in the same prison should not exceed 400. This does not mean that a prison should never accommodate more than 400 where there is the space to do so. On the contrary, it is fully recognised that if proper use is to be made of the prisons at present available, many more than 400 prisoners will have to be accommodated in some prisons.

However, where this is the situation, the Inquiry's recommendation would be met by operating two or more prisons within the same prison within the same prison perimeter. They would share the common facilities within that perimeter.

The days when it is appropriate for all the cells in a prison the size of Manchester to be able to opened by the same key are over. There should be different locks on the cells of each unit so that the loss of a set of keys will only give access to the cells of one unit. The units should be divided from each other by secure gates, preferably electrically operated. In the case of other areas in a prison where large numbers of prisoners congregate, there should be similar opportunities for containing prisoners within a defined area.

The security and management advantages of small units should result in a greater feeling of security for prisoners and for prison staff. They should therefore result in improved relations and in better justice for prisoners.

They should also enable the requirements of security and control, and the range of regimes offered, to be better attuned to the requirements of each part of the prison population. The result should be better relations, better control, better justice and a better balance between all three.

Remand Prisoners

It must be beyond dispute that only those for whom prison is essential should be there. This approach has influenced the Inquiry's consideration of whether there are groups of offenders who could be diverted from prison in greater numbers if alternative facilities were more fully available. The Inquiry has concentrated particularly on the position of remand prisoners. This is because they represent a significant proportion of the prison population and because they unjustly suffer some of the worst conditions in the prison system.

The Inquiry proposes the extension of the initiatives which are already being implemented in some, but not all, areas of the country to avoid unnecessary remands in custody. Those who have to be remanded in prison, as a matter of justice should be contained in conditions which, as far as this is possible, reflect the prisoner's remand status. These conditions must acknowledge that the remand prisoner is innocent unless and until proved guilty. They must reflect too the reasons for which the remand has been granted under the Bail Act 1976.

To emphasise the importance of these matters, the Inquiry recommends that there should be a separate Statement of Purpose setting out the Prison Service's responsibilities relating to remand prisoners. This Statement of Purpose should reflect the principle that remand prisoners should normally be part of the policy of the Prison Service to ensure that a remand prisoner spends his time while in custody in as constructive a manner as possible and that, to the extent that this is practicable, his employment, family and community connections should be kept intact. In order to further this policy, it is recommended that all remand prisoners, unless there is good reason for treating them otherwise, should be regarded as being equivalent to Category C rather than Category B prisoners.

A Grievance Procedure and Disciplinary Proceedings

Prisoners should know why a decision which materially and adversely affects them is being taken. This is essential to achieving satisfactory relations within prisons. If prisoners consider they have a genuine grievance, they should be able to have resort to a grievance procedure which has at its final stage the necessary degree of independence.

There should also be a more appropriate distinction drawn between disciplinary and criminal proceedings. Disciplinary proceedings should be capable of being appropriately disposed of by the exercise by a prison governor of his existing powers of punishment, subject to an appropriate right of appeal. It is not consistent with the Board of Visitors' watchdog functions for the Board of Visitors to be involved in adjudicatory proceedings.

The Inquiry's recommendation therefore involves:

(1) prisoners normally being given reasons for any decisions which adversely affect them to a material extent and the Prison Rules being amended to set out the details of that requirement;
(2) there being a legally qualified and independent Complaints Adjudicator who should be able at the final stages of the grievance procedure to make recommendations and, in cases of disciplinary proceedings, to determine an appeal;
(3) the adjudicatory role of Boards of Visitors being abolished; and
(4) serious criminal offences committed in prison being heard by the normal criminal courts.

Conclusion

What has been set out in this overview indicates the general approach of the Inquiry to the four questions with which this section began. It is not intended to give an indication of all the issues considered by the Inquiry, or all the proposals which the Inquiry has made. It is intended to identify the main signposts which the Inquiry considers the Prison Service should follow for the future.

In making its recommendations and in making its proposals the Inquiry has tried to be realistic and practical and to take into account the likely financial consequences. Some recommendations and proposals have financial implications, but not all should lead to greater expense.

It is partly with a view to avoiding unnecessary expense that the Inquiry has concentrated on methods of diverting from prison those who need not be there—although that was not the sole reason. There should be cost savings in reducing the involvement of prison officers in fields where their enhanced status is not required—although, again, cost savings are not the primary justification. The Inquiry has proposed the curtailing of censorship, partly because it recognises that the expense involved in censoring is out of proportion to the benefits. The proposals of the Inquiry to reduce the security status of remand prisoners, and the proposals which should have the effect of reducing the number of prisoners unnecessarily held within the highly secure dispersal system, should also lead to a reduction of expense. The alterations which the Inquiry proposes should be made to the grievance procedures and to disciplinary proceedings are deliberately designed to avoid unnecessary and disproportionate expenditure, although some additional costs would be incurred.

Finally, and most importantly, when drawing up the balance sheet of the cost of the improvements which the Inquiry believes should be implemented, it is necessary to remember that the objective is to remove the features of the existing prison system which result in instability and which lead to riots. The cost of the April disturbances here speak for themselves.

15

Strangeways: A Decade of Change?

Abstract This paper provides a personal assessment of what was achieved over the intervening decade since the publication of the Strangeways Report in 1991. It considers the 12 principal recommendations and examines the extent they have been implemented. It concludes that while in almost every area covered by the recommendations there have been some improvements, and in many the progress has been significant, the picture is disappointing when judged against what should have been achieved. It identifies management and overcrowding as the causes of the shortcomings. A discussion follows on the measures which might improve the prospect for the future to ensure there is adequate security and control of prisons, justice and fairness, and a constructive regime for prisoners.

Introduction

Ten years ago today, I finished a sentence of just under 12 months. I did not spend a year in prison but a year of my life was taken over by prisons. On the 31 January 1991, I handed the Strangeways Prison Report to the then Home Secretary. At that time the Prison Service was beginning to emerge from its appalling experience during the riots and anarchy, which erupted in Strangeways and then spread to prisons in a number of other parts of the country. The Report stated that its purpose was to answer four questions. They were:

(1) What happened during the six most serious riots?
(2) Were the six riots properly handled?
(3) What were the causes of those riots?
(4) What should be done to prevent riots of this type happening again?

---

* Originally delivered at the Law Society, London, on 31 January 2001. Published in its original form by the Prison Reform Trust, 'The Woolf Report. A Decade of Change'.

After ten years it could reasonably have been expected that the whole of my report would be only of historical interest. That is probably true of the first question but I am afraid that is still not so in relation to the remaining questions. Why should this be? The report was intended to provide signposts to guide the Prison Service as to the way forward. The way forward to a Prison Service which was equipped to play its proper role within the Criminal Justice System, a Prison Service which was well managed where relations between management and staff and staff and prisoners were based on mutual respect, and a prison system were there was a proper balance between security, control and justice.

The government of the day accepted the generality of the recommendations which Sir Stephen Tumin and I had made with the assistance of our excellent assessors. The Home Secretary, Kenneth Baker (now Lord Baker), was committed to improving the system on the lines proposed in the report. I believe it is fair to say there was a general consensus that the report offered a programme for constructive change, which should be implemented. There was undoubtedly a considerable feeling of optimism within prison circles. As prison numbers were falling there appeared to be an opportunity for fundamentally improving the prison system. The Prison Service supported by staff and officers at all levels seemed determined to seize the opportunity.

I went back to being a judge feeling reasonably confident we had with the help of a great many people produced a blueprint which had a good prospect of achieving what it set out to do. This was to produce a prison system, which would be secure, humane, just, and return inmates at the end of the sentences, back into society less likely and not more likely to offend again. Objectives which are hardly controversial.

During the following ten years my involvement with prisons was limited. I was however able to keep some contact with what was happening because the report resulted in my holding a number of offices in charities, for example the Prison Reform Trust who doggedly strive to improve the criminal justice system. I do believe these bodies are among the finest in the world and we owe those who work for them a huge debt of gratitude for what they achieved. Through my connections with these charities, particularly the Butler Trust, during intervening years I was aware of many excellent initiatives which were taking place within the prison system. I was also aware that prison numbers were rising relentlessly so that they have increased by approximately 50 per cent from their low point during that decade. As I indicated, publicly, I was extremely worried by the increase.

I knew it made overcrowding inevitable. I also knew that overcrowding is more destructive to an effective prison system, than anything else.

In his recent lecture to the Trust the Director General accurately described overcrowding as a 'scourge'. In addition, there has been the notorious escapes and problems over home leave. I was worried that the importance of moving towards the long-term objectives set out in the Report had been temporarily lost sight of.

When the tenth anniversary of Strangeways drew near I received a number of invitations to give talks under a similar title to that of this talk and I declined to do so. By then I was the Master of the Rolls and I did not consider that I was justified in doing so because of my limited involvement within the prison system.

Then I was appointed to my present office and that it seemed to me changed the situation. I was again involved in prison sentencing. It is judges and magistrates who send people to prison. It should be of the greatest importance to each judge and magistrate what happens to those who they send to prison whether they are in prison, on remand or under sentence. If you send someone to prison you have a responsibility for what happens to prisoners while in custody. If you have the privilege of holding my present office you have a responsibility to make known, in as constructive a manner as possible, concerns that you may have about the criminal justice system of which prisons are a vital part. The public is deeply troubled about crime and they, with justification, look to each part of the Criminal Justice System to provide them with the protection to which they are entitled. Prisons are a critical part of the Criminal Justice System. You cannot have an effective Criminal Justice System without effective prisons. I was aware that Lord Hurd, while the Chairman of the PRT, had once said of our prisons:

> It is our job, to break the destructive silence, and we must continue to do so, for a huge amount is still amiss.[1]

So although I cannot speak with the same authority as I did ten years ago having just having completed my sentence, I will give you my personal assessment of what has been achieved over the intervening decade. I will look at my 12 principal recommendations and examine the extent they have been implemented and I will then suggest measures, which might improve the prospect for the next decade.

---

[1] *Independent on Sunday*, 31 December 2000.

In making these remarks, I have the great advantage of having read two immensely instructive papers given to the Trust at a seminar held to mark the tenth anniversary of Strangeways. One was by Professor Morgan who was an assessor to the Inquiry and the other by Mr Narey, the former Director General of the Prison Service. Mr Narey's account appears to be admirably frank, balanced and helpful, and I can at least assume it is not biased against the Prison Service.[2] It helpfully sets out Mr Narey's assessment of the progress that has been made in relation to each of the 12 principal recommendations made by the Report. There are three initial points which I would make.

First, is as to security. In the intervening years, linked to overcrowding, at individual establishments there have been some extremely tense situations with which the Service has had to deal, but fortunately there has been no repetition of an incident on anything like the scale of Strangeways. The Prison Service deserves credit for this.

The second point is that in the intervening decade, as far as I am aware, there has been no authoritative criticism of the general thrust of the Report. The recommendations are still generally endorsed as setting out desirable objectives. The criticism, if any, is as to the detail. Again, as far as I am aware successive Home Secretaries and Prison Ministers have been supportive of the Report. This is true of Mr Michael Howard who at a time when I was expressing concerns about the impact of some of his policies wrote to me in his own hand assuring me that the reforms which I had recommended were safe in his hands. He was however subsequently concerned as to whether the reforms were diverting attention from security to which he gave priority. Of course all Home Secretaries, of whatever political complexion, at least since Winston Churchill, who made that famous remark about the way we treat our prisoners reflecting the moral fibre of the nation, have been in favour of improving conditions in prisons.

The third point flows from the previous points. It is that the lack of dissent is not surprising. Although perhaps I am not the person who should be saying this, the Report was doing no more than seeking to make sensible changes to the prison system designed to ensure that there would be an appropriate degree of security coupled with just treatment and constructive regimes. In other words, while recognising the importance of security and control, there also has to be justice and fairness and a constructive regime for inmates. Each of these elements supports the other.

---

[2] Martin Narey ceased to be the Director General of the Prison Service in February 2003. He became the first Chief Executive of the new National Offender Management Service in January 2004.

The difference between the Report and its predecessors and its successors is that it did not focus on one individual aspect of the system. Indeed, so far as our terms of reference permitted we dealt with the reforms in the context of the Criminal Justice System as a whole. I turn to the recommendations.

Criminal Justice Council

The first recommendation was the establishment of the Criminal Justice Council. The reason for the recommendation was that each part of the Criminal Justice System was acting independently of others. This is a subject of which Mr Narey can speak with great authority since he was the first secretary of the Council. He is in agreement with Professor Morgan's analysis. The Council has been established but it has struggled. He identifies some victories but says the problem was at the area level. I accept that there was and is this problem. But I fear it was inevitable for the reason he gives. As Mr Narey states it was 'nigh on impossible' to find a rational way in which you could have sensible coordinating bodies for 56 probation authorities, 42 police areas, 12 Prison Service areas and hundreds of Petty Sessional Divisions and, I would add, six Court Circuits. The sensible result that the agencies should each have the same boundaries is one the Inquiry could not achieve. However, more should be achievable and I would expect Auld LJ to address how this can be achieved.[3]

While recognising the limits of what has been achieved so far I do not regard this as an area of failure. The main Council has been in existence for ten years. Its first Chairman the Vice President, Lord Justice Rose, who is now retired, established a viable Council. Lord Kay has succeeded him. Over the ten years the Council has provided a forum in which discussion at the very highest level can take place between all the principal players in the Criminal Justice System. This is much needed improvement. As Mr Narey points out important rationalisation is now taking place 'which is very encouraging' and makes action between agencies possible which was not possible before. This is not just a question of bureaucratic tidiness; it goes to the heart of making the system work, as it should.

Take short-term prisoners and those on remand. They have the most impoverished time in prison. Why? Because in view of the short period they are in custody the programmes cannot be completed while they are there.

---

[3] See R E Auld, *A Review of the Criminal Courts of England and Wales* (HMSO, 2001).

But, if programmes in prisons were to be coordinated with programmes outside, after release a programme could be completed. Again there is considerable scope with cooperation to improve the arrangements for returning prisoners back into the community and so reducing the risk of prisoners reoffending.

More Visible Leadership

As to progress on the next recommendation, more visible leadership, I can answer more positively than the Director General can. I can say what he could not. That I have no reservations as to the quality of the leadership, which has been provided by successive heads of the Prison Service since Strangeways. It has been at least as good as I hoped and in Mr Narey's case is admirable. An agency has been established and that provides at least some space between ministers and the Service. As to increased delegation to governors, I have no reason to disagree with Mr Narey when he says the situation has been transformed. However, regrettably there are still real problems between different levels of management. I will return to this subject later. I am also pleased to know that prison officers are being given an enhanced role but I suspect more could have been done but for overcrowding.

Compacts

I turn to compacts or contracts. The importance of compacts is that they could develop the prisoner's sense of responsibility. They enable the prisoner to know what is expected of him and what he will get in return. Mr Narey deals with compacts and acknowledges the progress has been 'less dramatic'. Professor Morgan shares this assessment of the position. This is disappointing but hardly surprising because there are two parties to compacts. If the Prison Service does not believe it can deliver its side of a compact it is not going to enter into it. To do so would leave the inmate feeling he has been let down and the Prison Service could even be judicially reviewed. Sadly, the picture that Mr Narey draws is that across the Service as a whole the Service cannot deliver what the compact should provide. However, at least some establishments are achieving a great deal through compacts. I recently visited a most impressive Young Offenders Institute, Swinfen Hall. Their compacts are being used and the youngsters have a sense of dignity, which bodes well if their return to the community or entry into adult establishments can be properly arranged. Other establishments are using them in conjunction with the Earned Privilege Scheme and drug testing strategy.

There should be a national system of accredited standards

There was ten years ago a striking contrast between standards within prison establishments. Regrettably the national system of accredited standards which I recommended to combat this does not exist. Mr Narey indicates the position is changing and points to the performance standards. However in 1999–2000 the Service met less than half of its Key Performance Indicators which is hardly impressive.

Access to sanitation

At the time of Strangeways the humiliation and the degradation of slopping out was the norm. A recommendation for integral sanitation was made. It was thought to have been completed in 1996. But in 2001 four wings still did not possess it. In addition, in local prisons and remand centres some health care and segregation units still relied on slopping out. Why was this so? It was thought the wings were to be raised to the ground, as they deserved to be. Why did that not happen? The rise in prison numbers provides the answer. The size of the prison population meant that the wings, which were intended to be closed because they were not worth modernising, had to be retained. When is this shaming situation to change? No prospect in the short to medium term, but at least the Prison Service is seeking to provide 24-hour manual unlocking to provide access to sanitation on the wings. In addition I am told the Prison Service is applying for funds to introduce sanitation in such health care and segregation cells as are capable of receiving it. In the meantime, the Chief Inspector found at Portland, a young offenders institution, that slopping out had not ended in the induction and therapeutic wings and the young offenders were forced to live in 'disgraceful squalor' and in conditions described by the Governor as a 'moral outrage'.

Community Prisons

The next recommendation to which I turn is important. It is that there should be Community Prisons. The object being that prisoners would be able to maintain better links with their families if they were imprisoned locally. Better links with families would assist in their return to the community. It would also help with obtaining employment and accommodation on release.

In addition it would mean that it would be easier to maintain continuity in links with the probation service before and after release.

The facilities for visits have been improved in many establishments. Crèches are being provided for children (Kids VIP are here to be congratulated) but Mr Narey recognises there has been limited progress. The Prison Service also spends over £2m per annum on fares for family visits in order to mitigate the consequences of inmates being imprisoned at a place, which is far from home. This is admirable but of the concept of the Community Prisons I recommended Mr Narey says it is 'a dream' and I am afraid he is right. This is the position notwithstanding that Home Office research indicates that 'good family ties can reduce a prisoner's risk of offending by six times'.

I am told by the Prison Service that in accordance with the Report:

(1) 'where *possible* we aim to hold prisoners as close to their home community as *possible*';
(2) 'where *feasible* a cluster of prisons should provide separate establishments for women, remand prisoners, young male offenders and adult men'.

However, the reality is that of the approximately 65,000 prisoners, 26,000 are over 50 miles from their homes, 11,000 are over 100 miles from their home and 5,000 over 150 miles from their homes. This is again a consequence of overcrowding. Part of the problem is also the 'nimby'[4] factor. There is real difficulty in obtaining planning permission for new prisons. Mr Narey says rather wistfully: 'Nobody thought it a good idea to put three prisons on the Isle of Wight'; and adds ominously that he does not rule out a fourth. The desirability of Community Prison is not in issue. I realised this was a long-term project but the curse of overcrowding means the concept will remain theoretical for the foreseeable future. What is more, by building prisons in the wrong place we are institutionalising inappropriate accommodation and the increasing expense of funding visits. However, it is comforting that the Director General at least accepts that the concept of the community prison is a desirable goal.

I recently visited Wandsworth Prison. The Prison Inspector in his inimitable style gave Wandsworth a roasting in his report of 1998. The combination of the report and a new governor has proved to be a catalyst. Wandsworth has

---

[4] Otherwise known as 'not in my back yard'.

clearly changed its spots and it is a very different institution from that at the time of the last inspection. It now has an excellent feel and I was very pleased to note that the prison at Wandsworth describes itself as a Community Prison. I was also delighted that the Prison Officer's Association (POA) were supportive of the changes that were taking place in Winchester.

Prisons Should be Divided into Small and Secure Units

In order to achieve greater security I recommended that prisons should be divided into manageable units. This is being adopted in new prisons or prisons such as Strangeways which have had to be rebuilt, but with existing prisons the pressure to keep cells in use means limited progress. This is unfortunate not only because keeping prisoners secure is an important responsibility of the Service but also because security inspires confidence in the staff and inmates. Security is supportive of regimes so this is again a worrying consequence of overcrowding.

Improved Standards of Justice

At the time of Strangeways, justice stopped at the prison door. I regarded this as one of the worst aspects of the system. For the justice system to send people to prison where they would not be treated justly was intolerable. This is an area where it is claimed, with justification, that there has been substantial progress in implementing the reforms. There is now an Ombudsman (the present one being the admirable former Director of the Trust, Stephen Shaw). Boards of Visitors no longer have their disciplinary powers, which I considered were inappropriate for a body responsible for being the public's 'watchdog' within the prison. There is also now an established grievance procedure.

However, again Mr Narey acknowledges the situation is not what it should be. He recognises that the delay in handling of grievances was in danger of bringing the whole exercise into disrepute. An ineffective grievance procedure is probably as bad as no procedure at all. However, the delays are now coming down. Lets hope they continue to do so and stay down.

In addition, I would like to see changes to the Ombudsman Scheme and to the Board of Visitors. There is an association of Ombudsmen of this country and Ireland. I have tried to persuade them to accept the Prison Ombudsman as a member but they have refused to do so. As I understand the position, the reason for this is that they do not accept that the structure of the Prison Ombudsman is sufficiently independent of the Home Office. There is a risk of this perception being shared by inmates. It is absolutely essential that the integrity of the Prison Ombudsman be accepted. Anyone who knows the present Ombudsman and his predecessor would not have an iota of doubt as to their integrity and fairness. But it would be an advantage if they were answerable to someone else other than the Home Office. The Cabinet Office has conducted a review into Ombudsmen and I have suggested the Prison Ombudsman should report and be answerable to the Central Government Ombudsman.

The Board of Visitors are still undervalued by the Home Office and Service. I am confident that all their contribution is already extremely valuable. It could be far more positive if it was given the support that it needs. I recommended their profile should be raised by having a President. This was not accepted. At that time the Boards were not all of one mind. The proposal now has much stronger support. Ambov[5] is wholly in favour. Some of the annual reports I see are excellent. However, if their contribution appears to be undervalued this encourages under performance. Good leadership could make all the difference. I would also like to see the Boards doing more to combat the ignorance of their role. What about enabling young lawyers and others who are interested to spend a period working with a Board part time? Both sides would benefit. I would hope the Home Office would take the lead and allow some of their brightest high flyers to see what really happens in Prisons.

Remand Prisoners

I recommended a separate statement of purpose, separate conditions and generally a lower security categorisation for remand prisoners. This has not happened. The treatment of remand prisoners all too often means that they are at the bottom of the pack when they should be, as unconvicted prisoners, at the top of the pack. Because they are short stays they tend to qualify for the poorest accommodation. I cannot do better than cite Mr Narey as to the sorry position:

> although the population of remand has fallen very recently and there is some hope that this will be maintained, and although there are now performance standards for remand prisoners, conditions for most remand prisoners remain primitive.

---

[5] Association of Members of Boards of Visitors.

Mr Narey also accepts that the education, drug, offending behaviour programmes have only been of marginal benefit to those on remand.

Mr Narey provides no explanation for this state of affairs. This is a problem, which is calling out to be tackled. I am afraid I have seen nothing to suggest that any real action is yet planned.

The Impression Overall

What is my overall assessment of what has happened within the Prison System over the decade since I delivered the report? The picture is certainly not all black. In almost every area covered by the report's recommendations there have been some improvements and in many the progress has been significant. The physical conditions inside prisons have been transformed. Slopping out has virtually disappeared. Prisons are more just and more secure. There are telephones, television and better facilities for visits. Excellent work is being done to tackle solvent abuse with the involvement of prison officers. The need for the different parts of the Criminal Justice System to work together is recognised. Take Wandsworth, which I visited earlier this month. It was the subject of a damning report by the Chief Inspector in 1999. However, within 12 months new leadership meant I found it transformed from the establishment a decade ago. The prison staff were confident and the Prison Officers' Association cooperative. Regimes and time out of cells were satisfactory. There were many positive changes including induction courses and an energetic programme of suicide prevention involving the Samaritans and listeners touring the prison. There are other prisons where the same thing can be said. Taking into account overcrowding the Prison Service is entitled to at least one cheer and possibly two. The tragedy is that there was a prospect of doing so much more. We were on the way to creating a system of which the nation need not be ashamed and which would have made a positive contribution in the fight against crime. Judged against what should have been achieved it has to be said that the picture is disappointing. There is no difficulty in identifying the causes of the shortcomings. They relate to management and above all overcrowding and it is to those subjects I now turn.

The Management Problems

While the successive Director Generals have certainly provided more visible leadership there have been real problems over management. The problems have been linked to overcrowding and the stress this has placed on the system can be demonstrated in many ways: the high level of governor and staff absence due to sickness (according to the president of the Prison Governors[6] the sickness rate for governors 'virtually doubled in the last year'); the constant moving of the governing governors from one establishment to an other due to the need for crisis management (four governors in less than four years at Feltham tells its own story of management failure); the inability to make inroads on the high incidence of suicide; and the failure to develop across the system innovative good practices and the inability to maintain regimes. There is also the failure to tackle the remand problem, but I hope this is now high on the agenda. Nonetheless, undoubtedly there has been an improvement and I believe the Service is anxious to make further improvements and notwithstanding the problems I am confident this will happen.

I am confident that having to cope with an overcrowded system is compounding the problems with which management is faced. In addition I read the President of the Prison Governor's Association's description of the managerial climate as being characterised 'by fear, blame and a sense of impending doom'. I noted also that he put at least part of the blame on two things: the area management structure introduced by the Service while I was still working on my report; and the fact that governing governors 'do not feel trusted by Headquarters'. It would not be appropriate for me to try and identify the cure for the management shortcomings but on the second point I would repeat what the head of the Prison Service in Scotland illustrated to me at the time of Strangeways. He drew on a piece of paper two triangles, one with the apex at the top and the other with the apex at the bottom. The apex was the HQ and his message was that HQ should see itself at the bottom of the triangle supporting first the management and then the staff and not on the top of the triangle bearing down on management and staff.

Overcrowding

I come finally to overcrowding. Mr Narey, the former Director General, described it as a 'scourge'. I have described it previously as a 'cancer' but if an analogy with a disease is appropriate, and I think it is, then I would prefer to

---

6 Mike Newell, AMBoV, Winter 2001.

describe it as the AIDS of the Prison Service. I do so not to demonise AIDS but because it appears to have two features in common with overcrowding in our prison system. First, it debilitates the whole system and, secondly, we are still struggling to find a cure notwithstanding the expenditure of vast sums of money in trying to find the answer. It is because of overcrowding that we have still what Lord Hurd justifiably described as 'sick nicks'.

Overcrowding means prisoners are housed in unsatisfactory conditions. They are often miles away from their families so family ties suffer, notwithstanding the large sums paid out to subsidise the costs of visits. It means that programmes which have established and that reduced reconviction rates and prevent reoffending are neglected. Most importantly it results in the spasmodic delivery of education. For the consequence of this I again cite Mr Narey: 'This year the budget has been increased but the previous 2 years it had been cut. It is now focused on literacy and numeracy.' No one can complain about this since, as Mr Narey points out, 40,000 prisoners, 65 per cent of the prison population are ineligible for 96 per cent of the jobs. The position is even worse in some Young Offenders Institutions. Mr Narey cites Wetherby Young Offenders' Institution where 50 per cent of the boys were excluded from school from the age of 13. However, should we be in a position where to achieve what we need to do we have to cut other education, which is very important? Mr Narey confesses what has been happening by admitting he was almost lynched at Parkhurst by teachers who were enraged that he had shut down recreational classes.

My analogy of AIDS is not therefore an exaggeration of the scale of the problem. However, you might think that the problem should be simple to resolve. All you need to do is stop sending more people to prison and build more prisons and then you obtain the equilibrium, which should exist. Over the last decade this has been tried. We have at enormous long-term expense built or reopened 24 prisons, but half are already overcrowded. We are still planning even more prison building and also estimating an even larger prison population, though we already imprison more people than any country in Europe (other than Portugal).

We must remind ourselves of the figures, which are well known. After my report the figure went down to close to 43,000 before embarking on the continuously rising trail. Overall over the decade there was an increase of 50 per cent but in the case of women prisoners the figure doubled. The Home Office considers most of this increase can be attributed to a change in Crown Court sentencing practice. Over a third of women prisoners are there on their first conviction and the majority are young and have dependent children. Because of the overcrowding, education and probation contracts have been cut. Recent figures show at Holloway the women inmates have only nine hours purposeful activity each week.[7]

As to the future, the Home Office accepts that the figures are likely to rise. By 2007 the population was at least 78,000 and the female population increased by almost a further 50 per cent. Not only are we still going to have overcrowding ten years from now, but also the cost of housing the population is going to soar. In 2001 the annual cost of each prisoner was £25,000 per annum;[8] four prisoners increase the cost to £100,000, 40 prisoners to £1m; 100 to £2.5m; 1,000 prisoners to £25m; and for the 30,000 increase between 1991 and 2001, the cost increased to £750m. Do we think this a worthwhile expenditure especially if the system is going to remain inefficient because it is overcrowded?

What Should be Done About Overcrowding?

If by itself prison building is not going to provide a solution, is there anything else we can do to tackle overcrowding? Are there no signs of hope? In Germany, and possibly France as well, a simple solution was provided by the judges adopting an agreed programme of reducing the length of sentences. Although the judiciary, including the magistracy, has been adopting a more punitive approach to sentencing over the last few years, I do not consider it would be acceptable to follow those examples. Quite apart from statutory mandatory and automatic sentences the courts are subject to a well-established sentencing framework set by the Court of Appeal. A radical adjustment of that framework in this jurisdiction is the task of Parliament and not the courts alone.

This does not mean there is nothing we can and should do. During the Strangeways Inquiry, the then Director General said it was his belief:

> that the life and work of the Prison Service have, for the last 20 years been distorted by the problems of overcrowding. That single factor has dominated prisoners' lives, it has produced often intolerable pressures on the staff, and as a consequence it has soured industrial relations. It has skewed managerial effort and it has diverted managerial effort away from positive developments.

---

[7] Prison Reform Trust, 'Justice for Women: the Need for Reform' (2000).

[8] Today, the estimated annual cost of imprisonment is £37,500 per prisoner.

> The removal of overcrowding is, in my view, an indispensable pre-condition
> of sustained and universal improvement in prison conditions.

That is still true today if you substitute 30 years for 20 years. As a nation we
cannot allow it to be true for 40 years. We must be able to manage things
better. As with AIDS, what could be efficacious is a cocktail of treatments.
There will be many views as to what the cocktail should contain. My recipe
does not contain any novel answers. I would regard them as obvious.
The cocktail's credibility depends on the range of ingredients. I should also
acknowledge that insofar as they are in a position to do so the Prison Service,
the government and the Boards established by the government are already
seeking to supply most of the ingredients so far as it is within their respective
power to do so. My treatment is also a long-term remedy.

The combination of action I suggest for reducing overcrowding includes
the following.

(1) A programme designed to make it more difficult to commit crimes

The best deterrent for preventing crime is a high prospect of detection. This
requires more intense policing and the encouragement of better protection
for homes and attractive consumer items, especially mobile phones. The car
industry has shown what they can do to make cars more secure and the
telephone manufacturers must recognise they have a similar responsibility
to the public.

(2) The numeracy and literacy deficit both within and without the prison system has to be tackled

The beneficial effect of this on offending rates now appears to be proven.

(3) The credibility and effectiveness of community sentences has to be increased

It should be generally accepted that anything to tackle offending that could
be done in custody could be achieved more effectively in the community.
Judges and Magistrates already contend with some justification that they
only use custody as a last resort. But offenders may receive custodial
sentences because the judiciary does not believe there is any credible
community alternative. What has to be realised (and I include the government here) is that a short custodial sentence is a very poor alternative to a
sentence to be served in the community. It is far more expensive than a

community alternative. It places a disproportionately heavy burden on the Prison Service. It will do nothing to tackle the offenders' behavioural problems. It should be regarded as being no more than a necessary evil whose primary purpose is to obtain compliance with court orders.

Prisons and Young Offenders Institutions find it almost impossible to do anything constructive during a short sentence so they do nothing. The result is that a short sentence is a soft option. It is much more challenging for the offender to have to complete a community punishment.

Restorative justice should be accepted as more challenging for the offender than a short sentence. Having to face up to the consequences of what you have done to your victim and to have to do something for your victim is likely to be more constructive than lying on your cell bed for three months. The government in order to give credibility to community sentences has introduced a variant on 'two strikes and you're out'. Even in its modified form it is a retrograde step likely to increase the prison population. It would be preferable if a prisoner has to be punished for a breach that he should still have to finish his community sentence and serve the additional punishment as well. There could be power to remit the additional punishment if the community sentence is eventually successfully completed.

(4) More sentencing options have to be developed

The seamless sentence, which is served partly in custody and partly in the community, is such an option. The new detention and training sentence for young offenders is an example, although it appears to be increasing the use of custody. Would a training and detention order where the detention only has to be served if the offender does not complete his or her training be a viable option? The orders should not only be available for young offenders.

(5) The reintroduction of offenders into the community must be better managed than it is at present

This requires more longer-term support than is usually available now and closer cooperation between the Prison Service and the Probation Service. In particular, any training or drug- or offence-related programmes need to be able to be continued and matched in custody or in the community. This is essential if the cycle of imprisonment, release, further crime and a longer sentence is to be more frequently avoided.

(6) The provision of the programmes must be properly resourced

(7) The period prisoners are kept on remand should be reduced by building on what has already been achieved in bringing forward the date of trial

(8) The judiciary must play their part by reducing the use of custody to what is the acceptable and appropriate minimum

In particular when a custodial sentence is necessary the shortest sentence, which is appropriate within the relevant sentencing bracket, should be imposed. Frequently one month will achieve everything that can be achieved by three months and three months will achieve everything that can be achieved by six months and so on.

(9) The judiciary must be kept informed of the progress made by offenders in the case of both custodial and non-custodial sentences imposed by them

With the aid of technology, when it is available, it should not only be possible to achieve this but also for the same judge to be responsible for any post-sentence orders. The fact that an offender is aware that he will have to answer to the judge who imposed the original sentence could result in better compliance with the requirement of sentences.

(10) Sufficient secure and semi-secure hospital accommodation should be available to avoid those who need healthcare rather than prison to receive that care outside the prison system

Those who need healthcare should not land up in prison, as happens all too often at present, just because of the lack of any alternative.

(11) Prisons should not be used for the custody of those who are not being detained for criminal justice reasons

At Wandsworth they have had to provide a landing for asylum seekers. I have been informed that 500 asylum seekers are to be accommodated in prisons. This adds to overcrowding and the burdens of the Prison Service. In Wandsworth many of the asylum seekers did not speak English and I admired the cheerful way in which the staff were responding to the additional challenge, but this should not have been necessary.

(12) There should be a Board responsible for women involved within the Criminal Justice System

The Criminal Justice System's responsibilities in relation to women should be similar to that of the Youth Justice Board. It should regard it as its primary responsibility to contain the growth of the women prison population.

While I do not make any claims for the novelty of my recommendations, collectively they would undoubtedly reduce the prison population and at the same time result in more constructive sentencing. What, however, would have a greater effect on overcrowding would be an announcement by the government that it fully accepts the damaging effects of prison overcrowding and that it attaches high priority to it being tackled. The government could then set out its programme for containing the number of prisoners. The temptation to adopt a piecemeal approach would have to be resisted. For example, responding to public sentiment, there has been a number of initiatives to support the recruitment of more police officers. But an unintended effect of this is to cause prison officers to seek to join the police to the disadvantage of the Prison Service.

With the overt support of the government what has not been achieved over 30 years could now be achieved. The money, which would be saved by a reduction in numbers once the programme started, would fund a down spiral to replace the present upward spiral. The public would benefit from a diversion of resources into programmes to tackle offending and the closely related culture of drug and alcohol abuse.

There could not be a better time for such an initiative for conquering the disease of overcrowding. The review of sentencing by John Halliday on behalf of the Home Service has reported, as has Lord Justice Auld. The Judicial Training Board has the experience to take the programme forward with the judiciary. The creation of a Sentencing Review Panel could take the policy into account in its advice to the judiciary on the level of sentences. Such a policy would also assist the Youth Training Board to meet its objectives. An announcement would transform the morale of the Prison Service; it would make the whole of my report an historic document; and it would enable me to give up talking about prison overcrowding to the relief of a great many people who are present here this evening and know so much more about prisons than I do.

16

A Justice System the Community Owns

Abstract This paper emphasises the need for English courts to have closer links with the community. It highlights the current centralised nature of the courts and describes the Red Hook Project in Brooklyn, USA, where Judge Calabrese has dealt with cases that can blight a local community. No court in the UK has the facilities to play a community role in the same way as the Red Hook Court, where it is much easier to respond constructively to an offender's individual circumstances and find practical solutions to offending behaviour so that offenders leave court knowing exactly what they are supposed to do next. It concludes that were such a strategy to be implemented in the UK it would save years of adult offending and reduce the enormous costs to the state.

The message that the former Home Secretary, David Blunkett, once gave me was one that I considered extremely important. On behalf of the judiciary, I can assure the public that judges are absolutely committed to achieving the improvements to the justice system to which he aspired.

I have a friend who was a very good judge, but who, like me, has now retired. Before his retirement, if he was asked what he did, he would say he was a social worker. He did not give this answer because he was soft on crime. When appropriate, he could be as tough as old leather. He said it, partly, because he had found that telling people he was a judge provoked the wrong response but, more importantly, because his conception of a judge's role was that he was not there primarily to preside over trials and, when appropriate, to punish offenders. An important part of his role was to help solve problems in the society or the community in which he sat as a judge.

---

* This paper was originally given at the Criminal Justice Serving the Community Conference, Queen Elizabeth II Conference Centre, London, on 7 July 2003. Since then, a Community Court was opened on 20 October 2005 (having first dealt with cases in December 2004) sitting at Liverpool Magistrates' Court. On October 2006 it was announced there were to be 10 new community justice initiatives.

He would have been equally happy to describe himself as a community worker, because he was working with others to improve the community.

I mention my friend because, having visited the Red Hook Project in Brooklyn and having had the privilege of sitting in court with Judge Calabrese, it appeared to me that my friend's approach to judging was the Calabrese approach. Judge Calebrese's court does not deal with the serious crimes which will inevitably result in the offender being sent to prison to serve a long sentence. He deals with the sort of crimes that individually are not grave, but collectively can blight a locality. In relation to this sort of crime, it can be far more constructive for the community to try and tackle the causes of the offender's offending than to impose a conventional punishment. Without this approach, sentencers are forced to resort to the imposition of relatively minor sentences which do nothing to prevent future reoffending.

I learnt many things from the day I spent at Red Hook. One of the most important was that we might be making a mistake in this country by not appreciating that the courts, and all those involved with dealing with less grave crimes, should primarily be focussed on solving the problems of the community in which the crime took place. This is appropriate to a far greater extent in relation to such crimes than in the case of graver crimes where a clear message has to go out: 'If you commit a serious offence, you will be punished.'

A court performing this new role must have close links with its community. When I was a young barrister, the links between our local courts and the community were much stronger than they are today. The administration of justice was less centralised. Each court had its own probation officers who were often accommodated at the court. Each court had police officers who, for part of their career, worked day in and day out in the same court. Each magistrates' court had more autonomy and had its own clerk who was a pillar of the community. Borough Quarter Sessions were also much more locally focussed than today's Crown Court.

The changes which have taken place since those days have brought many benefits, but have also resulted in the courts becoming less connected with the communities that they serve. Many courts try to address this. Judges and magistrates visit local schools and community groups and schoolchildren are invited to visit the courts; courts have 'open-days'. But a court's relationship with its local community today is still not as close as it was 40 years ago. This is despite the fact that, because of our combination of lay magistrates and juries, our system should be very community-orientated.

Of course, there are courts in this country with very good liaison arrangements with local agencies and organisations. For example, a number of magistrates' courts have established diversion schemes designed to respond constructively to defendants with mental health difficulties. An illustration of the benefits of such an approach is provided by the experience of the Hampshire and Isle of Wight Magistrates' Courts Committee. This Committee has set up an area-wide scheme involving a variety of voluntary organisations, including MENCAP.[1] The scheme varies according to the needs of the particular court, but ensures that those with mental health difficulties are dealt with more expeditiously and in a broader range of ways than was the case previously. This has nothing to do with punishing offenders. Similarly, many good practices occur in our Youth Courts.

However, as far as I am aware, no court in this country has the facilities to play a community role in the same way as the Red Hook Court does. It was created out of an old school with the help of the community. Many, if not all, of the staff of the court themselves perform voluntary work in the community. Youngsters work in the court helping to sort out their peers who have gone astray. No court in this jurisdiction has all the facilities that Judge Calabrese will describe. It is so much easier to respond constructively to an offender's individual circumstances if the resources are actually available at the court. Practical solutions can then be found to the problems that underlie offending behaviour and the offender leaves court knowing exactly what he is supposed to do next.

In the case of juveniles, offending is often linked to problems within the family. If you are going to make any significant progress in tackling the juvenile's offending behaviour you have to tackle the problems of the family as a whole. As the former President of the Family Division, Dame Elizabeth Butler Sloss, pointed out, the division between our care and juvenile criminal jurisdictions has possibly become, from the best of motives, too rigid. She said:

> We must move to an overall appreciation that children in trouble need to be caught early and their problems dealt with in the context of the problems of their families. If we were able to do this we would have a chance to improve the behaviour of children; to reintegrate or in some cases, for the first time, integrate these children into the community and save years of adult offending with the enormous cost to the state. I should like to see the Youth Court given the jurisdiction to require the relevant local authority to investigate the family in accordance with the requirements of the Children Act and that in serious cases the local authority should be obliged to make a care application in the

---

[1] MENCAP is a UK learning disability charity, working with people with learning difficulties, their families and carers.

family court . . . The Home Office's recent White Paper on Anti-Social Behaviour contains some interesting ideas on working within the community as well as punishing offenders.[2]

A related issue is that magistrates and judges in this jurisdiction do not get the sort of feedback that Judge Calabrese receives when he decides upon a community disposal. Except in the case of a Drug Testing and Treatment Order, a magistrate or judge has little involvement with an offender once that offender has been sentenced. This needs to change— ongoing involvement helps both judges and offenders. Judges learn what works and offenders see that the judge who sentenced them has a continuing interest in their progress. When Judge Calabrese deals with an offender, on his computer in front of him is a running record of how the offender has responded to the court's orders. I take care not to use the word 'sentence' because in many cases, as I understand the position, the judge only passes a sentence if the alternative approach has failed or is in danger of failing.

At Red Hook it is not only the judge who adopts a different approach, but also the prosecutor and the defence lawyers. That is why Jennifer Etheridge's contribution is such an important part of what we will learn about here today. Both the prosecution and the defence put aside their usual short-term objectives; the prosecution is not primarily interested in obtaining a conviction nor the defence an acquittal. Instead, the prosecution, in the interest of the community, and the defence, in the interest of the offender, both appreciate they will fulfil their respective responsibilities better if they achieve an outcome that will solve the problems of the offender. They therefore cooperate to achieve this. I am happy to give a lead-in saying that we should be seeking a similar change of culture in this country.

I am delighted that former Home Secretary, David Blunkett, shared my enthusiasm for the 'community' approach and I hope that this enthusiasm will also be shared by future Home Secretaries.

---

[2] E Butler-Sloss DBE, 'Are we failing the family? Human Rights, children, and the meaning of family in the 21st century', the Paul Sieghart Memorial Lecture, given at the British Institute of Human Rights, King's College London, on 3 April 2003.

17

Do We Need a New Approach to Penal Policy?

Abstract This paper provides a detailed account of the numerous reforms implemented over recent years in the English Criminal Justice System. It suggests that while the government has made a huge commitment in trying to reduce crime and increase public confidence in sentencing, its efforts have been thwarted by the problem of prison overcrowding and rising costs of keeping prisoners in custody. It discusses the efforts that have been made to coordinate the different criminal justice agencies, such as the establishment of a Criminal Justice Board, the National Offender Management Service, and the Sentencing Guidelines Council, and focuses upon where the Criminal Justice System should be heading if it is to prevent the present situation from getting worse.

The contributions that Victor Mishcon, Lord Mishcon, has made to public life are as varied as they are numerous. That he was able to be the founder of one of the leading law firms in the country indicates his contribution to the law. Before becoming a member of the House of Lords, he made a significant contribution to the local government of Greater London. The fact that he has received honours from three countries as different as Sweden, Ethiopia and Jordan, is confirmation of his role in furthering international relations. What, however, makes this an intimidating evening for me is the fact that, when I became a member of the House of Lords, I witnessed and admired the eloquence, courtesy and style of his contributions to debates. He invariably was listened to with the greatest of respect. I, therefore, regard it as a singular privilege to be asked to give this year's lecture at my old college in his honour. I am particularly delighted that he is with us tonight. I know that

---

* Mishcon Lecture, originally given at University College London, on 22 April 2004.

his presence gives us all great pleasure. We wish him the best of health for many years to come.

It is, however, the health of the Criminal Justice System which is at the centre of what I have to say tonight. It is not possible to have a healthy society without a healthy Criminal Justice System. A healthy Criminal Justice System gives the public a sense of security. Crime will still be with us, but an effective Criminal Justice System will mean that a healthy society can accommodate this. Members of the public who have the misfortune to suffer the anguish of being victims of crime will, at least, have the reassurance and comfort of knowing that there is a real prospect of those responsible being arrested, prosecuted and appropriately punished.

Unfortunately, it has to be accepted that, for many years now, the public have had little confidence in the ability of our Criminal Justice System to ensure that justice is done. Regrettably, each part of the system has appeared to be failing the public. Far too few of those responsible for crimes were being detected and, of those who were detected, the percentage who were successfully prosecuted to conviction was regrettably low. When they were convicted, the sentences of the court, at least judging by the re-offending rate, were singularly ineffective. The whole system gave the impression that it was crying out for fundamental reform. In particular, there was a desperate need for the different agencies engaged in the system to work together to achieve the improvements which were needed. However, turning round a failing public service is notoriously difficult.

That this should be the position was particularly surprising, since when I cast my mind back over the 40 years and more since I commenced practice, the Criminal Justice System seems to have been continuously the subject of organisation and reorganisation, starting with the Dr Beeching reforms. I am not sure these were any more effective in relation to the Criminal Justice System than they were in the case of the railways. They certainly meant that some of the most charming courts in England and Wales met the same fate as some of our most attractive rural railway stations.

Over the last few years a real effort has been made to achieve the urgently needed coordination between the different criminal justice agencies that is the key to meaningful reform. More criminals are being arrested and the prosecution process has been significantly improved as a result of the Crown Prosecution Service working in close support of the police. This improved cooperation is reducing the number of trials that have to be adjourned or worse still abandoned. The late delivery of prisoners to court is being tackled. The needs of witnesses are being considered in a more constructive manner and more frequently met. The different services now realise the need for concerted action and this is being taken at all levels from the very top downwards. A Criminal Justice Board has been established to drive forward the coordination that is necessary. Each agency is represented at ministerial and at the highest official level and a senior judge, Lord Justice Kay, has been a member of the Board.[1]

There are reasons, therefore, for quiet confidence that there is about to be an increasing flow of criminal trials which result in the conviction of those who have committed crimes. This, in itself, should act as a deterrent to criminal conduct. My distinguished predecessor, Lord Taylor, was quite rightly convinced that the best deterrence to the commission of crime is the knowledge that there is a serious prospect of your being arrested and convicted if you indulge in crime.

The more direct objective of achieving the conviction of the guilty is of course so that they can be sentenced for the crimes they commit. Sentencing has been and still is a highly political subject. This is because it is of immense importance to the public and, in particular, to those who have the misfortune to be victims of crime. It is every bit as important that those who commit crimes should receive appropriate sentences as it is that they are convicted. An appropriate sentence is one that will not only punish the offender, but will also protect the public by reducing the incidence of reoffending.

There has been no shortage of reviews of penal process. There has been the enlightened report of a senior civil servant, John Halliday, *Making Punishments Work*. There has been a report by the Social Exclusion Unit of the Cabinet Office and a report by the All Party Parliamentary Penal Affairs Group among others. Finally, there is the report of Patrick Carter of 11 December 2003, *Managing Offenders, Reducing Crime: A New Approach*, to the Prime Minister.

Each report reveals a mind-blowing situation involving vast expenditure with little if any long-term improvement in the protection of the public. Tonight, my concern is not so much where we are, but where we should be going. But in order to identify the progress that is necessary you need to know something about the position from which you are starting. So let me remind you of some of the worrying facts about the present position. I do so from the valuable information that the Prison Reform Trust makes

---

[1] Now the late Lord Justice Kay.

regularly available to achieve its admirable objective of improving the present position.

On 5 March 2003 the prison population stood at its highest ever figure of 74,960. This figure is the result of a continuing increase in the prison population over a period of at least the last ten years. When I produced my report of the Strangeways Inquiry in 1991 the prison population was 42,000 and falling.

But worse is to come. By the end of the decade the Home Office projections predict a prison population of anything between 91,400 and 109,600. The Home Office are doing what they can to provide additional prison accommodation. Since 1995, over 15,000 additional prison places have been provided at a cost of more than £2bn. There is, despite this expenditure, a huge gap between planned useable operational capacity and the forecast prison population. At the end of February 2004, 85 of 138 prisons in England and Wales were overcrowded. At the end of November 2003, over 16,500 prisoners were doubling up in cells designed for one.

The average cost of keeping a prisoner in custody is over £36,000. But prison is ineffective in reducing reoffending; 59 per cent of prisoners are reconvicted within two years of being released. The Social Exclusion Unit came to the conclusion that reoffending by ex-prisoners costs society at least £11bn a year. Ex-prisoners are responsible for about one in five of all recorded crimes. All sections of the prison population are increasing. The worst figures are in relation to women where there has been an increase of 151 per cent over the last ten years.

Both the number of prisoners serving short sentences and the number of life-sentence prisoners have increased. By 31 July 2003, there were 5,427 prisoners serving life sentences, as compared with 3,000 in 1992. At any one time there are on average more than 10,000 prisoners serving sentences of 12 months or less. This is despite the fact that there is a uniform acceptance that sentences of this sort make little or no contribution to the reduction of crime.

I could go on providing you with more figures to a like effect but I have given you sufficient information to understand the position that we are now in. The inescapable conclusion is that, unless there is a dramatic change in the way that we deal with offenders, there is every likelihood of the position getting worse.

I emphasise that the poor results that are being achieved at present are not any reflection on the effort that is being made by the Prison Service and the Probation Service to tackle the problem. They are being given an impossible task. While considerable progress has been made in reducing escapes and the number of assaults, in other areas little has been achieved because of the direct and indirect consequences of overcrowding. Effort is being diverted into seeking to manage numbers at the cost of imaginative programmes to address reoffending. There is a continuous churning of prisoners. If it had not been for the Home Office adopting an early release programme involving ever-increasing numbers of prisoners leaving custody under electronic surveillance, the numbers of prisoners would be even greater. The period of sentences of imprisonment actually being served now bear little relation to the sentences imposed.

It is, however, the sentences which are imposed which still result in the continuous rise in the prison population. In the Carter Report it is stated 'the key explanation for growth in the use of prison and probation over the last decade is the increased severity in sentencing'.[2] He gives as an example that in 1991, 15 per cent of those found guilty of an indictable offence received a custodial sentence; by 2001 it was 25 per cent. There has been a similar increase in the use of community sentences. But Patrick Carter's conclusion is that:

> The increased use of prison and probation has only had a limited impact on crime. The deterrent effect of tougher sentences is weak: more important is the fear of being caught. Prison does reduce crime, but there is no convincing evidence that further increases in the use of custody would significantly reduce crime. Rehabilitative work can reduce the chance of reoffending but by only 5–10 per cent.[3]

It is the judiciary, including magistrates, who pass the sentences that produce the situation where, despite vast resources being expended, both the Prison and Probation Service are overwhelmed. However, it must be remembered that there has been continuous pressure upon the judiciary to increase sentences and, until recently, little, if any, effort in the opposite direction. Initiatives which might be justifiable in themselves are taken without regard to their knock-on effect on the situation as a whole.

There is no doubt that the government has made a huge commitment to trying to reduce crime and increase public confidence in sentencing. Its efforts have been thwarted by the chronic problem of overcrowding and, more recently, by a severe lack of morale and resources within the Probation Service. With the Probation Service, the trouble has been too much change that has been badly managed.

---

[2] P Carter, *Managing Offenders, Reducing Crime: A New Approach'* (HMSO, 2003), 11.
[3] Ibid, 15.

My primary concern in painting this sombre picture is not with the offenders who often find their regimes undermined by overcrowding, but with those who will be the victims of crimes because of our inability to tackle offending behaviour. We are not being sufficiently tough on the causes of crime.

Notwithstanding the gloomy statistics with which I have been peppering you, I do see what could be a bright light shining at the end of the tunnel. In responding to the report of Patrick Carter, the then Home Secretary, Mr Blunkett, stated:

> I believe that we now have a once in a generation opportunity to reduce crime by radically transforming the prison and probation services and those working in partnership with them.

Let me give the reasons why I think Mr Blunkett could be, and I fervently hope he is, right.

1. First of all, as a consequence of the Carter Report, another geological fault in the criminal justice system is about to be bridged. The Prison Service and the Probation Service are being combined into a National Offender Management Service.[4] This change is important and given time could be extremely positive, although the Probation Boards Association fear the immediate effect will be further damage to morale, loss of staff and recruitment problems. As against this, a chief executive of NOMS was already appointed. He was Martin Narey, who was undoubtedly the individual best qualified to make NOMS a success. He was an outstanding head of the Prison Service and had a firm grasp of what was needed.[5]

NOMS should be able to tackle one of the most intractable problems involved in offender management—bridging the return of an offender into the community after the end of a custodial sentence. The sentence needs to be a seamless whole, partly served in custody and part in the community. It is only if this happens that the benefits of programmes within prison can be made effective in the community. It is, for example, well established that the prospects of reoffending will be reduced if arrangements are made which enable the ex-prisoner to have accommodation and a job on release. Gallant efforts have already been made in some prisons such as Canterbury to ensure that prisoners will be released with these advantages, but the task will be made much easier with the establishment of a single service.

---

[4] Hereafter, 'NOMS'.
[5] Helen Edwards succeeded Martin Narey as Chief Executive of NOMS in November 2005.

NOMS will also be responsible for youth justice. Here the Youth Justice Board and Local Youth Offending Teams have already demonstrated how national leadership coupled with local delivery can produce results. I am confident that the lessons which are to be learnt from the way the Youth Justice Board worked with local offending teams will not be lost in the new organisation. I have also every expectation that NOMS will be receptive to the constructive comments that the Probation Boards Association has made. You cannot build prisons overnight and it takes time to train new probation officers, but the new service should turn out to be the foundation upon which an effective penal policy can be based.

2. The second positive change has been the introduction by the Criminal Justice Act 2003 of a spectrum of new community punishments. Community Orders can include an array of requirements.

The problem with community sentences in the past was that both the public and the courts were sceptical as to their efficacy. If the necessary preparation work is done to ensure that the new community punishments will be effective and properly monitored, they should inspire confidence in the public and the courts. This will have the advantage of the courts using them as an alternative to prison.

3. There are also new powers in relation to fines. Fines have the advantage over other sentences in that, if they are paid, they are not resource intensive. But their use by courts has dropped dramatically. Partly because enforcement has proved ineffective and partly, because there have only been limited sanctions available in the event of non-payment. As a last resort failure to pay a fine can lead to a result the court was seeking to avoid, namely imprisonment. However, the Courts Act 2003 provides for the introduction of an innovative new fine system which has already been launched in many parts of Europe. Offenders can either pay the fine by instalments or by a lump sum or have to do unpaid work instead. This, combined with wider powers of enforcement, should reduce the need to resort to imprisonment in default.

4. The fourth positive step is an innovation for which the Criminal Justice Act 2003 is the source. This is the creation of a power in the police and others to make the offender the subject of a conditional caution. It is important that the use of this power be properly monitored because one of its virtues, namely that the courts are not involved, means it is capable of being a source of abuse. Used appropriately, it has many advantages. First, it avoids the complexities and the delays of the court process for the less serious offender; secondly, if an offender

complies with the conditions he will not be left with the disadvantage of a criminal record; and finally, there is the fact that the Act requires the conditional caution to be used for the commendable purposes of facilitating the rehabilitation of the offender and ensuring that he makes reparation for the offence.

5. The next positive step is the establishing of a unified administration for the courts. The management of the magistrates' and Crown courts are being integrated to create a single court system. This is already resulting in closer relations between magistrates and the more senior judiciary. It should assist us in deciding how best to use available resources to punish offenders effectively.

6. Then there is encouragement to be had from the many constructive initiatives that are taking place to achieve positive outcomes once an offender's crimes have brought him to the attention of the authorities. An example is provided by restorative justice which can not only assist the offender to be rehabilitated, but also, to an extent which is surprising to those who are unfamiliar with the process, the victim as well.

7. There are also the positive things that are happening in our prisons, notwithstanding the difficulties caused by overcrowding. I refer in particular to the provision of education and training which means that a large percentage of prisoners who were unemployable when they entered prison have more hope of gaining honest employment when they leave.

8. The next and final point is the establishment by the Criminal Justice Act 2003 of the Sentencing Guidelines Council. The Council has the potential of being a most important development. It deserves a lecture of its own. I do not say this because its Chairman is, *ex officio*, the Lord Chief Justice, I do so because it is the key to achieving a sentencing framework in this jurisdiction that will protect the public from the immensely damaging consequences of crime. Assisting the Council to embark on the huge challenge with which it is faced is a daunting task. I regard it as one of the most critical responsibilities of my terms of office. For reasons I will explain, the Council must develop a more constructive penal policy while at the same time obtaining the confidence of the public, the judiciary, the other agencies in the justice system, the government of the day, the politicians, and at least a large section of the media.

The Sentencing Guidelines Council is just beginning its work. Prior to the creation of the Council, guidelines were given by the Criminal Division of the Court of Appeal. Guidelines are needed because, subject to exceptions that in practice have not met with success, Parliament does not fix the actual sentence to be served by a prisoner, but limits its role to setting the maximum penalty for an offence. In other words, Parliament establishes the framework within which a judge or magistrate imposes the appropriate sentence. This allows the judge or magistrate to tailor the punishment to fit the crime and in doing so to achieve, in the words of the Mikado, 'an object sublime'. While a sentence should be tailored to fit the crime, it must also bear an appropriate relationship to the sentences being imposed for the same offence and for other offences in other cases. This is the principle objective of the guideline judgments that have been given by the Court of Appeal in the past.

In recent times, the Court of Appeal has been assisted in its task by advice from the Sentencing Advisory Panel, under the chairmanship of Professor Martin Wasik. Now the Panel is to fulfil a similar role in relation to the Council. Both the Panel and the Council have a membership that is highly qualified to perform their respective roles. They, of course, include judges but also lawyers and non-lawyers whose collective experience means that they should be able to perform this task in a manner that commands respect.

The advantage of the Council over the Court of Appeal is that it is in a position to adopt a more proactive approach to the preparation of guidelines. Unlike the Court of Appeal, the Council is not constrained by the need to deliver its guidelines in the form of a judgment in a particular case. It can work systematically to produce a comprehensive code of guidelines for all courts that have to punish offenders.

Patrick Carter proposes, as one of his recommendations, a new role for the judiciary. He says:

> There needs to be greater emphasis on judicial self-governance, ensuring compliance with guidelines. In the short term, when capacity is fixed, the Sentencing Guidelines Council (SGC) needs to provide guidance that takes account of the capacity of prison and probation. Over the medium term, the Sentencing Advisory Panel needs to provide evidence of what works to reduce crime and increase public confidence. This will form the basis for adjusting the capacity of prisons and probation.[6]

The government in its response to the Carter report accepted this suggested approach. In *Reducing Crime and Changing Lives* it states, 'the change in sentencing practice depends critically on the role of the SGC and the judiciary.

---

[6] Carter, *Managing Offenders*, n 2 above, 31.

They have a pivotal role in helping ensure we can align the capacity of correctional services to deliver, with the demand placed upon them by sentencers'.[7]

In these remarks there is more than a suggestion that the judiciary need to change their practices in relation to sentencing. This can only happen with the full support of the SGC. It will be for the Council to decide the extent to which it can seek to ensure that the sentences imposed by all levels of the judiciary not only 'fit' the circumstances of the individual crime for which they are imposed, but do so in a way which uses available resources in an effective manner.

Carter adds that 'each year the Council should discuss the priorities for sentencing practice with the Home Office. It would then issue guidelines that ensure offences are treated proportionately to their severity, are informed by evidence on what reduces offending and makes cost-effective the use of existing capacity.'[8] In addition, Carter states that 'the Council needs to have responsibility for using the existing capacity of correctional services to the best effect'.[9] He also refers to the Panel producing for magistrates and judges up-to-date information on their sentencing practice and the impact on reoffending.

Having set out by no means all the promising signs that are at least on the horizon of the criminal justice system, I turn to consider whether my optimism is soundly based.

I have not forgotten the guideline which was given by the Court of Appeal over which I presided on 18 December 2002, that is just before the Christmas vacation. The date was to prove not unimportant. It was a guideline judgment as to the sentencing of burglars, and burglary is an offence that would be particularly distressing for householders at that time of the year. It was also the offence used by Carter as his example of upward drift in the average sentence. In view of this upward drift, and basing itself upon a recommendation of the Sentencing Advisory Panel, the Court suggested only a marginal downward adjustment to the then existing sentencing pattern. The guidelines caused an explosion of protest in the media. It was clear from the reports that my judgment had been misunderstood.

Looking back on the situation now, I stand by the judgment and I would not alter what I said. However, I do regard the media reaction a public relations disaster of a high order. It is to be hoped that in the case of guidelines

---

[7] D Blunkett (Home Office, January 2004), para 47.
[8] Carter, *Managing Offenders*, n 2 above.
[9] Ibid.

introduced by the Council there would be no repetition. The problem was that the media thought the burglary guidelines were being surreptitiously issued when attention would be diverted by the approach of Christmas. If the guidelines had not been contained in a judgment, the misunderstandings could have been more easily explained. In the case of guidelines issued by the Council, there will be less risk of misunderstanding. If, however, this is not the case, an information office could help to make the position clear. More importantly, in the case of the Council, the guidelines will be subject to a consultation process which should prepare the public for what is proposed and enable the public's views to be taken on board.

However, the lessons to be learnt from what happened should not be forgotten since any repetition would be extremely damaging for confidence in the Council. The experience emphasises the sensitivity of issues involving sentencing.

Part of that sensitivity is attributable to fact that our penal policies have not been more successful. If they had been I would expect the public and media to be less critical. Though I would stress the importance of the media informing themselves of the facts before they embark on vituperative attacks on individual members of the judiciary. In addition, they must appreciate that we give judges the task of passing a just sentence and, if they impose the wrong sentence, then it can be put right on appeal. The judge has to consider, not only the victim, but other issues including what is in the interests of the protection of the public as a whole.

The father of criminology, Sir Leon Radzinowitz, wrote a book at the age of 92 in which he stated: 'No meaningful advance in penal matters can be achieved in contemporary democratic society so long as it remains a topic of political controversy instead of a matter of national concern.'[10] He was right. It is my hope that the breadth and the distinction of the membership of the Council representing the police, the prosecution and the defence as well as the victims of crime will assist in making penal policy less of a political issue. There is also the fact that Parliament will have an involvement through the Council's relationship with the Home Affairs Select Committee.

It is critical that the Council, when exercising its wide discretion, should always frame its guidance within the principles of sentencing, which are now to be found in the Criminal Justice Act 2003. This will ensure that the legitimacy of the guidance is not in doubt. The principles include five purposes

---

[10] L Radzinowitz, *Adventures in Criminology* (Routledge, 1999).

of sentencing: the punishment of offenders; the reduction of crime; the reform and rehabilitation of offenders; the protection of the public; and the making of reparation by offenders to persons affected by their crime. These statutory purposes provide a broad, one could almost say visionary, approach to sentencing that has not been previously so clearly identified.

Then, importantly, there is the fact that the court must not pass a custodial sentence unless it is of the opinion that the offence, or the combination of the offence and one or more offences associated with it, was so serious that neither a fine alone nor a community sentence can be justified for the offence. Finally, there is the fact that the Council is required to have regard to:

(1) the cost of different sentences and their relative effectiveness in preventing reoffending; and

(2) the need to promote public confidence in the criminal justice system.

These statutory provisions ensure that it is well within the Council's area of discretion to make guidelines that will ensure that each of the principles to which I have referred form part of a new and more constructive penal policy. The Council cannot ignore the resources that are, and can be made, available for dealing with offenders—these resources are intimately linked to the effectiveness of sentences. While the Council has to live in the real world, it is independent of the government of the day and it must perform its role in the manner which it considers will best assist the courts. If there is a failure to make resources available where their provision is clearly possible, that failure will no doubt be given little if any weight by the Council. But the Council can be expected to accept that generally it is for the government of the day to determine how resources are allocated.

At the present time it is uncontroversial that there is a need for restraint in the use of prison and community sentences. The Council may take the view that NOMS should be provided with the time it needs to prepare for the community sentences and the other initiatives to which I have referred. If NOMS is given this opportunity, and is provided with the necessary resources, then the new community sentences should provide a brake on the increased use of prison in cases where custody is not necessary. If the brake can be applied, then over a period of time the gains should be massive. Increased public confidence in the criminal justice system and more effective use of the resources should follow. We will then have grasped the opportunity currently available to us and developed a new penal policy designed to tackle the grave problems that we currently face.

18

Making Sense of Sentencing

Abstract This paper discusses the need for the government to provide more resources for sentencing policy by identifying the resources that can be made available and then tailoring its policies to match those resources. It considers the purposes of sentencing and the role of the Sentencing Guidelines Council. Concluding while it is essential resources must be used in the manner which is most likely to provide the best protection for the public, it supports a more focussed role for sentencing that if used constructively could increase public confidence in community punishment and reduce reliance on imprisonment.

Introduction

I am deeply honoured to be the first Fellow of the first Fellowship established to celebrate the contribution to Criminology of the first Director of the First Institute of Criminology in the UK, Sir Leon Radzinowitz.

I must confess that I have reached a stage in life when I find it mildly encouraging that it was in 1998 Sir Leon published his last work on Criminology, *Adventures in Criminology*.[1] He was 92 years of age. He did so after he had devoted his life to the subject. Surely, with this experience the celebrated Father of Criminology in England would be able to provide all the answers. Alas, no, Sir Leon acknowledges that there is no single key to unlock the door either as to what causes crime or what are the cures for crime. Sir Leon was too wise to speculate on the answers.

You will not be surprised to learn that where Sir Leon feared to tread I am not intending to rush in. Instead, I am going to set myself a more modest but still a very important task and that is to identify the action that could be

---

* Originally delivered as the Sir Leon Radzinowitz Lecture at the University of Cambridge Institute of Criminology on 12 May 2005.

[1] (Routledge, 1999).

taken over the next four years to achieve, in the interests of the public, a more effective and strategic approach to sentencing. I am speaking out because it is timely for me to do so because the government is in the process of determining what should be, for the next four years, its policy as to sentencing.[2]

This is the right place to address these issues because this lecture is part of the celebrations to mark the opening of this magnificent new resource for criminology, an often neglected subject, and the right audience because criminologists have an important contribution to make to achieving the improvements that are needed to the criminal justice system.

While I am focussing on sentencing, I emphasise that real progress can only be made if criminal justice is treated as a whole. It is the judges who determine sentences within the framework provided by Parliament, but it is the police and the Crown Prosecution Service[3] who decide who comes before the courts and the judge needs the help of the advocates to identify the most constructive sentences. It is also critical what happens to the offender after the sentence. Here I welcome the establishment of the National Offender Management Service[4] as it should enable the Prison Service and the Probation Service, by working jointly as a single unit, to achieve more than they could separately.

We also knew that the government should have been able to make a running start because the Departments of State most involved in the Criminal Justice System were under the same leadership: former Home Secretary Charles Clarke, the previous Lord Chancellor and Secretary of State for Constitutional Affairs Lord Falconer, and the past Attorney-General Lord Goldsmith.[5] They each, together with their distinguished predecessors, helped to bring us to where we are now.

I can identify straight away what I would like a further contribution to be. The government should identify the resources that can be made available to support our sentencing policy for the next four years and then tailor its policies to match the resources available. In the past, policies have been embarked upon without sufficient attention being paid to whether or not the resources—I am

---

[2] See 'Introduction' in this book for a discussion of the progress achieved since 2005.

[3] Hereafter, 'the CPS'.

[4] Hereafter, 'NOMS'.

[5] Since this paper was originally given, Jacqui Smith has replaced Charles Clarke as Home Secretary, Jack Straw has replaced Lord Falconer as Lord Chancellor and Secretary of State for Constitutional Affairs (now Secretary of State for Justice), and Baroness Scotland QC has replaced Lord Goldsmith as Attorney-General.

not only referring to financial resources—are in place to enable the policy to be successfully implemented. In addition, the government should recognise that what is needed now is a period of consolidation. The system has reached the limit of the amount of change it can, for the time being, absorb. There is the need before implementing a new sentencing policy for there to be wide consultation with all those with a relevant practical and academic experience.

An Art or a Science?

This is not an expression of judicial conservatism. For the government to exercise the restraint in legislating I have suggested would be a radical change in government policy towards criminal justice.

The government should decide to exercise a self-denying ordinance and declare a closed season on sentencing legislation. I understand the desire to respond to public reaction over the latest horrendous crime, however, to resist this pressure would make a significant contribution to achieving the real gains that the government and judiciary would like to see.

While criticism of the judiciary is not confined to sentencing, it is the judicial role in relation to sentencing which creates the most public controversy. The man on the London Underground Circle Line will not second guess a judge's interpretation of a statute or a judgment awarding damages, but he does not hesitate to disagree with a judge's decision as to what is the appropriate sentence for a prisoner to serve. I make no complaint about this since I accept that there are no absolutes when it comes to sentencing; unless Parliament has made mandatory the sentence which should be imposed for a particular crime.

There are jurisdictions where effect is given to what I have just said and juries are given the task of determining the sentence, subject to limited rights of appeal. This happens even when what is at stake is whether the prisoner should be sentenced to death. This, it is said, is the democratic solution.

In this country we have chosen a different route. We give the task of finding the right sentence to magistrates and judges. We then place them under constraints that mean they are not entitled to pick a sentence out of the blue. First, the maximum sentence for any offence is established by Parliament. Within that statutory limit the sentencing judge must consider where in the scale of gravity the crime with which he is concerned fits into the extensive framework of sentencing for the whole range of crimes. To perform this task there has to be a careful analysis of the facts of the particular offence and this must take into account the consequences of the crime to the victim and any mitigating circumstances relating to the defendant.

Consistency is important and that is why the judge has to find the right pigeon hole in the complex structure I have identified. But the judge must, when the circumstances in the judge's opinion justify this, be prepared to impose the unconventional sentence if this is what the case requires. Judging must never be mechanistic.

While, therefore, the judiciary should take into account public opinion and criticism from whatever source it comes, and I include here the media, the police and politicians, they must in the end do what is their duty, which is to determine what is the correct sentence irrespective of the criticism to which this may give rise. It is the judge who will know all the facts and have the training and experience to enable him to determine what is the most appropriate sentence in all the circumstances, and his decision should be treated with the appropriate respect because of this.

It is sometimes said that sentencing is an art and not a science. Today, I prefer to say that sentencing is part art and part science. A judge has to combine both to achieve what are today the purposes of sentencing.

The Purposes of Sentencing

Those purposes are now set out in the Criminal Justice Act 2003 which radically revised the approach to sentencing. The Act was the culmination of two fundamental and distinguished reviews of the Criminal Justice System; the Auld Report and the Halliday Report. The Carter Report, which came after the Act, has also made a valuable contribution in this area.

The Act provides the focus for what I am discussing this evening. It sets out the purposes of sentencing in section 142(1) of the Criminal Justice Act 2003 as being:

(a) the punishment of offenders;
(b) the reduction of crime (including its reduction by deterrence);
(c) the reform and rehabilitation of offenders;
(d) the protection of the public;
(e) the making of reparation by offenders to persons affected by their offences.

These purposes are enlightened and should be uncontroversial. I accept that punishment should head the list but I applaud the attention that is given to the other purposes.

The extent to which we have been successful in achieving these purposes is also not controversial. Regrettably, we have not been doing as well as we should. I start with imprisonment because, although prison is also meant to deter, its primary purpose is to punish—the first statutory purpose. According to the most vociferous elements of the media, we should be sending more people to prison for longer.

This is despite the fact that the number of those sent to prison and the length to which they have been sent has been regularly increasing over a great many years. At the time of my Strangeways Report in 1991, the prison population was 42,000 and falling, while in 2005 it was 76,000 and forecast to rise. This is apparently wholly contrary to public perceptions, which believe the courts are unduly lenient. There has been an increase in punishment right across the board.

The issue is not whether we need imprisonment. We do, it is essential. It is one of the ways society can and should demonstrate its disapproval of serious crime. While an offender is serving his or her sentence it protects the public from further crime. However, even as a punishment it has limitations. Once the prisoner has become used to the clang of the prison door, prison makes little demand on most prisoners.

Positive steps in tackling offending behaviour can be taken in prison but they are able to be more successfully taken outside prison. A primary cause of prison sentences not being used more constructively is prison overcrowding. While overcrowding persists, it frustrates the ability of the Prison Service to deliver the contribution it could otherwise make to reducing crime and protecting the public by reforming and rehabilitating offenders. It is the primary explanation of why our prisons are not working better. Let me give some examples of the cancerous effects of overcrowding.

It is not easy to establish gainful employment in prisons and when they are overcrowded this is almost impossible.

The Prison Service is justifiably proud of what it can achieve through its educational programmes. However, the achievements could be greater, if it were not for the impact of overcrowding. The Prison Service are making ever greater efforts to ensure satisfactory arrangements are in place for the release of prisoners. If an offender is returned to society at the end of his sentence with increased skills, a job to go to and accommodation, the risk of that offender reoffending is significantly reduced. But again this is extremely difficult to achieve if an offender is being detained in a prison far from the community to which he belongs as a result of what is described as 'churning' within the prison system.

This is one of the reasons that I recommended in the report into the Strangeways Prison riots, and have continued since to advocate: the establishment of community prisons. A community prison has the advantage of the offender retaining his links with his family and the community to which he belongs. Although many governors tried to take this concept forward it is really not a practical prospect in current circumstances.

The Home Office in answer to my concerns about prison overcrowding will point to their prison building programme and I have to accept it is impressive. I do so with regret because it is hugely expensive but even if it is achieved it cannot hope to match the increase in prison numbers that the Home Office itself expects.

The present position just does not make sense. This is certainly not due to a lack of expenditure. According to the annual reports of the Prison Service for 2002–03 and 2003–04, the net expenditure on the prisons alone for the earlier year was £2,405m and for the later year, £2,105m. In addition, there was capital expenditure of £244m and £283m. There is to be added to these figures, the cost of the private prisons. There is also the cost of probation services. These are huge resources and the question must be asked: are we deploying them in the most advantageous manner? If we are not, then we must ask: why not?

The justification for this emphasis on ever-increasing use of imprisonment is that this is, so it is said, what the public demands. It is unfortunately the case that we have failed to persuade the public that there are many situations where community punishments can be more constructive in achieving the statutory purposes of sentencing than imprisonment. They are not an unconstructive let-off. Those who prefer the increased use of the custodial option are not apparently deterred by the fact that the cost of actually keeping the prisoner within prison averages roughly £37,500 per year.

However, from time to time I speak to victims and their families. When I do so I do not find that they are as unreasonable and as insistent on incarceration as the media suggests. Very few are crying out for the implementation of the biblical admonition 'an eye for an eye and a tooth for a tooth'. Surveys have shown that the public's perception is that the courts are much more lenient than is in fact the case; when the public are told what are the actual punishments imposed, they are genuinely surprised at their severity.

What will shock members of the public and victims is how unsuccessful we are at preventing reoffending. Here, the information provided by the Social Exclusion Unit in their report of 2002 is deeply disturbing. The figures speak for themselves.

The cost of reoffending by ex-prisoners is £11bn per year and around 58 per cent of prisoners are reconvicted within two years from their being released, the latter figure having remained approximately constant since 1990.

The story is not entirely bleak and there has been a significant drop in crimes of certain kinds. In general, however, we seem to be trapped in a vicious circle of offending, punishment, release after serving the sentence and reoffending.

How then do we break the vicious circle? Well I believe that the prospects of doing so are better now than they have been, at least over the period that I have been a judge. Let me explain why I am of that view:

(1) Parliament has told us what the objects of sentencing are.

(2) There is a greater realisation than there has been hitherto, that short prison sentences are not constructive and should only be used as a last resort.

(3) Our approach to juvenile offenders has been transformed by the establishment of the Youth Justice Board. The focus on offenders under 18 years of age has been producing positive results. It shows us that a more coordinated approach does produce results. Accordingly it is intended that what has been achieved by the Youth Justice Board in respect of young offenders should be extended to 18–20-year-old offenders.

(4) The same is true of women offenders. There has been a particularly sharp rise in the number of women offenders, particularly in connection with drug-related crime. There is a growing appreciation of the importance of addressing their specific needs.

(5) The position is the same in the area of those with mental health problems. It makes obvious good sense to tackle the substantial number of prisoners who have mental health problems in a more appropriate setting than prison.

(6) Then there is the piloting that is taking place on restorative justice projects. As this audience will know, restorative justice involves offenders taking responsibility for their crime and for making amends to their victims. Restorative justice in this jurisdiction is still in its infancy. However, those who have been involved are convinced that it has significant potential to make a difference. An impressive pilot involving the London Crown Courts has been quietly taking place with the support of the Home Office and an inspirational American Criminologist, Professor Lawrence Sherman. It is too early yet to establish with any degree of certainty that restorative justice reduces reoffending. However, what can be said is that it certainly is beneficial to victims. Victims should not be compelled to take part, but many of those who

do find it significantly ameliorates the damaging effect of what happened to them. I know from my own experience of having to reconsider the tariffs in respect of juvenile offenders detained during Her Majesty's pleasure that this can be true even in relation to the gravest crimes.

(7) Then, there is the contribution that can be made to sentencing by technology. The ability to create some of the advantages of a custodial sentence by the use of electronic tagging is undoubtedly an important development. I emphasise that this is not the only contribution that technology can make.

(8) Finally, there is now much closer consultation between the Home Office and the judiciary on legislative proposals and changes in government policy as to criminal justice. The judiciary set up a separate committee (the Rose Committee—named after its Chairman, the former Vice President of the Court of Appeal Criminal Division)[6] to achieve this. This assists in ensuring legislation will work in practice.

So from this more encouraging base, I return to the Criminal Justice Act 2003. Many of its provisions dealing with sentencing only came into force in April 2005.

They raise the possibilities of a more focussed role for sentencing. Constructively used they could increase the public's confidence in community punishment and help achieve a breakthrough in the undue reliance on imprisonment. Many of the provisions contained in the Act, if they are to achieve their purpose, will require a huge injection of resources in support of the community punishments.

I recognise that those resources are going to be hard to find and this means that it is essential that we have a very hard look at whether it really is necessary in the interests of the public to rely increasingly on imprisonment. I am confident this is not necessary. The government should make it clear that as a country we cannot continue to dissipate such a large proportion of the available resources on the use of imprisonment where there are more effective alternatives. In future the use of imprisonment should be focussed primarily on four situations:

(1) where imprisonment is necessary because the offender is sufficiently dangerous to make imprisonment essential for the protection of the public;

---

[6] Lord Justice Rose, now retired.

(2) where the crime is so serious that it can only be marked by a significant prison sentence;

(3) where what is needed (for example, in the case of significant white collar crime) is to mark the serious nature of the criminal conduct by a very short period of imprisonment in conjunction with other punishments. This is often referred to as a 'clang of the prison door' sentence; and

(4) finally, where the crime itself does not make imprisonment necessary but it becomes necessary because an offender will not comply with other sentences.

The alternative is to continue with the overcrowding that reduces the effectiveness of prisons and relies increasingly on executive release to avoid the prison system exploding as it did at the time of Strangeways.

Let me see how those four instances fit in with how I believe some of the provisions of the 2003 Act should be approached. I start with the provisions of Chapter 5 of the Act that apply to dangerous offenders.

Chapter 5 of the Act creates a new sentence of 'imprisonment for public protection'. This is a sentence that has most of the characteristics of a sentence of imprisonment for life. It extends to a great many offences, including motoring offences that are punishable with imprisonment of ten years or more. This range of offences is excessive.

Where the conditions identified in the Act are satisfied, imprisonment for public protection is mandatory. The sentence is for an indeterminate period and can involve the person sentenced remaining in detention after the period necessary for punishment and deterrence has been served, unless the Parole Board is satisfied that it is safe for that person to be released. Furthermore, even if the person is released, the release is on licence, with a consequential risk of recall.

The key to this sentence is a requirement that there should be 'a significant risk to the members of the public of serious harm occasioned by the Commission of further specified offences'. Courts will have to evaluate whether there is such a risk. Such a sentence is highly controversial and if it is to accord with acceptable principles the courts must restrict its use to cases where there really is such a risk. In doing this courts will be assisted by reports from the probation service. Those reports already as a matter of course give the opinion of the probation officer as to whether there is such a risk. However, the probation officer's assessment is not an assessment necessarily based upon his or her personal knowledge of the offender.

The sentence, in due course, will require a massive injection of additional resources for the Parole Board. The Parole Board is already involved in using more resource-intense procedures than was the case in the past to determine whether a life prisoner should be released. This is because of decisions of the European Court of Human Rights that make it clear that this is necessary if its procedures are to comply with Article 5(4) of the European Convention of Human Rights. In future, the hearings will have many of the trappings of a trial. The days when decisions on parole were based on a paper exercise are gone forever.

The cost of the Parole Board hearings is going to become a significant additional expense for the Home Office. In addition, it will place demands on judicial resources which it will not be easy to meet. The demands created by the new sentence will have to be accepted. Otherwise, the new sentence of detention for public protection could breach basic requirements of justice. This innovation meets my first justification for the use of prison but it adds to rather than reduces the burden on the Prison Service. More positive aspects of the 2003 Act exist in relation to other new sentences.

In the case of sentences of less than 12 months, there is the innovation of 'custody plus', a sentence combining a short period in custody plus a period on licence with a wide range of licence conditions. This can be used in a 'clang of the prison door' situation. There is intermittent custody which should enable a sentence to be custodial yet not interfere with the offender's ability to keep employment.

There is also a substantial improvement in the range of requirements that can be attached to a Community Order. There is the innovative requirement of unpaid work and there is an activity requirement that as its name suggests can require the offender to perform activities by way of reparation. Both these orders overcome the difficulties which can exist because of the offender's lack of resources to make amends otherwise. There are accredited programmes involving, for example, undergoing training. Finally, there are the prohibited activity requirements, curfew requirements, exclusion requirements, residence requirements, and possibly most important of all, mental health treatment, drug rehabilitation and alcohol treatment requirements. Electronic monitoring can then be used for ensuring compliance. This cocktail of requirements should go a long way to establishing a greater acceptance among the public of community sentences if, and only if, the orders are vigorously supervised and enforced.

I attach particular importance to the unpaid work requirement. One of the changes that has taken place in sentencing is the reduction in the use of a fine. This is a surprising development in the age of consumerism. The reduction in the use of fines is, I believe, at least in part attributable to a lack of resources of offenders and in part to a loss of confidence in fines due to lax enforcement. Enforcement is now being tackled and the inability to pay can be met by an unpaid work requirement. In addition, more can be done to make it worth the offender's while to pay fines promptly. We mitigate sentences by allowing prisoners parole. We should do the same for fines by allowing a reduction for prompt payment in accordance with the order of the court, whether payment is due by a lump sum or instalments.

The increased use of fines should be matched by the vigorous pursuit of the confiscation of the proceeds of crime from offenders who commit crime for acquisitive purposes.

These new community sentences could make the critical difference. However, we have to be on our guard against squandering any improvement. We must not take inappropriate action in other areas to meet popular demands for unjustifiable use of imprisonment in the case of offences where there are unintended but tragic consequences because of momentary inattention. Here there is a need to bear in mind Sir Tony Bottoms's wise comments 'the difficult task for policymakers is to recognise and build on modestly promising results of this kind, rather than succumbing to unrealistic demands for instant dramatic success stories'.

Sentencing Guidelines Council

Having established this new range of offences it was fortunate that the Act also created the new Sentencing Guidelines Council. Its task is to provide authoritative guidelines to courts on the level of sentencing, to enable sentencers to make decisions on sentencing that are supported by information on the effectiveness of sentences and on the most efficient use of resources. The Council is required by section 170(5) of the Criminal Justice Act 2003 to take into account:

(a) the need to promote consistency in sentencing;
(b) the sentences imposed by courts to which the guidelines relate;
(c) the cost of different sentences and their relative effectiveness in preventing reoffending;
(d) the need to promote public confidence in the criminal justice system; and

(e) the Council is also required to take into account the views of the Sentencing Advisory Panel.

Unlike the Court of Appeal, which had to wait for suitable cases, the Council can be, and is, proactive in preparing its guidelines. Again, unlike the Court of Appeal, the Council does not need to confine a guideline to a particular offence or series of offences. A guideline can be generic. Examples of this were the 2004 guidelines produced for reduction in sentence for guilty pleas and the critical question of seriousness.

The first guideline prepared by the Council dealt with the reduction in sentences for pleas of guilty. For many years, the courts had been in the habit of giving credit for a plea by reducing the sentences of those who plead guilty. The guidelines were only consolidating existing practice and establishing an open and clear structure which would encourage a more consistent response to a statutory obligation.

However, despite this, when the draft was first published, there was a hail of protest from many quarters who thought the guideline was a novel way of reducing sentences, the prison population and the proper reflection of the seriousness of offences, in particular in murder. However, after the consultation process had been completed, when the final guidance was published, the guideline was welcomed. That the guideline was modified as a result of the consultation process illustrates how the Council intends to operate.

Crimes vary in their seriousness both because of the type of offence involved and because of the gravity of the particular offence. Guidance as to how to approach this is provided by the seriousness guideline. It establishes relative culpability, identifying general aggravating and mitigating factors, and the approach to determining whether an offender has passed the community order or custody threshold.

In view of the scale of the changes made by the 2003 Act in relation to sentencing, it was decided that every judge who was engaged in sentencing should receive training from the Judicial Studies Board at a residential course. To assist in that training, the Council provided guidelines as to the preferred approach to the new sentences. The guideline is concerned with striking the right balance between the seriousness of the offence and the sentence most likely to prevent reoffending. In addition, guidelines dealt with the new release provisions for custodial sentences over 12 months which are set out in the 2003 Act.

In this way the Council is building upon the previous current sentencing guidelines cases. While this could take time to achieve because of the scale of the activity involved, in due course, there should be available to sentencers a code of guidelines. The Council has also published a compendium of still relevant guideline cases. Copies of the compendium have been distributed to all courts. In addition, it is included in the manual for legal advisors in magistrates' courts published by the Justices' Clerks' Society.

Over a period of time, the influence of the guidelines issued by the Council should be significant. An advantage of the guidelines is that in accordance with their statutory obligation, the Council must take into account the cost of different sentences and their relative effectiveness in preventing reoffending.

The Relevance of Cost

This brings me to a subject upon which there is still considerable debate. That is the extent to which the courts should take into account the resource implications of their sentences.

Those who argue that a court should not take account of resources, contend that once a court has decided on the just sentence, it is the responsibility of the government to ensure that the sentence is implemented. To curtail the sentence because of lack of resources is seen as a way of allowing the government to escape its responsibility. However, this approach assumes that there is only one 'just sentence' and unlimited resources. Both assumptions are wrong. While I consider, unsurprisingly, that more resources need to be devoted to criminal justice, I recognise that the Criminal Justice System is in competition with, for example, education and health for resources.

This is why it is essential that the resources that are available are used in the most effective way. If a community sentence, which is far less expensive, would be suitable for an offender, as a punishment for his crime and it would be constructive, it is wrong in principle to send him to prison. If there are no resources for drug treatment and training orders, it is pointless imposing such orders. The Council is required to take into account the cost effectiveness of different sentences in the drawing up of guidelines. Since courts are required to take into account the guidelines issued by the Council when sentencing, the courts indirectly are required by Parliament to do the same. It is wrong to say that to tailor sentences to the resources is to allow the government off the hook. The courts and the senior judiciary are quite capable of drawing attention to the effect of lack of resources.

What I have said about restricting the increase in the use of prisons is not only based on resources. It is based also on the fact that if there is a properly resourced community punishment that is a suitable alternative, the results of such a sentence are more likely than imprisonment to be in the interests of the public.

The position will remain that where resources are most urgently needed is for the Probation Service, now part of NOMS. The Probation Service is the key to tackling reoffending. This is so whether we are considering the person who is sentenced to a Community Sentence or the person who has been sentenced to imprisonment and is returning to the community. The role of the Probation Service is critical. We have to raise the standards of the Probation Service. The first priority is to improve their morale and effectiveness.

We now have more police; as a result more offenders are going to come before the courts. The courts in coordination with the other criminal justice agencies are providing a more effective service to victims, witnesses and defendants during the trial process. We must now tackle what is not being achieved by sentences that the courts impose. We must make inroads into the abysmal reoffending rates.

Success in doing this could transform the situation. Our efforts must not be deflected by the protests from those who ignore the reality of the situation we are in.

It follows that my recipe for bringing sense into sentencing involves:

(1) developing a consensus as to what resources should be available to the Criminal Justice System and ensuring that those resources are used in the manner which is most likely to provide the best protection for the public;

(2) using the platform that Parliament and the government have now provided to halt the continuing rise in the use of imprisonment and instead confining imprisonment primarily for the most serious offences and, in particular, for violent and dangerous offenders;

(3) making the broad range of community punishments really meaningful so that they prevent reoffending and inspire confidence in the public;

(4) providing more extensive drug and other substance abuse testing and training;

(5) relying more on properly enforced fines and the confiscation of the proceeds of crime; and

(6) avoiding further legislation except when it is absolutely necessary so as provide the courts and NOMS with the opportunity they need to absorb the changes that have been made and deliver an effective Criminal Justice System.

PART IV

Civil Justice

19

Access to Justice Final Report: Overview

Abstract This paper provides an overview of the *Access to Justice Final Report*, which was designed to meet the needs of the public in the 21st century by creating a comprehensive and coherent package for the reform of civil court proceedings. It aimed to improve access to justice and reduce the costs of litigation, reduce the complexity of the rules and modernise terminology, and remove unnecessary distinctions of practice and procedure. It recommended the courts should have the final responsibility for determining what procedures are suitable for each case; setting realistic timetables; ensuring the procedures and timetables are complied with; and ensuring that defended cases are allocated to short, medium or fast track systems.

The Principles

1. In my interim report[1] I identified a number of principles which the civil justice system should meet in order to ensure access to justice. The system should:

(a) be *just* in the results it delivers;
(b) be *fair* in the way it treats litigants;
(c) offer appropriate procedures at a reasonable *cost*;
(d) deal with cases with reasonable *speed*;
(e) be *understandable* to those who use it;
(f) be *responsive* to the needs of those who use it;
(g) provide as much *certainty* as the nature of particular cases allows; and
(h) be *effective*: adequately resourced and organised.

---

* This overview was originally published in the *Access to Justice Final Report* (HMSO, 1996).

[1] See *Interim Report to the Lord Chancellor on the Civil Justice System in England and Wales* (HMSO, 1995).

The Problems

2. The defects I identified in our present system were that it is too expensive, in that the costs often exceed the value of the claim; too slow in bringing cases to a conclusion and too unequal: there is a lack of equality between the powerful, wealthy litigant and the under resourced litigant. It is too uncertain: the difficulty of forecasting what litigation will cost and how long it will last induces the fear of the unknown; and it is incomprehensible to many litigants. It is too fragmented in the way it is organised since there is no one with clear overall responsibility for the administration of civil justice; and it is too adversarial as cases are run by the parties, not by the courts and the rules of court, all too often, are ignored by the parties and not enforced by the court.

The Basic Reforms

3. The interim report sets out a blueprint for reform based on a system where the courts, with the assistance of litigants, would be responsible for the management of cases. I recommended that the courts should have the final responsibility for determining what procedures were suitable for each case; setting realistic timetables; and ensuring that the procedures and timetables were complied with. Defended cases would be allocated to one of three tracks:

(a) an expanded small claims jurisdiction with a financial limit of £3,000;
(b) a new fast track for straightforward cases up to £10,000, with strictly limited procedures, fixed timetables (20–30 weeks to trial) and fixed costs; and
(c) a new multi-track for cases above £10,000, providing individual hands-on management by judicial teams for the heaviest cases, and standard or tailor-made directions where these are appropriate.

The Second Stage of the Inquiry

4. My general analysis of the problems in the present system, and the broad agenda for reform which I proposed in the interim report, have provided the foundation for the more detailed work I have carried out in the second stage of the Inquiry. This has concentrated on particular areas of litigation where, in my view, the civil justice system is failing most conspicuously to meet the needs of litigants. These areas are medical negligence, housing and multi-party litigation. I have also developed more detailed proposals on procedure and costs for

the new fast track. Another focus of special attention was the Crown Office List, which has a particularly important function in enabling individual citizens to challenge decisions of public bodies including central and local government.

5. In all these areas a particular concern has been to improve access to justice for individuals and small businesses. I am also concerned about the level of public expenditure on litigation, particularly in medical negligence and housing. In both of these areas substantial amounts of public money are absorbed in legal costs which could be better spent, in the one case on improving medical care and in the other on improving standards of social housing. An efficient and cost effective justice system is also of vital importance to the commercial, financial and industrial life of this country and I was anxious to improve this, especially because of the evidence I received that there was a substantial risk of the existing system changing our competitive position in relation to other jurisdictions. Finally, I was anxious to ensure that the judiciary and the resources of the Court Service were deployed to the best effect.

6. All the work I have carried out in the second stage of the Inquiry has confirmed the conclusions I reached in the interim report about the defects in the present system. This report therefore builds on the contents and recommendations of the interim report by:

(a) providing greater detail as to the principal recommendations in the interim report;
(b) identifying the problems in those areas which have received special attention during the second stage of the Inquiry and the solutions I am recommending to meet those problems;
(c) describing the new rules; and
(d) making clear any change in my approach since the interim report.

Rules of Court

7. An important part of my task in the Inquiry was to produce a single, simpler procedural code to apply to civil litigation in the High Court and county courts. This report is accompanied by a draft of the general rules which will form the core of the new code. In the second part of the Inquiry I have looked in detail at the specialist jurisdictions of the High Court with a view to accommodating them so far as possible within the general procedural framework embodied in the core rules. As a result of the work done by the Inquiry, it is apparent that a great many of the existing specialist rules are

no longer required. Work is continuing on the more limited body of special rules which are still considered essential. Here I await with interest the views of those engaged in the specialist jurisdictions who could not express a formal opinion as to what extra rules are still needed until they had seen the general rules which have been prepared by the Inquiry.

The New Landscape

8. If my recommendations are implemented the landscape of civil litigation will be fundamentally different from what it is now. It will be underpinned by Rule I of the new procedural code, which imposes an obligation on the courts and the parties to further the overriding objective of the rules so as to deal with cases justly. The rule provides a definition of 'dealing with a case justly', embodying the principles of equality, economy, proportionality and expedition which are fundamental to an effective contemporary system of justice. These requirements of procedural justice, operating in the traditional adversarial context, will give effect to a system which is substantively just in the results it delivers as well as in the way in which it does so.

9. The new landscape will have the following features:

Litigation will be avoided wherever possible

(a) People will be encouraged to start court proceedings to resolve disputes only as a last resort, and after using other more appropriate means when these are available.

(b) Information on sources of alternative dispute resolution[2] will be provided at all civil courts.

(c) Legal aid funding will be available for pre-litigation resolution and ADR.

(d) Protocols in relation to medical negligence, housing and personal injury, and additional powers for the court in relation to pre-litigation disclosure, will enable parties to obtain information earlier and promote settlement.

(e) Before commencing litigation both parties will be able to make offers to settle the whole or part of a dispute supported by a special regime as to costs and higher rates of interest if not accepted.

---

[2] Hereafter, 'ADR'.

Litigation will be less adversarial and more cooperative

(a) There will be an expectation of openness and cooperation between parties from the outset, supported by pre-litigation protocols on disclosure and experts. The courts will be able to give effect to their disapproval of a lack of cooperation prior to litigation.

(b) The court will encourage the use of ADR at case management conferences and pre-trial reviews, and will take into account whether the parties have unreasonably refused to try ADR or behaved unreasonably in the course of ADR.

(c) The duty of experts to the court will be emphasised. Single experts, instructed by the parties, will be used when practicable. Opposing experts will be encouraged to meet or communicate as early as possible to narrow the issues between them. The court will have a power to appoint an expert.

Litigation will be less complex

(a) There will be a single set of rules applying to the High Court and the county courts. The rules will be simpler, and special rules for specific types of litigation will be reduced to a minimum.

(b) All proceedings will be commenced in the same way by a claim.

(c) The claim and defence will not be technical documents. The claim will set out the facts alleged by the claimant, the remedy the claimant seeks, the grounds on which the remedy is sought and any relevant points of law. The defence will set out the defendant's detailed response to the claim and make clear the real issues between the parties. Both 'statements of case' will have to include certificates by the parties verifying their contents so tactical allegations will no longer be possible.

(d) During the course of proceedings the court on its own initiative, or on the application of either party, will be able to dispose of individual issues or the litigation as a whole where there is no real prospect of success.

(e) Claimants will be able to start proceedings in any court. It will be the court's responsibility to direct parties or to transfer the case, if necessary, to the appropriate part of the system.

(f) Discovery will be controlled; in a minority of cases the present scale of discovery will be possible but in the majority of cases there will be a new standard test for more restricted disclosure.

(g) There will be special procedures, involving active judicial case management, to deal with multi-party actions expeditiously and fairly.

(h) Instead of an irrational kaleidoscope of different ways of appealing or applying to the High Court against the decisions of other bodies, there will be a unified code.

The timescale of litigation will be shorter and more certain

(a) All cases will progress to trial in accordance with a timetable set and monitored by the court.
(b) For fast-track cases there will be fixed timetables of no more than 30 weeks.
(c) The court will apply strict sanctions to parties who do not comply with the procedures or timetables.
(d) Appeals from case management decisions will be kept to the minimum, and will be dealt with expeditiously.
(e) The court will determine the length of the trial and what is to happen at the trial.

The cost of litigation will be more affordable, more predictable and more proportionate to the value and complexity of individual cases

(a) There will be fixed costs for cases on the fast track.
(b) Estimates of costs for multi-track cases will be published by the court or agreed by the parties and approved by the court.
(c) There will be a special 'streamlined' track for lower value or less complex multi-track cases, where the procedure will be as simple as possible with appropriate budgets for costs.
(d) For classes of litigation where the procedure is uncomplicated and predictable the court will issue guideline costs with the assistance of users.
(e) There will be a new test for the taxation of costs to further the overriding objective. It will be that there should be allowed 'such sum as is reasonable taking account of the interests of both parties to the taxation'.

Parties of limited financial means will be able to conduct litigation on a more equal footing

(a) Litigants who are not legally represented will be able to get more help from advice services and from the courts.

(b) Procedural judges will take account of the parties' financial circumstances in allocating cases to the fast track or to the small claims jurisdiction.

(c) Limited procedures and tight timetables on the fast track, and judicial case management on the multi-track, will make it more difficult for wealthier parties to gain a tactical advantage over their opponents by additional expenditure.

(d) When deciding upon the procedure which is to be adopted the court will, if the parties' means are unequal, be entitled to make an order for a more elaborate procedure, conditional upon the other side agreeing to meet, in any event, the difference in the cost of the two possible procedures.

(e) The new approach will be supported by more effective sanctions, including orders for costs in a fixed sum which are to be paid forthwith.

There will be clear lines of judicial and administrative responsibility for the civil justice system

(a) The Head of Civil Justice will have overall responsibility for the Civil Justice System in England and Wales.

(b) The Presiding Judges on each Circuit will exercise their responsibility for civil work in conjunction with the two Chancery judges who will also oversee the business and mercantile lists.

(c) A nominated Circuit judge will be responsible for the effective organisation of each civil trial centre and its satellite courts.

(d) The new administrative structure will establish a partnership between the judiciary and the Court Service.

The structure of the courts and the deployment of judges will be designed to meet the needs of litigants

(a) Heavier and more complex civil cases will be concentrated at trial centres which have the resources needed, including specialist judges, to ensure that the work is dealt with effectively.

(b) Smaller local courts will continue to play a vital role in providing easy access to the civil justice system. Housing claims, small claims, debt cases and cases allocated to the fast track will be dealt with there, as well as case management of the less complex multi-track cases.

(c) Better ways of providing access to justice in rural areas will be maintained and developed.

(d) There will be a more straightforward system of appeals. Appeals with no real prospect of success will be eliminated at an early stage.
(e) The courts will have access to the technology needed to monitor the progress of litigation.
(f) Litigants will be able to communicate with the courts electronically and through video and telephone conferencing facilities.
(g) Trials will take place on the date assigned.

Judges will be deployed effectively so that they can manage litigation in accordance with the new rules and protocols

(a) Judges will be given the training they need to manage cases.
(b) Judges will be encouraged to specialise in such areas as housing and medical negligence, and will be given the appropriate training to ensure that they understand the legal and technical issues fully.
(c) Cases will be dealt with by the part of the system which is most appropriate. The distinctions between the county courts and High Court and between the divisions of the High Court will be of reduced significance.
(d) Judges will have the administrative and technological support which is required for the effective management of cases.

The civil justice system will be responsive to the needs of litigants

(a) Courts will provide advice and assistance to litigants through court-based or duty advice and assistance schemes, especially in courts with substantial levels of debt and housing work.
(b) Courts will provide more information to litigants through leaflets, videos, telephone helplines and information technology.
(c) Court staff will provide information and help to litigants on how to progress their case.
(d) There will be ongoing monitoring and research on litigants' needs.

The Funding of Civil Litigation

10. My Inquiry is concerned with the procedure of the civil courts. I have not dealt directly with the funding of litigation, but there are other developments in this area which will affect the new landscape I have just described. The most significant recent development in the funding of civil litigation is the current review of legal aid, on which there has been close cooperation between my Inquiry Team and the Legal Aid Reform Team.

11. It is essential that the reforms of legal aid should take into account and support the recommendations I am making. The reforms of civil procedure which I am proposing will be more effective if:

(a) legal aid funding is available for pre-litigation resolution and ADR (including the costs of an expert conducting expert adjudication of small claims and cases on the fast track);

(b) public funding is available for in-court advice services, especially on housing issues;

(c) legal aid is available for solicitors and barristers providing 'unbundled' legal services to parties conducting their own cases on the fast track;

(d) the Legal Aid Board's decisions take into account the court's allocation of a case to the appropriate track, and any directions of the court as to the future management of the case; in all cases but especially in multi-party actions;

(e) the legal aid reforms recognise the importance of ensuring the survival of efficient small firms of solicitors, particularly in remote areas.

12. In addition there is the availability of conditional fee agreements and the growth in legal expenses insurance. Both of these can help to make litigation more affordable, but they cannot in themselves deal with the underlying problems of excessive and unpredictable costs. Both conditional fees and insurance are, at present, available only in limited classes of cases. They will only become more generally available if costs are firmly controlled in the ways that I am proposing.

Implementation of My Reforms

13. The Lord Chancellor welcomed my interim report and has made plain his commitment to reform. Having accepted the thrust of my recommendations, he has established an implementation team and embarked on a programme of phased implementation.

14. In January 1996 the Lord Chancellor appointed the Vice Chancellor, Sir Richard Scott, to take on the duties envisaged for a Head of Civil Justice. This appointment is in itself a very important step. Sir Richard will be able to take charge of implementing many of the other recommendations. He will be able to provide the hands-on leadership for civil litigation which it has lacked in the past. He will be able to have an input into the selection of judges to be responsible for the handling of civil work at trial centres. He will be in a position to oversee the implementation of the other recommendations.

15. The Court Service, in consultation with the judiciary, has started to put into place the supporting structure which will be needed to introduce the new system of case management by the courts. This includes identifying the appropriate number and location of trial centres on each Circuit, and setting up a new arrangement for a partnership between the judiciary and administrative staff. The Judicial Studies Board is preparing for an intensive programme of training for judges involved in case management, based on a survey which the Board wishes to conduct to identify the special interests and needs of judges.

16. Some of my other recommendations which did not need to await this final report have already been implemented. The small claims jurisdiction has been increased to £3,000, except for personal injury claims, as from 8 January 1996. At the same time the test applied by district judges in considering transfer out of the small claims jurisdiction was modified, so that cases qualify for transfer if they are considered 'complex' rather then 'exceptionally complex'. The Judicial Studies Board is making arrangements to provide additional training for district judges in connection with their small claims work and has developed a protocol or best practice guide to promote the consistency of approach which I recommended. The option of paper adjudication, which I recommended, of benefit in particular to small businesses and the self-employed, is being considered by the Lord Chancellor's Department.

17. The effects of the increased jurisdiction are being monitored and research is being considered. I hope that the results of any monitoring or research will be published so that the effects of the increase in jurisdiction can be considered by all those involved, before any further increase is contemplated.

18. I outlined my proposals for an enhanced role for ADR in the interim report and the past year has seen further developments, including a pilot mediation scheme at Central London County Court and plans for pilot mediation and arbitration schemes at the Patents County Court. I also understand that the Lord Chancellor is considering providing assistance with the ADR pilot scheme being conducted by Bristol Law Society and researching the effects of this. I welcome the recent publication by the Lord Chancellor's Department of a plain English guide on ADR, *Resolving Disputes Without Going To Court*,[3] designed to make members of the public more aware of

---

[3] (LCD, 1995).

methods of resolving disputes which do not involve litigation. The new procedures I propose will emphasise the importance of ADR through the court's ability to take into account whether parties have unreasonably rejected the possibility of ADR or have behaved unreasonably in the course of ADR.

19. The interim report emphasised the importance of providing effective information, advice and assistance to all litigants and recommended that all the Civil Justice Review's recommendations in this respect should be implemented. Provision of such assistance until now has been very much a matter of local initiative and it says much for such local action that about one-third of all county courts now host advice schemes. The creation of the Court Service as an agency, with its emphasis on customer service, and in particular the new management structure, now provides an opportunity to take a more strategic approach. The provision of information and advice directs people to appropriate means of resolving disputes, enables them to understand how to progress their cases and contributes to the effective disposal of court business. Just as case management involves spending time to save time, so the provision of appropriate help to litigants will result in a better use of court and legal aid resources. It will also ensure that access to justice is a reality rather than a slogan.

Conclusion

20. In the course of the Inquiry there has been unprecedented consultation with all involved in the civil justice system. Over the last year, judges, practitioners and consumers have worked together to hammer out new ways of tackling problems and to contribute to what is proposed in this final report. I see a continuing need for such involvement in the process of implementation. Much has been done, but much more remains to be done. The continuing involvement of all those who use the civil justice system will be given coherence and leadership by the Civil Justice Council which I recommended in the interim report. Local user committees, a specialist IT subcommittee and working groups developing further detail for the new fast track would all come under its aegis. The Council would continue and develop the process of cooperation and creativity that the Inquiry has benefited from.

21. The civil justice system in this country urgently needs reform. The time is right for change. The public and businesses want change, and the majority of the legal profession agree. The judiciary has strongly supported my Inquiry.

I have been given a unique opportunity to help achieve the change which is needed.

22. My recommendations, together with the new code of rules, form a comprehensive and coherent package for the reform of civil justice. Each contributes to and underpins the others. Their overall effectiveness could be seriously undermined by piecemeal implementation. Their implementation as a whole will ensure that all the supporting elements of the civil justice system are directed towards the fundamental reform that is required.

23. Nevertheless, there should be a degree of flexibility in the approach to implementation. All the recommendations I have made, both in the interim report and in this report, are designed to meet the objectives for the civil justice system which I set out at the beginning of this overview. My detailed recommendations are based on a thorough review of the present system, including the wide consultation I have mentioned, but the objectives are of primary importance. The individual proposals should not be too rigidly applied if it is found that there are better ways of achieving the objectives. My overriding concern is to ensure that we have a civil justice system which will meet the needs of the public in the 21st century

20

Medics, Lawyers and the Courts—
A Defence of the Access to Justice
Recommendations

Abstract Commenting on the relationship between the medical profession and the courts, this paper discusses the recommendations in the *Access to Justice Final Report* and criticisms that were made of some of them, notably by Professor Michael Zander QC. It focuses upon the recommendations that were made for the improvement of handling medical negligence cases, as an example of the recommendations for the improvement of litigation generally. Professor Zander's opposition to the recommendations is described as 'misleading' and 'inaccurate', based on an unwillingness to accept that the civil justice system has serious faults—faults that most commentators have accepted exist. It concludes that the civil justice system does not meet the needs of patients or professional health carers, but the recommendations would improve the situation if they were to be fully implemented.

I am honoured to be allowed to give this lecture. I am grateful to have an opportunity to acknowledge publicly the extent to which I am indebted to the Royal Colleges in general and to the Royal College of Physicians in particular for the help they gave me during my recent inquiry into Access to Justice.

In this lecture I intend to say something about the recommendations I have made and about criticisms that have been made of some of them,

---

* This paper was originally delivered as the Samuel Gee Lecture at the Royal College of Physicians of London, on 13 May 1997. An original version of this lecture was published in the Civil Justice Quarterly ((1997) 16 CJQ 302). A shortened version of the lecture can be found in the Journal of the Royal College of Physicians of London ((1993) 31 JRCPL 686).

notably by Professor Michael Zander,[1] but before doing that I would like to make some comments on aspects of the relationship between the medical profession on the one hand and the courts on the other.

In my experience, the relationship has always been of a high order. The courts are very conscious that in many fields of litigation they depend on expert medical advice in order to come to a just decision. The general approach of the courts is to apply the standards which the medical profession adopt. Thus, we judge whether there has been negligence in the treatment of a patient by asking whether or not the medical treatment which is the subject of complaint accords with the standards which any recognised section of the medical profession regards as acceptable. If the treatment does accord with such a standard, then in general the judges do not categorise it as negligent. By adopting this standard the courts have managed to hold the balance fairly between the interests of the patient and the interest of the profession. By striking the right balance, the courts reduce the risk of proper medical practice being undermined by the fear of litigation and the need for compensation to be paid where treatment is of an unacceptable standard. In addition, the courts do not impose their ethical standards upon the medical professions. Wisely, on the whole they leave the medical profession to determine what is, and what is not, ethical behaviour.

However, because of the increasing complexity of society, members of the medical profession are from time to time faced with problems as to whether or not a particular course of treatment is or is not lawful. When the medical profession have problems of this nature, they can rightly expect the courts to provide them with an answer. It is primarily the responsibility of the courts to define what is lawful and what is unlawful behaviour. Furthermore, if the problem needs to be resolved urgently because the health of a patient is at stake, then the courts are under a heavy duty to ensure that it is resolved expeditiously. Here I believe the courts can take pride in what they have achieved with the cooperation of the legal profession.

First of all, the courts have significantly changed their attitude to giving advisory declarations in relation to medical issues. At one time it was the courts practice not to grant advisory declarations as to whether future conduct would or would not be lawful. This meant that a doctor could be faced with the choice of either not giving treatment or taking the risk of giving

---

[1] M Zander QC, 'The Woolf Report: Forwards or Backwards for the New Lord Chancellor' (1997) 17 CLQ 208.

treatment and having that treatment later condemned as unlawful. Now it is clearly established that if there is a doubt as to the lawfulness of treatment, the court can rule on this in advance of the treatment being given. As a judge of first instance, I was by chance involved in the three cases upon which the present approach is based. The first case, *Royal College of Nursing of the United Kingdom v Department of Health and Social Security*,[2] involved the Royal College of Nursing who were concerned as to what part a nurse could properly play in procuring an abortion without being under the direct supervision of a doctor. The second, *Gillick v West Norfolk and Wisbech Area Health Authority and the DHSS*,[3] was as to the lawfulness of doctors providing advice to children on methods of contraception when they were below the age which it was lawful to have sexual intercourse with them. The third case, *Attorney-General v Able*,[4] involved an issue as to what advice and assistance could lawfully be given to an individual who wished to terminate his life.

An area where it has been particularly important that the courts should be willing to grant advisory declarations is where a patient is unconscious as a result of an accident or illness and is incapable of stating whether or not he consents to a particular course of care. The law has laid down that in such circumstances a doctor may lawfully treat such a patient as long as he acts in the patient's best interest. Indeed, if the patient is already in his care he is under a duty to treat him. The case which made this clear was only decided in 1989.[5] That was a case in which it was obvious that it would be desirable to sterilise an adult woman of unsound mind and the court held it was law-ful for the operation to take place.

However, doctors are not entitled to impose treatment on someone who is of sound mind, however much treatment might be in his interest, if he does not consent to have that treatment. A patient may if he or she wishes starve him or herself to death. But what of a situation where what is involved is a decision as to whether to provide or to continue to provide treatment or care which could or might prolong the life of a patient if the continuance of the treatment is futile? Futile since it would not confer any benefit upon the patient. This was the issue that came before the court in a particularly acute

---

[2] [1981] 2 WLR 279.
[3] [1986] AC 112.
[4] [1983] 3 WLR 845.
[5] *F v The West Berkshire Health Authority (Mental Health Act Commission intervening)* [1990] 2 AC 1

form in relation to Anthony Bland,[6] the young man who was a victim of the Hillsborough football disaster. He was 21 years of age when the matter came before the House of Lords. He had been in a persistent vegetative state for three and a half years. The House of Lords drew a distinction between two situations. The first would be euthanasia and unlawful—bringing a patient's life to an end by positive steps, such as administering a drug to bring about his death. The second is not prolonging the patient's life by discontinuing medical treatment. This includes stopping artificial feedings and the administration of antibiotic drugs when it is known that the result will be that the patient will die. This is lawful. This is subject to a proviso which again involves the standards of the profession. The proviso is that responsible and competent medical opinion is of the view that it is not in the patient's best interest to prolong his life. Two members of the House, Lord Browne-Wilkinson and Lord Mustill, were especially concerned about having to reach a decision. This was because this is an area where it is particularly important that Parliament should review the law. They also recognised that the solution which was being provided was not ideal. Lord Browne-Wilkinson said:

> How can it be lawful to allow a patient to die slowly, though painlessly, over a period of weeks through lack of food, but unlawful to produce the immediate death by a lethal injection, thereby saving his family from yet another ordeal to add to the tragedy that had already struck them? I find it difficult to find a moral answer to that question.

As perhaps could be forecast, Parliament has not provided the legislation which their Lordships thought desirable and so the courts are still having to develop the law on a case-by-case basis.[7]

Since the *Anthony Bland* case, there have been a reasonably substantial number of other cases where similar assistance has been sought in the courts. Some of the cases have been variations of the *Anthony Bland* case. Others have raised different issues. There has been a case where a mother was in danger of inflicting injury upon herself and the loss of the baby she was about to have because she suffered from a needle phobia. The needle phobia was preventing her making any decision at all. The situation was extremely urgent and the court at first instance sat at 9.25 to 9.55 in the

---

[6] *Airedale NHS Trust v Bland* [1993] AC 789.
[7] It is noteworthy that in 2006 the House of Lords blocked a private member's bill that would have given terminally ill persons the right to assisted suicide.

evening so that it could grant a declaration. An appeal was heard on the same day from 11.00 pm to 1.00 am and a declaration granted by the Court of Appeal. The consequence was that later that morning the mother having learnt of the decision of the court voluntarily gave her consent and I am happy to say that she was delivered of a healthy child.

The courts also recognise that cases of this nature need a special form of case management. As the issues were often of a similar nature to those dealt with by the Family Division the cases were allocated to that Division so that the Family Division judges of the High Court could develop expertise in their disposal. Furthermore, the President of the Family Division laid down procedures which would ensure that they received the urgent attention they required. The consequence is a marked improvement in the ability of the courts to assist the medical profession and in so doing the interests of justice and the needs of the public. This is an example of what is now known as case management by the courts.

Turning to medical negligence litigation the story is not so happy. Medical negligence was given a high profile during my inquiry and has been the subject of a number of the recommendations which I have made. This is because medical negligence was one of the areas of litigation where it was obvious to everyone involved that the civil justice system was not working satisfactorily and radical change was desperately needed. I am confident that no one who has personal experience of this subject would dispute this diagnosis.

The recommendations I have made for the improvement of the handling of medical negligence cases are but an example of my recommendations for the improvement of litigation generally. If the general recommendations are not sound then I have to acknowledge my recommendations as to the hearing of medical negligence cases must be flawed.

It is because of this I now refer to a campaign of opposition to my recommendations upon which Professor Michael Zander has felt it right to embark. I do so, because if he is right in the criticisms which he makes, then the support which I have received from this College and the other Colleges has been misplaced. In addition, those who have been and are still working on carrying forward my reforms are engaged in a futile task. Among those to whom I am here referring are the medical and health practitioners, lawyers, and insurers who have been carrying forward the reforms as part of the Clinical Disputes Forum. They include a partner in a firm of well-known solicitors who conduct litigation on behalf of plaintiffs in medical negligence cases, who felt the inquiry into access to justice was such an important opportunity that she gave up her practice for nine months to work entirely voluntarily to assist in the preparation of my report.

I had been aware that Professor Zander had been concerned about my recommendations for some time. He is a friend and he has been punctilious in keeping me informed of the criticisms that he is making. If criticisms are constructive I welcome them. It is for that reason that I invited Professor Zander to address a meeting which was held in connection with my inquiry and I have also accepted an invitation to appear on the same platform to discuss my report. For the same reason I have deliberately restrained my response to his criticisms though I have observed they are becoming more strident as time passes. However, last week he gave a lecture for which he invited wide media attention which I am afraid I regard as being misleading and inaccurate. I therefore propose to devote part of the remainder of this evening to responding, insofar as time permits, to the criticisms which he makes.

As I understand his thesis, it is that there is nothing very much wrong with the way the civil justice system is working but, insofar as there is anything wrong, it is unlikely that anything can be done about it, because lawyers will not change their ways and, in any event, the recommendations which I have made will make the situation worse rather than better.

In making this root and branch attack on the reforms, Professor Zander recognises that he is, as he has said himself, a Cassandra figure. He said in his lecture last week, 'the Woolf project appears to have almost universal support including, so far as one can tell, that of the senior judiciary, the Bar and The Law Society as well as both the lay and the legal press'.[8] He adds that:

> ... one might have expected that of all people, practising lawyers would take exception to Lord Woolf's caustic view of the way that they operate. But neither the Bar or The Law Society has raised a peep of protest about this calumny. Indeed Lord Woolf's view was essentially not different from that of the independent working party set up in 1992 jointly by the General Council of the Bar and The Law Society.[9]

He is here referring to the report brought out under the chairmanship of Miss Hillary Heilbron QC and Mr Henry Hodge which reflected the views of 44 highly experienced practitioners. He suggests there has been 'remarkably

[8] Zander, 'The Woolf Report', n 1 above.
[9] Ibid.

little interest in awkward facts and analysis that suggest that this emperor is wearing no clothes'.[10]

In general I must confess the tenor of his lecture reminded me very much of the remark attributed to a 19th-century judge who was reported to have said 'reform, don't talk to me about reform, things are bad enough already'. Professor Zander concluded his lecture by saying, and I quote:[11]

1 The arguments I have been pressing are very strong ones and that they deserve an answer. But they have not been answered—perhaps because they are unanswerable.

2 That the new Lord Chancellor should say, 'I want to be told by someone in detail and addressing the facts and figures why Zander is wrong'. And I should be given an opportunity to reply to such an assessment of his argument. And let there be a reply to my reply and let this process go on until both sides have said what they have to say. Such exchanges or advice to the Lord Chancellor should be published and then let the Lord Chancellor decide which is the better argument.

3 A prudent approach might, for instance, lead us to stand by implementing the proposal made in 1979 by the Cantley Committee that attention should be directed first and foremost at the small minority of cases that plainly appear to be lagging. If a case has not been set down for trial within X months of issue of the proceeding a summons should be issued requesting an explanation. The court could then give whatever directions seemed appropriate in the light of what it was told about the reasons for delay. That would be a reform targeted at the right cases, as opposed to Lord Woolf's scatter-gun approach which would apply the reforms mainly to cases that do no need them.

If you heard his lecture you would no doubt be impressed by his eloquence but you should not have been impressed by the content. It was not based on any relevant practical experience. He is a distinguished academic and contributions from academics can be important. However, he has not conducted himself into the workings of the civil courts in recent times.

By contrast, although I of course accept this does not mean that my recommendations have any validity, they were produced after an intense two-year consultation process conducted with the assistance of an assessor with a wide-ranging experience of the subject with which my report deals. I was also helped by expert working parties of highly experienced practitioners and academic consultants of distinction whose findings supported my conclusions.

---

[10] Ibid.
[11] Ibid.

Those findings were that the civil justice system has become excessively adversarial, slow, complex and expensive. That this is especially true of litigation over alleged medical negligence in the delivery of heath care whether by doctors, nurses or other health carers. For example, there are five respects in which medical negligence actions conspicuously failed to meet the needs of litigants:

(1) The relationship between the costs of the litigation and the amount involved was particularly disproportionate. The costs were peculiarly excessive, especially in low value cases.
(2) Delay; the period which regularly elapsed before claims are resolved is more often unacceptable in the case of medical negligence claims than other classes of proceedings.
(3) Unmeritorious cases are pursued and clear-cut claims defended for longer than happened in other areas of litigation.
(4) The success rate is also lower than in other personal injury litigation.
(5) Finally the lack of cooperation between the parties to the litigation and the mutual suspicion as to the motives of the opposing party is frequently more intense than in other classes of litigation.

I emphasise that the system is not meeting the needs of patients or professional health carers. They are both being let down by the civil justice system at present. The pain is not only caused to the potential plaintiffs. It is caused also to those who have been responsible for delivering the health care of which complaint is made. All too often they find themselves in a nightmare situation. Their ambition throughout has been to help the patient but instead they find that they are the subject of hurtful allegations of negligent mistreatment. The allegations often only surface after the carer has ceased to have any real recollection of what happened. Frequently the carer feels intense frustration. They believe that if only they could have an opportunity of discussing the issues with the patient they could satisfactorily explain why things turned out as they did. However, outdated conventions as to behaviour makes this impossible. The concern is, that if there is an apology, or if even an explanation is given, this could be used in evidence against him or prejudice his position with medical defence bodies. The result is that patients feel let down. Treatment has gone wrong, sometimes because of unrealistic expectations as to what could be achieved and carers react defensively in respect of attacks from patients which they regard as unjustified.

I was convinced that a way had to be found for breaking down the barriers which divided the patient from his carers so that wherever possible litigation could be avoided. This could only help everyone involved. It would save on costs. It could result in those patients who deserve to be compensated receiving proportionate compensation voluntarily, and in an atmosphere which did not poison relations between the patients and those who had been treating them. Often, where things have gone wrong the need for treatment is at its greatest and the breakdown results in the professional feeling frustrated in not being able to provide that treatment.

The opposition of Professor Zander to my recommendations is based on his unwillingness to accept that the civil justice system has these serious faults. Faults that I and virtually all commentators are agreed the system suffers from. And his unwillingness to accept that, if the faults do exist, my recommendations will improve the situation. Let me therefore deal with these points in turn.

At the outset I should make it clear that all the blame for the problems which I believe exist is not to be laid at the door of the legal profession. However, too often in individual cases lawyers are at least partly to blame. More important as a cause of the problems is the disproportionate way the present adversarial system operates which encourages excessive delay, expense and unnecessary complexity. It is the system, not the lawyers, that explains, for example, the hostility and bitterness which distorts medical negligence litigation.

On the question of delay Professor Zander in his lecture relies on two reports which were into *personal injury* alone. One published almost 40 years ago[12] and the other is brief and published 28 years ago without any attempt at consultation.[13] Even 28 years is a long time ago. The Winn report as Professor Zander accepts did consider that delay was a problem and though not coming to identical conclusions substantially shared my views. Cantley was a limited exercise; there was no consultation and it took a more sanguine view of the position. Professor Zander suggests I may have not considered the evidence provided by those reports. I know not why he makes this suggestion but it is ill founded. I did, however, prefer to rely on the up-to-date statistics set out in my Interim Report and what I and my team found to be the position after what is suggested to have been the most extensive and thorough examination which has ever taken place into the civil justice system. I did not act as Professor Zander suggests on

---

[12] C Winn, *Report on Personal Injury Litigation* (1968).
[13] J Cantley, *Report of the Personal Injuries Litigation Procedure Working Party* (1979).

'unsubstantiated opinions' which I agree would be 'a recipe for getting things radically wrong'.[14]

The statistics included the following figures: High Court cases taking 163 weeks in London and 189 weeks elsewhere to proceed from issue to trial. In the county court dealing with smaller cases the figure was 80 weeks. These figures were, I emphasise, for the average case. Many would take substantially longer. Research for my inquiry by Professor Hazel Genn indicated that in medical negligence cases the average time from issue to conclusion was six years five months and in ordinary personal injury actions over four and a half years. To these figures have to be added the substantial periods, sometimes years, which is allowed to pass prior to the action being commenced.

I said in my report that the figures were unacceptable and as far as I am aware no one has sought to suggest the figures are inaccurate or, apart from Professor Zander, that my criticism is unwarranted. I was also concerned about the time cases were taking to settle. Here the figures available were for 1993. Of the cases which were set down for trial—that means they had gone through all steps necessary to make them ready for trial—only 13 per cent were determined after trial, 9 per cent settle at the door of the court or during the trial, that is, after all the expense has been incurred. I also referred to the research of Professor Genn which showed that the majority of cases took as long as four to six years to settle—larger cases took longer. Again, I regard the figures as unacceptable. In doing so, I have very much in mind the trauma that litigation can cause to those involved and why, especially in medical negligence cases it can leave both sides with a grave sense of the justice system having failed them. In minimising the problem as to delay, Professor Zander displays remarkable complacency.

Professor Zander however suggests that I am being 'Canute like' and defying reality in suggesting something can and should be done about this instead of recognising that 'the enterprise is hopeless'. He also categorises the failures of lawyers in this area as 'minor failures'. In expressing these views, he refers to the unfortunate experience in relation to the automatic strike-out provisions. They were introduced into the court rules in an effort to do something about the situation in 1990. The device was simple and crude. If a plaintiff allowed 15 months to elapse after the time when the parties had set out their case in writing in documents called pleadings before

---

[14] See Zander, 'The Woolf Report', n 1 above.

taking the steps necessary to enable the court to fix the date for trial, the action would be struck out automatically and they would have to apply for it to be restored. What was not foreseen is that in some 20,000 cases or more the plaintiff's lawyer would delay for over a year and a quarter to take the elementary step of setting down the case which is a condition precedent to the case coming to trial. I am at least here able to agree with Professor Zander that this result has been a 'disaster'; there have been appeals galore and actions for negligence and dissent from his conclusion as to what should be the response. Professor Zander suggests we should accept and I quote:

> ...there is really nothing that can be done about the problem other than the application of sanctions that are ridiculously out of proportion to the offence, a policy which, sooner or later has to be abandoned because it is manifestly unjust.[15]

The error that was made when the rule was introduced was not appreciating that there would be anything like this number of cases which it would affect. The error was understandable because the system could not provide the information which was needed to know otherwise. What then should be done? First, the lesson should be learnt that there will be a substantial number of the cases in which, contrary to Professor Zander's views, if the lawyers for the Plaintiffs are left to their own devices, they will delay taking even the most elementary steps in the interests of their clients.

Secondly, it must be accepted that in the interests of justice, as no one else can take the responsibility, the court must take the responsibility for seeing this does not happen.

Thirdly, it must be recognised that the solution is not to impose draconian sanctions except as a last resort but to achieve a situation where sanctions of this sort are not necessary because: (a) the court does not allow the situation to deteriorate to the extent that they become necessary; and (b) the court has the wider range of alternative sanctions I propose. Unfortunately, this will only be possible when the technology I have recommended is in place.

The experience with automatic strike outs is therefore not an argument against case management but for case management. Ironically, in relation to delay, despite his uncomplimentary remarks about my proposals and my own personal qualities (in addition to being 'Canute like' and indulging in 'scatter gun tactics', I am building castles on sand and proceedings like the

---

[15] Ibid.

Generals of the First World War, just thoughtlessly blundering ahead) Professor Zander does at least make two, and only two, positive proposals which I hope he will not be disappointed to learn are very much the same as my own. They are that dates for trial should be fixed at an early stage in a case's life and if a case is manifestly lagging behind schedule it should be called in for directions. Where we differ, is I do not restrict myself to these modest steps because delay is by no means the only subject which has to be tackled. There is in particular the need to reduce costs, to simplify the system, to remove disproportionate behaviour of differing kinds, and to divert cases from the courts when there is a preferable alternative method for resolving the dispute.

The research conducted on behalf of the inquiry established clearly that costs are disproportionate to the issues involved in litigation. They are substantially higher than those in some other jurisdictions, particularly Germany, with which comparisons were drawn as a result of the research conducted on behalf of the Inquiry by Adrian Zuckerman of Oxford. There is incontrovertible evidence that cases frequently involve costs of one party alone in excess of the amount in dispute. Unless they are assisted, large sections of the community cannot afford to go to court. This is again especially true of medical negligence litigation. Over 90 per cent of the cases which reached the stage of litigation are legally aided; 92 per cent of the successful litigants are legally aided. Yet the legally aided section of the community is no more vulnerable than other sections of the community to medical negligence. These figures must suggest if those other sections of the community were entitled to legal aid more actions would be brought which would succeed. Even as things were the April 1997 edition of *Health Law* estimated that the costs for 1996 to the Health Service were £170m and the outstanding contingent liability was £1bn (these figures include the awards of damages but a substantial part of the sum was costs). The author goes on to say: 'Legal aid does not secure access to justice or ensure compensation for deserving cases. Instead it impoverishes the health service.' Professor Zander ignores this situation; as he does the other situation namely housing where a similar waste of public expenditure can be demonstrated to be occurring. I do not believe he would do so if he had the opportunity that I had of learning at first hand from litigants, both patients and doctors and health carers, who are embroiled in this class of litigation what the experience is like. It is horrendous. Has it occurred to Professor Zander that the explanation for the failure of the lawyers and judges not to object to my 'calumny' which he finds so surprising, is that as practitioners they are all too well aware of what is happening on the ground and they agree with the diagnosis of the inquiry? Why does he make no mention of the consumer bodies who were adamant that radical action was necessary and who support my programme of reform? Are they unaware of the view of their members?

There are plenty of other diseases to which the system is prone, including the lack of certainty as to what will be the consequences of becoming involved in litigation, the fact that it fails to allow for the inequalities in resources of the parties and it is excessively adversarial. There are problems as to discovery and experts. However, as the remainder of diagnosis is not under specific challenge but ignored by Professor Zander I will turn now to the reforms or, should I say the medicine which I have recommended.

Professor Zander's criticism to date as far as I am aware is only as to two important elements of the package of reforms that have been recommended. They are the related subjects of the fast track and case management. However, the merits of those two recommendations can only be appreciated in the context of the recommendations as a whole. Among the most important of these recommendations are the reorganisation of the civil courts, the creation of a single Rule Committee for the civil justice system as a whole and the creation of the Civil Justice Council and the greater involvement of litigants in their own litigation. These recommendations are intended to provide the structure in which a radically reformed system can operate and to then enable that system to be kept under review.

Among the more specific recommendations are those as to protocols and expert evidence in the case of both of which my recommendations are designed to establish an agreed best practice.

The protocols are a wholly novel concept designed:

(1) to focus the attention of litigants on the desirability of resolving disputes without litigation;
(2) to enable them to obtain the information they need to settle the action or to make an offer to settle; and
(3) if settlement is not possible to enable the ground to be prepared for the action to proceed expeditiously.

The protocols will receive the support of the court and will be published in practice guides issued by the court. It is intended that they should be taken into account by the court if litigation results on the question of costs. They will be in effect a guide as to how to resolve disputes both prior to litigation and during litigation. It is essential, if the protocols are to have credibility, that they should be drawn up by a working group with unquestionable extensive practical experience of the problem areas of litigation to which they relate.

In the case of medical negligence the working body is known as the Clinical Disputes Forum. The Forum has members who are distinguished doctors, health carers, lawyers who act for plaintiffs and the defendants and insurers. Under this umbrella, representatives of the different interests, for the first time working together, have been struggling to find the right way forward and are reasonably close to agreeing a protocol which accords with my recommendations. Let me quote from a report they have prepared:

> At present there is often mistrust by both sides. This can mean that patients fail to raise their concerns with the healthcare provider at an early stage, and pursue a complaint or claim which has no or weak foundation due to a lack of sufficient information and understanding. It can also mean that patients become reluctant, once advice has been taken on a potential claim, to disclose sufficient information to enable the provider to investigate that claim efficiently and, where appropriate, to resolve it.

On the side of the health care provider this mistrust can be shown in a reluctance to be honest with patients, a failure to provide prompt clear explanations, especially of adverse outcomes (whether or not there may have been negligence) and a tendency to 'close ranks' once a potential claim is signalled.

If this mistrust is to be removed, and a more cooperative culture is to develop:

(a) health care professionals and providers need to adopt a constructive approach to complaints and claims. They should accept that concerned patients (or their representatives) are entitled to an explanation and an apology, if warranted, and, injured ones to appropriate redress, and that an overly defensive approach is not in the long-term interest of their main goal: *patient care*; and

(b) patients and their representatives should recognise that some degree of risk is inherent in most medical treatment (even the best practitioners make mistakes) and that misdiagnosis or unintended consequences of treatment can only be rectified if they are brought to the attention of the health care provider quickly.

The openness on the part of both parties, which the protocols will encourage, will in turn provide the information which is necessary for disputes wherever possible to be resolved by recourse to the now justifiably fashionable

Alternative Dispute Resolution (ADR). This could be dealt with in-house by hospitals. There is everything to be gained by the hospital using its resources to make available mediators and neutral claim evaluators at their own expense.

Both sides of the legal profession are now providing lawyers who are highly skilled in this activity. A pilot mediation scheme of this nature has already been set up. While it may be premature for the courts to insist on ADR, it is sufficiently established to justify the court taking into account an unreasonable refusal to resort to ADR when determining what costs should be awarded.

The courts have to offer more specialisation than they have hitherto. Judges in this country have always prided themselves on being generalists. However, society has become so complex and the issues so sophisticated, we must if we are going to deal with the work effectively have the necessary expertise. It takes time to instruct a judge who has no background knowledge of the intricacies of this area of negligence and time in court is expensive.

A single Master of the Supreme Court has already been earmarked to deal with the interlocutory stages of these cases in the High Court and the same thing should happen at major centres in other parts of the country. You also need a judge to try the case who understands the medical issues to which this litigation can give rise. It is for this reason I recommended and still do recommend that there should be a special list for cases of this nature in the High Court so that they can come before a judge whose experience they will respect. The judge must be on equal terms with the lawyers for the parties.

That brings me to a further problem area and that is as to expert evidence. I have been surprised but pleased by the interest the medical profession is taking in my recommendations as to expert evidence. I sense that the medical profession are not at all comfortable about the present situation. Here again there is an unhealthy polarisation. There is a tendency for medical experts to be categorised as plaintiffs or defendants experts. They are looked upon by the side which has instructed them—and this can be their own perception of their position—as hired guns, brought in to fight to the best of their ability on behalf of the side which is employing them. It is especially unfortunate that this should be the situation in medical cases because the court is dependent on medical advice for resolving the three issues: liability, quantum and causation, which are often particularly difficult in this area of litigation.

While there has been some improvement, it can still be difficult to find an expert if you are a plaintiff. This is because of the understandable reluctance, on the part of health care professionals, to criticise colleagues. The result is that those experts who are prepared to give reports on behalf of plaintiffs are diverted from their practice and become over dependent upon medico-legal reporting for their livelihood which can further undermine their independence.

My report seeks to improve the situation by making it clear that the experts first responsibility is to the court and not to the side that instructs them. For this reason reports are to be made to the court. However, I would go further.

There are some issues near the 'cutting edge' of medical science where there are two schools of thought. However, there are many areas where what is proper medical practice is not a matter of controversy, the issue is whether that practice has been adhered to. There are many issues as to quantum where one opinion is very likely to be very similar to another opinion. I believe there is scope for the joint instructing of a single expert, at least in the first place, in those cases where there is no controversial medical issue involved. A breakthrough is needed because at present both sides contend that they cannot trust the expert instructed by the other side and so instruct their own experts. This tends to make agreement of medical issues more difficult instead of less difficult. We need a more cooperative approach but that will only arise if the independence of the expert is clear. This really should not be a problem where those who are consulted are asked to advise because of their professional expertise and standing. At the present time one has the ludicrous position that because experts and those who instruct them are not trusted, the parties will not even agree to sequential as opposed to simultaneous disclosure of experts reports.

There should also be more frequent meetings between experts to resolve issues. Lack of communication between experts often explains their failure to reach agreement.

Changes of this nature represent a change of culture. They are suitable subjects for protocols. They will bring about significant changes to both costs and speed with which disputes can be disposed of. More importantly, they will help eradicate the suspicion which has been so destructive to the relationship between patient and carer.

I now turn to the two areas of the recommendations which are the subject for Professor Zander's attack. Case management is central to my recommendations because it is the means by which cases are handled in the court system. There is nothing new about it. It is an essential part of any system and is used with differing degrees in every developed system of civil justice. My recommendations are criticised because they call for more management by the court. This is exactly what is happening in Canada, New Zealand, Australia and has been happening in the US for a great many years. It is also part of civil systems. It is practical today to exert greater case management than in the past because of the advances in technology which makes it possible for courts to monitor the progress of cases. It was the absence of the ability to monitor cases which meant that it was not possible to implement the Cantley recommendation which Professor Zander finds so attractive. It is this change which explains in part why in my report I attach such importance to technology. The other reason is the savings to the system which it will achieve. As in medicine, technology opens new horizons.

While I favour the greater case management which is now possible I recognise that case management does involve the parties in more expense and so it can only be justified if the savings and other benefits which can be achieved justify that expense. Therefore, as Professor Zander does not acknowledge, 'hands on' case management is to be limited to those cases where it is likely to produce real dividends. Just because a medicine can be effective you do not use it unless it is justified.

In medical negligence cases, for example, it has a clear role to play which will undoubtedly be beneficial. It will weed out the hopeless cases which create unnecessary dislocation and expense to hospitals; it will ensure that discovery is controlled; it will confine the parties to the real issues and control expense by limited hearings; it will be used to encourage settlement and restrict the issues. Administrative arrangements have already been made to deal with the fear of Professor Zander that it will result in inconsistency of treatment by having the same procedural judge or Master to deal with all the cases in London and similar arrangements will need to be made outside London.

I believe that it would be difficult to find a practitioner who knows what he is talking about who would say that litigation of this sort would not benefit from selective case management. It is not the schoolmaster type of process which Professor Zander seems to have in mind. It is the court providing a forum in which the lawyers and the judge can work out the most satisfactory way a case can be dealt with and the judge then supervising the progress to trial in accordance with that programme. What the judge will prevent is parties not fulfilling their responsibilities, acting unfairly to a weaker party or acting unreasonably. Other types of litigation where case management is unnecessary will move directly to a hearing.

In support of his criticisms Professor Zander cites Sir Jack Jacob who he rightly describes as 'truly a master of civil procedure and wiser in these matters than any of us', but he makes no reference to the fact that in his Hamlyn Lecture of 1986 under the heading 'Prospects for the Future', Sir Jack set out in outline just the sort of changes that I am advocating as being necessary in the future.

The other source from which Professor Zander seeks assistance is the Rand Report on judicial case management in the US. Here the selective way Professor Zander cites from the report indicates that he has wholly failed to grasp the true nature of my recommendations or he has not fully absorbed the contents of the Rand Report.

I would not wish litigation in the field of medical negligence or in any other field to be handled in this country as it is in the United States. However, even if the situations are comparable, which they are not, I would not have anything to fear from Rand. First, Rand indicates that early case management reduces time to disposition. It also found that my approach as to early settling of a trial date and reduced discovery reduced both delay and costs. While early case management had an upward effect on costs, the overall effect was to reduce delay without having any significant effect on costs or the perception of fairness.

Why I am, however, particularly critical of the use by Professor Zander of the Rand Report is that its general conclusion is that it found little change in what was happening before 1990, the year in which it started its survey, and afterwards. The reason being that the act of Congress whose effect they were monitoring was loosely worded so judges could interpret what they were doing prior to the act as compliance with the act. Furthermore, as Professor Resnick, who really does know what she is talking about, has pointed out, the increase in costs detected by Rand in relation to early case management could be the consequence of Congress, making national rules apply to small cases when the rules are only appropriate for the large cases for which they were designed.

This unselective approach which Rand examined is wholly contrary to the thrust of my report. Remarks by Professor Zander suggest he has failed to grasp the elementary point that I am not recommending that case management shall apply to all cases where a defence is entered. In particular hands-on case management, in the sense that term is used by Rand, is intended to have no application to cases on the fast track. Yet he uses Rand to suggest in his lecture that lawyers would not use the fast track because of the additional expense to which they would be put by case management.

The fast track in its strict form will not be suitable for medical negligence cases. They are too complicated for application to the fast track. The virtues of the fast track would be beneficial for small medical claims such as claims against dentists if a suitably modified fast track could be devised. The virtues are that they provide a restricted procedure and a no frills form of litigation on a fixed timetable at a fixed cost. It provides a litigant with certainty as to what he is letting himself in for. A working group of volunteers are conducting an experiment in Birmingham to test whether a modified fast track could work in small cases. I should therefore deal briefly with the unjustified criticisms heaped on the fast track by Professor Zander:

(1) First, he seeks to apply the Rand conclusions to the fast track when they have no application.

(2) Secondly, he seems to think they are to be subject of the draconian sanctions when the idea is to call cases in for directions if the timetable is not kept in a way which will prejudice the fixed date of trial. It is, however, intended that if a lawyer wants more time he should apply in advance and not when time has already expired.

(3) Thirdly, he says lawyers are not capable of working to a timetable. This is not correct. Experience now exists that if timetables are set which are reasonable (and the fast track timetable is being drawn up in conjunction with those with great experience) then lawyers have no difficulty in complying with timetables and they welcome the certainty they produce.

(4) Then, he says, it will produce a sense of unfairness and prevent proper exploration of the issues. However, this is to ignore the alternative which can be no access to justice at all. It can also result in totally disproportionate litigation.

(5) Finally, he says that I am setting the fixed cost too high, citing against me Adrian Zuckerman, and then suggests the cost will be unfairly low. I do not see how he can make either of these criticisms since the cost is still the subject of consultation by the profession.

I know the fast track is unpopular with the Association of Personal Injury lawyers as they think of it is as a threat to their livelihood and I would wish to take their concerns into account insofar as it is in the public interest to do so, but I do not believe the Association would be happy about all of the criticisms which Professor Zander makes.

While I reject Professor Zander's criticisms I do not suggest the process of implementing my report is going to be easy. There are bound to be teething troubles. Modifications of detail will need to be made. My proposals are not written in stone. However, they do offer a practical programme to achieve a dramatic improvement in the way we handle civil litigation and in access to justice. That improvement should happen is important to the public as a whole. It is particularly important to medics and all whose work is the provision of health care and those who receive that care. A great many right thinking lawyers and medics have worked and are working hard in their valuable spare time to ensure the improvements come about.

This is why I do not apologise for spending so much of this lecture in answering that of Professor Zander's of two weeks ago. The issue is of great importance to the medical profession. It is right what is being sought to be achieved should be the subject to fair and balanced criticism. It is no part of my argument that the new Lord Chancellor should not conduct the review by Sir Peter Middleton which he forecast prior to entering office. It would, however, be unfortunate indeed if the Lord Chancellor were to call a halt to all the work that is in progress at the present time as Professor Zander suggests. To pay serious attention to what Professor Zander has said would be to give him credit he does not deserve. I regret having to say this of a friend but the fact is that his lecture was not a balanced consideration of this serious subject and ill-considered. Ill-considered because he is oblivious of what is in fact happening on the ground. Unintentionally, he could damage a process of change which is already taking place and which, while it will not be smooth, offers real hope for the future of judges, practitioners and insurance bodies up and down the land recognise.

21

Are the Courts Excessively Deferential to the Medical Profession?

Abstract This paper discusses how the relationship between the courts and the medical profession has changed in recent times. It suggests that the courts traditionally treated the medical profession with excessive deference, but that the position has changed and for the better. It explains why the courts were previously over deferential and relates the changes to the growth of judicial review, increasing litigation, increasing awareness of patients' rights, and well-publicised medical profession scandals. It concludes with a discussion of the Access to Justice reforms and how improved civil justice procedures have increased the ability of the courts to resolve medical issues justly.

Introduction

As a title to this lecture I deliberately pose a provocative question. My answer to it is that until recently the courts treated the medical profession with excessive deference, but recently the position has changed. It is my judgement that it has changed for the better. The situation is fluid because of the rapidity with which change takes place in the medical world. However, I consider that, as the situation is at present, the balance is now about right. What I propose to do here is give my explanation for the courts previously being over deferential and why this has changed. Then I would like to describe the nature of that change. Finally, I would like to set out what I believe to be the moral, the important moral, of my tale.

The over-deferential approach is captured by the phrase: 'Doctor knows best.' The contemporary approach is a more critical approach. It could be

---

* This lecture was originally delivered as the first Provost's Lecture at University College London, on 17 January 2001. A revised draft was published in the Medical Law Review ((2001) Med L Rev 1).

said that doctor knows best if he acts reasonably and logically and gets his facts right.

The Excessive Deference

What was the explanation for the excessive deference on the part of the courts? I would identify five factors which contributed to bringing it about.

(1) The first factor is that at the time when the foundation of our medical law was being developed by the courts, the practice of medicine gave rise to little controversy and the public, including the judges, extended to the medical profession what has been described as the 'presumption of beneficence'.

(2) The courts were then understandably reluctant to second-guess the conduct and opinions of respected professionals practising in their field of expertise. Generally, standards of behaviour within all professions were high. The reluctance was not confined to the medical profession. Judges displayed a natural reluctance to make findings of negligence against members of any honourable profession. By way of emphasis it is possible to point out that, if the courts were deferential to the medical profession, then they were even more generous to the legal profession. It is only recently that a barrister could be held liable for negligence and even more recently that an advocate could be liable for negligence in relation to the conduct of litigation.[1]

(3) The third factor was that practitioners appearing on behalf of claimants were usually generalists, who did not have the expertise to bring proceedings which were capable of challenging the Health Service or the medical practitioner. They would be aggressively defended by the bodies who insured their profession.

(4) Those bringing litigation against hospitals or practitioners or other health carers had difficulty in finding reputable experts prepared to give evidence against professional colleagues.

(5) Even by the 1950s and 1960s, in England, as elsewhere, the rate of medical negligence litigation was rising sharply as had the level of awards of damages. Judges were well aware of the horror stories emanating from the litigation culture of the US, which had resulted in the practice of

---

[1] *Arthur J S Hall & Co (a Firm) v Simons* [2000] 3 WLR 543, departing from *Rondel v Worsley* [1969] 1 AC 191.

defensive medicine, and the courts were anxious to avoid encouraging the importing of the same disease into this country.[2]

The Causes of the Change

What is it that has caused the change? I would identify the following causes.

First, today the courts have a less deferential approach to those in authority. The growth in judicial review has resulted in the judiciary becoming accustomed to setting aside decisions of those engaged on behalf of the Crown in public affairs, from a Minister of the Crown downwards. By comparison the medical profession and the Health Service were small beer.

Secondly, while there has been the huge growth in the scale of litigation, including actions brought against hospital trusts and the medical profession, the proportion of successful medical negligence claims in England is put at only 17 per cent. The courts became increasingly conscious of the difficulties which bona fide claimants had in successfully establishing claims.

Thirdly, there had developed an increasing awareness of patients' rights. The public's expectations of what the profession should achieve have grown. Like it or not, we have moved from a society which was primarily concerned with the duty individuals owed to society to one which is concerned primarily with the rights of the individual. You may find this difficult to accept, but judges do move with the times, even if more slowly than some would like. The move to a rights-based society has fundamentally changed the behaviour of the courts.

Fourthly, the 'automatic presumption of beneficence' has been dented by a series of well-publicised scandals. The judges were not oblivious to these scandals.[3] The deterioration in confidence by the public and judges alike is evidenced by an increase of more than 30 per cent in the number of complaints made to the General Medical Council,[4] the profession's disciplinary authority. The number had risen from some 3,000 in 2000 to

---

[2] Note, for example, *Sidaway v Board of Governors of the Bethlem Royal Hospital* [1985] AC 871, Lord Scarman at 887 and Lord Diplock at 893.

[3] The scandals which spring to mind are the events prompting the Bristol heart babies inquiry; the conviction of serial killer Dr Shipman; the case of Dr Robertson, who stole an elderly patient's savings; and the disgraced gynaecologists Dr Ledward and Dr Neale.

[4] Hereafter, 'GMC'.

a total of 4,300 in 2001.[5] The future of the GMC itself has been called into question. Almost daily there are reports in the media suggesting that there is something amiss with our health treatment.

Fifthly, our courts were aware that courts at the highest level of other Commonwealth jurisdictions, particularly Canada and Australia, were rejecting the approach of the English courts.[6] They were subjecting the actions of the medical profession to a closer scrutiny than the English courts, yet this was not obviously followed by such an excessively litigious culture as to be found in the US.

Sixthly, medical negligence litigation was revealed as being a disaster area. The Health Service and the insurance industry had to be required to change their approach to handling litigation. They appeared to consider that every case was worth fighting. The cost of medical negligence litigation was estimated by the Secretary of State at £300m for the year 1996–97. The annual cost of medical negligence litigation is estimated to be at least equivalent to building, running and staffing one new hospital annually.[7] The litigation was particularly bitter and often singularly unproductive. In most litigation you have at least one satisfied party, but with medical negligence you tended to end up with two more embittered parties. The scale of the litigation indicated that the Health Service was not giving sufficient priority to avoiding medical mishaps and treating patients justly when mishaps occurred. It was clear to be relied on to resolve justified complaints justly.

Seventhly, recently a series of cases have come before the courts that raised fundamental questions of medical ethics. There were questions about the right to life and the right to terminate life;[8] questions about the patient's

---

[5] 'Protests over doctors rose by a third', *The Times*, 12 October 2000, 12; 'Carey in attack on arrogant surgeons', *The Times*, 19 October 2000, 9. In 2006, the General Medical Council received 4,980 complaints. See 'Record complaints against doctors', BBC online, 10 July 2006.

[6] See, for example, *Reibl v Hughes* (1980) 114 DLR (3d) 1 (Canada), and *Rogers v Whitaker* (1992) 109 ALR 625 (Australia). The position was even more striking within the civil law jurisdictions on the continent. In particular, in Germany, where the common law approach was regarded as being inconsistent with the patient's right of self-determination: see, B S Markesinis, *The German Law of Torts, A Comparative Introduction* (3rd edn, 1994/7), 476. Again, there was no explosion of litigation.

[7] M Brazier and J Miola, 'Bye-Bye Bolam: A Medical Litigation Revolution?' (2000) 8 Med L Rev 85 (arguing that Bolitho and other developments herald a medical revolution whereby less deference is paid to the decisions and opinions of doctors); at note 4 they review the evidence on the cost of medical negligence litigation.

[8] See, for example, *Re A (Children) (Conjoined Twins: Surgical Separation)* [2000] 4 All ER 961; *NHS Trust A v M; NHS Trust B v H* (2000) 58 BMLR 87. It is to be noted that in 2006 the House of Lords blocked a private member's bill that would have given terminally ill persons the right to assisted suicide.

right to refuse treatment[9] and the professional's duty to treat the patient;[10] questions about the allocation of scarce resources;[11] and questions about who should make decisions about the care of people who are incapable for one reason or another of making decisions for themselves.[12]

Questions such as these, of which the *conjoined twins'* case[13] provides the most dramatic example, provoke heartfelt and real disagreement among members of the medical and legal professions as well as members of the public. They arise, at least partly, due to the extraordinary pace of the advance in medical knowledge, skill and technology. It was clear that the professions, as well as the public, were seeking assistance from the judges. The courts had to grapple with points of law which are bound up with the most fundamental ethical and spiritual questions, and they have had to do this under the intense glare of media scrutiny. The courts, having had to struggle with issues such as these, were prepared to adopt a more proactive approach to resolving conflicts as to more traditional medical issues.

Eightly, a final influence that will be of increasing importance and probably played a part in the case of some of the factors I have already mentioned was first the proposal for and subsequently the incorporation into English domestic law of the European Convention of Human Rights. This development elevates the position of the English courts as arbiters of public values when considering fundamental questions raised in cases concerning, for example, abortion and euthanasia.[14]

The Changes

Having attempted to identify the influences which have successively been at work, I would like next to illustrate how they operated in practice. I take as my starting point the *Bolam* test which has had a profound impact on professional liability, not only in the case of the medical profession, but across the board. I will unfairly rename the test as being 'any responsible group of doctors know best'.

---

[9] *St George's Healthcare NHS Trust v S* [1999] Fam 26.
[10] *R v Portsmouth Hospital NHS Trust, ex parte Glass* (1999) 50 BMLR 269.
[11] *R v Cambridge HA, ex parte B* [1995] 1 WLR 898.
[12] *Re F (Mental Patient: Sterilisation)* [1990] 2 AC 1.
[13] *Re A (Children) (Conjoined Twins: Surgical Separation)* [2000] 4 All ER 961.
[14] Hansard, HC, cols 165–166 (24 March 1998). D Irvine, 'The Patient, the Doctor, the Lawyers and the Judges: Right and Duties' (1999) 1 Med L Rev 255 at 261–263 (overview of which Convention rights bear on medical law questions).

The touchstone of liability for medical negligence in England has for sometime been McNair J's famous jury direction in *Bolam v Friern Hospital Management Committee*.[15] The House of Lords have affirmed its importance at least five times since 1980, and notably in 2005.[16] McNair J began by observing that in a case involving a special skill and competence, such as the skill and competence of a doctor, the test of negligence is whether the defendant has exercised the skill of an ordinary skilled man professing to have that special skill: 'A man need not possess the highest expert skill at the risk of being found negligent . . . it is sufficient if he exercises the ordinary skill of an ordinary competent man exercising that particular art.'[17] Those words have not caused real problems. The important passage came later. It concerns the relation between negligence and actions or advice which conform to the standards of common medical practice or opinion. McNair J said: 'He is not guilty of negligence if he has acted in accordance with a practice accepted as proper by a reasonable body of medical men skilled in that particular art . . . '[18] Notice the words 'responsible body of medical men'. McNair J went on to comment on cases in which there is a difference in medical opinion: 'Putting it the other way round, a man is not negligent if he is acting in accordance with such a practice merely because there is a body of opinion who would take a contrary view.'[19]

In Canada the courts modified the *Bolam* test.[20] The courts accepted that the question of the standard of care should initially be judged by that of common professional practice since in many cases it would be unwise to

---

[15] [1957] 1 WLR 582. *Bolam* was a case in which the plaintiff patient had undergone electroconvulsive therapy without having been administered with a relaxant drug and without having been subject to any physical restraint to control the convulsive movements. In the course of therapy he sustained a fractured hip which was the cause of his complaint. At that time expert opinion varied as to the use of drugs and physical restraint as well as to whether patients should be warned of the risk of fractures. See, *Bolam*, 87 and *Bolitho Royal Hospital* [1998] AC 232, 239.

[16] *Whitehouse v Jordan* [1981] 1 WLR 246; *Maynard v West Midland RHA* [1984] 1 WLR 634; *Sidaway v Bethlem Royal Hospital* n 2 above; *Bolitho v City & Hackney HA* [1998] AC 232; *Simms v Simms; A v A (a child)* [2002] EWHC 2734, [2003] 2 WLR 1465; *R (Leslie Burke) v General Medical Council* [2005] EWCA Civ 1003, [2005] 3 WLR 1132. See also the Privy Counsel decision of *Chin Keow v Government of Mayalsia* [1967] 1 WLR 813.

[17] See n 15 above, 586.

[18] Ibid, 587.

[19] Ibid.

[20] The standard of care applicable to a medical professional was formulated in similar terms in *Crits v Sylvester* in 1956, which was affirmed by the Supreme Court of Canada: (1956) 1 DLR (2d) 508; aff'd (1956) 5 DLR (2d) 601. That Court more recently confirmed in *Lapointe v Hôpital Le Gardeur* (1992) 90 DLR (4th) 7 (though the case was decided under the Quebec civil law) that the standard of care allows for differences of opinion.

disagree with medical professionals on technical questions of medicine or health care practice. However, in Canada it was appreciated there need to be limits placed on that proposition and it is in fixing those limits that the courts in England and in Canada followed different paths.[21]

Why the *Bolam* test has attracted considerable criticism is not fairly levelled at McNair J's statement. The problem lies in the way his words have been subsequently understood. *Bolam* has been taken to mean that a doctor will not be negligent so long as he acts in accordance with common professional practice or opinion. There are many cases in which actions for medical negligence have been dismissed on the basis that the doctor conformed to accepted professional practice. Further, if there is a difference of professional opinion then it is enough that he acted in accordance with one of the bodies of opinion. I do not say that the test has always been formulated this bluntly, but that this is how it has often been understood. One example is to be found in Lord Scarman's speech, which was the judgment of the House, in *Maynard v West Midlands RHA*.[22] There he said that 'a judge's "preference" for one body of distinguished professional opinion to another also professionally distinguished is not sufficient to establish negligence in a practitioner whose actions have received the seal of approval of those whose opinions, truthfully expressed, honestly held, were not preferred'.[23] Notice the absence of any reference to the quality of the honest and truthful opinion.

In another case Lord Scarman said, in connection with decisions concerning diagnosis and treatment, that 'the law imposes the duty of care; but the standard of care is a matter for medical judgement'.[24] For these reasons it has commonly been thought in England that it is a sufficient defence to a medical negligence claim for the doctor to lead the honest evidence of other doctors to the effect that they would have done the same thing.

In Canada, the courts are appropriately respectful of medical professional opinion, but the courts have also recognised that there are questions related to medical practice that naturally fall within the comprehension of a layman. A good example is professional practice in relation to safety precautions. Expert evidence may be needed to illuminate the extent of a particular risk,

---

[21] *Crits v Sylvester* ibid; qualified in *Dale v Munthali* (1976) 78 DLR (3d) 588 at 594, aff'd (1978) 90 DLR (3d) 763; *Lapointe v Hôpital Le Gardeur* ibid, 15.

[22] [1984] 1 WLR 634.

[23] Ibid, 639.

[24] *Sidaway*, n 2 above, 881.

but once that is understood a layman will often be able to evaluate whether adequate precautions have been taken against that risk. Coyne J A's remarks in *Anderson v Chasney*[25] are interesting. He said that if general practice were a conclusive defence, a group of professionals 'could legislate themselves out of liability for negligence to the public by adopting or continuing what was an obviously negligent practice, even though a simple precaution, plainly capable of obviating the danger which might result in death, was well-known'.[26] The surgeon in that case inadvertently left a sponge inside the patient child's throat, and the child suffocated. It transpired that it was common practice, in that hospital at least, not to count the sponges used in an operation, and not to attach strings or tape to them. If these precautions had been taken then the overlooked sponge would have been noticed.

What emerges from the Canadian case law is a distinction between matters requiring technical skill and expertise and which, therefore, fall within the exclusive professional competence of doctors, and conduct which does not involve medical expertise, and which a layman is therefore in a position to evaluate.[27]

The English courts have at times been less circumspect in reviewing the activities of members of professions other than the medical profession. For example, it was held by the Privy Council that a conveyancing practice followed by Hong Kong solicitors was negligent because it created an obvious and avoidable risk of fraud by the lender's solicitor.[28] But in the case of the medical profession the *Bolam* approach was extended by the House of Lords in 1985 in *Sidaway v Bethlem Royal Hospital*[29] beyond cases involving allegedly negligent diagnosis or treatment to questions as to the extent of the medical practitioner's duty to inform patients of the risks of a proposed treatment.

Here the differences between the law in Canada and in England are greater. In *Sidaway*,[30] cutting through the differences of opinion of the members of the House, the majority thought complaints about inadequate disclosure of the risks of treatment should be resolved by application of the test in *Bolam*. In anything but exceptional circumstances, a patient is only entitled to be told so much as a responsible body of medical opinion judges

---

[25] [1949] 4 DLR 71; aff'd [1950] 4 DLR 223.
[26] Ibid, 85.
[27] *ter Neuzen v Korn* (1995) 127 DLR (4th) 577.
[28] *Edward Wong Finance Co Ltd v Johnson Stokes and Master* [1984] AC 296.
[29] See n 2 above.
[30] Ibid.

to be prudent. I say that there might be exceptional circumstances because Lord Bridge thought that there might be cases where disclosure of a particular risk was so necessary to an informed choice that it would have to be disclosed whatever actual medical opinion might be.[31] In practice, however, the case came to mean that patients were entitled to know only what their doctor thought they should.[32]

Canada took a different course: the approach is to ask what a reasonable patient would want to know. Doctors are under a duty to ensure that their patients receive the information they need to give an informed consent to surgical and other health care decisions. In particular, the physicians must discuss with their patients the nature of their illness and of the recommended treatment, disclose the material risks involved in that course of action, and discuss any alternatives as well as the consequences of doing nothing.[33] I suspect that this is what most responsible doctors have for generations been in the habit of doing.

In the 1992 case, *Rogers v Whitaker*[34] the Australian High Court also rejected the approach in *Sidaway* and chose to follow Canada. The court opted for a mixed objective and subjective approach: the extent of the requirement of disclosure will depend in Australia on the extent to which a particular patient demonstrates an interest in being told. Since *Rogers v Whitaker* was decided the New South Wales Court has held that the *Bolam* test is not only the wrong test where disclosure of risk is concerned, but it is also the wrong test in relation to decisions concerning treatment and diagnosis.[35]

Happily, the House of Lords in *Bolitho v City & Hackney HA*[36] has signalled a greater willingness to evaluate professional medical practice

---

[31] Ibid, 900.

[32] The last sentence is supported by the trend of Court of Appeal authority: *Blyth v Bloomsbury HA* [1993] 4 Med L Rev 151, and *Gold v Haringey HA* [1987] 2 All ER 888. Today, this has to be considered in light of *Chester v Afshar* [2004] UKHL 41, [2005] 1 AC 134. The House of Lords decided that the duty to warn is owed by a doctor to a patient who consents to being operated on. The law which imposes the duty to warn has at its heart the right of the patient to make an informed choice as to whether, and if so when and by whom, to be operated on. The duty is owed as much to the patient who, if warned, would find the decision difficult as to the patient who would find it simple and could give a clear answer to the doctor one way or the other immediately. To leave the patient who would find the decision difficult without a remedy, as the normal approach to causation indicated, would render the duty of care useless in the cases where it might be needed most.

[33] *Reibl*, n 6 above; *Arndt v Smith* (1997) 148 DLR (4th) 48.

[34] See n 6 above.

[35] *Lowns v Woods* (1996) Aust Torts Reps 81-376.

[36] See n 15 above.

than it has shown in the past. The infant patient had been admitted to hospital suffering from respiratory difficulties. These difficulties eventually led to cardiac arrest which resulted in serious brain damage. At one point a nurse summoned the supervising doctor because of concerns about the child's condition. On the telephone the doctor seemed alarmed, but she then negligently failed to attend or to send a deputy. It was common ground that if the doctor had attended and had intubated the child so as to provide an airway, the respiratory failure leading to cardiac arrest would not have occurred.

The defence was put on the basis of causation, the point being that even if the doctor had attended, she would not have intubated the child. This in turn required consideration of whether intubation would have been proper professional practice in the light of circumstances then known about the child. Conflicting expert evidence was led on this point. The trial judge concluded that he was not entitled to prefer one body of distinguished and truthful expert opinion over another. On this basis he decided that the doctor would have come up to a proper level of skill and competence if she had attended the child but not intubated him. That being so, the appeal was dismissed and the claim did not succeed.

Controversially, the House of Lords upheld the trial judge's decision on the facts, but explained the *Bolam* test in a way that is less deferential to medical expert opinion than the test has sometimes been understood. Critically, Lord Browne-Wilkinson, giving the only speech, said that a court is not bound to hold that a 'doctor escapes liability for negligent treatment or diagnosis just because he leads evidence from a number of medical experts who are genuinely of the opinion that the defendant's treatment or diagnosis accorded such sound medical practice . . .'.[37] He drew attention to the fact, which I highlighted earlier, that in *Bolam* itself McNair J said that in order to avoid liability a doctor must have acted in accordance with a 'responsible' or 'reasonable' body of opinion.[38] From this Lord Browne-Wilkinson inferred that, in rare cases, it would be negligent to act in accordance with a professional opinion which 'is not capable of withstanding logical analysis'.[39] He drew particular attention to decisions which might attract careful scrutiny.[40]

---

[37] Ibid, 241.
[38] [1957] 1 WLR 583, 587–588 respectively.
[39] See n 15 above, 243.
[40] Ibid.

Although initially there was doubt as to this, it is my belief that the courts are going to take Lord Browne-Wilkinson's injunction to review the logical basis of expert medical testimony seriously.[41] This has been doubted but I am attracted by an article not least for its title, 'Bye-Bye Bolam', which takes a different view.[42] Certainly I would expect the 'logic' approach to be applied to questions of informed consent. Unlike Canada, the approach in England is not categorical. Instead, the courts will test the logical coherence of any professional practice or medical opinion. In reality it is unlikely that a court will find an opinion on a highly technical topic to be illogical, and to this extent many cases will be decided similarly in England and Canada. But still there will be cases in England, but not Canada, where the court evaluates the rational basis of a medical opinion on a technical point. Equally, in England, but not in Canada, there will be cases where the court defers to a medical practice on a matter involving the balancing of risks and benefits even though the judge himself would have decided differently.

Even where the matter is one of common sense, the question in England is not whether the judge would have done things differently, rather it is whether what the doctor has done is logical and defensible. The difference in approach may well be explicable because of the greater involvement of juries in Canada.

Did the House of Lords in *Bolitho* pitch the standard of review at the right level? Lord Browne-Wilkinson said that a responsible body of medical opinion is one that can withstand 'logical' analysis. However, I can see it will enable a court to distinguish between two sets of medical opinion. When faced with conflicting expert evidence, what a court regularly does is to select the reasoning of the expert which is most logically persuasive.

It seems clear that in England *Sidaway* will now have to be read in light of *Bolitho*.[43] A doctor's decision not to disclose risks will now have to be subjected to logical analysis, and if he has withheld without a good reason information that should have been disclosed then he will be liable even

---

[41] See my judgment in *Penney v East Kent HA* [2000] Lloyd's Rep Med 41. *Marriott v West Midlands HA* [1999] 1 Lloyd's Rep Med 23. See also, *Reynolds v North Tyneside Health Authority* [2002] Lloyds Rep Med 459. Gross J disregarded expert evidence where there was a failure to examine the claimant's mother properly during childbirth, causing the claimant's asphyxia, and resulting cerebral palsy.

[42] Brazier and Miola, n 7 above.

[43] The commentary I refer to includes: A Grubb and I Kennedy, 'Consent to Treatment: The Competent Patient' in I Kennedy and A Grubb (eds), *Principles of Medical Law* (OUP, 1998), 171–174; J Keown, 'Burying Bolam: Informed Consent Down Under' [1994] CLJ 16; Brazier and Miola, n 7 above.

though his decision may have been consonant with ordinary professional practice. That was my view in *Pearce v United Bristol Healthcare NHS Trust*, which was decided in 1999.[44] Basing my judgment on the speeches of Lord Bridge and Lord Templeman in particular, I suggested there was normally a duty to mention significant risks involved in treatment.

In addition I have pointed out that it is an important part of the court's task to distinguish between opinion and fact. The explanation for a conflict in medical opinion is frequently based on a different interpretation of the underlying facts. It is always the courts and not an expert's task to find the facts. This is so even if it is necessary to have expert evidence in order to interpret the facts.[45]

Beyond Medical Negligence

I have mentioned already that the courts are nowadays, with increasing frequency, being asked to adjudicate on legal points bound up with fundamental and emotive questions of medical ethics. The willingness of the courts to take on this task has been of particular value to the medical profession and all those involved in the provision of health care. To provide this assistance the courts had to radically develop its power to grant declarations.

The first case was brought in 1980: *Royal College of Nursing v DHSS*.[46] It was brought by the Royal College of Nursing[47] of the UK against the Department of Health. The RCN was concerned that its members were being asked to perform, unsupervised by a medical practitioner, acts in connection with termination of pregnancy which were unlawful notwithstanding the Abortion Act 1967. This was because section 1(1) of that Act only allowed pregnancies to be 'terminated by a registered medical practitioner'. I granted a declaration that the nurses were acting as part of a medical team and therefore acting lawfully. The House of Lords agreed by a majority of three to two.

It was on the peg of the *RCN* case that Mrs Gillick initiated her proceedings in *Gillick v West Norfolk & Wisbech Health Authority*,[48] challenging the legality of a DHSS circular setting out the circumstances in which it was in order for a medical practitioner to provide children under the age of 16

---

[44] *Pearce v United Bristol Healthcare NHS Trust* [1999] PIQR P53.
[45] See *Penney*, n 41 above.
[46] [1981] AC 800.
[47] Hereafter, 'RCN'.
[48] [1986] AC 112.

with advice as to the use of contraceptives without the agreement of the parents of the child. The appropriateness of the giving of such advice was highly controversial. Mrs Gillick suggested she was much concerned, as a mother of daughters, with this practice. Again, I granted a declaration.[49] Again, the Court of Appeal disagreed[50] and the House of Lords by a majority allowed the appeal.[51]

The decision's greatest significance was probably the light it threw on the relationship between teenage children and their parents. Here I believe the case was constructive because the House of Lords (particularly Lord Scarman) did not deal with the issue in black-and-white terms. Instead, the issue was described as a situation where the responsibility of the parents, and therefore their power to intervene, withered with the increasing ability of the child to take responsibility for his or her own actions.

The next case of interest is the *Attorney-General v Able*.[52] It constituted approval of the new advisory role of the courts since the Attorney-General was asking the court's advice as to whether to send out request pamphlets on how to take your own life constituted aiding and abetting suicide if the recipient followed the pamphlet's advice. Ironically, I refused the plea of the Attorney-General that the conduct was unlawful. To do so would amount to a finding that Mr Able had committed a criminal offence and it seemed to me only a jury should perform that task. There was no appeal.

The real break through was in *Airedale NHS Trust v Bland*.[53] The case involved the question as to whether the hospital could lawfully discontinue life-sustaining treatment designed to keep alive a patient in a persistent vegetative state where there was no prospect of a recovery. The House of Lords concluded that the doctors could discontinue the support measures and granted a declaration to this effect. Without the declaration the doctors would have been at risk of prosecution.[54]

More recently, the Court of Appeal decided the case involving two conjoined twins named Mary and Jodie.[55] The issues that case involved and the decision of the court are so well known that I need not set them out.

---

[49] [1984] QB 581.
[50] [1985] 2 WLR 413.
[51] See n 48 above.
[52] [1984] QB 795.
[53] [1993] AC 789.
[54] See *R v Bingley Magistrates' Court, ex parte Morrow* (1995) 3 Med L Rev 86.
[55] *Re A (Children) (Conjoined Twins)*, n 8 above.

I only draw attention to the case, fascinating though it is, because it is a good example of this novel jurisdiction in action.

The importance I attach to these cases, which I regard as important, is the fact that the Court of Appeal decided to receive evidence on the ethical issues involved from the Archbishop of Westminster. The Court was right to do so. The Court also received evidence from the Pro Life Alliance in the conjoined twins case. There can be many situations when evidence from groups representing important sections of the public assist the court to come to the correct decision. Yet public interest intervention is still uncommon in England. The House of Lords does consider petitions for leave to intervene, but leave has only been granted in a limited number of cases; the best known of these being Amnesty International's intervention in the *Pinochet* case.[56] There have been medical cases before the House in which intervenors, such as the Mental Health Act Commission and others, have been allowed.[57]

I recognise that there are real dangers in taking too liberal an approach to allowing interventions. Interventions can complicate cases, they tend to diminish party control, and there is a danger that one man's lawsuit will become a platform for another man's political posturing. But I think that public interest interventions can also bring real benefits—the benefits to be derived of listening. This is particularly true in medical cases raising questions with an ethical dimension, as the JUSTICE working party pointed out.[58] I agree with Professor Philip Bryden of the University of British

---

[56] *R v Bow Street Metropolitan Stipendiary Magistrate, ex parte Pinochet Ugarte (Amnesty International and Others Intervening) (No 3)* [2000] AC 147.

[57] See, for example, *Re F (Mental Patient: Sterilisation)* [1990] 2 AC 1 (Mental Health Act Commission); *R v Bournwood Community and Mental Health NHS Trust, ex parte L (Secretary of State for Health and Others Intervening)* [1999] AC 458 (Secretary of State for Health, Mental Health Act Commission and Registered Nursing Homes Association); *R (Leslie Burke)*, n 16 above.

[58] One notable English study was published by JUSTICE in 1996. The JUSTICE working party included a number of distinguished members. They looked at current English law and practice, and compared it with the practice of the courts in Canada and the US, as well as the practice of the European Court of Human Rights. The working party paid close attention to the need for controls on public interest intervention, but concluded that there were good reasons for clarifying and extending the scope for intervention in the English courts. The controls proposed by the working party were modelled on the Supreme Court of Canada's procedure. That is to say, intervention would be by leave of the court and ordinarily restricted to written submissions only of no more than 20 pages. The working party also proposed that the court have the power to invite intervention from any party which in its view might assist in its deliberations. The JUSTICE working party's recommendations were not well received in all quarters. See JUSTICE, *A Matter of Public Interest: Reforming the Law and Practice on Interventions in Public Interest cases* (1996), Ch 2 (arguing that England should expand and clarify the rights of third party public interest intervenors; the working party, chaired by Laws J (now Laws LJ), favoured adopting the Supreme Court of Canada's procedural model). See also, K Schiemann, 'Interventions in Public Interest cases' [1996] PL 240 (strongly worded critique of the

Columbia when he writes that 'the willingness of courts to listen to intervenors is a reflection of the value that judges place on people'.[59]

The Moral

Preaching in St Paul's Cathedral on the 200th anniversary of the Royal College of Surgeons on 11 October 2000, the then Archbishop of Canterbury, Dr George Carey, called on surgeons to exercise the gift of humility, particularly when making life-or-death decisions. He noted that humility has sometimes been lacking, and that this has tended to erode public confidence as well as professional morale. I agree and accept that judges must also show humility, especially when seeking to resolve ethical issues which go beyond their traditional role.

A problem which complicated the court's task in medical negligence cases which my *Access to Justice* reforms[60] were intended to tackle was the excessively adversarial nature of the proceedings. This created unnecessary expense and delay. The result was that the vast majority of cases were brought by legally aided litigants. This was not because more wealthy patients were never the subject of negligence, they just could not afford the financial risks involved.

Horror stories abounded of very seriously injured patients spending years in the litigation process only for the defendants to throw their hand in at the last minute before the trial. Frequently, claimants during the inquiry told me that they were not bringing the proceedings for money. What they wanted were two things: an apology and to prevent others suffering as they had done.

With the help of the Royal College and a number of well-intentioned doctors, the reforms have done a great deal to change the culture. A new culture is required. A culture where if a patient unfortunately had an unsatisfactory outcome the medical carers were able to sympathise with the patient. They needed to recognise that because patients felt they had been a victim of medical malpractice this did not justify withdrawing treatment.

JUSTICE report); and R Charteris, 'Intervention: In the Public Interest' [2000] SLT 87 (arguing that Scottish courts should allow public interest intervention—good summary of the issue and comparative survey).

[59] P Bryden, 'Public Interest Intervention in the Courts' (1987) 66 Can Bar Rev 499, 509.

[60] See, H Woolf, *Access to Justice: The Final Report to the Lord Chancellor on the Civil Justice System in England and Wales* (HMSO, 1996).

It meant that those who had the responsibility for treating the patient were under a particular duty to achieve the best result possible for the patient. To achieve this the courts could not leave the proceedings in the hands of the parties. The courts had to take the ultimate responsibility for ensuring that the proceedings were conducted with reasonable expedition and in an open and proportionate manner.

One facet on the reforms is that the expert evidence is now given, whenever appropriate, by a single or joint expert. In addition, all experts now owe their primary duty to the judge and not the parties. The improved procedures increase the ability of the court to resolve medical issues justly and reduce the need for the courts to rely on the intrusive *Bolam* approach.

This brings me finally to the important moral, which I would draw from the story. It is that it is unwise to place any profession or other body providing services to the public on a pedestal where their actions cannot be subject to close scrutiny. The greater the power the body has, the more important is this need. That is why the appellate system within the courts and the fact that the judiciary administer justice under the cleansing scrutiny of the public are so important.

The task of analysing the scandals to which I have referred is the responsibility of others and my views are no more authoritative than the views of an interested onlooker. However, I do believe that Dr Carey's call for humility was very wise. I cannot help believing that the behaviour of those involved in the scandals betrays a lack of appreciation of the limits of their responsibility. They were not motivated by personal gain but they had lost sight of the limits on their powers and authority. They acted as though they were able to take any action they thought desirable irrespective of the views of others.

The problem with *Bolam* is that it inhibited the courts exercising a restraining influence. The courts must recognise that theirs is essentially a regulatory role and they should not interfere unless interference is justified. But when interference is justified they must not be deterred from doing so by any principle such as the fact that what has been done is in accord with a practice approved or by a respectable body of medical opinion. It is all a question of getting the balance right and this is what I hope the courts have now established. I have suggested what I believe to be the position today. A case decided tomorrow could show I have been too optimistic. In addition, as a result of scientific advances medical ethical problems of a new dimension are arising continuously. I have no doubt that those problems are not problems which are ideal for the courts to resolve. They are best tackled in the first instance by expert bodies such as the Human Fertilisation and Embryology Authority. The courts' role is to regulate the regulators. However, whether this will happen must be doubtful. What I can say is that the courts will do their best to meet the challenges with which they will undoubtedly be faced.

22

Are the Judiciary Environmentally Myopic?

Abstract This paper discusses the development of environmental law in England, explaining that while it has an identifiable core, it has no clear boundaries. It considers the various proceedings that can be used to enforce environmental legislation and suggests that the existing situation is unsatisfactory. It recommends the establishment of a new environmental tribunal, or 'one stop shop', with general responsibility for overseeing and enforcing the safeguards provided for the protection of the environment. This, it concludes, could lead to faster, cheaper and more effective resolution of environmental disputes.

Introduction

It is a great honour to be invited to give this lecture associated as it is with the nature of Professor Garner. The judiciary have claimed considerable credit for their contribution to the development of administrative law. However, that credit has to be shared with a small group of outstanding administrative lawyers who marked out the path which the judiciary followed. Among that small group is Professor Garner. I can personally vouch for the contribution which he made to the development of administrative law. As Treasury Junior in the 1970s, I regularly relied on his distinguished textbook for the most acceptable arguments to support the validity of government action. However, even with this help I was not always successful. Indeed, I believe that my only qualification to give this lecture tonight is that I probably hold the dubious record of having lost more planning cases on behalf of the Secretary of State for the Environment in one day than any other member of the Bar. I had the

---

* This lecture was originally given as the 5th Garner Environmental Law Lecture at Church House, Westminster, on 23 October 1991. The Garner lectures are named after the late Jack Garner who was a leading environmental lawyer. A revised version was published in the Journal of Environmental Law ((1992) 4(1) JEL 1).

painful experience of sitting in the Court of that great planning lawyer, the late Mr Justice Ramsay or Jack Willis while he delivered four separate elegant judgments, quashing decisions of the Secretary of State in relation to different planning appeals.

The inaugural lecture, only four years ago, marked the establishment of the United Kingdom Environmental Law Association. I attended that lecture, which was given by the then President Lord Nathan,[1] attracted by its association with Professor Garner. I was glad that I did so. Not only because of the learning displayed in the lecture 'Fencing your Eden'; nor only for the fascinating description of the journey of the caterpillar in Mrs Voss's tin of peas (which in turn attracted the attention of the Dorchester Magistrates, the Divisional Court presided over by the Lord Chief Justice and the Lord Chancellor in the House of Lords), but because it made me aware that there was an area of the law which could be properly identified as being environmental law.

My previous ignorance was probably excusable since in delivering a paper the same year,[2] at a conference jointly organised by the American Bar Association and the Institute for European Environmental Policy, Richard Macrory, your then Chairman, stated that 'the term, "environmental law" is hardly recognised in academic or practitioners circles'. The explanation given for this was that while the subject 'has an identifiable core such as pollution and nature conservation, it has no clear boundaries'.

I suspect that even those responsible for founding this Association and inaugurating these lectures, with the invaluable support of Legal Studies and Services Ltd, could not have anticipated the importance which was going to be attached to the development of a system of environmental law in this country.

In the 1970s and 1980s there was a clearly perceived need for the public to be better protected against the abuse by public bodies and their ever-increasing powers. The dramatic development of administrative law which then took place was the response. In the short period which has elapsed since the establishment of this Association, it has become increasingly clear that the public has even greater concern about the threat to the environment. A problem which should concern us all is whether our legal system is capable

---

[1] The current Chairman of the UK Environmental Law Association is Daniel Lawrence.

[2] R Macrory, (1989) 4 Connect J of Int L 287.

of adopting, as it did in the case of administrative law, so as to provide an effective means of protecting the environment.

What is Environmental Law?

It could be suggested that the initial difficulty is that while environmental law is now clearly a permanent feature of the legal scene, it still lacks 'clear boundaries'. However, it may be that, again as in the case of administrative law, it is preferable that the boundaries are left to be established by judicial decision as the law develops. After all, the great strength of English law has been its pragmatic approach. It has always been concerned more with remedies than with principles.[3] However, environmental law does not fit conveniently into any existing legal compartment. It is easier to identify the areas of the law with which it is not concerned than those with which it is concerned. For my own purposes I regard it as being concerned with our physical surroundings rather than our political or social surroundings. I recently attended a conference in Northern Ireland. The political environment was such that I was advised to travel to another part of the UK using a *nom de plume*. A situation I regarded as highly undesirable. However, enforcing our laws in a way which changes the political environment is not my present concern. Equally, I am conscious that some have attributed teenage hooliganism in some of our cities to the social environment in which these youngsters have been brought up. This again identifies a problem which deserves the attention of lawyers but is not a subject which I am addressing here. Instead, taking advantage of my experience I want to focus on how we can best strengthen and maintain the fences around our Eden to which Lord Nathan referred in the first Garner Lecture.

At the present time, for this purpose we rely upon no single legal procedure or remedy. Instead, we rely in part on the long-established common law actions for private and public nuisance; in part on the public law procedure of judicial review; in part on statutory appeals and applications and generally on the criminal law. Combined, these procedures provide a formidable armoury. However, at the present time, their deployment can and occasionally does result in an embarrassing succession of proceedings. Take, for example, the consequences of an explosion onboard an oil tanker which is

---

[3] Lord Wilberforce, in *Davey v Spelthorne Borough Council* [1984] AC 262, 276, pointed out 'English law fastens not on principles but on remedies'.

discharging its cargo at a terminal close to an urban area; a serious disaster, but a disaster of wholly different proportions to those which can only be too readily anticipated after what occurred at Chernobyl.[4] If our conventional procedures and remedies are to be employed to deal with this sort of situation then a multiplicity of proceedings follows. First of all the relevant Minister sets up an inquiry to investigate what has happened and makes a recommendation, depending on the scale of the incident the inquiry is likely to be conducted either by a judge or a distinguished Queen's Counsel. Pending the outcome of the inquiry other proceedings are likely to be delayed if not deferred. If there is a death there will be an inquisition before a coroner, who will be either medically or legally qualified, and a jury. There is likely to be at least a real possibility of criminal proceedings, which may result in charges of manslaughter against companies if recent experience is anything to go by. Finally, and following in the rear there will be scores of civil proceedings by those who have been unfortunate enough to suffer personal or other injuries and those whose property has been damaged.

In the conduct of the respective proceedings each of the tribunals will have to exercise caution not to frustrate the ability of the other tribunals to do justice. The inspector may have difficulty in hearing certain evidence because of the need to avoid prejudicing criminal or civil proceedings. The coroner will be faced with the same problem. The costs of the differing proceedings may be enormous but at the end of the day, the real problem may be traced to a failure of the regulatory bodies which have been set up to do their task properly. This in turn may direct attention as to the suitability of our present procedures and cannot be tackled by looking at the problem in a piecemeal manner. What is required is a fundamentally new approach.

Indications of the approach which is required are provided by developments which are already occurring, I am glad to say, in the academic world. At least one of our universities has developed a centre of environmental law. Thanks to the sponsorship of Denton, Hall, Burgin and Warrens a Chair in Environmental Law is about to be established, not at one of the well-known law schools within the London University, but at the Imperial College of Science's Centre for Environmental Technology. An admirable initiative with what, at first sight appears to be a surprising base. In fact its connection

---

[4] In 1986, a nuclear reactor exploded at the Chernobyl Nuclear Power Plant. This was the worst nuclear power plant accident in history, severely impacting upon the environment in western Soviet Union, Europe and as far as eastern North America.

with Imperial College is no more than a recognition that environmental law raises problems to which a multi-discipline approach, including a proper involvement of technology and science may be the appropriate response. In relation to the environment, even the media is becoming constructively involved. I read with interest recently that if I was a young instead of an old lawyer I could submit this lecture to *The Times* and, if only its quality were greater, have a prospect of a share in the £6,000 prize *The Times* is offering for a contribution on environmental law.

The new approach was reflected in your choice of lecturer last year. Even when he is a non-practising lawyer of the distinction of Sir Denys Henderson, the former Chairman of ICI, he is not the obvious choice for a lecture in law.

A different aspect of environmental law is also apparent from your choice of lectures. I was not present at the second lecture which was given by Ludwig Kramer, but thanks to the *Journal of Environmental Law*[5] I have been able to read that lecture which brings home the extent to which this area of the law is already and will continue to be dominated by developments within the European Community. The European dimension in itself creates tensions for our existing institutions and our traditional approach. There is a danger which has to be acknowledged of our traditional common law approach being undervalued by the Community partly because in the majority of other member states' legal systems there is nothing comparable.

The Capacity of the Judges

Although they would not have regarded themselves as deciding environmental law cases, the English judiciary have of course been providing remedies for environmental interference with an occupier's enjoyment of land as long as Queens Bench Courts have existed. However, as Ludwig Kramer made clear in his lecture, a nuisance action is rather different from what is now generally recognised as being the proper subject matter of environmental law. In a nuisance action a plaintiff is seeking to protect or to receive compensation for interference with his purely personal property rights. The primary focus of environmental law is not on the protection of private rights but on the protection of the environment for the public in general. An action for nuisance can be framed so as to protect not only one occupier of a single site, but a number of

---

[5] L Kramer, 'The Open Society, its lawyers and its environment' [1989] 1(1) JEL 1.

occupiers of different sites. However, this was not what it was primarily designed to achieve.

The old action for nuisance, if what I read is correct, may well be about to develop additional dimensions. This could be a consequence of proceedings being brought by those who live within the fallout area of the noise, dust and traffic pollution which are inevitable consequences of the docklands development. If such or similar actions are brought, they will require different treatment from the traditional nuisance action. Arrangements will have to be made and can be made to cope with the number of plaintiffs and possibly defendants. A single judge may have to be nominated to deal with all the actions. He will have a rather different task to perform than a judge normally trying an action for nuisance. In the ordinary way, a judge has to assess whether or not what is complained of is anything more than a reasonable use of the adjoining occupier's property. Since nuisance 'is the law of give and take the Court is inevitably concerned to some extent with the utility or general benefit to the community of the defendant's activity'.[6] It is only if the court after balancing the competing interests of all parties considers the interference is excessive, that the court will intervene.

Where a judge is holding the balance between the interests of two residential occupiers, no one would question his competence to draw that balance. However, where, as a result of legislation passed by Parliament, you are concerned with the consequences of the decisions of a statutory authority which are designed to achieve the regeneration of a large area of derelict land, different considerations are involved in deciding where the balance lies. The French *Conseil d'Etat*, whose members have a different background and experience to that of an English judge, may be better equipped to play this role than an English Court. For example, I understand that when the *Conseil d'Etat* is considering a proposal affecting the environment, it is evaluated by employing what is known as the Braibant balance sheet, named after a senior member of the *Conseil d'Etat*, which involves setting out the benefits of the scheme on one side of the balance sheet, the disadvantages of the scheme on the other side of the balance sheet, and comparing the results. If the balance is substantially against the proposal, then the *Conseil d'Etat* intervenes. This is the approach which may be required for resolving the larger scale of nuisance actions to which I have referred. However, considerations which should and would have to be

---

[6] See *Winfield and Jolowicz on Tort* (13th edn, Sweet & Maxwell, 1989), 375 *et seq.*

weighed by a judge in such an action are ones which in other areas of the law the judiciary have regarded themselves as ill-equipped to perform.

The Capacity of the High Court

It is now necessary to consider the approach which the High Court adopts both on statutory appeals from the decisions of ministers and when a statutory appeal is not available on judicial review. When deciding cases brought before the High Court by either procedure, the High Court has consistently turned its face against considering the merits of the decision, but instead has confined its attention to scrutinising the procedural process adopted by the ministers in reaching their decisions. It is because the judiciary are not regarded as competent to determine the sort of issues which frequently have to be taken into account by ministers in coming to their decisions that the judges are required to avoid reviewing the merits of decisions of public bodies, irrespective of their importance to the public. The constitutional theory is that as to political policy and aesthetic considerations it is preferable for Parliament, not the courts, to join issue with ministers as to the merits of their decisions. This, I recognise, can give the impression that judges are ignoring or at least giving limited attention to these important considerations. Thus, the title of this lecture. As always happens, you agree to give the lecture many months in advance and then postpone the preparation of the lecture as long as possible. There comes a stage as the date draws near when you are pressed to at least provide a title. At that stage you have probably not more than some idea about what you are going to talk about but you try and think of some suitable umbrella which will give you as much flexibility as possible. In this case, when I was being pressed for the title for this paper, I had just read the decision of the House of Lords in the case[7] which SAVE had lost in respect of their opposition to the new Palumbo building at the Mappin and Webb site in the City of London close to the Bank of England. I was concerned that I had in part been responsible for SAVE being saddled with a huge bill of costs as a result of their determined opposition to what they regarded as a wholly erroneous decision. The issue before the High Court, as the House of Lords pointed out, was a strictly limited one. It was as to whether the admitted shortcomings in the Minister's reasoning were remedied by his implied adoption of the detailed and admirable reasoning of

---

[7] *Save Britain's Heritage v No 1 Poultry Ltd* [1991] 1 WLR 153.

the inspector. Simon Brown J,[8] at first instance, and the House of Lords, came to the conclusion that the Minister's decision was not effective. I had been a member of the Court of Appeal who came to a different conclusion. Lord Bridge in his speech in favour of allowing the appeal, with which the other members of the House of Lords agreed, concluded by saying:

> The public controversy over this case arises from differences of opinion about traditional and contemporary architectural styles. These arouse strong feeling but are no concern whatever of the courts. It is a trite observation that can bear repetition in a case like this, that our concern is solely with the legality of the decision making process, not at all with the merits of the decision.[9]

Lord Ackner also made it clear that aesthetic judgments were for the Secretary of State and not the for the members of the House of Lords.

This is the traditional and, in the present situation, probably the only possible approach of our courts. However, whether it satisfied the members of SAVE is a different question. I have little doubt as to how they would answer questions posed by my title. I accept that the desirability of the judicial role being limited in this way is debatable. It does not need to be limited to this extent as is shown by what happens in the US and in Australia.

However, I have no doubt that the role of the English judge should be so limited unless we are prepared to change our courts in a way which I would not contemplate. It does not however follow from this that there should not be some review of the Minister's decision which is not as restricted as that which is at present possible before the courts. It only means it should not be by judges, or judges sitting alone without help from those who have broader experience of the issues involved. In the *SAVE* case it happened that what was involved was an aesthetic judgment and it is questionable as to whether the Minister was as qualified as his inspector to take that decision or, dare I say it, better qualified than a judge.

Even if judges are required to continue to take a restricted, or in accordance with the title of this lecture, a myopic approach, there remain problems. No doubt reflecting the public's concern with the environment there was in the 1990s an amazing volume of new legislation which was designed to tackle environmental problems. This legislation is going to give rise to fresh problems which will require the attention of the High Court making use of

---

[8] Now Lord Brown, Lord of Appeal in Ordinary.
[9] *Save Britain's Heritage*, n 7 above, 171

its existing jurisdiction. An idea of the scale of the legislation is indicated by the recent planning acts. In 1990 we had the Town and Country Planning Act 1990, the Planning (Listed Building and Conservation Areas) Act 1990, the Planning (Hazardous Substances) Act 1990 and the Planning (Consequential Provisions) Act 1990. If that was not sufficient to occupy the environmental lawyer, we had the Planning and Compensation Act 1991.

To the legislation to which I have already referred there is to be added the Hazardous Substances Act 1990.[10] This Act also provides for appeals to the Secretary of State[11] and for a further statutory appeal to the High Court[12] by any person aggrieved by the decision of the Secretary of State.

However, paramount among this legislation is not a planning act but the Environmental Protection Act 1990 with its integrated pollution control, its new structure for the control of the disposal of waste and its consolidation of the provisions relating to statutory nuisance, accompanied by improved public access to information. The legislation gives a formidable array of new powers to the Secretary of State and other regulatory bodies.[13] He is to make national plans with regard to the release of substances into the environment.[14] There are provisions which enable enforcing authorities to issue enforcement notices and, for example, section 12 requires that a notice shall be issued where in the enforcing authority's opinion the continued operation of a process involves the risk of serious pollution of the environment. There are powers of appeal to the Secretary of State and those appeals may be dealt with by an inspector in much the same way as planning appeals are dealt with by inspectors. However, unlike the planning and the compulsory purchase legislation the Act does not provide for an appeal to the High Court against a decision of the Secretary of State. The same is true of the appeal provisions in respect of the control and handling of waste contained in the Act. When the High Court is given no express power to control the manner in which the Secretary of State and the enforcing authorities perform their functions under the Act, they become subject to the supervision

---

[10] Which, as the former editor of the *Planning Encyclopaedia,* Professor Malcolm Grant, pointed out at the time (para 270030), 'unstitches and divorces the control over hazardous substances from planning powers notwithstanding the fact that the draftsman of the 1986 Act (Housing and Planning Act 1986) had gone to considerable pains to integrate the new regime over hazardous substances with the planning provisions of the (then) 1971 Act'.

[11] Hazardous Substances Act, s 21.

[12] Ibid, s 22.

[13] For example, the Secretary of State has power to set quality standards and quality objectives for the release of substances into the environment, ibid, s 3.

[14] Ibid, s 3(5).

of the Court on judicial review and it is not difficult to identify provisions which will be a fruitful source of additional litigation on judicial review. For example, that processes involve 'a serious risk of pollution of the environment' could well be the subject of debate even with the Court's present limited area of concern. Furthermore, the resolution of such litigation is not going to be a simple task. Many of the provisions of the Act reflect the European dimension[15] to which I have already referred. For example, in order to consider whether a minister had misdirected himself as to the law, it may well be necessary to also consider the European Community regulations to which the Act is giving effect.[16] This creates the problem that in ascertaining the legal position the judge is not able to confine himself to consideration of the language of the legislation in the same way that he can when he is considering domestic legislation which does not have a European dimension.

In the light of this flood of legislation which in turn is inevitably going to produce an ever-expanding mushroom of subordinate legislation, the question arises as to how well the High Court is equipped to deal with the additional litigation which this legislation will generate adopting its existing limited role.

I suspect that I am as enthusiastic a supporter of the present judicial review system as anyone. However, I am very concerned as to how it is coping with its existing workload, never mind what is in store. Initially there were four judges nominated to decide these cases who had a background in administrative law practice; now there are 18.[17] But still the increase in the workload has resulted in a most undesirable backlog. Extremely urgent cases can still be dealt with remarkable expedition but other cases are taking 12 to 18 months to be heard once they enter the warned list. Worse is in store as the number of judicial review applications is already increasing at the rate of 10 per cent per annum compound. The result is that for every

---

[15] There have been some significant domestic environmental statutory developments since this paper was originally given. See, for example, the Environment Act 1995, the Planning and Compulsory Purchase Act 2004 and the Natural Environment and Rural Communities Act 2006. It is also to be noted that a new Planning Bill was introduced in the House of Commons on 27 November 2007.

[16] So far as this is possible within our existing rules of construction, domestic legislation must be construed to accord with this country's European Community obligations. Even where it is not possible to establish a match, an applicant can contend, because the European regulation or directive is of direct effect, the courts are required to give precedence to the European legislation.

[17] In 2007 there were 37 judges, including judges of the Chancery Division and Family Division of the High Court, who act as additional judges of the Queen's Bench Division when dealing with cases in the Administrative Court List.

case disposed of, two or three cases enter the warned list. The general picture so far as judicial review is concerned is therefore one of increasing delays. The importance of this to environmental issues is underlined when it is remembered that the Environmental Protection Act 1990 depends upon judicial review for its control of the activities of environmental enforcement bodies. This cannot be regarded as anything other than an unsatisfactory situation. It is particularly so because the record of both central and local government with regard to enforcing environmental measures has not always been what it should. With regard to the powers previously contained in the Control of Pollution Act 1974, in their report, the House of Commons Environmental Committee in 1989 stated:

> Never, in any of our inquiries into environmental problems, have we experienced such consistent and universal criticism of existing legislation and of central and local government as we have during the course of this inquiry.[18]

Locus Standi in the High Court

Sections of the public may therefore wish to take up the cudgels for the benefit of the public as a whole and seek to obtain an order compelling a government department or regulatory agency to fulfil its duties. If this happens, the litigant will be required to show that he or she has *locus standi*. Where European Community legislation has direct effect, then as we stated in the *Factortame* case:

> It is for the national courts in application of the principle of cooperation laid down in Article 5 of the EEC Treaty to ensure the legal protection which persons derive from the direct effect of provisions of Community law.[19]

Accordingly, in those areas where our legislation is giving effect to Community obligations those adversely affected by the non-compliance with the legislation should be able to obtain a remedy in the courts. However, in general it is the domestic principles as to standing which have to be applied. They differ depending upon the procedure which is being invoked and the remedy which is claimed. If the would-be litigant has been subjected to common law nuisance then there should not be any difficulty with regard to standing but there may be difficulties in establishing liability because

---

[18] HC Environmental Committee Report (HMSO, 1989).
[19] *R v Secretary of State for Transport, ex parte Factortame Ltd (No 2)* [1991] 1 All ER 70.

the proposed defendant may be able to claim that what occurred was the necessary consequence of a performance of statutory obligations. The position is the same with regard to public nuisance. Here the prospective plaintiff will have to establish that he has suffered special damage over and above that of the community at large. If our would-be litigant wishes to bring an ordinary action for a declaration, he or she will have to establish that some private law rights of theirs have been infringed. Failing which he will not have standing unless he can persuade the Attorney-General to consent to relator proceedings being brought in his name.[20] If the proposed defendant is a Secretary of State or government department, the prospects of obtaining such consent is indeed remote.

The next possibility is a statutory appeal to the High Court if there is an express provision contained in the relevant legislation. If there is a provision it will usually require that the appellant or applicant be a 'person aggrieved' by the decision which will normally have been taken by a Secretary of State or an Inspector on his behalf. The approach of the courts to the question as to who is a 'person aggrieved' has changed over the years. A more generous approach is now adopted than once was the case. The same is true of judicial review. As a result, I had come to accept that both on judicial review and on a statutory appeal it was unlikely that if an application had real merit, it would ever be refused on the basis that the applicant had insufficient standing. This is what I interpret to be the message from the House of Lords decision in the leading case of *R v IRC, ex parte National Federation of Self Employed and Small Business Ltd*.[21] I was compelled, however, to rethink this approach to *locus standi* as a result of the decision of Schiemann J[22] in *R v Secretary of State for the Environment, ex parte Rose Theatre Trust*[23] and the distinguished lecture which the same judge gave extra-judicially on the subject to the Administrative Law Bar Association.[24] That was the case which concerned the remains of the Elizabethan theatre on a site which was ripe for redevelopment and where the development had been postponed to enable the excavations to take place which resulted in the discovery of the theatre. The Secretary of State refused to designate the remains as a listed building under section 1 of the Ancient

20 *Gouriet v Union of Post Office Workers* [1978] AC 435.
21 [1982] AC 617.
22 Now a Lord Justice of Appeal.
23 [1990] 2 WLR 186.
24 See K Schiemann, *'Locus Standi'* (1990) PL 342.

Monuments and Archaeological Areas Act 1979 and an attempt was made to challenge the Secretary of State's decision on an application for judicial review. The applicants were clearly concerned about the question of *locus standi* and they constituted themselves as a trust company with the object of preserving the remains of the theatre. Schiemann J concluded that the decision not to apply the Act to the remains was 'one of those governmental decisions in respect of which the ordinary citizen does not have a sufficient interest to entitle him to obtain leave for judicial review'.[25] As an individual citizen would not have *locus standi* so the judge concluded an aggregate of individuals could not claim sufficient interest not possessed by any of its members[26] so the trust had no *locus standi* to bring the application. The problem which the decision creates is that if the trust did not have *locus standi*, who would? It is difficult to see that there would be anybody who could bring proceedings. In the *Rose Theatre* case this did not matter because the application was, in any event, without merit. However, the position would be exactly the same if the decision of the Secretary of State had been manifestly unlawful. Until a higher court has an opportunity to consider the correctness of Schiemann J's approach, it is not possible to say whether there is a real impediment to the enforcement of environmental obligations. It would be inappropriate for me to speculate as to what view a higher court would take. It has, however, to be recognised that the fact that there is such a high number of applications for judicial review nowadays means that it will be tempting for the court to use the requirement of *locus standi* as a protection against the flood.

A restricted view as to who has a sufficient interest would have a particular impact in the environmental law field. Many of the activities of public bodies which would be amenable to judicial review affect the public at large in an identical manner. The same argument as in the *Rose* case could therefore be relied upon.

The Problem with Statutory Appeals

While statutory appeals to the High Court share with judicial review problems over *locus standi*, the statutory appeals do not have the same problems over delay. The reason is that while this is not intended, in practice they are

---

[25] [1990] 2 WLR 186, 202.
[26] Ibid, 201–202.

rarely heard by High Court judges. Instead, they are heard by Deputies who are usually experienced practitioners in the environmental field, particularly planning, who sit for a few weeks at a time as Deputy High Court Judges. The admirable manner in which they dispose of their cases shows the advantage of having a specialist tribunal. However, there is a disadvantage inherent in the service which they provide. If as occurred in the case of statutory appeals and judicial review in the past, the decisions are taken by the same number of judges, then consistency should result and principles should be propounded which develop the framework provided by legislation. Our planning law today shows the influence of Lord Widgery CJ, Lord Bridge and Willis and Forbes JJ. This beneficial process is difficult to achieve in the present situation where there are a considerable number of cases being decided by many different part-time judges who only sit for short periods at a time.

The Criminal Courts

Turning to consider the involvement of the criminal law, the legislation to which I have referred to earlier creates a considerable number of statutory offences. Some of those offences are to be dealt with by magistrates but others are liable to be dealt with on indictment by a fine or imprisonment and are triable by the Crown Court. Where an offence carries a sentence of imprisonment, then I certainly would not wish the case to be tried otherwise than in the criminal courts. However, I do have reservations as to whether the criminal courts are the appropriate tribunal to determine some of the offences created by environmental legislation. Take, for example, the offence which arises in consequence of section 6 of the Environmental Protection Act 1990. That section prohibits the carrying on of a proscribed process except under an authorisation. The authorisation is normally subject to an implied condition that in carrying on the process to which the authorisation applies the person carrying it on must use the best available techniques not entailing excessive costs, inter alia, for rendering harmless any other substance which might cause harm if released into any environmental medium. Whether the process which is being used is 'the best available technique not entailing excessive costs' must be a difficult question of judgement and the problems of determining this could be extremely challenging for a lay tribunal in environmental matters. The fact that the Act unusually for a criminal offence places the onus of proof in regard to such matters upon the defendant does not resolve the problem. In addition, it may well be difficult for a lay tribunal to exercise the salutary power contained in section 26 of the Act of making an order that the matters giving rise to the offence should be remedied.

I recognise the need for sanctions to enforce compliance with legislation designed to protect the environment. However, I do question the appropriateness of the criminal courts having to deal with issues of this sort where all that is at stake is the imposition of a financial penalty.

A different aspect of the same problem has been highlighted by the disasters which have occurred and which did not involve an environmental dimension but could readily have done so. If, in such a situation, a company is responsible for the disaster there is naturally a desire on the part of those adversely affected to see that company punished. For this purpose it has been thought necessary to charge companies with manslaughter.[27] I question whether this is the ideal manner in which to deal with this problem. If an individual, be he a director, a chief executive or a chairman of a company, is guilty of such wrongdoing that he deserves to be tried for the serious offence of manslaughter, then so be it. However, in the case of a company, there are problems which make a criminal trial on a charge of manslaughter hardly the ideal process for determining the responsibility and punishment of a company. In this connection, I draw attention to the powers available to the European Commission to directly or indirectly punish commercial concerns who contravene European Community regulations in other areas.

Coroners

So far as coroners are concerned, they perform an admirable function where there is no alternative public investigation of the cause of a sudden death. However, without, I hope, unduly detracting from the importance of the role performed by coroners, it is reasonably clear that in determining complex issues they do not provide an entirely satisfactory forum.

Inspectors

It is also necessary to say a word about the present role of inspectors on appeals to Ministers. In the past the Minister, or more accurately his unidentified official, would normally be the decision-making body; the decision

---

[27] It is noteworthy that it is expected a new Corporate Manslaughter and Corporate Homicide Act 2007 will be implemented on 6 April 2008.

being based on a report prepared by an inspector he appointed. Particularly where the Minister was himself the promoting authority there was naturally considerable dissatisfaction with the procedure. However, changes were made and now it works reasonably well. In practice, however, certainly in the planning field, the involvement of the Minister is purely nominal. In the vast majority of cases he delegates to his inspector the task of deciding the appeal and the inspector, who is frequently a one-man tribunal, conducts the proceedings as he sees fit, subject to the supervision of the High Court either on a further statutory appeal or on judicial review. The question that arises here is whether or not it would be preferable for what is the reality in the majority of cases to be accepted as being the legal position in all cases? It may be suggested that the disadvantage of adopting such an approach is that it would inhibit the Minister injecting his views as to policy into the decision. This, however, does not need to be the consequence. Even where an independent body is given a decision making role, it still may be required by statute to follow policy guidance given by the Minister. It is of course possible for the inspector to come to a wrong decision. This is, however, true whoever takes the decision and there is something to be said for instead of having a limited right of appeal, as at present, for there to be an extended right of appeal before an expert tribunal which could investigate the issues in a way which would not be appropriately done by a judge.

A Possible Alternative

Having examined the existing situation, I suggest it does reveal an unsatisfactory picture. A High Court, overburdened already and without the specialist input to deal with an influx of complex environmental issues; problems of multiplicity of proceedings; the criminal courts which have more than enough work already having to deal with quasi-criminal offences giving rise to technical crimes which do not fit easily into the structure of a criminal trial. The next question therefore is whether there is a better solution than that which is offered by the legal system at present? This is the type of question which is best suited to the sort of examination that was conducted by the Law Commission into judicial review[28] and I am not qualified to do more than offer the following tentative comments. I have already made it clear that I do not believe matters would be improved by broadening the jurisdiction of the High

---

[28] See *Report on Judicial Review and Statutory Appeals* (Law Com No 226) (1994).

Court so that judges are no longer required to adopt their existing restricted approach to environmental problems. In other areas of the law, even where the issues are more readily susceptible of judicial decision, for sensible practical reasons the issues are now determined by tribunals and I suggest that consideration at least should be given to adopting the same approach to the complex issues to which environmental law gives rise.

The enforcement of one aspect of environmental law was the subject of a report by Mr Robert Carnwath QC[29] to the Secretary of State for the Environment and his recommendations resulted in the Planning and Compensation Act 1991. Mr Carnwath discussed the desirability of a radical solution to the undoubted problems which exist at present. He considered four ideas in particular. The first was to make unauthorised development a crime; the second was a new planning enforcement tribunal; the third was the substitution of the existing enforcement procedures by remedies provided by the Court; and the fourth was to give third parties rights they do not have at present. He rejected each idea but it is interesting to note that he only rejected the idea of a new planning enforcement tribunal because his terms of reference confined his consideration to planning enforcement alone. If he had been concerned with a wider canvas, he makes it clear his views may have been different. He says:

> Ideally there should be one Court or Tribunal, able to interpret and apply the law, to make orders, and to impose penalties for their disobedience. At present those functions are divided between two administrative agencies (the local authorities and the planning inspectorate) and various courts—criminal and civil. Planning enforcement, like some other forms of administrative or environmental control, lies awkwardly between the civil and criminal areas of jurisdiction.[30]

Later he adds:

> I can see a case for a form of Tribunal which is able to encompass the whole range of planning appeal and enforcement work, including the levying of penalties. Alternatively, there may be a case for reviewing the jurisdiction of the various Courts and Tribunals which at present deal with different aspects of what might be called 'environmental protection' (including planning), and seeking to combine them in a single jurisdiction.[31]

---

[29] Now a Lord Justice of Appeal and Senior President of Tribunals. See *Enforcing Planning Control* (HMSO, February 1989).
[30] Ibid.
[31] Ibid.

A New Tribunal

I commend these conclusions for further consideration. They conclude with the views I had independently formed looking at the problem on a wider canvas. In doing so I have very much in mind my own recent experience of conducting an inquiry which had nothing to do with the subject matter we are discussing tonight but which demonstrated to my satisfaction that there are areas of the law where the inquisitorial approach can have considerable virtues, as can a seminar. There could be great benefits in having a tribunal with a general responsibility for overseeing and enforcing the safeguards provided for the protection of the environment which is so important for us all. The tribunal could be granted a wider discretion to determine its procedure so that it was able to bring to bear its specialist experience of environmental issues in the most effective way. If the issues from the outset warranted the attention of a High Court judge, architect, or surveyor, he could be appointed to determine the issue helped by permanent members of the tribunal. The High Court judge could, as in the case of the Employment Appeal Tribunal, be the President of this Tribunal or he could be a judge who, as a result of sitting in the Tribunal, has experience of environmental issues. He could have the responsibility of initially finding the facts and making general recommendations very much on the lines which are now adopted by judges when appointed to hold inquiries.

In addition, the Tribunal could be given the responsibility for making the ancillary decisions which can arise out of the facts investigated by the inquiry. For example, where a death results the inquiry could be given the responsibilities of the Coroner's inquisition; where compensation is appropriate, this could be dealt with in its entirety or, where this is more sensible, the inquiry could determine only the question of liability. Where punishment is required the Tribunal could have the power to impose penalties. Obviously, care would have to be exercised to avoid inhibiting the performance by the Tribunal of its primary role. However, as long as the Tribunal has control over its own procedure it could refer to others, including the courts, issues which it is appropriate for them to determine.

Frequently the issues involved would justify the use of a multi-disciplined adjudicating panel. The procedures should be as informal as the nature of the inquiry permitted. The Tribunal could have a broad discretion over who could invoke the jurisdiction of the Tribunal and who could represent the parties. When the issues warranted this, independent counsel could be instructed to act on behalf of the Tribunal and members of the public who would not otherwise be heard. The Tribunal would need to have its own investigatory resources supported where appropriate by the police. In the case of issues of a lesser dimension inspectors, who would be part of the Tribunal, could perform a similar role to that which they perform at present. There could be within the structure of the Tribunal a system of appeals which differed in their scope as the circumstances required. Finally, there could be an appeal on a point of law, probably only with leave, to the Court of Appeal so as to ensure the maintenance of the necessary standards of justice and to achieve the proper development of the law.

Conclusion

It is not possible to do more than give a taste of the possible Tribunal that I have in mind. I hope however I have said enough, some would say too much, to whet your appetite. To indicate that what I am contemplating is not just a court under another name, nor is it an existing tribunal under another name. It is a multi-faceted, multi-skilled body which would combine the services provided by existing courts, tribunals and inspectors in the environmental field. It would be a 'one stop shop' which should lead to faster, cheaper and the more effective resolution of disputes in the environmental area. It would avoid increasing the load on already overburdened lay institutions by trying to compel them to resolve issues with which they are not designed to deal. It could be a forum in which judges could play a different role. A role which enabled them not to examine environmental problems with limited vision. It could however be based on our existing experience, combining the skills of the existing inspectorate, the Lands Tribunal and other administrative bodies.[32] It could indeed be an exciting project.

We are fortunate that at the present time the Law Commission are re-examining our administrative procedures but not alas environmental law which goes beyond administrative law. It is still to be hoped that as a result of this examination, recommendations will be made which are important to the future of environmental law as well as the development of judicial review. If the Commission are successful in doing this, part of the credit will be due to those who have had the foresight to establish this Association, which has assisted in elevating environmental law to a status which reflects its importance to us all.

---

[32] Professor Jack Garner and Professor Malcolm Grant both drew my attention to precedents for my proposal of a multi-faceted tribunal. In the case of Professor Garner to that which exists in Denmark, and in the case of Professor Grant to that which exists in New South Wales.

23

Environmental Law and
Sustainable Development

Abstract This paper identifies the dramatic scale of the changes that
have taken place in environmental law in the intervening years since the
5th Garner Lecture was delivered in 1991 [see Chapter 22 above]. It discusses how the threat to the environment has increased, recognising
that development must be restricted to that which is environmentally
sustainable. It calls for a judicial system that meets the needs of the environment as encapsulated in the Johannesburg principles on the role of
law and sustainable development, and advises how this could be achieved.
It concludes that we need a global legal framework to restrict development to that which is sustainable backed by a global means of enforcement. Until this is achieved, however, it could be sensible to consider
having specialised environmental courts at the regional level.

I am deeply honoured to have been invited to take part in this important
conference. I am most grateful for the invitation of Chief Justice Dr Mamdouh
Fathi Naguib and Deputy Chief Justice, Justice Adel Omar Sherif of the
Supreme Constitutional Court of Egypt. I could not have been more hospita-
bly received.

I am particularly delighted to be here because it provides me with an opportunity of meeting the judiciary from a number of Arab nations with whom
I have regrettably not previously had any connection. This is unfortunate
because it is my firm belief that the judiciary of different jurisdictions have
an immense amount to learn from each other. Our legal systems may differ.

---

* Originally given at The Needs Assessment Meeting for the Chief Justices of the Arab Countries
on Training of Judges and other Legal Stakeholders in the Supreme Constitutional Court of Egypt
and the United Nations Environmental Programme, in May 2004.

They may fall on one side or the other of the divide between the common law and civil law systems or they may be a mixture of both systems or even unrelated to either of those systems. Yet, the problems with which they are confronted today are still very similar. How to ensure that all sections of the public can obtain access to justice from our courts? How to deal with ever mounting case loads? How to protect the public from increasing crime? How to deal with terrorist offences and in particular, in the case of such offences, how to balance the rights of the individual against the need of the state to protect the public from terrorist attacks? How to ensure the independence of the judiciary and finally how to protect the environment, the subject of this conference? Some of these problems are purely domestic but protection against crime and the environment are becoming increasingly recognised as problems, which transcend national barriers. They are problems, which no jurisdiction can successfully tackle by itself and this explains why conferences of this nature are so important.

Indeed a recent judicial symposium between Egyptian and British judges in London in relation to problems relating to family law demonstrated how judges of different jurisdictions can find new ways of achieving justice for parents and children of broken marriages when this might otherwise have proved impossible.

Another example of what can be achieved by international judicial cooperation is provided by a conference in Helsinki of all the Attorney-Generals and Chief Justices of the European Union which I was attending before I came to Cairo. There was a long agenda of issues relating to criminal law on which we were seeking means of cooperation. The week before that, I was engaged in dialogue in the Hague with very brave judges from Iraq in Holland in the hope that exchanging views would assist them. Now I am very much looking forward to our discussion over the next two days.

There could be no more appropriate city in which to discuss our twin topics of sustainable development and the environment than Cairo in view of the environmental problems with which Egypt is faced. How do we reconcile the demands of tourists like myself who want to travel up the Nile and visit the most magnificent antiquities with the need to preserve those antiquities in the interest of future generations? The well-being of the Nile is critical not only to Egypt but its neighbours as well. How do you ensure that it continues to serve all the nations through which it flows? Today these are no longer problems of politicians and statesman alone, they are problems of judges as well.

In 1991, not much more than a decade ago, I gave a lecture under the title 'Are the judiciary environmentally myopic?'. My title was meant to be provocative. It was intended to indicate that perhaps our judiciary should be more proactive in protecting the environment. I started off the lecture by pointing out that, in the UK, environmental law was still hardly recognised even in academic and practitioners' circles let alone by judges. We had a developed system of planning control but it took a narrow view of its role.[1] It was concerned with land uses and sight lines. It was not engaged in confronting the massive problems such as global warming with which we are faced today. Our general law and the remedies that our courts could supply were largely the ones which were available to adjoining occupiers under our private law action of nuisance. This was designed to deal with the interference by a landowner with the enjoyment by a neighbour of his land. It worked very well in sorting out neighbourhood disputes but it was quite inadequate to deal with the widespread damage, which could be caused to the environment on a national and even international scale.

We have, however, developed a process of judicial review of the actions of public bodies that has proved increasingly effective in controlling abuse by public bodies. It has been helped to do so by the relaxation of the requirements as to standings. To bring proceedings it is no longer necessary to establish a special interest in the outcome beyond that of your fellow citizens, in other words, *locus standi* before the proceedings were possible. This meant that a citizen who wished to take up cudgels for the benefit of the public as a whole in order to compel a government department that was otherwise unlawfully threatening to take or restrain from taking action could usually do so.

Judicial review is not the specialist machinery that a modern state has to protect the environment in the 20th let alone the 21st century. In my lecture I therefore recommended the establishment of a special tribunal to deal with environmental issues. I said:

> What I was contemplating was not just a court under another name, nor an existing tribunal under another name. It is a multi-faceted, multi-skilled body which would combine the services provided by existing courts, tribunals and inspectors in the environmental field. It would be a 'one-stop shop' which should lead to a faster, cheaper and more effective resolution of disputes in the

---

[1] 'For a critique of the UK planning inquiry system and suggestions on how it could be renovated, see H Woolf, 'The Courts' Role in Achieving Environmental Justice' (2002) 4(2) JEL 70

environmental area. It would avoid increasing the load on already overburdened existing institutions by requiring them to resolve issues with which
they are not designed to deal. There was needed a forum in which judges could
play a different role. A role that did not restrict them to examining environmental problems with myopic or limited vision.[2]

The creation of such a body would have been an exciting project. But it is a
project that it is still only on the horizon in the UK. In the meantime, the
primary need has changed. A problem that was largely national has become
at least international and probably global. Disasters such as the aftermath of
escape of nuclear material from the reactors at Chernobyl made it clear that
more extensive action was needed than I had contemplated.

The International Court of Justice vividly painted the scale in its Advisory
Opinion on the Legality of Nuclear Weapons:

> ... the environment is under daily threat and that the use of nuclear weapons
> could constitute a catastrophe for the environment ... the environment is not
> an abstraction but represents the living space, the quality of life and the very
> health of human beings, including generations unborn.[3]

The International Court of Justice made a similar point, in a judgment involving
a dispute over the Danube between Hungary and Slovakia, the *Gabčíkovo-
Nagymaros* case.[4] The Court having referred to the 1997 Watercourses
Convention, that now reflects customary international law, stated:

> The Court is mindful that, in the field of environmental protection, vigilance and
> prevention are required on account of the often irreversible character of damage
> to the environment and of the limitations inherent in the very mechanism of
> reparation of this type of damage.[5]

Throughout the ages, mankind has, for economic and other reasons,
constantly interfered with nature. In the past, this was often done without
consideration of the effects upon the environment. Owing to new scientific
insights and to a growing awareness of the risks for mankind, for present
and future generations, of pursuit of such interventions at an unconsidered
and unabated pace, new norms and standards have been developed, set forth
in a great number of instruments during the last two decades. Such new

---

[2] H Woolf, 'Judiciary Environmentally Myopic?', Chapter 22 in this book.
[3] International Court of Justice, 'Advisory Opinion on the Legality of Nuclear Weapons' (1996),
para 29.
[4] *Gabčíkovo-Nagymaros* case, 25 September 1997.
[5] Ibid, [140].

norms have to be taken into consideration, and such new standards given proper weight, not only when States contemplate new activities but also when continuing with activities begun in the past. This need to reconcile economic development with protection of the environment is aptly expressed in the concept of sustainable development.

The ideal would be a global legal framework that restricted development to that which is sustainable backed by a global means of enforcement. However, while this should continue to be a long-term ambition, because of the difficulty in achieving it, we must also consider building upon the more modest foundations, which already exist. Indeed, for the time being a more modest approach has a considerable amount to commend it. This is because it should enable developments to take place within the different States and jurisdictions, which are suited to their respective state of development and the problems that they face. We need to achieve progress on as many fronts as possible. If that progress has to be at differing speeds this should be accepted as long as progress in achieving greater control of environmentally damaging development continues.

As is now generally recognised we must concentrate on restricting development to that which is environmentally sustainable. A balance needs to be struck and if the other arms of government do not accept their responsibility for doing this the judiciary despite being the weakest arm of government can be forced to take action. Of course what is possible in one jurisdiction is not possible in another.

There have been extremely fruitful meetings between the English judiciary and the Indian judiciary during which we have had described to us the proactive action taken by the Indian Supreme Court to protect the environment that I freely acknowledge could not be taken by English courts. The Supreme Court of India has shown what can be done in the absence of 'black letter weapons' in the judicial armoury. The right to life under the constitution has been interpreted as giving each individual a right to a healthy and pollution-free environment. The Court has abandoned strict principles of 'standing' and recognised the rights of citizens generally to raise issues of public importance. This made possible 'public interest litigation' an important tool in promoting environmental protection.

The Supreme Court of India has been willing to devise new remedies, for example putting in place expert committees to supervise environmental measures and monitor performance. In the *Vellore Citizens' Welfare* case, it was held that principles of 'sustainable development', including 'the precautionary principle' and the 'polluter pays' principle, were part of

Indian law. In response to a petition complaining of pollution of the water supply to the claimants' area by untreated effluent from tanneries, the Court ordered the government to set up an authority and to confer on it the powers necessary to remedy the situation; it also established arrangments to enable families who had suffered to be compensated by the polluters.

Again the Indian Supreme Court have restricted pollution levels in Agra to protect the Taj Mahal. Even more strikingly, basing themselves upon the protection of the right to life, the Court has outlawed the use of petrol in public service vehicles in Delhi thus significantly improving the atmosphere in the most creative way. Even if such action would be a step too far in most jurisdictions the example the Court has provided should deter an inclination for judiciaries to be excessively reticent.

If there is to be progress, whether at the national, regional or international level, then an important part of the structure within that which is going to take place is provided by international treaties. Here the United Nations has played a constructive role. This started with the United Nations conference on the Human Environment in Stockholm in June 1972. It followed concern about 'the continuing and accelerating impairment of the quality of the human environment'. It resulted in the Declaration of Principles for the preservation and enhancement of the human environment which were intended to provide 'a common outlook and . . . common principles to inspire and guide the peoples of the world and the preservation and enhancement of the human environment'. It was an important benchmark which required States to cooperate in developing international environmental law. It set the scene for legal and institutional development. Even more important was the UN Conference on Environment and Development which took place in Rio, Brazil. The Rio Declaration was an important benchmark in the development of international environmental law. The principles, which were set out, have been adopted with regularity by both national and international courts. The Rio Declaration, whilst recognising that it was necessary to differentiate between responsibilities that States have, again underlined the importance of political, economic and specifically legal cooperation between States. Principle 11 committed all States to 'enact effective environmental legislation'.

The road from Rio led to Johannesburg. For my purposes it was the Global Judges' Symposium on Sustainable Development and the Role of Law that took place on the eve of the World Summit on Sustainable Development that was of the greatest significance. Some 120 judges from around 60 countries attended. At the end of the meeting the judges adopted the 'Johannesburg principles on the role of law and sustainable development'. The Johannesburg principles affirmed that:

> ...an independent judiciary and judicial process is vital for the implementation, development and enforcement of environmental law and that members of the judiciary, as well as those contributing to the judicial process at the national, regional and global levels, are crucial partners for promoting compliance with and the implementation and enforcement of international and national environmental law.

The Johannesburg Principles also called for a programme of work. This included:

> ... the improvement of the capacity of those involved in the process of promoting, implementing, developing and enforcing environmental law, such as judges, prosecutors and legislators and others to carry out their functions on a well-informed basis equipped with the necessary skills, information and material.

I believe it is that exhortation that has been the catalyst for the convening of this great regional meeting of the Chief Justices of the Arab countries. Will you be able to respond to the challenge set at Johannesburg? I hope so. The question that we have to ask ourselves is how do we as judges go about translating the Johannesburg principles into practical, workable measures that can be used effectively at the regional level?

What are Possible Mechanics for Implementing Aims Set Out in the Johannesburg Principles?

Cooperation between States

Cooperation between States and the sharing of knowledge can play a key role. The cooperation can take place at various levels. I was pleased to learn of the cooperation that is taking place between my country and Egypt under the SEAM or the Support for Environmental Assessment and Management Programme. It is an example of what can be achieved at a relatively modest cost, at £6.2m over the years 2000–05. It supports the development of environmental action plans; it provides assistance in managing municipal waste; it provides environmental projects to help the poor and cleaner production. It accompanies the other admirable initiatives that the Egyptian authorities are taking for example because of the close links between tourism, conservation by establishing protected areas, and establishing codes of conduct in sensitive areas.

The cooperation of States is also enhanced by their becoming parties to treaties and conventions, such as those to which I have referred.

An administrative and legal framework that acknowledges and promotes the importance of protecting the environment

What can be done will depend on the resources available to the individual State. However, good practice can provide its own dividends, as has been demonstrated by those countries including Egypt that are developing ecotourism.

National courts have an important role to play in the development of the law and its application within a given jurisdiction[6]

For example, where international environmental law has not been implemented adequately through national legislation or administrative law making, the courts can play a key role whether by applying international law: (i) directly, as the rule of the decision; or (ii) indirectly, as a means of interpreting national law.[7]

The Indian Supreme Court has set an excellent example but it is not alone. Examples of judicial ingenuity are also found in the decisions of other Supreme Courts around the globe. In the *Eppawlea* case from Sri Lanka, a government proposal to lease a phosphate mine to a US company for 30 years conflicted with principles of sustainable development and had not been subject to adequate environmental assessment. The Sri Lankan Supreme Court emphasised the importance of public access to environmental information, and drew on the policies of the European Commission and the Rio Declaration to provide back-up to the fundamental rights guaranteed by the constitution.

In *The Oposa*, the Supreme Court of the Philippines confirmed the right of a group of Philippino children to bring an action on their behalf and on behalf of future generations complaining of excessive timber felling operations permitted by the Department of Environment. Their right to do so

---

[6] See S D Murphey, 'Conference on International Environmental Dispute Resolutions: does the world need a new international environmental court?' 32 GW J Int'l L & Econ 333.

[7] See M Anderson and P Galizzi (eds), *International Environmental Law in National Courts* (BIICL, 2002), 9.

was based on the right to a 'balanced and healthy ecology' incorporated in the 1987 constitution of the Philippines.

A ready exchange of information between the judiciaries of different countries as to the best method of resolving environmental disputes

As an example, in Europe a working party has been set up to establish a new European Union Forum of Judges for the Environment. Its inaugural meeting recently took place in Luxembourg. It will be open to judges from all the States within the expanded European Union and EFTA. Its purpose: exchange of information on issues of environmental law arising under the EU Treaty or decisions of the European Court of Justice. It is hoped that information exchange will improve judicial responses to environmental issues in each individual member state.[8]

Among Commonwealth countries there have also been recent initiatives aimed at information sharing and the expansion of judicial awareness of environmental issues.[9]

Of great importance has been the work of the UN and, in particular, the United Nations Environment Programme[10] in this field. In Nairobi, in February 2003, there was a session of the governing council of UNEP in which it considered how best the principles outlined in Johannesburg might be implemented. Aside from the convening of country-specific programmes of work for strengthening judicial capacity of which the Cairo conference is one example, it called for the production of a training manual in environmental law. The fundamental beliefs underlying the project were that: (i) the environment is the great challenge; (ii) time is running out; (iii) the principles that should guide our response to the environmental challenge— sustainable development, precautionary principle, public trusteeship—form a shared pool of knowledge that is now recognised in one form or another by most of the legal systems of the world; and (iv) by comparison to governments that can be here today and gone tomorrow, judges are, in relative terms, a stable body.

---

[8] See draft version of 'Judicial Protection of the Environment—at Home and Abroad', paper for Institute of Advanced Legal Studies, given by R Carnwath (27 April 2004), 3.
[9] Ibid.
[10] Hereafter, 'UNEP'.

International bodies to enforce international environmental law

The International Court of Justice is fully capable of hearing cases involving international environmental disputes.[11] However, in recent years the limited success of enforcing rules of international environmental law against deviant States has led to calls for the creation of a global international environmental court or tribunal capable of issuing binding and enforceable decisions against such States. No such tribunal has, as yet, been set up and there are no signs that one is imminent. However, in the EU where, in general, there are relatively developed codes of environmental practice and systems for monitoring their compliance, the European Court of Justice can enforce compliance with European enviromental directives. Here too, however, exchange of information plays a key role. There is also increasing emphasis on access to justice and public access to environmental information, both the subject of the Aarhus Convention of 1998. Article 9 of the Convention requires member States to ensure that members of the public with sufficient interest have access to a court or other independent tribunal to challenge the substantive or procedural legality of any decision. Any such procedures must, in basic terms, be swift, effective and economic.

A *Handbook on Access to Justice under the Aarhus Convention* has also been published. The stated purpose of the Handbook is 'to look at possibilities in the field of applying the access to justice principles of the Aarhus Convention, as expressed through real cases drawn from the UNECE region'.[12] The Handbook acknowleges that, whereas environmental cases were virtually unheard of a generation ago, EU courts and tribunals, encompassing a number of different legal traditions, are now increasingly hearing environmental cases. The Handbook provides a number of case studies that cover a wide range of problems relating to access to justice and equally provide a useful guide as to how justice may best be administered. The Handbook has proved a useful tool for the judiciary across Europe and its

---

[11] In 1997 the ICJ issued its most important decision concerning international environmental law in the *Gabčíkovo-Nagymaros* (Hungary/Slovakia) case. In that case, Hungary tried to convince the ICJ that a legal obligation, contained in a 1977 treaty, to cooperate with Czechoslovakia in the building of certain dams along the Danube River could be set aside once Hungary realised that the project would have adverse environmental effects. The ICJ found, inter alia, that 'newly developed norms of environmental law are relevant for the implementation of [the 1977 Treaty]' and the parties could, by agreement, incorporate them into a joint contractual plan pursuant to the treaty.

[12] S Stec (ed), *Handbook on Access to Justice under the Aarhus Convention* (Hungary, March 2003), 17.

example bodes well for the utility and success of the UNEP training manual in environmental law.

Where there is no regional court that is satisfactorily enforcing environmental law it could be sensible to consider having a specialised environmental court or tribunal. Here the basic question is: what makes environmental law so special that a separate environmental court or tribunal might be of benefit? Environmental law is a 'specialist' area of law but it is difficult to say exactly what it is. Not least because each judge present no doubt has his own views on this subject that differ from all the others.[13]

That said, although the concept of 'environmental law' may be without clear boundaries and even though its definition may be problematic, I suspect we would all recognise an environmental case when we see it. In addition they tend to have similar characteristics: (i) their technical complexity, particularly in relation to scientific issues which would respond to a multi-disciplinary approach; (ii) they can raise difficult policy issues; (iii) they may involve both the criminal and civil law; and (iv) public and private interests may be involved.[14] It is the combination of these features that is significant[15] and explains why an environmental or 'green' court with broad powers to secure the protection of the environment has attractions.

What Should be the Features of an Environmental Court?

An environmental court could have the following features:[16]

(1) a wide jurisdiction: a specialist, but widely defined, jurisdiction relating to the environment;

(2) an integrated role: environmental dispute resolution often involves a number of agencies due to functional distinctions, which are now no longer relevant or logical. Hence, jurisdiction should go beyond any single environmental sector and between types of suit, e.g. public law; civil action; enforcement; criminal prosecution;

---

[13] See 'The environment and international law: defining terms' in P Sands, *Principles of International Environmental Law* (2nd edn, CUP, 2003), 15.

[14] See further 'Towards an Environmental Court', note to H Woolf from R Carnwath.

[15] In certain jurisdictions besides New South Wales, for example, New Zealand, Denmark, Ireland and Sweden, there are already environmental courts of some description, albeit based on different models.

[16] Adapted from 'Environmental court project: final report' (DETR, 2000), section 1.

(3) independence and procedural effectiveness: the court should be independent of government and politically unbiased; hearings should be open to the public; there should be clear, practical and effective procedural rules; and the court should have the power to make binding awards;

(4) specialist judges: members should be specialists in environmental issues, from different disciplines and need not necessarily be lawyers;

(5) high level of access by the public: a lack of private rights in the environment makes this necessary. Environmental protection is about broader social values, and providing broad rights of access to a specialised court to protect those values is needed;

(6) informality: it should have procedures that enable those who lack funding and expertise to participate effectively. A largely inquisitorial process could be most effective; and

(7) costs: a 'one-stop' environmental court could keep costs down.

Conclusion

Let me end this talk as I begun by thanking my hosts again for allowing me to address you. It has given me the opportunity of identifying the dramatic scale of the changes in environmental law that have taken place since I gave that lecture in 1991. In the intervening years the threat to the environment has increased but so has our ability to meet the challenges. Most important of all is the fact that from my prospective the judiciary is far better qualified to meet the challenges with which they are faced today than they were a decade ago. If the judiciary of the world continue to work in ever-closer collaboration we can meet the future with confidence.

PART V

International Legal Systems

24

The International Role of the Judiciary

Abstract This paper considers the transformation of the role of the English judiciary in recent times and its significance internationally. It explains that it is necessary to improve the observance of the rule of law throughout the world, and supports judging that involves comparative analysis between different jurisdictions, particularly in the field of human rights. It concludes by emphasising the importance of international cooperation between the judiciaries of different countries, and suggests that each country can do more to help other countries by providing appropriate training.

I am delighted to be in Melbourne attending another great Commonwealth Law Conference. Commonwealth Law Conferences are hugely enjoyable occasions and that is certainly true of this event. The hospitality, even by Australian and Victorian standards, is exceptional. If I may, I will single out for praise just one member of the organising committee. I do so, because he has taken on a special role in relation to judicial contributions. I refer of course to Justice Bernard Teague. From my personal knowledge, I am able to pay justifiable tribute to Bernard for his indefatigable work to make the conference a success.

However, as I fear you are about to learn over the next 35 minutes, not everything that happens at Law Conferences is enjoyable. We attend because we find that what we learn assists us to perform our role in our own countries more effectively whether the role is that of a judge, a lawyer or an academic.

For the judiciary, certainly for the English judiciary, that role has been transformed during my judicial lifetime, which has just entered its 25th year. Until the 1970s, the role had hardly changed in over a century. A judge's

---

* This lecture was originally delivered at the 13th Commonwealth Law Conference in conjunction with the 33rd Australian Legal Convention, Melbourne, Australia, on 16 April 2003.

concern was to decide cases, but little more than that. The general attitude to reform was encapsulated in the oft-quoted remark by a judge of the previous century: 'reform, reform, do not talk to me of reform; things are bad enough already'. Trials were conducted almost exclusively orally and were extremely adversarial. Rumpole was not entirely a figment of a barrister author's vivid imagination. Such advocates could be readily identified at the Bar. One of my favourites at the time was Sam Stamler QC—not so much a Rumpole of the Bailey, but a Rumpole of the Strand. Today oral advocacy has a lesser role and written advocacy has become far more significant. However, the changes in the judicial role upon which I want to focus today are much more significant.

Just as the common law has been evolving with increasing rapidity, so has the role of the common law judge. The judge's responsibility for delivering justice is no longer largely confined to presiding over a trial and acting as arbiter between the conflicting positions of the claimant and the defendant or the prosecution and the defence. The role of the judiciary, individually and collectively, is to be proactive in the delivery of justice; to take on new responsibilities, so as to contribute to the quality of justice.

At the forefront of these new responsibilities is achieving access to justice for those within the judge's jurisdiction. But it is not on a judge's many new domestic responsibilities that I want to concentrate today. Rather, it is the international dimension of the judiciary's new responsibilities that I wish to stress. Chief Justice Murray Gleeson made reference to these new responsibilities in his admirable article, 'Global influences on the Australian judiciary', in the *Australian Bar Review*, when he said:

> In an open society, a nation's legal system, and its judiciary, will always be exposed to international influences. Even when unrecognised, or unacknowledged, they will be reflected in the substantive and adjectival law applied by judges, in the structure and status of the judiciary, and its relationship with the other branches of government.[1]

The judiciary to which I am referring here are not the judiciary of the growing number of international and supernational courts and tribunals that are being established in different parts of the world. This is not because I do not support the contribution those courts and tribunals are making towards upholding the rule of law, on the contrary, I recognise their contribution is critical. These courts—for example, the long-established International Court

---

[1] (2002) 22 Aust Bar Rev 1.

at the Hague, the European Courts of Justice and of Human Rights, the new International Criminal Court, and the Special Court for Sierra Leone— deserve our strongest support. We should provide that support by ensuring that international courts are properly resourced and are supplied with judges to serve upon them of the highest calibre from amongst the legal communities of our respective jurisdictions and, wherever practical, from amongst our own judiciaries.

But today, rather than members of international courts and tribunals, I am referring to the judiciary who day by day in each of our jurisdictions are responsible for providing justice to members of the public. It is my contention that all judges in every jurisdiction are, by the way they undertake their responsibilities, contributing to the quality of justice internationally.

Today no country is cocooned from its neighbours. Human beings do not live in hermetically-sealed containers. While we remain citizens of our individual nations, what happens in any part of the globe can affect us all. We not only have a global economy, we are part of a global society. As SARS[2] has dramatically demonstrated, the health of any nation can be at risk if an infection afflicts any other nation. The same can be true of justice and the observance of the rule of law. The process may be slower, the rate of contagion not so high, but the spread of infection from one legal system to another is likely to be unstoppable unless a cure for the disease is found.

Terrorism and crime are no respecters of national borders. It is where the rule of law has broken down that terrorism takes root. Crime thrives where law enforcement is weakest. It is no accident that the citizens of countries which observe the rule of law do not have to seek asylum.

A theme which has justifiably reverberated through the halls of this building since the conference started on Monday is that the observance of the rule of law is critical to progress in both the underdeveloped and developed worlds. Cherie Booth expressed admirably my own sentiments when she said that the rule of law, based as it is on human rights values, is the key which can unlock greater economic and ethical wealth. The problems confronting the different nations in the Commonwealth are far from identical. However, Cherie Booth was making the point that, if real progress is to be achieved, it is necessary to improve the observance of the rule of law in every part of the Commonwealth and, indeed, of the globe.

---

[2] Severe Acute Respiratory Syndrome. This illness became an uncontrollable pandemic around the world from February 2003, when it struck its first known victim, Johnny Cheng, in Hanoi, Vietnam.

In February 2003 I attended the All Africa Conference on Law, Justice and Development in Abuja, Nigeria. Kofi Annan, Secretary General of the United Nations at the time and James Wolfensohn, then President of the World Bank, were both due to attend. Not surprisingly, in view of what was happening in other areas of the world, they were not able to do so, but papers were delivered on their behalf. Both recognised the importance of establishing effective justice systems in the developing world. I was particularly impressed by the comments of James Wolfensohn. Amongst the things he said were:

> [What] we know is absolutely critical—absolutely critical—in that there should exist a legal and judicial system which functions equitably, transparently and honestly. If these forms of legal and judicial systems do not exist in Africa, there is no way that you can have equitable development.

And:

> Africa needs strong, well-established rule of law regimes to enable it to trade itself into prosperity and out of poverty.

Kofi Annan expressed very much the same views.

Many of the countries to which reference was being made at the All Africa Conference were Commonwealth countries. The state of the legal systems within those countries should be, and I believe is, very much a matter of concern to the more prosperous and better developed members of the Commonwealth. But it is not only out of self-interest that we feel outraged when we see the system of justice being traduced within another member of the Commonwealth. We know that the citizens of that country should, like our own, be protected by a system of justice that shares the values of our own. While in some Commonwealth jurisdictions, such as South Africa, the common law has a less dominant role, what should not differ from one country to another is the adherence to the rule of law.

I hope it is clear from my earlier comments, that I believe that the way in which the rule of law is administered by a judge in one jurisdiction either contributes to, or detracts from, the observance of the rule of law generally. Without taking away from the importance of this central thesis, I wish to turn now to the more direct contribution that is made by the judiciary of each of our jurisdictions. I will also mention the legal professions within our jurisdictions, whose contribution is equally important.

Perhaps the most obvious example of the type of contribution to which I am referring is that which the judiciary make to their own jurisprudence by referring to the jurisprudence of other jurisdictions when they give judgment. This is particularly true in the field of human rights because those rights represent international norms. One of the reasons why I am personally enthusiastic about the European Convention of Human Rights being made part of our domestic law via the Human Rights Act 1998 is that it has enabled the judges in my jurisdiction to play a part which in the ordinary course of their duties trying domestic cases had hitherto been unavailable; namely contributing by their decisions to the evolving international jurisprudence of human rights. In the past, British judges could do this in the Privy Council, but that provided limited opportunities. Now they can join the great majority of judges in other jurisdictions in making a direct contribution.

As a member of the Privy Council, I had a limited exposure to the jurisprudence of other members, but nothing like that which I had later. The new exposure of our judiciary is of particular importance since, until the European Convention became part of our domestic law, there was no common law jurisdiction which directly gave effect to the Convention in its courts. The Republic of Ireland had its Bill of Rights, of course, and has done an admirable job in keeping the common law flag flying in Europe though its contribution, as will be appreciated, has been that of a close relative of the Commonwealth rather than that of an actual member of the family.

Another example is provided by the Commonwealth Conference. The great majority of those attending are domestic practitioners or, like myself, domestic judges. However, by our discussions we are learning how to achieve higher standards of justice in our own jurisdictions.

On the Sunday prior to the conference, we had a meeting of Chief Justices of common law jurisdictions. One of my colleagues expressed surprise that I was able to be here after having already spent a week at a conference in Sydney. I answered that I would not have considered myself to have been doing my duty if I had not been able to make arrangements to be here, an opinion about which, I fear, you may already have reservations. Personalities aside, I am quite satisfied that attending conferences of this nature is part of the essential preparation of the judiciary for their duties. I say this in relation to what they can contribute and receive. Contribute not only in the business of the meetings, but also during the social events because of the ideas which informal exchanges of views can generate. The international contacts that are made can provide reference points for consultation and guidance for future development.

Another opportunity for exchanging views, the benefits of which I can vouch for personally, are the exchanges which take place now with increasing frequency between the judiciary of two or more jurisdictions. I know, for example, that my decisions have been influenced by the exchanges I have had with my Indian colleagues. Initially, I was astounded by the proactive approach of the Indian Supreme Court, but I soon realised that, if that Court was to perform its essential role in Indian society, it had no option but to adopt the course it did and I congratulate it for the courage it has shown.

I believe we have a responsibility to learn from each other not only in regard to substantive law, but also in relation to practice and procedure. When considering procedural reforms of our legal systems it would be a foolish reporter who did not look at the experience overseas. I certainly did so for my report on Access to Justice and, as you would expect, I received most generous assistance wherever I turned—in particular, from the different jurisdictions in Australia.

Another benefit that can result from judicial exchanges is an improvement in international judicial cooperation. Sometimes this can be achieved by establishing international conventions. Such an approach is ideal if everyone is willing to participate and agree. Then, the judiciary's role can be limited to merely providing advice on what would be the most appropriate form for the convention to take. However, there can be a particular reason for a country not being prepared to join a convention, even though there is a real need for practical cooperation between two jurisdictions.

When this happens we have found that the judiciary can themselves, through direct contact, achieve what may be necessary. In the UK we now have a substantial Pakistani community. In the past there have been difficulties because of the lack of a convention to which Pakistan is a party to regulate the position where a marriage breaks up and a parent takes a child back to Pakistan, or vice versa. Until recently, there was no simple process of obtaining the return of the child. The court procedures could be slow and ineffective. Fortunately, a solution was found. The President of our Family Division[3] made a visit to Pakistan and a delegation of Pakistani judges made a return trip to England. Out of this exchange, a protocol was established between the two judiciaries on their own initiative. The Protocol provided that, in the absence of special reasons, a child would be returned to its former country of residence so that issues as to care could be dealt with by the courts of that country. To ensure the smooth operation of the protocol, each country has identified

---

[3] When this lecture was given, the President of the Family Division was Dame Elizabeth Butler-Sloss; the post is now held by Sir Mark Potter.

a senior judge and has agreed that these two individuals will liaise if any difficulties arise. My informant tells me that the protocol is working well with considerable benefit to the children involved. It is intended to replicate the model with other countries that are not parties to the Hague Convention.

Another example is provided by the arrangement which exists between France and the UK to achieve better judicial cooperation in relation both to criminal and civil matters. Each country now sends a liaison judge to the other country so as to facilitate cooperation between the two legal systems. This has made a significant contribution to an improved understanding between two jurisdictions, one of which is of civil and the other common law. We have realised that not only do we have to learn from other common law systems, but also from the civil systems as well.

I regard it as important that, where we can, we should harmonise our legal systems, again not only with other common law jurisdictions, but also with civil jurisdictions. In this regard it is without doubt true that the European Union and the European Convention are acting as catalysts. This is not, as is sometimes suggested, to the disadvantage of the links with Commonwealth and common law jurisdictions. In fact, it enables us to bring added value to our interchanges—a continental flavour. Our civil procedure is now much closer to the French. As I like to describe it, it is situated somewhere in the middle of the English Channel, au milieu de la manche.

I turn now to what is perhaps the most important part of a judge's international responsibilities—making a contribution to other systems. The position, as I see it, is briefly as follows. If I am right that the legal systems of different jurisdictions are dependent upon each other, then the judiciary are not only responsible for promoting the quality of justice in their own jurisdiction, they are equally, so far as practical, responsible for making a contribution to the jurisprudence of other jurisdictions.

Individual judges and lawyers have in the past and, I hope, will continue in the future to make significant contributions to other jurisdictions, particularly with a view to enhancing the observance of human rights. In this regard, I am especially proud of the work done by the English Bar and solicitors to obtain justice for those on death row in the United States. I know that the Australian and New Zealand judiciary go and sit in the small jurisdictions in the Pacific area which do not have the resources to provide the quality of judges that they themselves would wish from amongst their own citizens. The UK is, I believe, the only jurisdiction providing judges prior to retirement to the Court in Hong Kong, although Australia and New Zealand provide very distinguished retired members of the judiciary. The Special Court of Sierra Leone has amongst its judges a number of members who were judges of African States. These examples should be precedents for other smaller jurisdictions to follow. It is an approach which enables them to demonstrate that their judiciary has the necessary quality and independence, but which is not inconsistent with national pride—a real disadvantage of appeals to the Privy Council.

In addition, I am sure we could do more to help each other by providing training. The training of judges needs to be in the control of judges from the country concerned, but judges from other jurisdictions can provide assistance when required. I know a great deal of valuable assistance is being provided already by and to different jurisdictions. I was particularly impressed by the contribution being made by Australia's Federal Court to the Indonesian judiciary and was extremely grateful to Chief Justice Michael Black for allowing me to witness the 'graduation ceremony' for the members of the Indonesian judiciary who most recently completed a training course in Australia. For the new democracies of Eastern Europe, where the judicial and legal systems are still recovering from the cold war days, there are already many similar programmes in place.

Before coming to Melbourne I attended the 5th Worldwide Judicial Conference in Sydney. At that conference, the Hon Clifford Wallace, who has worked as hard as Justice Kirby to improve the standards of justice throughout the world, made a suggestion that I would warmly endorse. He suggested that each developed jurisdiction should pair up with one of the jurisdictions of the emerging democracies to mentor that jurisdiction as long as this was required. I believe he had very much in mind the precedent of the relationship between Indonesia and the Federal Court of Australia to which I have already referred. He would welcome volunteers.

It should not be thought that the benefits of such programmes are all one way or that it is only small countries that have need of assistance. I have had the good fortune relatively recently to visit three large jurisdictions— much larger than my own—at particularly opportune times. In each case, I have witnessed the start of a process of change prompted by those countries realising that adherence to the rule of law is of critical importance to their future development.

The first country was South Africa, which I visited in 1994 soon after Nelson Mandela had been released. I went to Bloemfontein with three colleagues for a conference on human rights at the South African Court of Appeal presided over by their Chief Justice. The conference was between the judges of South Africa and the judges of other African jurisdictions. We met for the first time in the library of the Court—the visiting judges, most of whom were black, in their lounge suits and the white judges of South Africa in their black robes. Initially the two groups stood apart, but then merged and started to talk avidly. From that meeting, I believe, grew the tree which now flowers as one of the great Commonwealth Courts, the Constitutional Court of South Africa.

The second country was China. I made two visits about 15 years apart. The change was dramatic, brought about, I believe, by exposure to foreign legal systems. On the first visit, although the Vice President, who was head of the Supreme Court, was interested in the Western legal systems, he had no conception of how a legal system could operate. On the second visit in 2001, there was a hunger for advice so as to develop a system of justice which would support China's growing trade.

The final country was Russia. The World Bank held a conference there last year on reforms of legal systems. As a result of the visit, I was convinced that Russia was committed to adherence to the rule of law. The conference was due to be opened by President Putin. In the event, he could not attend. I was one of a privileged few flown in his private jet to meet him in Moscow at the Kremlin. I was astonished to find that this was not a private meeting, but was to be broadcast on Russian television. I had been told that the President would welcome a question on human rights and the question I posed on capital punishment certainly received a positive response.

But to return closer to my chosen subject. A case in the UK which I believe demonstrated a defining realisation of the importance of the interactive responsibilities of our judiciary was the General Pinochet litigation. Passing over the reasons for there having to be two hearings of the appeal, I believe the result of the case sent a strong message as to how different jurisdictions, Spain and the UK, could require even one of the most powerful citizens of another State to return home to be held to account for his possible guilt of crimes against humanity.

My Scottish colleagues have recognised the need to be innovative in order to overcome geographical hurdles to achieve justice. I refer to their response to the Lockerbie terrorist incident. The decision to sit in a Scottish enclave in Holland was a remarkably imaginative way of enabling justice to be achieved for the relatives of the victims on the flight which happened to be passing over Scotland at the time the bomb exploded.

It is the fact that challenges posed by novel situations of this nature can be overcome that makes the judicial role today so rewarding. They are achievements for the jurisdictions involved, but more importantly they contribute to the accumulated experience across all jurisdictions. If it has been done once, it can be done again. These contributions result in the reach of the rule of law extending more rapidly today than ever before.

We must not, however, be complacent. In recent years, there have been deeply worrying threats to the independence of the judiciary in some jurisdictions. Commendably, in a few other jurisdictions, and particularly in South Africa, the senior judiciary have publicly joined the protest of the UN rapporteur, politicians and the media. Others have, in private, provided support. However, it could be helpful if, in these situations, the collective voice of, say, the Chief Justices of the Commonwealth could be heard. But how could this be done? There is no organisation of Chief Justices in existence at present to take on this responsibility.

After much thought, I have come to the conclusion that it is doubtful whether such an organisation is practical or even possible. The need is intermittent, but when it arises it is urgent. There is a regular turnover in those who hold the office of Chief Justice. It is most unlikely any general mandate could be given without a meeting of those in office at the relevant time. Opinions could differ as the nature of the problems differ. Certainly the desirability of finding an answer requires this issue to be on the agenda.

What I have said emphasises the importance of, not only lawyers, but judges as well coming together at such conferences, the event last week in Sydney and the Chief Justice's meeting on Sunday, to discuss issues such as this. As Chief Justice Murray Gleeson also said in the article to which I referred earlier: 'Engagement between Australian judges and their overseas counterparts, whether of a civil law or common law background, is essential.'[4] I entirely agree and would adopt the same words in relation to the British judiciary. And I suspect the other Chief Justices present would do the same in relation to their judiciary. This is an important reason, among the many reasons, why I am so grateful to the organisers of this conference and my Australian colleagues for this opportunity to become more 'engaged' during my visit to Australia.

---

[4] See n 1 above.

25

The Rule of Law and the Development of a Modern Economy in China

Abstract This paper focuses on the importance and requirements of the rule of law in relation to China's developing legal system and emerging modern economy. It explains that the Chinese economy requires effective and economic methods to resolve the disputes that are the inevitable consequence of commercial activities. It discusses the use of mediation and alternative dispute resolution throughout China's history and promotes its continued use under the Uniform Contract Law, arguing that it can make more commercial sense to decide cases out of court, saving time, cost and being less stressful than adversarial proceedings. It concludes that a developed state which is properly administered should be able to comply with the rule of law to support an effective market economy that efficiently serves those engaged in commercial activities both within the state and internationally.

I am deeply honoured to have been invited to give this lecture in the Great Hall of the People. I am delighted that it is possible for this to happen during my visit to China to attend the 22nd Congress of the Law of the World at the invitation of the President and Chief Justice of the Supreme People's Court of the People's Republic of China, H E Mr Xiao Yang.

The fact that this congress is taking place in Beijing at the present time emphasises the importance that the People's Republic of China, wisely, now attaches to the exchange of views between lawyers and jurists from different countries with different governmental and legal systems.

We are here today because a group of Chinese and British individuals, over 50 years ago, had the foresight to establish a body which aptly describes

---

* Lecture originally delivered in the Great Hall of the People, Beijing, China, on 7 September 2005.

itself as the 'Icebreakers'. The 'Icebreakers' had a vision. The vision was that the People's Republic of China would re-establish itself as a leader among the nations of the world. The 'Icebreakers' believed that by working together they could, in a modest manner, contribute to China achieving its rightful position as a global power. I understand that your premier, Mr Wen Jiabo, recently revalidated the Icebreaker mission, indicating that there are reasons why there is a greater need for icebreaking to take place between the West and China in the present era.

I would strongly endorse this view. One of the key areas where the icebreaking mission exists is in relation to the rule of law. I would like to thank Chairman Mr Jiang Enzhu, who has been a pioneering Icebreaker for many years, for providing me with the opportunity to give this lecture. My gratitude is also due to the 48 Group Club, whose members are British Icebreakers, for supporting my visit and this lecture. They no doubt thought it was appropriate that I should give this lecture because I am about to become the Chairman of the Council of University College London. University College also has a vision as to its role. The vision is that it should be a global university.

This is the third time that I have had the privilege of visiting your country. Each of my prior visits has been for a limited period. I therefore recognise that I only have the most limited knowledge of this vast country. However, the developments that have taken place over the period spanning my visits are truly remarkable.

On my first visit in 1986 I had the good fortune to be entertained by the Vice President of the Supreme People's Court. He wore military uniform and was not a lawyer. Although we had the most useful discussion, it was apparent that our approach to the role of courts was very different. When I came back in 2001, I found the situation was very different. Huge progress had already been made in developing an independent and properly func-tioning legal system. I had, on that occasion, the opportunity to talk to those engaged in drafting this country's new legislation. I also had the opportunity of meeting Chinese academic lawyers and jurists. Already on the present visit, I have been able to observe something of the great progress that has been made over the intervening four years.

If over the same period of nearly 20 years a visitor from China had made a visit to my country, he would not have noted anything remotely like the same scale of change. London, to the visitor, would look very much the same today as it did 20 years ago. There are some new buildings, but nothing like the extent of the development that has taken place in Beijing and Shanghai.

However, although the ordinary tourist would not be aware of this, changes have been taking place in our society over the last 20 years which are significant, although nothing like as significant as those that have occurred here. Included in those are changes relating to the responsibilities of our judiciary, in particular its responsibilities as to upholding the rule of law. In my lecture, I am therefore going to draw attention to these changes in the hope that our experience may be of value to you as you confront the challenge of adapting to a new situation characterised by:

(a) the development of a socialist market economy;
(b) all round social progress; and
(c) China's accession to the WTO,

so that by the year 2010, China will have a fully related socialist system of laws with Chinese characteristics.

I will make my remarks with a considerable degree of diffidence because I appreciate the scale of the differences that exist between the challenges which you confront and those that have been confronted by my country. Not least among those is the relative size of our countries which is reflected in the fact that the population of the UK is completely dwarfed by that of China, which is nearly twice as large as that of the whole population of Europe. In addition, I am only too aware that although the subject of my lecture is limited to the role of the rule of law in the development of a modern economy, the role of the rule of law can never properly be assessed in watertight compartments. This is because its role is all embracing. It affects every part of society. This is a quality it shares with the economy itself. It is unusual if one sector of a country's economy is successful and other sectors do not prosper as well. So if the economy of a country benefits from its observance of the rule of law other aspects of its society will do so as well. The obverse position is equally true. This makes the subject of my talk one with wide implications.

I am also conscious that there are differences in the ages of our legal system. I believe your first law code was the Fajing (cannon laws) of approximately 400 BC. England cannot claim that it had anything like such a code until 1,400 years later when a king known as King Alfred the Great promulgated his code in the 880s AD. Furthermore, it was not until about the 12th century that England had anything resembling a fully integrated legal system.

Yet, in England, like China, we are proud of our legal history and traditions. In particular, we are proud of our role in developing the common law, which has subsequently spread around the globe so that it today forms the foundation of the legal systems of about a third of the nations of the globe, including countries as large and as powerful as India and the United States.

An explanation of this development is the ability of the common law to change incrementally so that, notwithstanding the differences between the countries in which it had been adopted, it has been able to evolve and grow to serve the different requirements of many different nations. A feature of each of those countries is that, although their histories and societies may be very different, they all at least report to and adhere to the rule of law, though the extent of their development may affect their ability to do so.

An effect of this shared reliance upon the common law is that shortly after I return to London, I will join representatives of the majority of those countries in another legal conference, the Commonwealth Law Conference, which I hope will be a great celebration of the principles of the common law, and the rule of law.

Though dwarfed by comparison with the challenges that China is in the process of meeting, I believe the changes that have taken place in the English judicial system may be of relevance to China. In part, this is because, in both countries, old entrenched systems are being radically changed to meet modern conditions and, in particular, the difficulties created by the economic developments that are taking place around the globe.

In the UK there is hardly an institution which recently has not been subjected to considerable reform. We have been experimenting with the devolution of power. We have been grappling with the problems created by the increasing scale of a single legal order covering a confederation of European separate States. We have been confronting the consequences of the need to cope with the impact of the international competition on what were our traditional industries—that is a consequence of my country being part of the global economy. Traditional industries that, in the past, formed part of the engine room of the British economy, have disappeared—not least because of the competitive advantages of countries such as China. The problems of our respective jurisdictions may differ in their source and scale, but they are not unconnected.

Where we have been fortunate, is that we have not been subjected to the sort of problems which were created by China's Cultural Revolution. This has meant that our legal system has benefited from continuity since 1215. It has firm foundations which have been a huge advantage when making the changes needed to meet the current demands of society. These changes, as I will explain, have been significant. There has been a transformation of the extent to which public officials can have their decisions reviewed by the courts. Our civil procedure over the last decade has been fundamentally changed and our criminal procedure is now being subject to a similar process.

Among our traditions is a continuous adherence to the rule of law: an adherence which stretches in an uninterrupted line from a compact which was entered into in 1215 by a feudal king, King John, and his feudal barons, until the present day. That compact, which is known as Magna Carta, is revered throughout the common law world. It contains what common law jurisdictions claim is the source of the rule of law today.

The rule of law embraces principles of basic justice that speak for themselves, and I cite here chapters at the heart of Magna Carta, because they contain many of the core features of a society that today adheres to the rule of law. Those chapters are as follows:

20. For a trivial offence, a free man shall be fined only in proportion to the degree of his offence, and for a serious offence correspondingly, but not so heavily as to deprive him of his livelihood.
38. In future no official shall place a man on trial upon his own unsupported statement, without producing credible witness to the truth of it.
39. No free man shall be seized or imprisoned, or stripped of his rights or possessions, or outlawed or exiled, or deprived of his standing in any other way, nor will we proceed with force against him, or send other to do so, except by the lawful judgement of his equals or by the law of the land.
40. To no one will we sell, to no one deny or delay right or justice.
45. We will appoint as justices, constable, sheriffs, or other officials, only men that know the law of the realm and are minded to keep it well.

What is significant about those chapters is that they had nothing whatsoever to do with what could be described at that time as Western democracy. Neither King John nor the barons had any conception of the nature of a democracy and even if they had, they would have been at one in rejecting it. But as democracies developed, including that of the UK, the rule of law ensured that democracy operated effectively. Adherence to the rule of law ensured that, within a democracy, individual rights did not suffer as a result of abuse of power by the majority. However, it does not follow that because the rule of law had, and has, an important role to play in a democracy, it cannot have a role in other forms of government. It is a requirement for any form of developed society and will contribute to the efficiency of any society.

Trade can and will take place with and in a society that does not observe the rule of law, but that society will have to pay a price for not observing the rule of law. The risks inherent in trading with that country will be greater than those involved in trading with a country that does observe the rule of law and because of this, those prepared to trade or invest in a country that does not observe the rule of law will look for greater rewards to compensate them for incurring the greater risk involved in doing this. If they do not obtain at least the prospect of the greater profit to compensate for the additional risk then, in a global economy, when practical, they will trade and invest elsewhere.

While the rule of law can contribute to the great majority of the different aspects of society, it has an obvious and critical role in relation to the proper functioning of the economic well-being of a society. There is nothing novel in this. For some time it has been recognised by the World Bank that the establishment of an appropriate judicial and legal infrastructure has a critical role to play in assisting in the alleviation of poverty in third world countries. The rule of law provides the framework a country needs for the development of its economy. In addition, observance of the rule of law contributes to good governance which is so often absent in undeveloped countries.

On my visit to China in 2001, after I had given a talk, I was asked about the distinction between 'rule by law' and 'the rule of law'. What is meant by 'rule by law' is easier to describe than what is meant by 'the rule of law'. Different commentators would not necessarily agree on what is the distinction between the two concepts, but they would certainly agree that they are not the same.

Most commentators would agree that rule by law involves little more than requiring observance of the law irrespective of what may be the content of the law. At least part of the distinction between the concepts is, therefore, that rule by law lacks the essential basic qualitative requirement which is at the heart of the rule of law. It is this qualitative requirement which is so important when it comes to the contribution that the rule of law can make to a successful society in the contemporary world.

What, then, are the requirements of the rule of law? There is no universally accepted statement of those requirements and their precise nature can differ depending upon the constitutional situation in a specific State. However, it can be safely said that the minimum requirements are:

1. That there should be access to a court to resolve disputes by any individual whose legal interests are adversely affected by a dispute.

2. That the court should be presided over by an independent and unbiased individual (the judge) who is reasonably competent to resolve the dispute.
3. That the court will hear and determine this dispute within a reasonable time and give a reasoned judgment for its decision.
4. That there are reasonably effective methods of enforcing the court's decision, once it has been given.
5. The court's procedures should be fair and reasonable.
6. The law applied by the court should be reasonably certain, readily ascertainable, proportionate and fair.

In relation to mercantile disputes, the requirements are likely to be primarily procedural, though the substantive law must not be confiscatory in nature. Certainly, those engaged in economic activities are most likely to be concerned about the absence of satisfactory procedural arrangements.

Here it is relevant to refer back to the procedural changes to which I referred earlier. One of the most radical changes to our civil law has been the development and introduction of the new Civil Procedure Rules in 1999. These reforms are still referred to by a number of English lawyers as the 'Woolf Reforms' because it was my task to make the report and recommendations that led to them.

The new Civil Procedure Rules are a complete code covering all matters of civil procedure, from pre-action behaviour, through to the conduct of cases that go to trial, to the orders and costs that are awarded post-trial. Before the development of this code our civil procedure rules were fragmented. There was no clear organisation. They were mostly to be found in previous decisions of the courts in a variety of different cases over a long period of time. The previous rules encouraged litigation that was often too costly, in that costs, the expenses incurred by the litigants,[1] often exceeded the value of the claim; too slow in concluding cases; too unequal between the powerful, wealthy litigant and the under resourced litigant; too uncertain in forecasting what litigation will cost and how long it will last; and too incomprehensible to most litigants. Added to these problems the system was too adversarial as cases were run by the parties, not the courts.[2]

---

[1] 'Costs' here refers to the costs of representation (e.g. barristers' and solicitors' fees) incurred by the parties to litigation.

[2] The running of the case involves deciding on the timetable for the exchange of documents, holding of hearings etc within a case. Under the new Civil Procedure Rules, it is now the responsibility of the court to manage the case (for example, by making timetable directions).

The unification and standardisation of a whole myriad of separate rules and procedures into one code based on definite principles is perhaps a similar process of reform to that which China has gone through in relation to contract law. China's Uniform Contract Law, also enacted in 1999, and our Civil Procedure Rules have in common that they are supportive of the rule of law, particularly in the economic field. They contribute to the creation of the framework of law which is so important for the successful encouragement of trade and investment.

Additional support of the rule of law is provided by Mediation and Alternative Dispute Resolution. What the economy requires is effective and economic methods to resolve the disputes that are the inevitable consequence of commercial activities. Often it is more sensible for parties to resolve their differences outside the court. To commercial parties who may wish to trade with each other in the future, the possibility of a future relationship is often jeopardised by acrimonious and costly court proceedings. It is also the case that the parties are often more likely to find a solution that suits both of their interests when they attempt to settle than when they leave it to the potential lottery of litigation. And, of course, settlement can be much quicker, cheaper and less stressful than embarking on adversarial proceedings. Not only can this benefit the parties, but the court's time can be better resourced to deal with those really important cases that genuinely require judicial intervention. However it is essential that if a dispute is resolved the resulting agreement or decision in the arbitration can be effectively enforced. The need for effective methods of enforcement is a subject to which, at least in my jurisdiction, we are inclined to pay too little attention.

I appreciate that there is no need to lecture to you on the benefits of mediation. I am aware that Chinese law has traditionally placed particular emphasis on this way of resolving disputes throughout China's history. I understand that well over 2000 years ago the official administration of the Western Zhou Dynasty included the post of Mediator for the purposes of 'solving disputes among the people and harmonising their relations'. It has been said that Confucius's doctrine of 'benevolence, rites, loyalty and tolerance' (circa 500 BC) provided the moral framework for the mediation of civil disputes. During the Han Dynasty between 206 BC and 220 AD there developed a mediation institution for the resolution of civil disputes consisting of the Three Elders, an elderly and wise farmer, handicraftsman and businessman. After the Revolution in the 1950s China developed a network of Peoples' Mediation Committees that resolved a variety of disputes including contract and property disputes.

Apart from a brief period during the Cultural Revolution, China's embracement of mediation has continued. Article 385 of the Uniform Contract Law includes a clause requiring parties to attempt to resolve their disputes through mediation, then arbitration, and finally only through litigation in the people's courts where an agreement has not been reached. China has also taken steps to enable mediation in international contracts and allowing the parties to a foreign economic contract to choose the law that will apply to disputes. I understand that China has recently implemented measures aimed at resolving disputes in domain name registration on the internet, demonstrating the applicability of mediation to the new technologies.

A developed State which is properly administered should normally be able to comply with the requirements of the rule of law that I have set out, insofar as this is necessary to support an effective market economy that efficiently serves those engaged in commercial activities both within the State and internationally.

So far as the UK is concerned, we start off with considerable advantages, first of all, because of the way our system has been developed both by Parliament and the judiciary over many, many years, and secondly, because of the quality of our judiciary and legal profession.

In England and Wales we are assisted by having a strong and independent legal profession made up of two separate branches—solicitors and barristers. Entry into the professions is highly competitive and those that are admitted will generally have earned their admission by having achieved academic distinction. The standards of education and training within the profession are also rigorous: practising barristers and solicitors cannot rest on their laurels—they must actively maintain their professional education whilst they are working.

The judiciary are, on the whole, appointed from the practising legal profession. The majority of judges were among the most successful in their field within the profession before they became judges. They bring to the judiciary significant, relevant experience. Most importantly, they bring with them a culture of sturdy independence and total incorruptibility.

As far as I am aware there has never been a suggestion that any of the judges for whom I have been responsible have been involved in any way in corruption. No High Court judge has ever had to be removed from office.

This is a remarkable record. It is part of the explanation why so many countries choose to conduct financial transactions in or with the City of London.[3]

London has the necessary legal infrastructure that is required by a financial centre. The legal profession and the judiciary are deeply involved in the provision of legal services not only to those who live and trade in the UK but those from abroad as well. Although it has no separate building, and its facilities are not the most up to date (but hopefully will be improved in the near future), the Commercial Court acts, to a significant extent, as a court for the resolution of commercial disputes that often have limited or no connection with the UK. On average, two-thirds of the disputes which are resolved by the Commercial Court will have one party who is unconnected with the UK. It is a similar story in other specialist jurisdictions, such as within the Technology and Construction Court.

A key reason why individuals and companies choose, not only to conduct their business in the City of London, but to settle their commercial disputes here, is our country's longstanding adherence to the rule of law. People elect to trade in London and have their disputes resolved there because they know that the law that governs their transaction, or which will be applied in their proceedings, will not be charged on a whim or selectively applied; they know that the courts will uphold the law independently; fearlessly and without bias; and they know that any judgment of the court can be enforced. If one is looking for practical, economic illustrations of the value of the rule of law, one need look no further than the City, and courts, of London.

A similar picture is provided by a much smaller jurisdiction from which I returned in August 2005, namely Singapore. Coincidently, I was giving the Singapore Lecture that was given by your Chief Justice in 2003. As a matter of policy Singapore has ploughed huge sums, proportionate to its resources, into providing state of the art legal services. Singapore appreciates that its success as a commercial and trading nation without natural resources other than its location and as a port depend in part on the quality and reputation of its legal services. The same is true at least partially of why Hong Kong attaches such importance to the one nation two

---

[3] For readers unfamiliar with the 'City', it is an historic part of London and represents the financial centre of the UK.

systems principle. Of course, Singapore and Hong Kong are both far smaller than even my country, but even so I believe the importance they attach to the rule of law and the quality of their legal systems demonstrates their view of the commercial benefits that flow from having legal systems that adhere to the rule of law.

26

The Rule of Law and Harmony in China

Abstract This paper provides an account of the 'Icebreakers' visit to China, from which a lecture is included in this book [see Chapter 25]. It discusses the development of China's legal system in recent times and China's genuine ambition to adhere to the rule of law and human rights, vital for a country that seeks to meet its obligations as a member of the World Trade Organisation and achieve its economic ambitions. While China still has some way to go to meet the requirements of the rule of law, it is making progress; there is now an acceptance of the need to produce clear accessible laws to improve enforcement of laws and to train more lawyers and judges. It concludes by emphasising the importance of spreading the standards of the common law to China, drawing upon the role that Hong Kong's legal system has played to China's overall success, and promoting China's relationship with the UK.

It was in 1271 that Marco Polo set out on his travels following in his father's footsteps. Three and a half years later, having travelled 5,600 miles, having crossed the Gobi desert, he arrived at what is now the city of Beijing. Then it was Cambaluc, the site of the winter Palace of Kublai Khan.

On 3 September 2005, I left Heathrow on a similar voyage of exploration but by British airlines. I arrived in Beijing next morning Beijing time. The hardships were a short delay and the food provided by British Airways, because of the Gate Gourmet strike.[1]

Marco Polo fell in love with the capital which was to become Beijing. He marvelled at the palace in particular. He described it as 'the greatest

---

* Lecture originally given in the Middle Temple, London, on 28 September 2005.

[1] A strike by workers at the in-flight caterer Gate Gourmet when the caterer terminated the employment of 670 staff. Eventually, in a deal agreed between union officials at the Transport and General Workers' Union and managers at Gate Gourmet, 144 workers were forced to take compulsory redundancy.

palace that ever was'. He added: 'The rooms are all gilt and painted with figures of man and beasts all executed with such exquisite art that you regard them with delight and astonishment.' This description could be applied, not inappropriately, to the Great Hall of the People where we were entertained, first during the 22nd Congress of Law of the World and second as the guests of the People's Congress. In both capacities we were right royally entertained. We banqueted (the record was 18 courses) off gold plates, using gold-tipped chopsticks (alas no easier to use than their more vulgar cousins).

If the object of the entertainment was to impress, then that objective was undoubtedly achieved. Both at Beijing and then subsequently in Shanghai, like Marco Polo we were dazzled by what we saw. We were also hugely appreciative of the courtesy that was extended to the delegates from over 50 countries. A young mentor judge was attached to each visiting Chief Justice and accompanied him throughout his visit. Vice Presidents of the Supreme Court were at the airport to greet us and to say goodbye both at Beijing and Shanghai.

I tell you this not because I want to encourage tourism to these fine cities. I do so because the exceptional hospitality does say something about our hosts' present attitude towards the law and justice.

The theme of the congress was Law and Harmony. Great emphasis was placed by our Chinese hosts on both, but especially on the importance of the rule of law. We had a most impressive opening address by the President of China in which he stressed the importance to China of not only the rule of law but human rights in a socialist democracy. The Chief Justice of China who played a leading role in the conference made a series of addresses which followed the approach of the President. A similar approach was adopted by representatives of the National People's Congress who I met independently of the conference.

In addition to jointly chairing a session on the reform of the United Nations, I was the Presiding Judge at a mock trial which took place before Chief Justices of seven different jurisdictions.[2]

The issue at the trial arose out of cross-border pollution caused by the use of coal-powered generators. The complainant country was developed and prosperous while the polluter was an underdeveloped country dependent on

---

[2] The Chief Justice of Nigeria, the President of the Supreme Court of Germany, Chief Justice of Philippines, a Chinese judge who was a judge on the Yugoslav International Criminal Court, the Chief Justice of Mozambique and the Chief Justice of Pakistan.

the revenue it could earn from exporting electricity. Two of the advocates were very experienced American trial lawyers and four were Chinese. The Chinese advocates were young and their performance was adequate. There was a huge audience who stayed throughout the trial.[3] They were impressed that I produced a judgment which found in favour of all three parties! My robes were much admired—especially my Chain of Office.

I draw attention to the mock trial because of the size of the audience, their obvious thirst for knowledge and the fact that the great majority of the members of the audience were young.

The day after the end of the part of the congress taking place in Beijing, instead of travelling directly to Shanghai, my party stayed a further day in Beijing so we could attend a meeting which also took place at the Great Hall of the People. It was originally to be hosted by Chairman Mr Jiang Enzhu of the PCP Foreign Office Branch, but he had explained before I arrived that he was unable to attend because he had to accompany Mr Wen Jiabo, the Premier of China, on a visit to the United States. However, the meeting was admirably hosted by two Vice Presidents of the Party. In explaining his absence, and in answer to a letter from me, Chairman Jiang made the following comments which are worth repeating:

> As you mentioned our states come from very different histories and cultures. During the past thousands of years China has been a feudalistic state. The socialist democracy and the rule of law have been carried out for only about a dozen years. To adapt to the situation characterised by the development of a socialist market economy, all round social progress and China's accession to the WHO, China is strengthening legislation and improving its quality and will have formulated a socialist system of laws with Chinese characteristics by the year 2010. Since 1979, the National People's Congress and its Standing Committee has legislated more than 200 pieces of effective law. But we still have a long way to go. So I believe your lecture and your experiences are absolutely valuable and helpful to the Chinese lawmakers and other people concerned.

This carefully worded paragraph expresses the official position as to the developments taking place in China with admirable clarity and deserves close attention since I believe it expresses accurately present Chinese policy. It certainly formed the background to our meeting.

---

[3] Approximately 750.

That this meeting took place was due to the quite remarkable initiative of the Perry Brothers, for which I am extremely grateful. The Perry Brothers are leading members of a group of Chinese and British individuals who over 50 years ago had the foresight to establish a body which aptly describes itself as the 'Icebreakers'. The British members are also called the '48 Group'. The Icebreakers had a vision. The vision was that the People's Republic of China would re-establish itself as a leader among the nations of the world. This was at the time that the People's Republic was being shunned by most of the Western nations. The Icebreakers believed that by working together they could in a modest manner contribute to China achieving its rightful position as a global power. The Chinese Premier recently revalidated the Icebreaker mission, suggesting that there is still a role for the Icebreakers.

Certainly it was clear at the meeting and at the dinner in the evening that the Icebreakers are regarded with particular esteem by senior Chinese officials. At the meeting, about 20–30 Chinese officials who were present studied my paper with the closest attention and subsequently asked perceptive questions. Arrangements were also made for us to have a working lunch with the All China Law Society. The officers of that Society did not conceal that there were short comings in the Chinese legal system but were positive about the progress that was being made.

It is relevant to mention that the Supreme Court building is almost as impressive as the Great Hall of the People's Congress. In addition to the Supreme Court, in Beijing the Chinese are in the process of building what by report is a superb new High Court. This will no doubt match the new High Court in Shanghai which we visited. That building had been already erected for a year, but was so pristine it was hard to believe it had received much use. It is not only large but built to the highest standards. So at least in Beijing and Shanghai the Chinese are investing in building modern Courts which put our efforts in this country to shame.

Before I describe my overall impressions, I would like to say something of my previous visits to China because they provide the context for my views.

I had been to China on two occasions prior to my recent visit. The first visit was just over 20 years ago. On that occasion in Shanghai, my Chinese host took me to what I was told was the first trial of a mercantile case in Shanghai since the Cultural Revolution. Remarkably the case started precisely when I arrived and finished precisely at the time that I had to leave. Even more remarkably, if my translator was correct, there were three conflicting accounts of what was the issue in the case that involved two parties, both State-owned collectives. There was the claimant's case, there was the defendant's case which did not address the claimant's contentions and there was the judgment which did not discuss either the issues raised by the claimants or the defendants. I came away with a clear impression that what I saw had no more reality than the mock trial in which I had been involved in Beijing on my latest visit. However, it was nonetheless interesting that even 20 years ago, the authorities were anxious to show that legal rights of commercial enterprises could be protected by the law in the People's Republic.

My next visit was in 2001, 15 years later. There was no doubt that considerable progress had been made since then. This was not entirely surprising because I had been assured on my previous visit that China, whose legal system had been decimated in the Cultural Revolution, was planning in time to train one million lawyers. In 2001, I was closely questioned by the technocrats who had been charged with producing China's new legal system. They were aware of the procedural reforms in England for which I am responsible. Their questions indicated that my inquisitors were highly intelligent and intent on creating a viable legal system as soon as possible.

However, after a lecture which I gave, a professor, with malice aforethought, asked me to deal with the distinction between rule *by* law and rule *of* law. The obvious implication in the question was that China at that time was not interested in rule of law, but was prepared to sign up to rule by law.

The difference between the situation in 2001 and on my recent visit was as great, if not greater, than the difference between the situation on my first visit and on my second visit, 15 years later. On the recent visit the change in the way people were dressed was striking. Chairman Mao suits were out. There was also the explosion in extremely impressively modern buildings which, particularly in Shanghai, were often of outstanding architectural merit. The buildings confirmed the extent of the commercial activity which is now taking place in China. You had no doubt that you were in a country in the midst of an industrial explosion.

The new court buildings also indicated, that at least in the two highly developed cities I visited on my latest trip, that there are the trappings of a modern court system to accompany the emphasis that my Chinese hosts were placing on their desire to establish China as a country that adheres to the rule of law.

Such adherence is of course critical if China is to have a legal system which will support China's economic ambitions. It is also necessary if

China's global reputation as a nation is to match its size and power. Finally, it is of great importance if China is to meet the growing expectations of its own people.

As to these requirements, the impression that I formed on my latest visit was either that China has now a genuine ambition to adhere to the rule of law, or everything that I saw and heard was no more than window dressing for the benefit of the visitors from overseas. Was it a convenient charade or was the reality that China is seeking to be true to its obligations as a member of the WTO?

Unlike on my second visit, on my recent visit it was clear that my hosts fully appreciated the importance of China being committed to having a legal system which meets the requirements of the rule of law and were well aware of what such a commitment involves. I therefore thought that this was no charade and that China was intent on doing what was necessary to achieve the legal system and the adherence to the rule of law that is essential if China is to move forward to the next stage of its progress towards reaching its full potential.

On 2 June 2005 the *Financial Times* published an interesting article by Jean-Pierre Lehman. He indicated that the outlook for China could be much more questionable than that of India notwithstanding its high rates of GDP growth. Transparency in corporate governance he considered was vital for shareholders and creditors to ensure that assets are being properly managed. As to China's stock market he regarded it as questionable as to whether it is possible to have a properly functioning stock market in a non-democratic society. China's current system he suggested combined dictatorial politics with market economics and this was not a sustainable combination. He also said it was necessary for there to be a strong foreign presence and referred to Japan's example where there were incestuous inbred forms of corporate governance. China, he contended, must evolve a political and administrative system and especially the rule of law that will strengthen rather than undermine its market economic system. He refers to the example of Hong Kong which he considered had maintained that great buccaneering Chinese capitalist risk-taking entrepreneurial spirit that has been such a driving force in Asia's economic miracle.

As to these views having regard to my limited experience and the fact I am no economist I hesitate to comment. However, as a lawyer, I can draw attention to the part Hong Kong's legal system has played in its success. Here, however, it may be relevant to point out that while at the Congress

I noted the respect the Chinese judiciary accorded to Andrew Li, the Hong Kong Chief Justice.

As to this, I was told by an impeccable source that a very senior Chinese official had been heard to say that it would be more productive if in China more emphasis was placed on the advantages of the two systems and if in Hong Kong more emphasis was placed on the benefit of one nation.

I myself could not say for certain at the end of my visit what was the extent to which as yet the judiciary in the senior courts in China are in fact independent of the influence of the wishes of the highest level of the Party if there was the wish to interfere. Is there still the tradition of the courts being subservient to the Party which you would expect in a socialist State? I am not certain. Yet, as against this everything I heard on this visit from the highest level downward suggested that China was determined to change and to embrace the rule of law at least so far as this was possible in a socialist democratic State.

Criticisms can be made of the Chinese legal system as it exists at the present time. However, I had the very firm impression that huge strides had been made by the Chinese from a very low starting point towards creating a legal system which would accord with the requirements of the rule of law.

If I may hark back to my first visit, on that occasion I also met the then President of the Supreme Court of China. He was a soldier wearing military uniform. I was able to have a long conversation with him because he gave a banquet in my honour at which we sat next to each other. Apart from the fact that he was not a lawyer, his views of the criminal process were rather different from my own. He attacked me because he contended our system of trial was unfair. He explained why he thought this. He considered it was unfair to publicly trial anybody who was not guilty because of the pressures and loss of face this inevitably involved. In China they had a preferable practice. They first came to a conclusion internally whether the defendant was guilty and it was only if they decided that he was, that he would be placed on public trial. For me the trial was not in fact a trial but an opportunity for the public to be informed of what he had done and what sentence was to be imposed.

I can accept that some who have been tried in this country and found not guilty would recognise that the President had a point. However, despite this, the Chinese approach at that time was wholly inconsistent with what is normally regarded as the requirements of a trial in accordance with the rule of law. The conversation that I had with the President would never take place today. The judges I met were not only highly intelligent, they were fully conversant with and adopted a more conventional approach to what a trial involved and had been competently trained, some I am glad to say in this country under the innovative scheme of the Lord Chancellor. These experiences are but a part of the explanation for my finding it difficult to believe that the whole exercise to which I and my colleagues were subjected was a charade.

In any event, even if it would be more realistic to recognise a degree of window dressing was involved, I consider it is almost inevitable that the Chinese judiciary would, at least over a period of time, be influenced by and give effect to what they were being regularly told are the virtues of rule of law. In other words the rhetoric to which they are now being exposed from their leaders eventually will achieve a situation where the reality matches the rhetoric.

The Chinese accept the need for clear accessible laws and have already made great progress in producing that legislation. I was given a gift of 22 volumes in English containing the legislation which they have passed so far. The job is being done with significant skill.

The officials are also aware of the problems with enforcement and accept that action is needed. However, here there is real difficulty because of the sheer scale of the country. The Beijing writ is not readily accepted in many of the provincial cities and I was given the impression that there was little at this stage that central government can do, but while, perhaps a more muscular approach could be adopted, there is already a genuine effort to improve the situation. While there are likely to continue to be problems for some time, this is unlikely to be the permanent situation.

Enforcement is a problem in relation to both orders made by the court and orders made in arbitration. Arbitration is flourishing. But ultimately if the process is to be effective, there must be the machinery for enforcement. My hunch however is that given time China will sort out the provincial problems not only in relation to enforcement but also in relation to the corruption that it is still said is endemic in parts of the country.

The British firms who have established themselves in China are doing very well. I was particularly grateful to Simon Davies of Linklaters who attended some of the events to which I have referred. I have no doubt that the presence of firms, such as Linklaters, with their experience of commercial transactions is very beneficial to the legal system in China. They set standards for the provision for legal services in the main cities in which they are present. Many if not all of the British firms have made arrangements with Chinese firms. However, it is unfortunate that in recent times if a Chinese lawyer has worked for a foreign firm, the Chinese lawyer has had to give up his practising qualification as a condition of doing so. I do not believe this is in the long-term interests of anyone. It deters young Chinese lawyers going to work for foreign firms which deprives them of beneficial experience. It means that the Chinese firms are not subject to the rigours of proper competition. Legal services are provided by the foreign firms but only as a result of their entering into arrangements with their Chinese counterparts, which is not the most efficient way of providing those services.

I am afraid in my discussions, I was not given any indication that the present rules are about to be relaxed. However, I would hope that this is a temporary phase attributable to an understandable desire of the officials to protect the very much smaller Chinese firms which have now been established.

Although there are already a great many more lawyers than there had been when I made my previous visit, there is still a great need for more lawyers and judges, particularly in the specialist areas such as intellectual property. Our party included, Malcolm Grant, the Provost and President of University College London (UCL), and Michael Bridge, the Dean of the Law Faculty at the time. They were anxious to ascertain what UCL could do to assist in this situation. I detected considerable enthusiasm from our Chinese hosts for initiatives in this area. One project which was discussed was creating in conjunction with Peking University a chair in English Law in China and Chinese Law in London. This could produce twin centres of excellence which could allow students from both jurisdictions to prepare themselves for the difficulties in studying in the other jurisdiction created by language and cultural differences.

Our different histories mean that we have in depth the necessary expertise and professional legal culture which China lacks. The Icebreaker vision is I am glad to say still alive and it is my hope and belief that both our legal systems would benefit from closer cooperation on the training of the lawyers needed to support the commercial revolution now taking place in China. As always, resources are a problem in this country. We are slow in recognising the importance of investing in maintaining the advantage that our historic role provides. If we do not do so other countries will step in and provide what we are so well placed to provide.

It is my hope that our law firms will rise to the challenge, not least because they are well aware of the potential that China provides for the profitable provision of legal services. They know what is needed if they are to be capable of reaching their full potential in China. Working alongside and supporting the universities, they could ensure that both countries benefit from having available the young lawyers who have the required skills to fulfil the needs that exist.

Our meetings made it clear that this would be very welcomed by the Chinese side. It would be important in spreading the standards of the common law in China, a country which is going to be of the greatest importance to all our futures.

There is no doubt as to the potential of the Chinese Students. From the discussions I had at the reception, which the British Council and the Consul General arranged for me to address in Shanghai, the benefit that accrues to the few young Chinese lawyers who have had the opportunity of studying in this country is clear. They hunger for further opportunities to do so.

It must be in the long-term interests of both our countries that our respected lawyers of the future have an opportunity of learning about each other's legal systems. It is my belief and hope that this meeting this evening and the contacts that were made during our visit will result in the action being taken which is needed to enhance and develop the links which exist already. We must not allow the immense opportunities to be lost by default.

However, to keep this talk within any sort of bounds I must finish here. I do so misquoting the words of Marco Polo: 'I have only told the half of (not) what I saw' but what is possible.

INDEX

abortion 24, 354
  see also right to life
academic exchanges 425–6
academic training 89–97, 161–2
access to justice 7, 71, 195–200
Access to Justice Final Report 1996
  basic reforms 312
  criticisms of the Report 323–4, 327–9,
    331, 332–5, 338–42
  funding of civil litigation 318–19
  implementation of reforms 319–22
  interim report 311–12
  medical negligence *see* medical
    negligence cases
  principles 311
  problems 312
  protocols 335
  recommendations 314
    civil justice responsive to needs of
      litigants 318
    clear lines of judicial and
      administrative responsibility 317
    cost of litigation more affordable,
      predictable and proportionate 316
    judges deployed effectively to
      manage cases in accordance with
      protocols 318
    litigation avoided wherever
      possible 314
    litigation less adversarial and more
      cooperative 315
    litigation less complex 315–16
    parties of limited means able to
      conduct litigation on more
      equal footing 316–17
    structure of courts and deployment
      of judges designed to meet
      litigants' needs 317–18
    timescale of litigation shorter and
      more certain 316
  Rules of Court 313–15
  second stage of the inquiry 312–13

Ackerman, Bruce 220
Ackner LJ 41, 163, 368
Addo, Michael 151
administrative law 24, 25, 26, 43, 227–30
  see also public law proceedings
ADR (Alternative Dispute Resolution) 178,
  195, 315, 320–1, 336–7, 412
advisory declarations 194, 324–5
Africa 210–11, 212–13, 398, 402–3
Al Fayed, Mohamed 134
Alfred the Great (King of England) 407
Alliot, John 4
All Souls Justice Report 33, 34, 36, 42, 60,
  62, 147
Alternative Dispute Resolution (ADR) 178,
  195, 315, 320–1, 336–7, 412
American Bar Association 110
Annan, Kofi 210, 398
anti-discrimination
  legislation 227–8, 234–5
anti-semitism 225
Arab nations 381–2, 387
Arden J 169
assisted suicide 24, 355
Association of Law Teachers 89
asylum 9, 113, 128–30, 144–5, 172, 224,
  231–2, 233, 235, 275
Attorney General, office
  of 15, 21–2, 172–4
Auld J 263
Australia 109, 223, 225–6, 228, 234, 351,
  396, 401, 402
Australian Adminstrative Review
  Council 42

Baker, Kenneth (Lord Baker) 13, 260
barristers, political careers of 119
Beeching (Lord) 4, 5, 137, 166, 282
Belmarsh Prison 114
Bentham, Jeremy 149
Bill of Rights 72, 77, 85–7, 225–6, 234
  influence of Magna Carta 108

Bingham (Lord) 94, 107, 180
Black, Michael (Chief Justice) 402
Blackstone, Sir William 82, 165
Blair, Tony 5
Bland, Anthony 326
Bloody Sunday 205
Blunkett, David 11, 12, 277, 280, 286
B'nai B'rith Anti-Defamation
    Commission 225
Bolingbroke (Viscount) 164
Booth, Cherie 397
Bottoms, Sir Tony 303
Braibant balance sheet 366
Bridge (Lord) 50, 51, 66, 144, 176,
    354, 368, 374
Bridge, Michael, 425
British and Irish Legal Information
    Institute (BAILI) 154
Brooke LJ 179
Brown (Lord) (formerly Simon
    Brown J) 141, 194, 368
Browne-Wilkinson (Lord) 326, 352, 353
Bryden, Professor Philip 356
BSE ('mad cow' disease) 204
Burger, Warren (Chief Justice) 140
burglary 158, 290
Butler Sloss, Dame Elizabeth 279
Butler Trust 260
Buxton LJ 230

Calabrese, Anthony O
    (Judge) 278, 279, 280
Canada 348–50, 351, 353
Canadian Charter of Rights 86–7
Cantley, J 331, 339
Carey, Dr George (Archbishop of
    Canterbury) 357, 358
Carnworth, Robert 377
Carter, Patrick 283, 285, 286, 289
case management 183–4
certiorari 33, 49, 61, 65, 79
Chagos Archipelago 109
Chancery Division 47
Charles I (King of England) 107
Chernobyl 364, 384
Child Poverty Action Group 75
China 211–12, 403, 405–7
    academic exchanges 425–6
    British firms 424
    Chinese lawyers working for

        foreign firms 425
    criminal process 423
    enforcement of court orders 424
    history of the legal system 407
    mediation 412–13
    Perry Brothers 420
    rule of law 418, 419, 421–2
    travels of Marco Polo 417–18
Churchill, Sir Winston 224, 236, 262
Circuit Judges 183
Citizens' Advice Bureaux 96–7
City of London 97, 414
Civil Justice Report 13
civil procedure 90–1
Civil Service 56
Clarke, Charles 10, 173, 294
clerks 189
Clifford Chance 161
Clinical Disputes Forum 327, 336
Code Civil (France) 115
Coke, Sir Edward 107–8
Collins, Paul (Judge) 170, 177
Commercial Court 414
common law jurisdictions 194,
    212–13, 407–8
Commonwealth appeals 86, 215, 402
Commonwealth jurisdictions 397–8
Commonwealth Law
    Conferences 395, 399
community links 277
    feedback after sentencing 280
    mental health 278–9
    problems of centralisation 278
    Red Hook Project 277, 278, 279, 280
community prisons 265–7, 298
community sentences 273–4, 287,
    298, 302
compensation 59–64
conditional cautions 287–8
Confucius 412
Conseil d'Etat (France) 72, 174, 366
Constitutional Affairs
    Committee 128, 129
constitutional change 14–15, 72, 120
    abolition of Lord Chancellor's office 14,
        15, 111–13, 120–6, 135–6, 168–71
    absence of a written constitution 118–19
    devolution 92, 126, 146–7
    influence of Magna Carta 107–15
    proposed Supreme Court 126–7

contraception 24, 355
control orders 10, 173
Cooke, Sir Robin (Lord Cooke) 80, 84
coroners 375
court administration 136–9, 166–7, 178,
    179, 184, 202, 288
  access to justice reforms *see* Access to
      Justice Final Report 1996
  see also judiciary
Cowen, Sir Zelman 223–4
Coyne, J A 350
Craig, Paul 70
Cresswell J 179
crime prevention 273, 283
Criminal Justice Council 263–4
criminal proceedings 11–13, 197
  environmental law 374–5
  public confidence 282
Cromwell, Oliver 108
Crown Prosecution Service 180, 282
Cumming-Bruce LJ 20

damages 59–64, 94
Danube (River) 384
Davies, Simon 424
de Smith, S A 25, 64
declarations of rights 194
declaratory relief 46–59
  judicial review and 48, 49, 50
  retrospective 57–8
Denham J 152
Denning (Lord) 19–20, 26, 43,
    44, 45, 47, 59, 90, 132
  recitation of *Runnymede* 106
developing world 209–13, 397–8
devolution 92, 126, 146–7
Diplock (Lord) 36, 37, 38, 47, 49
Divisional Court 46

economic loss 93
Eden, Sir Anthony 110
Edward I (King of England) 103
Egypt 381, 382, 387–8
Ellenborough (Lord) 119, 227
emergency legislation 220
environmental law 362–5
  capacity of the High Court 367–70
  capacity of the judges 365–7
  coroners 375
  criminal courts 374–5

Egypt 381, 382, 387–8
features of an environmental
    court 391–2
India 385–6
inspectors 375–6
International Court of Justice 384
Johannesburg Principles *see*
    Johannesburg Principles
judicial review 370–1, 383
  locus standi in the High
      Court 371–3, 383
manslaughter 375
nuclear weapons 384
nuisance actions 365–6, 383
Philippines 388–9
planning legislation 369, 374, 383
pollution control 369, 385–6
proposed global legal
    framework 385
proposed new Tribunal 376–9, 383–4
Rio Declaration 386
SAVE 367, 368
Sri Lanka 388
statutory appeals 373–4
UN Conferences 386
UN Environment Programme
    (UNEP) 389
waste disposal 369
World Summit on Sustainable
    Development 386
Etheridge, Jennifer 280
ethical decisions 200–1, 324–7, 346–7, 354–
    7, 358–9
ethical standards 96
European Community law 85
  environmental law 371
European Court of Human
    Rights (Strasbourg) 62, 70, 86,
    168, 214, 217–18, 219, 226, 232,
    302, 397
European Court of Justice
    (Luxembourg) 70, 397
European Union
  environmental disputes 389, 390
  membership qualifications 211
Evershed (Lord) 110
evidence 91
expert evidence 337–8, 358

Falconer (Lord) 12, 15, 121, 171, 294

(Al) Fayed, Mohamed 134
fines 287, 303
Forbes J 374
France 72, 76, 115, 174, 366, 401
Frankfurter, Felix 95
Fraser (Lord) 41, 143
freedom of expression 152, 153, 231
freedom of information 150
French Revolution 109

Garner, Jack 361
Genn, Professor Hazel 332
Gibson, Sir Peter 23
Gleeson, Murray
    (Chief Justice) 396, 404
Glidewell, Sir Iain 180
Goldsmith (Lord) 294
Grant, Malcolm 425
Greenpeace 75
Guantanamo Bay 114
gypsies 231

habeas corpus 33
Hale, Sir Matthew 77
Halliday, John 283
Hamlyn Lectures 19–20, 45
Heilbron, Hillary 328
Henderson, Sir Denys 365
Henry II (King of England) 104–5
Henry III (King of England) 103
Henry VIII (King of England) 154, 168
Henry LJ 177
High Court
    environmental actions
        capacity 367–70
        locus standi 371–3
High Court judges 182–3
Hodge, Henry 328
Hoffman (Lord) 213
Home Office 171, 172
homosexuals 229, 230
Hong Kong 415, 422–3
Hope (Lord) 119, 217
House of Lords, proposed Supreme Court
    and 126–7
Howard, Michael 262
Hoyt, Hon William L 205
Human Fertilisation and Embryology
    Authority 200, 359
human rights 7–8, 85–6

anti-discrimination
    legislation 227–8, 234–5
developing world 209–13, 397–8
English law and 213–21
fragility of liberal democracies 225–6
freedom of expression 152, 153, 231
inclusion in legal education 92–3
international role of the judiciary 401
private and family life 230
protected rights 111, 146–7, 199
right to life 200–1, 325–6, 346–7,
    355–6
see also asylum; immigration;
    prison conditions; terrorism
Hungary 384
Hurd (Lord) 261, 271
Hutton Inquiry 152

Ibbs, Sir Robin 56
immigration 8–9, 128–30, 195,
    224, 231–2, 235
Imperial College, London 364–5
India 71, 109, 212, 219, 234, 385–6, 400
Indonesia 402
information technology 178–9, 180, 183
injunctions 64–7
Inland Revenue 3
Inner Temple 2
Innocent III (Pope) 102, 104
International Court of Justice 384, 396–7
International Criminal Court 397
inquiries 140, 204–5
Iraqi war 114, 194
Irish constitution 150, 151, 152, 399
Irvine (Lord) 13, 108–9, 111, 123, 139, 149,
    158, 168, 185
Israel 66, 215
Italy 72
IVF treatment 200–1

Jacob, Sir Jack 339–40
James I (King of England) 107
Jeffreys, George (Judge) 136
Jews 105, 229
Jiang Enzhu 406
Johannesburg Principles
    cooperation between states 387–8
    exchange of information between
        judiciaries to resolve environmental
        disputes 389

framework to acknowledge and promote
importance of protecting the
environment 388
international bodies to enforce
international environmental
law 390–1
role of national courts 388–9
John (King of England) 101–2,
104, 105, 409
Jolowicz, Professor J A 91
judges' clerks 189
Judges Council 186–7, 190–1, 207
judicial appointments 122, 125–6,
177, 178, 186, 413
High Court judges 182
judicial exchanges 185, 400
judicial inquiries 140, 204–5
judicial review 7–8, 24, 27, 29, 30
absence of other constitutional
safeguards 145–6
attitude of public bodies 30–2
declaratory relief and 48, 49, 50
decline in deference to authority 345
defence of the public-private
divide 74, 75
differing intensity of review 144–5
enlargement of scope 143–4
environmental actions 370–1, 383
explosion in applications 34
immigration policy 8, 144–5
injunctions and 64, 65
privatised bodies 56, 76
Remedies in Administrative Law
(Law Commission, 1976) 70, 74
role of the judge 131–3, 199
safeguards against abuse 33–42
Takeover Panel 51, 55
tensions between executive and
judiciary 140–3
Judicial Studies Board (JSB) 92, 304
analysis of training needs 181
corporate governance arrangements 191
creation 175–6
proposed expansion of role 177, 186
remit 176–7, 192
training judges in case management 320
judiciary
access to justice and 195–200, 396
see also Access to Justice Final Report
1996

assisting judiciary of other
jurisdictions 206
broadcast appearances and
statements 156–7
career development 186
case management 183–4
Circuit judges 183
Commercial Court 414
common law jurisdictions 194, 396, 399
community role *see* community links
complaints against 205
conduct of inquiries 204–5
consultation on proposed
litigation 194–5, 202–3
contribution to the quality of justice 396
disciplinary processes 154
discretion 196, 199
environmental law cases 365–7
High Court judges 182–3
image 188
incorruptibility 413–14
independence of 121, 123, 124, 150,
152, 153–4, 162, 413
effect of the Human Rights Act
1998 162–3
international situation 404
separation of powers and the Lord
Chancellor 163–7
international role 396–7
contribution to other
jurisdictions 401–2
cooperation between
jurisdictions 400–1
judicial exchanges 185, 400
reference to jurisprudence of other
jurisdictions 399
part-time judges 181–2
performance appraisal 187–8
personal support 189
political careers of 119
press office 159
promoting confidence 206–7
providing knowledge about the legal
system 206
relationship with media 149–59
relationship with medical profession *see*
medical negligence cases; medical
profession
relationship with Parliament 133–5
representative of society 186, 193

judiciary (*cont.*)
  role in judicial review 131–3, 199
  running the courts 136–9
  terms of service 185–6
  traditional responsibilities 194–5, 396
  training 203, 204
    see also Judicial Studies Board; legal
      education
  unpopular decisions 155–6, 236, 295–6
  welfare 203–4
jury system 91, 194
Justice All Souls Report 33, 34,
    36, 42, 60, 62, 147

Kay LJ 263, 283
Keith (Lord) 62–3
Kennedy, J F (President) 140
Kilmuir (Lord) 156, 157
King, Martin Luther Jr 224, 236
Kipling, Rudyard 106
Kramer, Ludwig 365
Kublai Khan 417

Latin 195–6
Law Commission 94, 197, 203
    *Remedies in Administrative
      Law* (1976) 70, 74
law libraries 117–18
law reporters 154
Laws LJ 109
legal aid 318, 334
legal correspondents 154
legal education 89–97, 161–2
  Judicial Studies Board *see* Judicial
      Studies Board
Leggatt, Sir Andrew 180
Lehman, Jean-Pierre 422
Lester (Lord) 72, 234
Li, Andrew 423
libraries 117–18
life-sentence prisoners 284
life-support mechanisms 200, 325–6,
    346–7, 355
Linklaters 424
litigants in person 197
litigation 195
  access to justice reforms *see* Access to
      Justice Final Report 1996
  medical negligence cases *see* medical
      negligence cases

Lloyd (Lord) 176
Lockerbie plane crash 403
locus standi 200, 371–3, 383
London, City of 414
Lord Chancellor
  abolition of office 14, 15, 111–13,
      120–6, 135–6, 168–71
  historical office 165–7

Mackay (Lord) 13, 90, 129, 139, 157
Macrory, Richard 362
'mad cow' disease 204
Magistrates Association 171
magistrates' courts 278–8
Magna Carta
  contents 103–7, 409
  historical background 101–3
  influence 107–15
Maitland, F W 164
mandamus 33, 49, 79
Mandela, Nelson 212
Mann, F A 82
Mansfield (Lord) 119
manslaughter 375
McNair J 348, 349, 352
media, judiciary and 149–59
mediation 412–13
  see also Alternative Dispute Resolution
medical ethics 200–1, 324–7, 346–7,
    354–7, 358–9
medical negligence cases 324, 327, 330
  Alternative Dispute Resolution
      (ADR) 336–7
  automatic strike-out
      provisions 332–3
  case management 338–40
  causation 352
  Clinical Disputes Forum 327, 336
  costs 334, 346
  delay 331
  disclosure of the risks of
      treatment 350–1, 353–4
  excessively adversarial nature 357
  expert evidence 337–8, 358
  failure to attend 352
  fast track 340–1
  fixing dates for trial 334
  informed consent 351, 353
  mistrust 336
  standard of care 348–50

medical profession
    decline in deference towards 345–7
    determining whether treatment is
        lawful 324–7
    excessive deference towards 343–5
mental health patients 231, 279, 299
MI5 153
Middleton, Sir Peter 13, 342
Ministry of Justice 14, 125–6, 127, 171–2
minorities *see* racial discrimination;
        religious discrimination; sex
        discrimination; sexual orientation
Mishcon (Lord) 281
Monopolies and Mergers Commission 77
Montesquieu (Baron) 164–5
Morgan, Professor Rod 262, 263, 264
MPs, previous legal careers of 119
Muslims 229
Mustill (Lord) 81, 326

Naguib, Dr Mamdouh Fathi 381
Narey, Martin 262, 263, 264, 266, 268–9,
        270, 271, 286
Nathan (Lord) 362, 363
National Offender Management Service
        (NOMS) 286–7, 292, 294
national security *see* terrorism
National Service 2
Neill, Sir Patrick 142–3, 147
New Zealand 77, 86, 215, 401, 402
Nigeria 212–13
Nile (River) 382
NOMS (National Offender Management
        Service) 286–7,
        292, 294
non-custodial sentences 12
non-pecuniary loss 94
nuclear weapons 384
nuisance actions 365–6, 383

O'Connor, Sandra Day 110
Ombudsman 62, 78, 134
overseas jurisdictions 185, 206
Oxford Circuit 3, 5

Paine, Thomas 109
Pakistan 400
parliamentary sovereignty 82–4, 133–4
Parole Board 302
patient's rights 345

Pearl, David 177
Perry Brothers 420
personal injury litigation 331
Philippines 388–9
Phillips (Lord) 105, 170, 204
Pilgrim Trust 110
Pinochet (General) 403
Pitchers, Christopher 177
planning legislation 369, 374, 383
pollution control 369, 385–6
Polo, Marco 417–18
prerogative writs 33, 37, 46, 49, 72–3, 79
Presiding Judges 5–6
prison conditions 12–13, 224, 231, 242–3
    control on number of prisoners
        within a prison 253–4
    education and training 288
    healthcare 275
    life-sentence prisoners 284
    mental health 231, 279, 299
    numeracy and literacy deficit 273
    overcrowding 260–1, 270–3,
        284, 297–8
    recommended programme of
        action 273–6
    reintroduction of offenders into the
        community 274
    sanitation 254, 265
    short-term prisoners 263–4
    women prisoners 271–2, 276
Prison Ombudsman 267–8
Prison Reform Trust 283
Prison Report 1991 13–14
    central problems of the Prison
        Service 242–5
    community prisons 265–7, 298
    compacts 264–5
    Criminal Justice Council 263–4
    criticisms of the Prison Service 240
    enhanced status of prison officers 251
    'Fresh Start' 246
    grievance procedure and disciplinary
        proceedings 257
    head of the prison service 249–51
    implementation of
        recommendations 269
    improved standards of justice 267–8
    links with the community 254–5
    management problems 269–70
    more visible leadership 264

Prison Report 1991 (*cont.*)
  outline of the Inquiry 239–42, 257–8,
    259–60
  overtime 246
  prison conditions 242–3
    control on number of prisoners
      within a prison 253–4
    sanitation 254, 265
  relations with prisoners 252
  relationship between headquarters and
    establishments 251
  remand prisoners 256, 268–9
  riots of 1990 239, 244
    preventing repetition 245–8
  small units 255–6, 267
  staff absence 270
  staffing levels 246
  standards within prisons 252–3, 265
  structures for consultation across the
    criminal justice system 248–9
private law proceedings 29–30, 43
privatisation 56, 76
Privy Council 86, 126, 215, 216, 402
pro bono legal services 96–7
Probation Service 306
prohibition 33, 49, 65, 79
public inquiries 140, 204–5
public law proceedings 27–30, 43, 69–70
  arguments for a Bill of Rights 85–7
  attitude of public bodies 30–2
  defence of the public-private
    divide 73–80
  growth of public law 70–3
  incorporation of European law 85–6
  parliamentary sovereignty 82–4
  rule of law 82–4
  ultra vires rule 80–1
  see also judicial review; remedies
public protection 301–2
Putin, Vladimir 403

racial discrimination 225, 227–9
Radzinowitz, Sir Leon 291, 293
Ramsay J 362
Rand Report 340
rape victims 156
Rastafarians 229
Rawlinson (Lord) 22
Red Hook Project 277, 278, 279, 280
regulatory bodies 55, 56

Reid (Lord) 81
religious discrimination 229
remand prisoners 256, 268–9
remedies
  damages 59–64, 94
  declaratory relief 46–59
  injunctions 64–7
  judicial review *see* judicial review
  prerogative writs 33, 37, 46, 49,
    72–3, 79
restorative justice 288, 299–300
retrospective relief 57–8
Revenue Junior 3, 6
right to life 200–1, 325–6,
  346–7, 355–6
rights-based society 345
Rio Declaration 386
Rose LJ 263, 300
rule of law 82–4, 121, 225
  China 418, 419, 421–2
  definition 410–11
  developing world 209–11, 397–8
  effect on economy and trade 410
  influence of Magna Carta 108, 409
  responsibility of judiciary 206
Rodger (Lord) 119
Runnymede 102, 106–7, 110, 111
Russia 212, 403

same-sex couples 230
SARS (Severe Acute Respiratory
  Syndrome) 397
SAVE 367, 368
Saville Inquiry 204–5
Scarman (Lord) 72, 349
Schiemann J 373
Scott, Sir Richard 319
scutage 104
Sedley LJ 92, 134
Senior Salaries Review Body 185
sentencing 11–13, 158, 275, 283, 293–5
  community sentences 273–4, 287,
    298, 302
  continuing involvement with
    offenders 280
  cost considerations 305–7
  fines 287, 303
  imprisonment for public
    protection 301–2
  increased severity 285

public opinion 295–6, 298
purposes 296–303
Sentencing Advisory Panel 289, 290
Sentencing Guidelines Council (SGC) 288,
    289–92, 303–5
separation of powers 118, 131, 166–7
sex discrimination 227–8
sexual orientation 229, 230
Shaw, Stephen 267
Sherif, Adel Omar 381
Sherman, Professor Lawrence 299
Shipman, Dr Harold 204
Sierra Leone 397, 402
Sikhs 228–9
Silkin, Sam 132
Simon Brown J (now Lord
    Brown) 141, 194
Singapore 414–15
Slovakia 384
Slynn, Gordon 21, 22
small claims procedure 197, 320
Social Exclusion Unit 283, 284, 298
socio-legal issues 93
South Africa 212, 219, 398, 402–3
Special Immigration Appeals
    Commission 195, 232–3
Sri Lanka 388
standing 200–2
statutory appeals 373–4
Stevens, Dr Robert 119
Strangeways Prison Report
    see Prison Report 1991
Straw, Jack 134
Sumner, Christopher 177
Sunkin, Professor Maurice 162
Supreme Court, proposal for 126–7
Susskind, Richard 179

Takeover Panel 51, 55, 76, 80
Taylor (Lord) 283
teenage contraception 24, 355
telephone judges 163
Templeman (Lord) 80, 89, 354
terrorism 10, 172, 220, 224, 232,
    235, 382, 397
Toohey, Hon John L 205
transsexuals 229, 230
Treasury Junior ('Devil') 6–7, 20–3
Trevor, Sir John 136
Tumim, Sir Stephen 247, 260

ultra vires rule 80–1
United Nations Charter 108, 109
United Nations Conference on
    Environment and
    Development 386
United Nations Conference
    on the Human
    Environment 386
United Nations Environment Programme
    (UNEP) 389
United States
    Constitution 108, 151, 164
    legal education 95–6, 161–2
    Warren Court 71
universities 94–6, 97, 161–2
University College London 2, 149
Upjohn (Lord) 89, 90

victims 288, 298, 299–300
voluntary organisations 279

Wade, Sir William 25–6, 36–7, 38,
    50, 70, 71, 130, 198–9
Waller LJ 177
Wandsworth Prison 266–7, 275–6
Warren Court (United States) 71
Wasik, Professor Martin 289
waste disposal 369
Wate CJ 77
Wen Jiabo 406, 419
Westminster Constitution 150
Wideyer J 24
Widgery (Lord) 7, 23, 176, 374
widows 104
Wilberforce (Lord) 38, 42, 48–9, 62
Willis, Jack 362, 374
Winn LJ 20, 331
Wolfensohn, James 210, 398
Wolsey (Cardinal) 168
women prisoners 271–2, 276, 299
Woolf (Lord)
    Access to Justice Reforms 7, 71
        see also Access to Justice
            Final Report 1996
    Civil Justice Report 13
    Criminal Procedure Committee 11, 12
    development and introduction of Civil
        Procedure Rules 411–12
    ICI case 57
    Inner Temple 2

Woolf (Lord) (*cont.*)
    Oxford Circuit 3, 5
    Prison Report *see* Prison Report 1991
    Revenue Junior 3, 6
    Sentencing Guidelines Council 11, 12
    Treasury Junior ('Devil') 6–7, 20–3
World Bank 210, 211, 398

Yang, Xiao 405
Younger LJ 54
Youth Justice Board 299

Zander, Professor Michael 324, 327–9, 331,
    332–5, 338–42
Zuckerman, Adrian 334, 341